THE BOOK
OF THE 22:

THE ALL-AMERICAN
CALIBER

BY SAM FADALA

STOEGER PUBLISHING COMPANY

DEDICATION

This book is dedicated to Dale A. Storey, maker of accurate rifles, and to Dr. Lou Palmisano, co-inventor of the 22 PPC cartridge and devotee of precision shooting.

Edited By: Kenn Oberrecht

Production Editor: Charlene Cruson Step

Cover Photo and Design: Ray Wells

Published by Stoeger Publishing Company
55 Ruta Court
South Hackensack, New Jersey 07606

ISBN: 088317-149-X
Library of Congress Catalog Card No.: 89-90654
Manufactured in the United States of America

Distributed to the book trade and to the sporting goods trade by Stoeger Industries, 55 Ruta Court, South Hackensack, New Jersey 07606.

In Canada, distributed to the book trade and to the sporting goods trade by Stoeger Canada, Ltd., Unit 16, 1801 Wentworth Street, Whitby, Ontario L1N 5S4.

ABOUT THE AUTHOR

Sam Fadala is a technical editor for Wolfe Publishing Company's *Handloader/Rifle Magazines*. He is a frequent contributor to *Gun World* and Harris Publications's shooting annuals. His work has appeared often in *Outdoor Life*, *Sports Afield*, *Petersen's Hunting*, *The American Hunter*, and many other national magazines. Fadala is the hunting editor of *Muzzleloading Magazine* and a field editor for *Handgun Illustrated*. He has authored 12 books, including *The Rifleman's Bible* (Doubleday), *Winchester's Model 94 30-30* (Stackpole), and *Game Care & Cookery* (DBI Books). Sam Fadala lives in Wyoming with his wife Nancy and their children.

PREFACE

The 22: The All-American caliber—that's what this book is all about. All 22s, from the tiny BB cap to the powerful 226 Barnes. It's about ammo history, plinking, practice, beating the flinch, target shooting, varmint control, benchrest precision, and the quest for the one-hole group (with tested data on the super-accurate 22 PPC). Picking the right 22-rimfire rifle, the right 22-centerfire rifle, 22-rimfire sidearm, and the 22-centerfire pistol. The book covers 22-rimfire and 22-centerfire accuracy (supported with tested handload data), 22-rimfire games, silhouette games, small-game harvesting, and you name it if it deals with the 22.

Most of all, this book is about *shooting*. Big-bore rifles are fired now and then. They are sighted in, resighted, and range-tested. But the 22 is an everyday companion, a sidekick, a handgun or rifle serving its master frequently, any time of the year. From small-game hunting to backcountry survival, the 22 caliber is at home. A couple of boxes of 22-rimfire ammo and a peaceful hour in which to shoot them is therapy for many busy shooters.

This is a fact book, a practical book, a reference, but the data are often strung together with the threads of real-life adventure. Every shooter remembers his first 22, and the experiences that have shaped a lifetime of marksmanship and outdoor enjoyment. You never outgrow a 22-rimfire rifle or handgun. No shooter could be bored with the high-intensity, quantum-velocity 22-centerfire cartridge. The little 22 caliber is emperor of the cartridge world, and in this book, we explore every facet of that world.

—Sam Fadala

CONTENTS

1 AMERICA'S FAVORITE SHOOTING

Three and a half billion of anything is a lot—be it billions of botflies, bottlecaps, burgers or . . . cartridges. More than 3.5 billion 22-rimfire cartridges are pinged away annually in the United States alone—add two billion more for the rest of the globe. That's a lot of shooting. The 22 rimfire is the most popular cartridge in the world, and although it may not be the most important round in the realm of shooting—big game cartridges harvest more meat, and centerfire smallbores win more benchrest matches—it's the most universal and for many shooters the best-loved.

The little 22 rimfire is no good for stopping the charge of an enraged rhino, or dropping a big buck 'cross-canyon, or winning Wimbledon. But the pipsqueak is almost perfect for many important shooting tasks. It's ever-popular because it's ever-useful. No round does more for the penny than the 22 rimfire, one of the most highly developed cartridges ever produced, with multivariations on the theme. You can relax with a 22—relieve stress, sit back awhile, concentrate on a tin can or paper target with that mild-mannered, low-noise, no-felt-recoil 22-rimfire rifle or handgun; there isn't enough "kick" in a 22 to knock a gnat off the barrel.

The 22 rifle or sidearm is a teaching tool. It serves well for smaller varmint and pest control at modest range. The 22 is a favorite for harvesting the littler edibles. The most popular small-game animals in the country, the cottontail rabbit and tree squirrel, are often hunted with the 22-rimfire rifle, and sometimes the 22 handgun. The 22 cartridge shines for serious paper punching, from the local club shoot to the Olympics, as well as informal target shooting, even in the basement. It's a plinker's delight. When affairs of State invaded his serenity, one famous man calmed his nerves and cleared the cobwebs from his mind with a good session of 22-rimfire plinking. Who? Abraham Lincoln. Honest Abe enjoyed many quiet shootfests with his little 22-rimfire rifle.

Games—some serious (the Olympic Biathlon), others just for fun (tin can circle-shooting)—are always great pastimes for the marksman with a 22 rifle or sidearm. The 22 rimfire is just right for serious practice, from improving gun handling to learning long-range bullet drift and drop as the bullet describes its parabola. Twenty-two rimfire cartridges range from the diminutive BB Cap, the CB Cap, Short, Long, Long Rifle, through the 22 Winchester Rim Fire (WRF), all the way to the powerful 22 Winchester Magnum Rimfire (WMR), with jacketed bullet, capable of cleanly harvesting the hard-to-hunt wild turkey and bristly Southwestern javelina, the little wild pig of cactus and catclaw land.

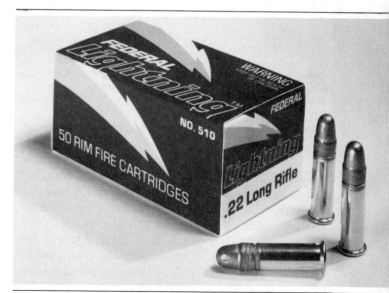

The 22 Long Rifle cartridge, one of the most highly developed cartridges in the world, and still undergoing study and change. Shooters fire billions of 22-rimfire rounds annually.

Scenes like this one dominate the small-game hunting season. Users of the common 22-rimfire rifle or sidearm build many fine memories in the field.

As a survival firearm—with bush pilots, military personnel, explorers, and others who tread the lonely reaches of the outback—the little 22 rimfire has made great impact, not only as a sidearm, but also as a compact, takedown rifle. The Charter Arms AR-7 Explorer rifle has served well in this capacity for many years, the entire firearm ensconced within its own floatable stock. A silver dollar bets well against a stale doughnut that a wilderness hunter with an AR-7 will harvest small edibles with this little semi-automatic rifle.

Cottontail rabbits are legal fare over much of the year in many areas. Old Long Ears, the jackrabbit, may not provide an epicurean delight at the dinner table; however, wanderers of the desert say the dark meat tastes better in proportion to a hiker's hunger. But you don't need to be lost to enjoy a survival-type 22 firearm; many big-game hunting camps are well-served by a small, handy rifle or sidearm of the survival design. Even in this admittedly minor capacity as wilderness and camp gun—not one in a million of us will trudge a wilderness path in need of food—the little 22 rimfire serves the shooter faithfully.

THE ALL-AMERICAN CALIBER

The 22 is the All-American caliber. After the rimfire, there is the superb 22 centerfire. Beginning

The 22 is at home on many fronts. Here, the author's son, John, carries a Marlin Model 39A rifle on an exploring venture.

where the great 22 WMR leaves off is the mild 22 Hornet, followed by many other centerfire 22 caliber cartridges, from the efficient 22 PPC, which, along with the 6mm PPC, may well be the most accurate cartridge in the world, to the super-fast 220 Swift and 22-250 Remington rounds, to the omega among 22 wildcats, the big-game-powerful 226 Barnes, firing a tower-like 125-grain 22-caliber bullet of super sectional density and high ballistic coefficient. One hunter reported numerous one-shot harvests with his 226 Barnes rifle, and though the use of any 22-caliber firearm is rightfully questionable for big game, the 226's record of conquests, including a grizzly bear with one shot, give the cartridge enviable credentials in the big-game field.

While the 22 rimfire is the most popular cartridge in the world, the 22 centerfire is quite likely the most interesting. Fellow writer Kenn Oberrecht said it well as he reminisced about his favorite cartridge type—the 22 centerfire: "I remember as a youth looking through the window of the local sportshop where the proprietor displayed the then-new Remington short-action Model 722 rifle chambered for the 222 Remington cartridge. The little rounds resembled miniature 30-06 Springfield ammunition. I finally owned one. Initially, I was in love with it. Later, the little 222, along with a 218 Bee and a 22-250, became a passion with me."

There is seemingly no end to the different varieties of 22-rimfire rifles. The Charter Arms AR-7 semi-automatic is a takedown model that fits into its own buttstock.

The popular 22 is not a rimfire only. The 22 centerfire plays a large role in the theater of shooting. John Fadala took these jacks from long range using a Sako varmint rifle in 22 PPC USA caliber.

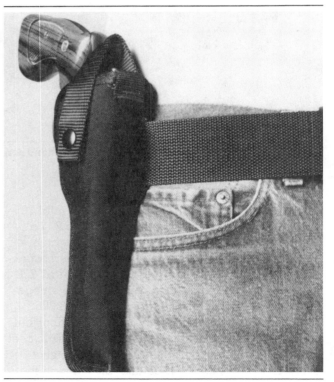

A sportsman can get a lot of use from a 22-rimfire sidearm in the backcountry. Such a firearm—pistol or revolver—is relatively small and easily carried.

Precision shooting with a 22-centerfire rifle (above) is a sport unto itself, either in the varmint field or at the range. Whether rimfire or centerfire, the 22 remains ever-popular because it is ever-useful; the Ruger 223 Remington semi-auto rifle (below) is just one of numerous types.

Many of us have found the 22 centerfire a passion. Lately, the 22 PPC has been mine. In the Sako Vixen varmint rifle, the little cartridge produces groups of only one-third inch center to center from the 100-yard bench. Even with "mass produced" ammo (turned out on an RCBS Auto 4×4 press), groups of one-half inch center to center are commonplace.

Bullet-makers of America will tell you that the 22 jacketed projectile is extremely high on sales, certainly among the top few missiles on their long list. Handloaders love it. The 22 centerfire rifle (and now pistol as well) offers not only startling accuracy, but scintillating velocity and high ballistic performance. Trajectory is low. Bullet ricochet is minimal. Noise levels can be sharp with the "hot" 22 centerfire, but it delivers nothing close to the thunderous clap of a big-game rifle. The milder 22 centerfires are even less boisterous in their report. Many shooters fire 22-centerfire rifles and pistols for pure enjoyment. Other shooters study the hotshot smallbore for its full potential in velocity and performance. Still others use the 22 centerfire for serious long-range varminting, the control of species that cause damage to the ecosystem—woodchucks, prairie dogs, ground squirrels, jackrabbits and other mammals. And then there are the benchresters, whose goal is to achieve the still-mythical one-hole group, where each bullet will pass through the circle left by the missile before it. Many benchresters look to a 22-centerfire cartridge to someday reach this elusive pinnacle.

Every shooter owns a 22, has owned one, or will. The All-American caliber continually gains fans in the circle of shooters. The 22 rimfire remains the most popular cartridge in the world, while its bigger brother of centerfire design continues to delight—and amaze—shooters with its long-range precision capability, tight-grouping, flat trajectory and high-energy delivery. Shooters in every country fire the 22: Russia, Canada, New Zealand, Australia, Africa, Mexico, and every segment of Europe. In America, the 22 rimfire is king. The 22 centerfire is queen.

And now on to the 22-rimfire and 22-centerfire cartridges and the guns that shoot them.

2 THE MAKING OF A LITTLE GIANT

Louis Nicholas Flobert, a Frenchman who lived from 1819 to 1894, is credited with the "bulleted breech cap" invented about 1831, it is believed. The French patent No. 3589 of July 17, 1846, illustrates a unique "cap and shot" gun using an unusual type of percussion cap. However, Flobert actually manufactured ammunition for his BB Cap from 1835 to 1847. Later, his patent No. 8618 resulted in an improved rimfire cartridge. The tiny BB Cap cartridge was chambered in smoothbore pistols and petite "parlor rifles" designed to curb ennui, or boredom, during evening visitations of the genteel French class, who divided their polite conversation with a little target shooting in the front room.

Flobert's BB Cap was essentially a round ball combined with a common percussion cap. Some sources reveal that Flobert's BB Cap had extra priming mixture around its rim for added power. Even so, the entire head of the Flobert case constituted the primer. The BB Cap is noted as a hallmark in shooting because the little cartridge and its guns appeared in the 1851 London Crystal Palace Exhibition. At the Exhibition, Horace Smith and Daniel B. Wesson, then of Springfield, Mass., took interest in the BB Cap design. They carried the idea back to the United States, where they expanded upon it. For a time, they built certain Flobert firearms as well, according to some researchers; however, this information is subject to proof, which seems lacking. Incidentally, some experts feel that Flobert's BB Cap reached our shores before Smith and Wesson went to England. Such is gun history.

Flobert's BB Cap contained no powder. The round ball was propelled downbore by the detonation of the cap alone. Smith and Wesson developed a case with a hollow rim. During manufacture, the rim was filled with wet priming mixture, which dried within the entire inside edge of the case;

The BB Cap (two shown here flanking a 22 Long Rifle cartridge) started the rimfire machine in motion. Flobert's BB Cap is manufactured to this hour.

Rimfire cartridges carry priming mixture located around the rim of the cartridge, hence their name. The 22 Long Rifle rimfire cartridge, center, is flanked by two 22 CB Cap cartridges.

The 22 Short serves several useful functions, including close-range plinking and small-game hunting. Shown is the 22 Short hollow-point high-velocity cartridge with one 22 Long Rifle (left) for comparison.

The 22 Automatic Rifle (Winchester Automatic) cartridge, flanking the 22 Long Rifle for comparison, fit only the Winchester semi-automatic rifle, Model 1903.

therefore, a firing pin striking any portion of the rim detonated the mixture. This in turn set off a small powder charge within the case. Because the cartridge was fired by being struck on the rim, it became known generically as a rimfire-type round. Smith and Wesson claimed that the original Flobert BB Cap could not withstand the pressure developed by a powder charge, because the case ballooned out upon firing, thus becoming stuck in the firearm's chamber. On August 8, 1854, the pair obtained U.S. Patent No. 11,496, similar to a French patent of 1845. The Smith and Wesson patent was for a "self-contained" cartridge, but not the 22 Short. It was 1857 before the 22 Short was born as the "S&W 22 Rim Fire."

By November of 1857, the Smith & Wesson company had its first production revolver, the seven-shot tip-up No. 1, in 22 Short caliber, although the cartridge itself would not be patented for another three years. The great popularity of the revolver and the 22 Short cartridge prompted many manufacturers to supply 22 Short ammunition to the shooting public. Charles D. Leet's company offered 22 Short ammo by July 1, 1860. The company built rimfire ammo from 22 Short through the big 58-caliber Storm rimfire round. Smith, Hall and Farmer offered a 22 Short. The Allen & Wheelock Company did too, and rimfire rounds headstamped "A&W" are still existent. Union Metallic Cartridge Company (UMC) built rimfire ammo, including the Short, from 1867 through 1875. From 1867 to 1871, Winchester Repeating Arms Company (WRA) produced the Short along with its rimfire ammo. The

Phoenix Metallic Cartridge Company sold the Short from 1874 through 1876. The U.S. Cartridge Company also sold the Short and, as noted below, was involved in the development of the 22 Long Rifle round.

The 22 Short, in turn, parented a series of 22-rimfire rounds, including the 22 Long and 22 Extra Long. It was the grandparent of the 22 WRF (Winchester Rim Fire), the 22 Winchester Automatic, and many other variations, including the most famous 22 rimfire of them all, the 22 Long Rifle. Most of these rounds have followed the dodo bird into extinction, but others have become classics. The ammo history of the little 22-rimfire giant is extremely convoluted, with hundreds of different designs. The Short may have prompted the invention of many important big-bore rimfire cartridges as well as 22 rimfires, including B. Tyler Henry's 22 Flat Rim Fire, U.S. Patent No. 30446, October 16, 1860. The 44 Flat made such an impact that for many years Winchester headstamped an "H" on its rimfire ammo in honor of Henry. Ballistics of the 44 Flat were fairly anemic: a 216-grain bullet propelled by 26 grains of black powder for a muzzle velocity of about 1200 feet per second (fps). But tubular magazines held a great many 44 Flats for high "firepower."

Early 22-rimfire ammunition was good. The thin copper case upset nicely against the walls of the chamber, offering an excellent gas seal at the breech. Unlike the paper cartridges that preceded them, the new rimfire metallics could be fairly well-protected against moisture invasion by crimping the mouth of the case well into the shank of the lubricated lead bullet.

An extension of the 22 Short case was inevitable. The resulting round fired essentially the same 22 Short bullet, but instead of a .392-inch to .445-inch case length, the new longer cartridge had a case length of .599 inch to .618 inch. This was the 22 Long, which surfaced in 1871 (according to record). As with the Short, the Long was loaded with black powder. However, the extra case capacity gave the Long a velocity advantage. The Short case contained about three grains of black powder. The Long case held about five grains.

If the Long was good, an Extra Long should be even better. That line of thinking brought the 22 Extra Long to life in about 1880. One source gives the Extra Long a six-grain charge of powder behind a 40-grain projectile. Winchester's catalogue of 1916 lists the 22 Extra Long as firing a 40-grain bullet backed by seven grains of powder. Many other 22-rimfire cartridges came—and went. Of them, the 22 Winchester Automatic and 22 Remington Automatic were among the most limited in use. The first was chambered in Winchester's semi-automatic rifle of 1903; the round could be fired in no other rifle. The second was chambered for Remington's Model

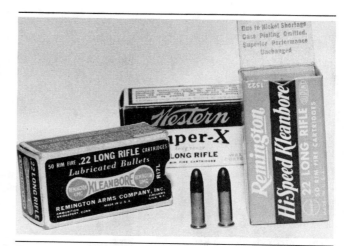

The 22 Long Rifle rimfire cartridge took over as the most popular rimfire in the world.

16 Automatic, introduced in 1914. No other rifle was ever chambered for the 22 Remington Auto. Both fired 45-grain bullets at about 903 fps muzzle velocity when they first appeared.

The 22 WRF arose in 1890, together with the Winchester Model 1890 pump-action rifle. Remington's version of the cartridge, the 22 Remington Special, employed a round-nosed bullet, as opposed to Winchester's flat-point. But it was ballistically identical to the WRF. Either fired a 45-grain lead projectile at a muzzle velocity of about 1100 fps initially, and as high as 1400 fps with later loadings. There was also a 40-grain hollow-point bullet offered in 22 WRF for a while. The cartridge was chambered in a number of rifles and sidearms. It was more powerful than the 22 Long Rifle; however, the 22 WRF was not noted for sterling accuracy. It was also more expensive to shoot than other rimfire cartridges. Quietly, it slipped away from ammo manufacturers' lists, no longer to be found on the gunshop shelf. Winchester resuscitated the 22 WRF cartridge with a fresh run in late 1986. That the cartridge will remain in production is questionable, however. After the current supply is exhausted, the WRF may once again become difficult to find, picked up primarily at gun shows, often at collector's prices.

BIRTH OF THE 22 LONG RIFLE

The facula in the bright aura of 22-rimfire development deserves the lion's share of this brief history. But relating the chronology of the great 22 Long Rifle cartridge with total accuracy is impossi-

Considering inflation, cost of 22 Long Rifle ammo has "held the line" quite well over the years. These popular brands are still available, although not in the specific styles depicted here. Note statement on Remington box: "Due to Nickel Shortage Case Plating Omitted. Superior Performance Unchanged." Twenty-two ammo has had to keep pace with the times, including wartime demands.

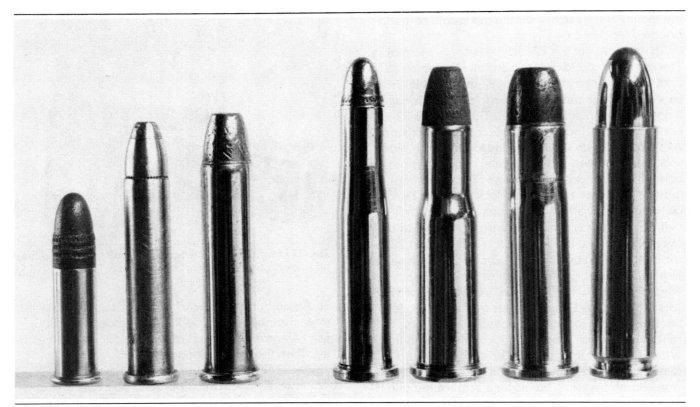

The 22 WCF, Winchester Center Fire, promoted great interest in the development of the "hot" 22 centerfire cartridge. It is shown here in the center, flanked by three cartridges on each side. The rounds (from left to right) are the 22 Long Rifle, 22 WMR, 25 Stevens, 22 WCF (centermost), 25-20 Winchester and 30 M1 Carbine Service cartridge.

ble. A serious student of firearms history soon learns that shooting chronologies are eel-slippery and phantom-elusive. However, the year 1887 is most likely the birth date of the 22 Long Rifle cartridge, granting that it may have been 1888 before ammunition was readily available at the crossroads gunshop.

Joshua Stevens and W. M. Thomas are credited with the development of the 22 Long Rifle in the literature. Having studied arms history for several decades, I have as much faith in dates and inventors as I do little green men from space. Too often, the truth finally emerges from hiding like a teasing child. The J. Stevens Arms & Tool Company is credited with birthing the 22 Long Rifle. However, researcher Thomas Schiffer believes that the U.S. Cartridge Company worked with Stevens. So do I.

Peters Cartridge Company is often named as the first manufacturer of the round. But Peters's company history shows no metallic cartridges manufactured in its plant in the 1880s.

Ely of England first manufactured the 22 Short as

the .230 rimfire, incidentally. Others called it the 5.6mm rimfire. It was the late 1860s before the name "22 rimfire" gained prominence in the U. S.

A September 13, 1888, issue of Shooting and Fishing magazine sheds more than a few rays of light on the matter. An article by Ralph Greenwood entitled "More About The .22 Caliber Long Rifle Cartridge" includes quoted information from the J. Stevens Arms & Tool Company: "We kept calling upon the Union Metallic Cartridge Co. to produce a good .22-caliber long cartridge. Finally, after a year or two had passed, Mr. Hobbs sent up a box of long rifle cartridges and wished us to give them a good test."

I would conclude from this that Mr. Schiffer's surmise is absolutely correct. The Union Metallic Cartridge Company produced the first 22 Long Rifle ammunition.

Initially, the bullets keyholed from rechambered 22 Short barrels, the twist being too slow to stabilize the Long Rifle's 40-grain projectile. But that was overcome with a 1:16 twist in subsequent test rifles.

These tests were conducted in 1885, incidentally, and were written about in 1888. The 22 Long Rifle cartridge had appeared in *Shooting and Fishing* prior to September of 1888, and the usual date of inception—1887—seems close enough for all practical purposes.

Peters was not the first company to produce the 22 Long Rifle round then, but the firm did manufacture a great deal of 22 Long Rifle ammunition using King's Semi-Smokeless powder. Peters's first ammo was uncrimped. Accuracy problems were associated with bullet crimping. However, around 1900 the company introduced the "22 Smith & Wesson Long," which was actually a crimped 22 Long Rifle cartridge. Crimping was an important improvement, because uncrimped 22 ammo worked poorly in revolvers; the bullets sometimes dislodged from the mouth of the case, thereby impeding the progress of the cylinder.

Peters continued to offer uncrimped 22 Long Rifle rounds as well, such as their 1919 semi-smokeless "NRA" ammo. Later, a machine was devised to pull bullets from sample rounds, recording the exact amount of pressure required to unseat the projectile from the mouth of the case. This step allowed uniform bullet crimping. Improved grouping with crimped bullets was now possible because of uniform seating friction, since consistent resistance of the bullet as it is held in the case is important to accuracy.

THE SWITCH TO SEMI-SMOKELESS AND SMOKELESS POWDERS

The first 22 Long Rifle rounds loaded with five grains of black powder were soon supplanted not only with semi-smokeless powder, but with smokeless propellants as well. Lesmok was noted in some literature as a 50/50 mixture of smokeless and black. Colonel Townsend Whelen reported that Winchester's target grade Lesmok EZXS ammo was loaded with a mixture of 85% black, 15% smokeless fuel. The ammo was very accurate. Peters widely used target 22 Long Rifle ammunition of 1920, "Indoor Tack Hole," was loaded with 2.6 grains of FFFFg semi-smokeless powder, according to Phil Sharpe. A year later, "Outdoor Tack Hole" emerged, loaded with 3.15 grains of FFFg (not FFFFg) semi-smokeless powder. The bullet was crimped in order to insure "competent primary ignition and combustion." Semi-smokeless 22 Long Rifle ammunition remained available for many

years. But smokeless powder eventually eclipsed semi-smokeless powder.

Hercules No. 1050 smokeless powder was used in certain 22 Long Rifle ammunition of the early 1930s, one load noted as 1.5 grains of powder for a muzzle velocity of 1085 fps. Hercules No. 1101 smokeless was also used then. Velocity was registered as 1300 fps in a 22 Long Rifle round containing 1.9 grains of this powder. Although smokeless powder delivered improved muzzle velocity, some target ammo remained loaded with semi-smokeless powder into the late 1930s. While semi-smokeless powder was hygroscopic (attracting moisture), it did not appreciably add to corrosion problems, because the priming mixture was corrosive anyway. But three important 22 Long Rifle improvements were on the way.

First, priming mixtures became non-corrosive. Second, smokeless powder totally replaced semi-smokeless powder. Third, bullet lubrication grew more sophisticated. Bullets could be electroplated with copper to prevent bore leading. However, such bullets increased bore wear. Whelen noted a barrel life of "only" 50,000 rounds with copper-plated bullets, as opposed to a barrel life of 250,000 rounds with plain lead missiles. Accuracy was on the increase now. Ballistics were upgraded. The 22 Long Rifle Lestayn load of the 1940s developed 1070 fps muzzle velocity with the standard 40-grain bullet.

By the 1950s, muzzle velocities were in the neighborhood of 1200 to 1300 fps, as they are today for high-velocity 22 Long Rifle ammo. Of course, something else changed too as time marched on: the cost of 22-rimfire ammunition. In 1871, the 22 Long

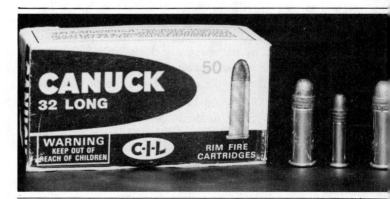

The 32 Long was one of many rimfire cartridges that did not withstand the test of time, even though it was quite useful in its own niche. Two 32 Long rounds, with a 22 Long Rifle in the center for comparison, are shown here.

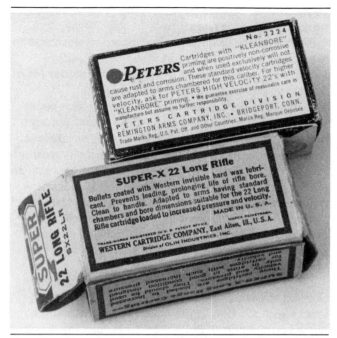

The 22-rimfire cartridge changed dramatically with the popularity of smokeless powder and non-corrosive priming. The statements on the backs of these mid-'50s 22 Long Rifle boxes indicate non-corrosive priming, lubed bullets and high velocity.

cost $7.30 for 1,000 rounds. In 1932, 22 Long Rifle ammunition was priced at 70 cents per hundred rounds, about the same. The year 1939 showed no increase; 22 Long Rifle ammo sold for 32 cents per 50 rounds. In 1951, fifty rounds of 22 Long Rifle ammo sold for 58 cents. In 1956, the same ammo ran 70 cents per 50 rounds. By 1969, the marksman paid 85 cents for 50 shots. Today, "plinker grade" 22 Long Rifle ammo is about a buck a box, with major brand names running closer to a dollar and a half per 50. Considering that a large pizza and pitcher of beer can severely damage a $20 bill, 22 ammo is still quite reasonably priced, especially for such a highly developed and reliable product.

By 1945 there were 130 varieties of 22 Short cartridges, 106 different loadings of the 22 Long, and a whopping 157 variations of the 22 Long Rifle. Modern refinements have reduced these numbers. Ammo-crafters discovered what works best, eliminating marginal loads from their cartridge lists. However, the 22 Long Rifle cartridge, especially, remains in transition. Students of accuracy are continually striving toward more cartridge precision. Rifle accuracy is improving with the ammunition.

Recent developments include a better "lockup" for the bolt-action rifle, for example. Standard grade over-the-counter 22 ammo is extremely reliable and accurate. The end of 22 rimfire improvement is not in sight.

Remember that Flobert's 1831 design produced a cartridge in which the entire head was a primer. Later, the Smith & Wesson rimfire functioned via a priming mixture contained in the rim, with ignition caused through indentation of the rim from firing-pin pressure. The percussion cap that was the body for Flobert's BB Cap metamorphosed into a primer that fit into the center of the cartridge head. Thus was born the centerfire (first called "central fire") cartridge. That centerfire rounds would be built in caliber 22 was as certain as the rising of the sun.

Even before there was a 22 Long Rifle rimfire cartridge, there was a 22 Extra Long centerfire, for which the single-shot Maynard Model of 1882 was chambered. The cartridge is listed in Winchester's 1916 catalogue with a 45-grain lead bullet and eight grains of black powder. The primer was the long-obsolete O type. Ballistics were mild—about 1100 fps muzzle velocity with the 45-grain bullet. While the 22 Extra Long centerfire gained nothing over its rimfire brothers, the case could be reloaded many times over; therein lay its value.

However, the 22 Extra Long centerfire was superseded by the 22 WCF (Winchester Center Fire). This cartridge emerged around 1885, chambered in Winchester's Model 1885 single-shot rifle. Winchester's catalogue of 1908 shows a "22 Winchester Single Shot" cartridge with a 45-grain bullet at 1481 fps muzzle velocity. Winchester's 1916 catalogue still listed the 22 WCF, with a 45-grain bullet and 13 grains of black powder. Remington chambered the 22 WCF in its famous rolling-block, single-shot rifle as well, but by 1936 the 22 WCF was moribund. The cartridge was especially important because it proved to be the light that illuminated the path to the 22 Hornet. The Hornet, in turn, suggested the hot 22 centerfires we enjoy today. Another important 22 centerfire of the early days was the 22-15-60 Stevens, introduced in 1896. This old blackpowder designation means 22 caliber, 15 grains of powder, with a 60-grain bullet. The 22-15-60 Stevens was chambered in the excellent Stevens 44 and 44½ rifles. The round does not seem to hold much historical significance; however, its 60-grain bullet propelled by about 15 grains of black powder would have been quite effective on small game and var-

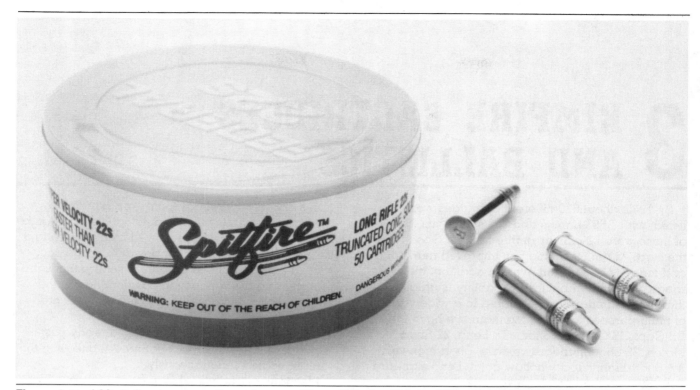

The variety of 22-rimfire ammo continues to grow. Hyper-velocity 22 Long Rifle ammunition, such as these Spitfires, marks another specialized offering for the shooter.

mints at modest range.

Although these early 22 centerfires were comparatively short-lived on the market, they remained active among reloaders for a number of years after the ammo companies dumped them. An old Ideal loading handbook listed three .226-inch-diameter bullets as "standard for the new .22-15-60 Stevens Straight," showing that reloading interest quickly followed the cartridge's invention. The reloader cast and sized the lead bullets and loaded his cartridges according to data that included 15 grains of FFg black powder, 12 grains weight of King's Semi-Smokeless, or five grains of Du Pont's No. 1 smokeless powder for the 22 Stevens.

Ideal also offered bullet moulds and data for loading the ".22-10-45, .22 Extra Long C.F. and .22-13-45 W.C.F." These bullet moulds remained available long after the above rounds were obsolete. Reloading interest promoted ballistic improvement. Wildcatting was the answer to greater 22 centerfire performance. The chapter on 22 centerfire wildcatting deals with many important developments that furthered the cause of high velocity, flat trajectory and long-range energy retention.

In 1912, the Charles Newton cartridge called the "Imp" was brought out commercially as the .22 High-Power for the Savage Model 99 lever-action rifle. Based on a necked-down 25-35 Winchester case, the factory cartridge propelled a 70-grain bullet at about 2900 fps muzzle velocity. Handloaded ammo did a little better. The 22 Hornet appeared in the late 1920s. In 1935 the shooting world was brought to attention by a sharp crack in the air—the 220 Swift had arrived, firing a 48-grain 22-caliber bullet at over 4000 fps. The smaller 219 Zipper was in the field by 1937, and a year later the even smaller 218 Bee was available. By 1950 one of the most successful 22-caliber centerfires came off the drawing board, the accurate 222 Remington. In 1957 the U.S. Army was studying an experimental 22-caliber cartridge to be adopted as a military round in 1964. The 223 Remington is, today, one of the most popular 22 centerfires. And in 1965, Remington would have its name on the headstamp of an old, but ballistically excellent cartridge, the 22-250. These centerfire 22s set the stage for some of the most accurate and efficient long-range shooting ever accomplished.

3 RIMFIRE CARTRIDGES AND BALLISTICS

By 1945, about 670 different cartridges were listed, with 1,623 names and 953 synonyms. Many of these were 22-caliber rimfire rounds. Good from the start, 22 rimfire ammo has improved markedly, and today is better than ever. In addition, the range of 22-rimfire ballistic capability is greater than ever. Rimfire 22s are offered in a wide variety of multi-purpose loads. In the main, we have the 22 BB Cap, CB Cap, CB Short, CB Long, 22 Short Match, 22 Short standard velocity, Short high velocity, Short high velocity hollow point, Long standard velocity, and the Long high velocity.

Among 22 Long Rifle ammo, here are some of the variations: pistol match, match grade, subsonic, standard velocity, high velocity, high velocity hollow point, and hyper-velocity. A late 1986 factory run of 22 WRF ammo from Winchester may never be repeated; however, there exists in this country and Canada many thousands of sound rifles so chambered, and 22 WRF ammo is still important to a number of rimfire fans. Finally, there is the powerful 22 WMR (Winchester Magnum Rimfire), which deserves, and has, its own chapter (Chapter 17) in this book.

The author chronographed all ballistics data presented here. All rimfire ammo proved statistically reliable, with verification through actual target shooting. Considering how rapidly 22-rimfire ammo is crafted, and in such quantities, the ammo companies deserve high praise for excellence of product. Not one misfire occurred during the myriad testing sequences, in which virtually thousands of rounds were eventually fired.

The manufacture of 22 ammunition is mostly automated. First, each case is exposed to a machine that deposits the correct amount of wet priming mixture into the base of the case. A little tool inserted into the mouth of each case distributes the priming mixture around the interior rim. After the cases dry for several days, they are handled a thousand at a time with full automation. Each case is charged with powder, followed by exposure to a sensing device that tests for powder-charge accuracy. If there is but one case in the entire thousand that shows a discrepancy in powder charge, the entire batch is temporarily rejected until the problem is corrected.

Bullets await the charged cases, already positioned in a large block for seating. All bullets in the run are seated simultaneously.

Mechanical and visual inspections follow. Then the finished ammo is moved on for packaging, with appropriate code numbers that relate specific loading information for each run. In some factories, the rate of production exceeds several million rounds per day. Finally, the ammo is test-fired. The larger ammo companies test-fire millions of rounds annually in their quest for quality control.

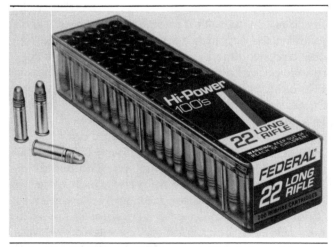

High-velocity 22 Long Rifle ammunition is boxed in many ways today, including the plastic 100-pack, as shown here.

NOTES ON BALLISTICS

Rather than have the reader flip pages to locate a chart, appropriate ballistics data appear with the cartridge under discussion. All velocities were registered at 10 feet from the first chronograph screen and are not "worked up" for muzzle velocity. Barrel length is noted. Ballistics figures always appear sequentially as follows: lowest velocity in the string/highest velocity in the string/extreme spread of velocity in the string/average velocity in the string/standard deviation in feet per second (fps). If the data read 1246/1277/31/1257/12, this means:

a low velocity of 1246 fps in the string,
a high velocity of 1277 fps,
an extreme spread of 31 fps,
an average of 1257 fps,
a standard deviation of 12 fps.

Strings of five shots were fired unless otherwise noted. Elevation of the test site was around 6,000 feet above sea level. Temperatures ranged from 50 to 75 degrees Fahrenheit. Standard deviation remains a valid figure in looking at ammo potential, in spite of the many statements to the contrary. Most of the argument against standard deviation reliability comes when ballistics students try to apply rules of standard deviation from educational methods. However, standard deviation in ammo-testing gives a valid picture of variance. The less variance, the better. The lower standard deviation figure, the better chance for the ammo to prove consistently reliable. Naturally, accuracy is a function of many factors. No matter how low the standard deviation is, accuracy from a worn or damaged barrel, or with poor bullets, may be impossible. Many factors are listed in the chapter on centerfire accuracy. Most of these pertain to rimfire

A vast array of 22-rimfire ammunition gives the shooter numerous choices.

accuracy as well and will not be repeated here.

BB Cap. The current BB Cap differs from the original Flobert design in that a very tiny powder charge is used. My test ammo in this configuration was produced by RWS, the box being marked "100 Flobert-Patronen BB Caps, 6mm." Although called 6mm, these BB Caps are indeed 22 caliber. They have a diminutive powder charge captured beneath a thin cardboard wad. The round ball weighs 15.5 grains. The BB Cap is no toy, and although it can be fired in the basement of the home when all safety requirements are observed, the ballistics of the BB Cap demand great respect.

The little 15.5-grain round ball departs the muzzle at 812 fps from a 22-inch barrel for a muzzle energy of 22.7 foot-pounds, seemingly nothing, but in fact, it is sufficient force to cause severe harm when misused. Accuracy in the test rifle was acceptable at 20 yards; however, too few target sessions were fired to give a solid picture of actual group size. Suffice it to say that a shooter can expect to hit the common tin can every shot at 20 paces if he does his part. The BB Cap is good for quiet plinking and close-range garden-pest control where the demands of shooting safety are met. Incidentally, a sample BB Cap from 1940 contained a round ball of 18 grains weight. Standard deviation was not re-

corded for the BB Cap. The standard deviation for the CB Cap is recorded below.

CB Cap. Again, the RWS brand was tested. The box read, "100 Flobert-Patronen CB Caps, 6mm." Bullet diameter was 22 caliber. This CB Cap has a small powder charge behind a sharply pointed bullet weighing 16.0 grains. Case length matches the RWS BB Cap. Velocity data from a 22-inch barrel was: 891/988/97/948/41. Actual muzzle velocity would be around 950 fps, giving a muzzle energy of 32 foot-pounds. The CB Cap is sufficient for close-range cottontail-rabbit hunting, as well as garden pests where safety and law allow its use. A sample CB Cap from the 1940s contained a standard 29-grain Short bullet.

22 CB Short. The Winchester 22 CB Short low velocity was tested. From a 22-inch barrel, the 29-grain solid-point bullet achieved the following ballistics: 729/763/34/743/15. The muzzle velocity would be a shade over 750 fps for a muzzle energy of 36 foot-pounds. Accuracy and power are sufficient for very close-range plinking and small-game and pest hunting. Tests in a barrel one inch longer consistently gave a slightly lower muzzle velocity, indicating that the extra barrel length constituted drag. In a 25-inch barrel, the figures read: 699/714/15/708/5. The good standard deviation in both

Ballistically, the little 22 Short, even in the hollow-point version, is well behind the 22 Long Rifle round. However, both cartridges serve with distinction in their own arenas.

tests verifies Winchester's excellent quality control.

22 CB Long. Federal Cartridge Company and CCI offer the CB Long cartridge. The function of this round is low velocity, very mild report, and good close-range accuracy for pest control in confined areas, as well as small-game harvesting with head shots. The CB Long fires the 29-grain bullet commonly found in the Short cartridge. Standard deviation was not recorded for this round; however, a muzzle velocity of 745 fps was registered from a 22-inch barrel. The CB Long's case precludes erosion of the Long Rifle chamber, for those who may be concerned about shooting shorter cases in the longer chamber.

22 Short Match. General short-range target shooting may be conducted with this 22 Short cartridge, the advantage of the littler round being its mild report. While the common rifling twist of 1:16, one turn in 16 inches, is best-suited to the Long Rifle's 40-grain bullet, the 29-grain projectile was surprisingly accurate from the 1:16 test barrel. Groups of one ragged hole were registered at 25 yards with a target rifle firing RWS Short R-25 ammunition with a 28-grain bullet. Muzzle velocity was not tested. However, RWS shows 566 fps for this load. Recoil was nil. Noise was minimal. While accuracy tests were conducted with a rifle, the intended use of the R-25 is rapid-fire pistol shooting for serious competition.

22 Short Standard Velocity. This is a good load for close-range pest and small-game hunting. The RWS loading achieved a muzzle velocity of about 850 fps. Plinking where low report is desired is another viable use for the 22 Short standard velocity round.

22 Short High Velocity. Currently, bargain-priced 22 Long Rifle ammunition is often cheaper than 22 Short high-velocity ammo. Therefore, it is difficult to recommend this round for its intended purposes: plinking, close-range small-game hunting, and pest control. There are still a few rifles around that were chambered for the 22 Short only, and in these firearms this high-velocity load works well, provided that the rifle remains in sound and safe shooting condition. The Short high-velocity cartridge is quiet, however, and sufficiently accurate for plinking and other short-range 22-rimfire duties. Its ballistics closely resemble the excellent 22 Short hollow point discussed next. Special 22 Shorts are generally a thing of the past. In the 1950s shooters had the Peters Thunderbolt and Remington Rocket Short. These came in flat packs, like Chicklets chewing gum, 28 cartridges per container. The little bullet zipped away at 1600 fps muzzle velocity. The bullets contained "Q-99," an ingredient that promoted frangibility—these bullets broke up readily, with little tendency to ricochet.

22 Short Hollow Point. An excellent short-range small-game load, this is the round I use in the cottontail coverts of the West, where shooting distances are close and headshots preferred. Remington 22 Short hollow-point ammunition fired a 27-grain bullet from a 22-inch barrel as follows: 1040/1068/28/1049/10. With a standard deviation of only 10 fps and an average muzzle velocity of about 1050 fps, the Short hollow point has ample power for small game and pests with well-placed shots. Accuracy is more than adequate for such work. A longer barrel produced a slightly lower muzzle velocity. From a barrel three inches longer, these results were obtained: 1012/1055/43/1038/16. Quiet, yet effective, the 22 Short hollow point is far more effective than often credited.

22 Long Standard Velocity. RWS offers its 22 Long with reduced charge for those who desire modest velocity and low report from a Long round. Results are ballistically similar to the CB Long, but the cartridge is not placed in the CB category; therefore, it is presented here. Results from a 22-inch barrel firing a 28-grain bullet are as follows: 883/925/42/907/17. Average velocity at the muzzle would be about 910 to 915 fps. Such subsonic speeds should eliminate muzzle crack.

22 Long High Velocity. Negatively criticized, the 22 Long is maligned by the poison pens of gun writers everywhere as absolutely worthless. It is thought of as a combination of the 22 Short bullet with the 22 Long Rifle case. Physically, this is true. But, chronologically, it is impossible for the Long to have been parented by the joining of the 22 Short and 22 Long Rifle, because the 22 Long Rifle was not yet invented when the Long was already in use all over America. Although the cry from all quarters seems to be "Kill the Long," this shooter does not concur.

I own a particularly handsome Model 12 Remington pump-action 22 rifle that fires Longs perfectly, while jamming with Shorts or Long Rifles. Simply, some older rifles function well with Longs. Furthermore, while it's true that for all practical purposes the Long delivers no better ballistics over the Short, it does so from a longer case. For those concerned with eroding the Long Rifle chamber through using

Greg Thompson with a cottontail harvested by a 22-rimfire bullet. Ballistically, the 22-rimfire cartridge is just about ideal for close-range small-game hunting.

the Short, but who still wish to have Short ballistics for special reasons, the Long is just right. Remington's high-velocity Long produced these results: 1122/1139/17/1129/8, another typical high-quality Remington product. With a muzzle velocity of about 1135 fps—remember that the above data were derived at 10 feet from the first chronograph screen—the Long is perfectly adequate for modest-range small-game hunting with well-placed shots.

22 Long Rifle Pistol Match. Several companies the world over offer 22 Long Rifle cartridges geared for serious pistol match competition. RWS's Pistol Match ammo renders a muzzle velocity of about 885 fps from a match handgun. This ammunition works quite well in the revolver, and was tested in a Ruger Single Six with perfect satisfaction.

22 Long Rifle Match. Match-grade ammunition offers more than low standard deviation. It is very accurate ammunition because bullet precision is high. Today's 22 ammo is so excellent that in initial tests, certain standard-grade 22 Long Rifle rounds delivered standard deviations of match quality. However, in benchrest shooting, the match ammunition proved its worth, generally producing the better groups from match rifles. An example of match-grade precision is revealed in CCI's Long Rifle Competition Green Tag ammo. From a 22-inch barrel, results were: 1112/1149/37/1128/13 in one 10-shot string. Another 10-shot string derived: 1120/1150/30/1134/9. Further strings rendered equal or better figures with very high consistency. Target shooting proved the merit of CCI Green Tag 22 Long Rifle ammo. Eley 22 match-grade ammo was also tested with excellent results. This ammo has been imported from England for some time.

RWS target-grade ammunition was also tested. Results from a 22-inch barrel were: 1184/1201/17/1191/7. Note that match-grade ammo operates at about the speed of sound. This velocity has been deemed conducive to accuracy by ammo engineers. Remember, however, that lower velocity ammo does not always give quieter results as compared with standard-velocity or even high-velocity 22 Long Rifle rounds, because the air traveling around the base of the projectile (a sort of slip-stream effect) may, in fact, break the sound barrier even when the actual bullet velocity is below the speed of sound.

22 Long Rifle Subsonic. In an attempt to offer a 22 Long Rifle load with a standard 40-grain bullet at a reduced velocity and noise level, the subsonic load

This is a greatly enlarged photo of a 22 Short hollow-point bullet recovered from a small-game animal. The "mushroom" of the projectile aids in dispensing the bullet's energy.

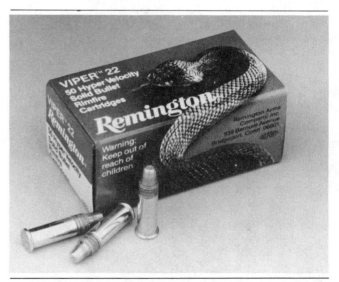

Muzzle energy ratings are increased by these hyper-velocity rounds.

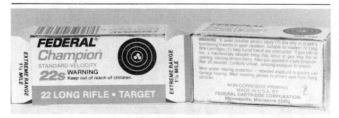

In spite of the ballistic superiority of the high-velocity 22 Long Rifle round, it is the standard-velocity cartridge that fares better in the wind (by as much as 50 percent less wind drift).

was invented. RWS offers its Subsonic with a 39-grain hollow-point bullet, because the company saw a need for a quiet Long Rifle load for close-range varmint control. Accuracy of this round proved very high. Ballistics are entirely adequate for the intended purpose. From a 22-inch barrel, results were: 958/982/24/971/10. From a 25-inch barrel, ballistics were: 989/1036/47/1011/20.

The 22 Long Rifle hollow-point was right for harvesting this jackrabbit. The expanding bullet imparted sufficient energy to drop the hare with one shot.

22 Long Rifle Standard Velocity. This is an excellent load for general shooting, practice, plinking, small game with head shots, and any other 22-rimfire work not requiring the ultimate in velocity and energy. Now and again, bargain-priced 22 Long Rifle standard-velocity ammo is on sale. It makes a good buy. Accuracy of standard-velocity ammo is proved so. Its 40-grain bullet gave the following results from a 22-inch barrel: 1057/1090/33/1071/13. CCI standard-velocity yielded: 1085/1120/35/1105/16. Remington's standard-velocity 22 Long Rifle averaged about 1100 fps also. The excellent Hansen 22 Long Rifle standard-velocity cartridge developed the following ballistics with its 40-grain bullet: 1114/1134/20/1124/7.

22 Long Rifle High Velocity. Twenty-two Long Rifle ammo delivers muzzle velocities generally in the 1250 fps domain. These tests did, however, reveal muzzle velocities in the 1100 fps class with ammunition marked "high velocity." Velocities of 1200 to 1300 fps were difficult to distinguish between in the field. The older Federal Power-Flite Long Rifle high-velocity ammunition gave an average muzzle velocity of about 1265 fps. The new version of this ammo, called Federal Hi-Power, was just shy of 1300 fps by chronograph test. The "bargain brands" of 22 Long Rifle ammo in general tested well. So did most (all but one) foreign makes from a 22-inch barrel. A few examples of foreign-made ammo include—

Sovereign Tiger Cat high velocity (Mexico): 1189/1269/80/1219/30;
Seeker 22 Long Rifle high velocity (Philippines): 1231/1244/13/1237/4;
Charles Daly 22 Long Rifle high velocity (Argentina): 1145/1205/60/1171/23;
Valor 22 Long Rifle standard velocity (Yugoslavia): 1083/1167/84/1113/46.

There are many other high-grade 22 Long Rifle products from overseas and across the borders. Canadian shooters have an excellent product in the Imperial line, with standard-velocity, high-velocity, hyper-velocity, target, and many other loadings. A request for Imperial test ammo was denied due to lack of importation to the U.S.; however, respected shooters of that country provided data that showed a 22 Long Rifle load with an average muzzle velocity of about 1260 fps and a hyper-velocity load reaching about 1500 fps. Australia's Stirling brand is well thought of, as is South Africa's Swartklip Products 22-rimfire ammunition.

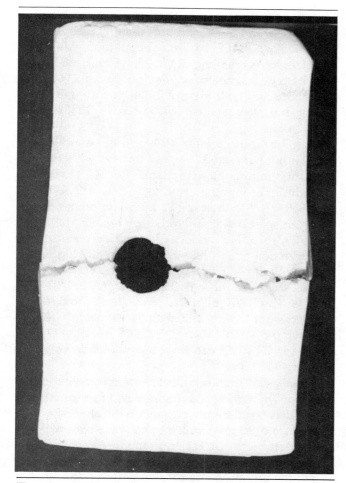

The impact of the 22 magnum rimfire bullet split this bar of soap into two pieces.

22 Long Rifle Hyper-Velocity. Match-winning accuracy has not been associated with this faster-than-normal 22 Long rifle ammunition. However, high performance has. When Winchester's Xpediter 22 Long hyper-velocity ammo was available, I bench-tested it against the same company's target-grade offering. A weighted average compiled from several five-shot groups gave the Xpediter two-inch center-to-center clusters at 50 yards. Winchester's match 22 Long Rifle registered groups of half that size consistently. On the other hand, the 29-grain hollow-point Xpediter missile left the muzzle at over 1650 fps. It had zip. But the company, noted for ammo of fine accuracy, dropped the Xpediter.

Today, several hyper-velocity 22 Long Rifle rounds are worth considering for higher-than-normal muzzle velocity and energy. On a practical

field test of Fiocchi's 22 Long Rifle Wasp load, a decided advantage was noted over regular Long Rifle ammunition in terms of cleanly dispatching rodents. The Fiocchi Wasp propelled its 37-grain hollow-point bullet as follows: 1419/1464/45/1444/20. With an average muzzle velocity of about 1450 fps and a bullet only two grains lighter than the usual 22 Long Rifle hollow point, this hyper-velocity ammunition proved its worth. Accuracy was ample for varmint shooting up to 75 yards. Shots at greater estimated distances were not attempted with any of the 22-rimfire ammo tested.

In 1979, Remington introduced its Yellow Jacket hyper-velocity round with a 33-grain hollow-point bullet of truncated-cone design. Accuracy proved to be very good. In 1982, the company announced another hyper-velocity cartridge: the Yellow Jacket, again with a truncated-cone bullet, this time 36 grains in weight. Accuracy was again very good. Chronographed ballistics from a 22-inch barrel yielded: 1437/1490/53/1472/22. The low standard deviation was correctly indicative of this ammo's performance. Then, in 1982, Remington brought out its Viper hyper-velocity 22 Long Rifle loading, another "hot one" with a muzzle velocity (the author's test) of 1410 fps. In a revolver with a 6½-inch barrel, muzzle velocity with the Yellow Jacket was 1300 fps as opposed to 1100 fps for a 22 Long Rifle high-velocity load. Hyper-velocity ammo is excellent for its intended purpose—greater stopping power within 22-rimfire range.

22 Long Rifle Shot. From a smoothbore barrel, 22 Long Rifle shot cartridges are far better performers than often credited. On the trail, we have successfully used shot cartridges in revolvers for harvesting small edibles at close range. The tiny individual pellet sizes used in 22 Long Rifle shot cartridges preclude serious "shotgunning" with them. Dust is the smallest size noted. The pellet size of dust is only .04 inch. There are 4,565 pellets in one ounce of dust. No. 12 shot is next in size with a pellet diameter of only .05 inch. No. 11 shot is .06 inch in diameter. Compare these with No. 8 shot, limited generally to hunting smaller upland birds, at .08 inch diameter; dust or No. 12 is tiny indeed. Currently, 22 Long Rifle shot cartridges are loaded with No. 11 or 12 shot sizes at muzzle velocities of about 1050 fps muzzle velocity for light duty at very close ranges only.

22 WMR (Winchester Magnum Rimfire). The 22 WRF (Winchester Rimfire) cartridge propelled a 45-grain

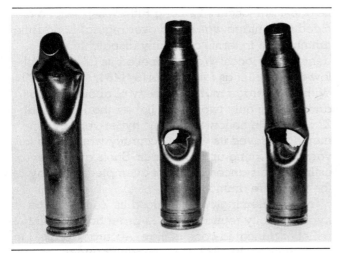
Indicating various levels of 22-rimfire power, these three brass cartridge cases were struck with three different types of 22-rimfire cartridge. The case on the left was hit by a 22 CB Cap. The center one was struck by a standard-velocity 22 Long Rifle round. The case at right was hit by a high-velocity 22 Long Rifle bullet.

bullet at 1300 (up to 1400) fps. The newer WMR round is capable of driving a thinly jacketed bullet of 40 grains weight at up to 2100 fps muzzle velocity. All tested 22 WMR ammo proved sufficiently accurate and powerful for small-game and varmint hunting at 125 to possibly 150 yards. The cartridge has also proved itself on wild turkeys and javelina. A later chapter is devoted to hunting these species with the 22 WMR round with full-metal-jacket and hollow-point projectiles. Federal offers a special load with a 50-grain jacketed hollow-point bullet.

Muzzle velocity from the long barrels is 1650 feet per second. In the 22-inch barrel, ballistics were: 1500/1522/22/1509/11. This ammunition was very effective for varminting out to 150 yards, and would also be a good choice for javelina. Federal's 40-grain jacketed hollow-point bullet provided the following ballistics results: 1872/1912/40/1885/15, another fine load.

With the 40-grain full-metal-jacket Federal load, we cleanly harvested two wild turkeys with two shots and minimal loss of meat. The CCI Maxi Mag 40-grain hollow-point tested as follows: 1814/1889/75/1859/31. Winchester's 22 Magnum ammo with 40-grain solid bullet derived these results: 1802/1831/29/1823/11. The latter were quite accurate in a Marlin bolt-action rifle. RWS brand 22 Magnum loads with the 40-grain hollow-pointed soft-point bullet registered these ballistics: 2087/2110/23/2097/9. The RWS full-metal-jacket load provided the same general results, with the 40-grain bullet achieving a 10-foot velocity of 2025 fps. Shot cartridges in 22 WMR use No. 11 shot. Muzzle velocity is about 1150 fps.

Twenty-two rimfire ballistics are interesting and diverse. The various 22-rimfire cartridges and ballistics discussed here will provide the shooter with hard-core data from which to base his own cartridge selections. Data pertaining to 22-centerfire rounds fit in later. Some of the most exciting shooting today emanates from 22-centerfire cartridges chambered in pistols as well as rifles, and these ballistics will be handled individually in the pertinent chapters to come.

4 RATTLESNAKE NIGHTS AND THE LOUISIANA BULLFROG MAN

My father worked the swing-shift, four in the afternoon to midnight, herding out of a small shanty next to the railroad tracks in the remote east yard. His switchman job allowed my brother and me to tag along. The lonely stretch of territory out of town was a good place to be when we were boys.

I had a 22 rifle. My brother was too young for one that first year on the east end, but before our third year of going to that huge patch of land east of Yuma, Arizona, he also owned a 22 rifle. Long summer days gave us many hours of shooting light. There were jackrabbits in the uninhabited desert that lay in the distance on both sides of the tracks. We soon learned their haunts and ways and hunted them successfully. But our major targets were the ground squirrels that lived along the railbed. "Damn gophers burrow down along the rails and undermine the bed," the yardmaster had told my father. "Tell your boys to thin out as many of those damn gophers as they can."

We took on the work with great enthusiasm.

"'Hear you've been getting a lot of those damn gophers," the yardmaster praised when he came by the shanty from time to time. There was no such thing as a ground squirrel to the yardmaster, and the only way he could say "gopher" was with the expletive attached in front of the name. If professor jackrabbit was the best teacher of a youth with a 22 rifle, the ground squirrel was at the very least an apt tutor. We agreed that only head shots counted, and we were careful to dispatch the pests quickly with clean hits. I don't know how much good our varmint control program did for the railroad track bed, but the program did us a lot of good—it taught us how to shoot accurately and safely.

When the sun went down, the "gophers" did, too, deep into their burrows along the trackbed. As the cooling of the evening air sent the critters away, it invited another denizen of the desert to approach the rails. Rattlesnakes, lured by the iron warmed in the hot sun all day, moved out of the desert to lie alongside the heated metal ribbons. Sidewinders were prevalent, but so were the much larger diamondbacks. Equipment was simple—a broom handle, with no metal catching hook attached, and bare hands. My brother controlled the beam of the flashlight, its rays glancing from the polished iron rails like ricocheting bullets in a B western movie. "There's one!" You never became anesthetized to the sudden sighting of a rattler stretched along the railing half hidden under the cover of darkness. One glance at the serpent, and the adrenalin flowed.

The snake might remain sedentary by the warm tracks. Then a gentle nudge with the long broom handle would animate the rattler into a buzzing coil like live barbed wire. A quick swipe of the stick shuttled the reptile away from the track and down onto the sandy sides of the railbed. The bare stick was positioned where head and neck join to hold the creature down, and then the snakeman "walked the stick." This meant tiptoeing along the length of the wooden wand until the toe of the boot was about six inches from the "sharp end" of the snake. There was only one immediate danger—the shifting desert sand. If the sand were soft enough, the snake might slip its head out from under its wooden detainer. Often, this is just what happened, and a quick jump back was the only maneuver that prevented a bite.

The stick was hit plenty of times. Venom shined from it in the flashlight beam. The snake might retreat toward the familiar desert. Hopefully, the new earth held fast and the rattler was pinned under the stick on the next try. When his head was in reach of my hand, I tightened anxious fingers around his neck. The broad head precluded the snake's slipping through my fingers and sinking its

Gophers, jackrabbits, and rattlers like the one above were among the many animals that "tutored" the author's early shooting lessons with the 22 rifle.

fangs into my arm.

As my brother and I reminisce about our "rattlesnake nights," the blood runs cold in our veins. We wouldn't grab a rattler behind the head in the dead of night on a sandy railbed these days for all of the apples in the state of Washington. Anybody who catches a dangerous snake with his hands is asking for serious trouble; our lack of caution was foolish. At that time there was no knowledge of the electric shock method for treating snakebite, either.

Collected snakes were in gunnysacks, trans-ported to town, and there they were traded to the man who ran the secondhand shop. He probably sold the reptiles to a biological supply house for hard cash. We didn't care. The trade item offered by the proprietor of the secondhand store was better than money. He traded 22-rimfire ammunition for our snakes. Twenty-two ammunition often became a medium of barter for us in turn. A water canteen, a hat, a piece of hunting hardware, all could be obtained with trade ammo. Trading 22-rimfire ammo was nothing new. In the 1930s, 22-rimfire swapping was a common practice.

Our 22 rifle-shooting interest continued to be varmint-oriented, mainly ground squirrels and jackrabbits. Then the Louisiana Bullfrog Man came to town. His son and I were schoolmates. "'Want to go hunting with my dad and me?'' the boy asked. Sure I did, and I learned the value of a 22 rifle for "making meat.''

First trip out took us to a 100-acre stretch of tangle and undergrowth along a major canal. The patch of ground was known as the Old Golf Course, and perhaps it had once been just that. However, that bit of geography had become home to cottontail rabbits, as well as raccoons and sundry other small animals.

The Louisiana man carried a 22 rifle, always the same one. It was a single-shot Remington Rolling Block Model 4. Nothing but 22 Short ammo ever entered its chamber. A box of ammo stood for 40 to 50 edibles. The Louisiana Bullfrog Man didn't hold

with spending too much ammo in plinking.

He knew the limitations of his little rifle, its range, and its power. He never exceeded those limitations. Vast experience had taught him the trajectory of the 22 bullet. He had translated that experience into a "feeling" for how to hold on each shot. As a great outfielder knows without calculation how to throw the ball accurately to home plate, the seasoned hunter knows his sight picture. Marksmanship was the byword.

Experience with jackrabbits had given me a good handle on "long-range" 22 rifle shooting, but my skills were unpolished and crude compared with the Louisiana man's abilities. More than marksmanship, he knew how to hunt small game. He knew the ways of the animals and where they might be at any given time of day. If it was legal and edible, the animal was on the man's hunting list.

"You can make a living with a little rifle like

As a youngster, Sam learned how to shoot accurately and safely with his 22 rifle, working on "varmint control" with his brother. Here, Nicole Fadala, his daughter, takes aim with her single-shot 22-rimfire rifle.

this," the hunter said. "I helped my folks make a living with this very rifle back in Louisiana—along with a fishing pole," he added. The veteran hunter patted the worn stock of the four-pound, 38-inch-long Remington, and reaching inside a pocket, his hand brought forth a single box of 22 Short cartridges. "Head shots are the only ones that count," he said.

The 22 Short hollow-point cleanly dropped more running rabbits than I could assess. The marksman was confident of his aim. When he hunted along a ditch that ran parallel to the main canal, his keen eyes searched both sides of the waterway, the steep bank leading to the water, and the bank running to the miniature jungle of undergrowth on the other side. He mounted the little rifle to his shoulder the way a painter strokes a canvas with his brush, just one graceful sweep, and then Spttt!, there'd be another edible for the bag. His aim was deliberate on running game. I held my breath waiting for him to pull the trigger, but when he finally did, his hit vs. miss ratio made an enviable record.

Bullfrogs were high on his list of food procured with the 22 rifle. The Louisiana Bullfrog Man often strolled alongside a flowing drainage canal, his feet padding slowly on the dusty trail, in rhythm with the coursing water. Peering down into the murky water, his eyes strained to penetrate the gray liquid. The angle downward was steep, the banks of the miniature canal soft. There was no chance for the 22 Short bullet to hop off the water and up the bank. He would eventually pause. The iron-sighted rifle was slowly mounted, and . . . spat! One of us darted down the bank and into the water to retrieve the long-legged prize. I never pulled a bullfrog out of the drainage ditch that didn't have a neat 22 caliber hole head-centered.

Frog leg dinners. They were delicious. Fried rabbits and turtle soup were equally good. The little rifle made half a living for the Louisiana man. He taught us conservation of the resource, and wise use. He taught us, too, the value of the common 22-rimfire rifle. We never forgot the lessons.

The Louisiana Bullfrog Man wanted to get his son, and his son's friends, started right. The outdoors became a blackboard for our education, with the little 22 rifle our chalk and pointer. Our teacher instructed quietly, but with strict rules that never had to be quoted more than once. Had we learned school lessons as quickly, teachers would have stuck gold stars on all our papers. Twenty-two rifles and a set of carefully thought-out rules taught us well. The 22 was a rifle for all seasons. I said you never outgrow a 22 rimfire rifle. We didn't. And now about picking the right 22 rimfire rifle for your needs.

5 CHOOSING THE RIGHT 22 RIFLE

Each rifleman chooses the appropriate 22 long arm (rimfire or centerfire) to match his particular needs. That is why this chapter is arranged not according to firearm action type—such as bolt-action, lever-action, or slide-action—but rather according to the function the rifle serves, i.e., small-game hunting, close- or long-range varminting, match shooting, and so forth. There is crossover, of course. Local target matches have been won with the lever-action 22 rifle, for example, especially when the marksman used a Marlin 39A combined with the specific ammunition that his individual rifle "liked best." But most shooters will tackle a shooting contest with a target rifle, a small-game hunt with a small-game rifle, and a silhouette shoot with a silhouette rifle, using the right tool for each job.

There's a trace of bias coloring certain recommendations here. But even those personal preferences extend from experience, not whim. The goal here is to sway no shooter, but rather to remind him of the various types of 22 rifles at his command. There are many in both rimfire and centerfire persuasion.

THE RIMFIRE 22 RIFLE

The Starter 22 Rifle. The single-shot 22-rimfire rifle remains an excellent choice for the beginner, an example being the scaled-down Chipmunk bolt-action model with a barrel length of 16 1/4 inches and an overall length of 30 inches. The rifle weighs only 2.5 pounds. The Iver Johnson Li'l Champ is another bolt-action single-shot 22 of miniaturized dimensions to suit the junior shooter.

Since mental maturity may outrun physical growth in the early years of childhood development, be certain that your young shooter can cock the plunger-type single-shot rifle before choosing one for training. A little girl who proved herself mentally prepared to shoot a 22 rifle under supervi-

sion could not set the cocking plunger of her rifle. Her practice rifle had to be cocked for her before she could fire any shot. That extra step broke the smooth flow of the shooting sequence, as well as the girl's concentration. Her learning of the function and the sighting procedure of the rifle were impaired.

Marlin's Model 15Y Little Buckaroo is a single-shot bolt-action rifle that cocks with the working of the bolt. There is no plunger. The rifle is short—about 33 inches overall. Break-open single-shots have always been highly regarded for beginners, too. For example, the Savage Crackshot with falling-block action is easily operated by the smaller marksman.

Single-shots are not the only intelligent choice of

The modern Varner single-shot rifle is a replica of a much older Savage model. The single-shot rifle is still the beginner's choice as well as a fine piece in the hands of the expert marksman.

A Marlin Model 15Y "Little Buckaroo" rifle is sized for the young shooter. It does not require the cocking of a plunger.

22-rimfire rifles for the beginner, however. Although a single-shot rifle is excellent for plinking, informal target work, even high-competition matches and serious small-game hunting, most shooters eventually want a repeater. (Many veteran shooters do keep a single-shot rifle on hand, however.) For this reason, it's wise to consider one of the smaller repeaters as a training rifle for the young shooter. The Anschutz Woodchucker 22 rifle is a bolt-action repeater designed for the young marksman. Its clip holds five shots. A 10-shot clip is also available. However, the rifle can be single-loaded very smoothly, due to its loading port design. The downsized Woodchucker has a 12-inch length of pull.

More important than the style of the beginner's rifle is the manner in which the rifle is handled and the teaching methods employed for its use. However, a firearm that does not fit the shooter carries built-in discouragement. Imagine your own rifle

Bill Fadala handles a Weatherby 22-rimfire semi-auto rifle. The semi-automatic 22 is currently a popular action style.

having an 18-inch length of pull, a weight of 27 pounds, and a 36-inch barrel. Such oversized dimensions would spoil any chance for consistently good shooting. The young (and smaller) shooter saddled with "Dad's rifle" is outfitted just as properly as Dad would be with the imaginary 27-pound rifle above.

Plinking. Any 22 rifle will serve the plinker. However, the semi-automatic (self-loading) 22 rifle makes a lot of sense for tin-can rolling and shooting games. Just because the rifle will fire each time the trigger is pulled (until the magazine runs dry) does not mean that splattering lead in the direction of the target and backstop is prudent. The semi-auto can be aimed as carefully as any other rifle type— and it should be aimed for each shot. But when the shooter desires, the semi-auto is capable of accurate and fast repeated fire—with safety—making its type quite enjoyable for plinking. The Marlin Model 70 semi-auto 22-rimfire rifle used for this book's plinking tests was fired 1,000 times (two bricks of Federal's standard velocity ammo) without a hitch. Consider any rifle style for plinking, but try a self-loader before making a final decision.

Practice. The only difference between plinking and informal practice is transfer value. The practice session should be carried out in such a manner that each event in that session pertains to a later situation in the field or on the range. Furthermore, it's a good idea to practice with the 22 rifle that you'll use on the small-game hunt, the target match, silhouette shoot, or other event. Such use breeds familiarity. In turn, rifle familiarity breeds better shooting. It is also a good idea to practice on targets similar to the "real thing," whether the real thing is a cottontail rabbit cutout, a bull's-eye, or a silueta profile. Therefore, the proper 22 rimfire practice rifle is the actual rifle used by the shooter for "serious" marksmanship.

Small-Game Hunting. The Louisiana Bullfrog Man used a Remington single-shot rifle for all of his small-game hunting, and he was a very successful "pot hunter." However, a repeater makes more sense most of the time. Here, action style simply does not matter, *but rifle fit does.*

Choose a small-game 22 rifle that you can wield like an extension of your personality. You may find many rifles that fill the bill. You may find few. Before buying your 22 small-game rifle, handle it. Handle it as much as possible. If you can, borrow a rifle before buying, and practice with it. The rifle

The used 22-rimfire rifle comes in all styles. This Winchester Model 75 Sporter is a high-class rifle that has not been made for many years, but it can be found advertised in *The Gun List* and other used-gun outlets.

should mount to shoulder with silk-smooth motion. You should not have to shift your face on the comb of the stock in order to reposition the rifle in relation to your body. Not to get carried away with this—shooters bend, too, and there is nothing wrong with having to get used to your 22 hunting rifle. But that rifle should fit you well.

I'm forever gravitating to the bolt-action 22 rifle for small-game hunting, although I never will abandon my older slide-action models for field work. The Remington Model 541-T bolt-action, for example, offers a fantastic trigger pull, along with top accuracy. Browning's A-Bolt is also very accurate and reliable, and it has a 15-shot clip option. My Model 75 Winchester Sporter, which has been out of manufacture for years, finds its way into my hands every cottontail season.

Choose your own 22 small-game tool based on how it fits you, how well you shoot and handle the rifle, its reliability of action, and, finally, your particular hunting conditions. If shots at running game are called for, a well-sighted semi-auto may be just right. If most shooting occurs on sedentary squirrels, a stable, accurate (scoped) boltgun may be the ticket.

Varmints. The 22-rimfire rifle is as capable on varmints as the marksmanship and stalking ability of its owner. Although seldom applied so, a 22 rimfire can drop even the coyote within the range limitations of the cartridge. Prairie dog control on a nearby ranch means carrying my 22 PPC in a Sako Vixen rifle, or a similar outfit. However, ensconced safely in the vehicle rides a 22 rimfire rifle—always. True, that rifle has been a Model 12 Remington pump gun, but more often it is a bolt-action model with a good scope sight. That type of rifle—bolt-action, scope-sighted—makes a lot of sense for 22-rimfire varminting. Rapid fire is seldom required. High accuracy is. Not to suggest that super accuracy is unattainable in the self-loader, slide-action, or lever gun—it is. However, the bolt-action rifle chambered for the 22 rimfire or 22 magnum fills the bill neatly for 22-rimfire varminting, personal prejudice duly noted.

Target Shooting. Target shooting ranges from local matches to the Olympics. The 22 rifle must meet the conditions of the match. For example, the Anschutz Model 1803 D Match Rifle, at a weight approaching nine pounds with sights, is engineered for serious competition; but it does not function identically with Anschutz 1813 Super Match rifle, which weighs

close to 16 pounds and has an international type stock with a multitude of stock dimension adjustments. Then there is the Anschutz Model 1827B Biathlon rifle, geared to that particular Olympic event. It even has a snow cap to protect the rear sight. The Beeman/FWB Ultra Match Free Rifle is also specially suited to serious target shooting. Any 22-rimfire rifleman entering high levels of competition will choose his target rifle based upon the actual event of his interest. Specialization is the byword. The nine-pound Anschutz Biathlon rifle is matched to its event. The 14-pound Beeman Ultra Match rifle is also matched to its intended competition.

Silhouette Competition. Silhouette shooting, or *Silueta* to use the original Spanish name, calls for its own rifle style. Although this is a target-shooting event, sanctioned matches are not normally conducted with the target rifles one would find at other shoots. Several stringent rules apply to the silhouette rifle; therefore, the rifle becomes a very specialized tool. Consider the Beeman/Krico Silhouette Rifle—it has a five-shot clip, rather than being a single-shot. The barrel is 21 inches long, not 27 1/4 inches long, as found on the Anschutz 1811 Match Rifle. The Beeman/Krico 340 Silhouette rifle weighs 7 1/2 pounds—compare that with the heft of the other target rifles. The rifle meets NRA official rulings, as does the Anschutz Model 54.18 MS Silhouette Rifle, another specialized shooting machine made especially for the *silueta* match.

The target rifle must exhibit superior accuracy, of course. However, there is much more to a 22-rimfire target rifle than a precision barrel. Triggers must be up to competition standards. As noted in the forthcoming accuracy chapter, no matter how excellent the barrel, it takes a proper trigger to realize the rifle's potential. The target rifle must also be built to the specifications of the particular event. There is even a special Super Running Boar Target rifle (by Anschutz) and a Walther Running Boar Match Rifle for their particular competitions. Therefore, the target rifle is chosen in accord with the rules of the event. As noted earlier, while a local competition may be won with a non-match rifle, odds are the shooter who walks away with first place will have captured the match with a rifle geared especially for that specific shooting event.

The Survival Rifle. The survival rifle is used often as a standby unit, especially in the big-game hunting camp. My own survival rifle is a Charter Arms

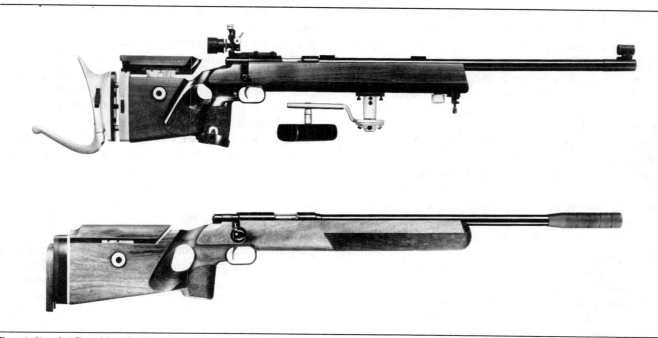

Specialized rifles, like the Anschutz Model 1413 (above), are for serious competition. Such a rifle would be the obvious choice for the competitive marksman. Another specialized rifle, the Anschutz Model 1408-ED, is for the running boar match and is designated "Super" Running Boar.

with flotation stock. The little rifle goes where I go. It is entirely self-cased, with barrel, action, and even ammo resting within the confines of the hollow stock. This peep-sighted rifle can be used to collect an incidental small-game or mountain-grouse dinner for the hunting camp, or to harvest meat for survival. Bush pilots who may have to live off the land for a while in a forcedown often carry survival rifles. These compact rifles take up little space and are feather-light and very reliable.

The little Charter Arms rifle was given my standard test devised to put various rifles through their paces—two bricks of ammo fired without benefit of cleaning. The self-loading rifle shot its 1,000 rounds without a single hangup. There are other 22 survival rifles, including the Springfield Armory M6 Scout Survival Rifle, a combination firearm with over/under barrels that offers a choice of 22 Long Rifle, 22 WMR, or 22 Hornet, along with a 410 shotgun tube. The break-down Savage Model 24 may be purchased with a 22 Long Rifle (also Short and Long) barrel in combination with a 20-gauge shotgun barrel. The 24-C over/under has a trap buttplate that holds a 20-gauge shotgun shell and 10 Long Rifle rounds.

Wild Turkey and Javelina. Of the rimfire clan, only the 22 WMR (Winchester Magnum Rimfire) cartridge meets the ballistics requirements for wild turkey and javelina. In fact, the use of the 22 rimfire, including the Long Rifle in its most persuasive loadings, is denied by law on either of these game animals in most areas. There are numerous rifles chambered for the 22-magnum cartridge, and all of them work well for these two larger species. Marlin offers several good rifles in 22 WMR caliber, including the little Model 25MB "Midget Magnum" with its 16 1/4-inch barrel, 34 1/4-inch overall length, and lightweight heft of only 4.75 pounds. A Marlin Model 25 used for testing proved entirely reliable and quite accurate.

Lever-actions are also available in 22 WMR. Winchester's sturdy Model 9422 Magnum WIN-CAM rifle with a camouflage-style laminated stock is built for heavy-duty work. It's an excellent choice for wild turkeys or javelina. Marlin's Model 1894M carbine is chambered for the 22 WMR cartridge too.

An interesting tool for the turkey hunter is a combination rifle. There are several of these. Tested was the Savage Model 24 with 22 WMR rifle barrel combined with a 20-gauge shotgun barrel. It worked well.

The Heckler & Koch Model 300 Auto Rifle is chambered for the 22 WMR round. As the name implies, this is a self-loading 22 Magnum rifle. It has a five-shot magazine and weighs 5.75 pounds.

A multitude of excellent bolt-action 22 WMR rifles were tested, among them the Anschutz Bavarian, a handsome and well-made model offering interesting lines and high-grade accuracy.

The 22 WMR rifle chosen for javelina or wild-turkey hunting is usually scoped. A variable scope makes sense, because either of these trophies may be encountered at very close range in dense cover. Then the wide view of the variable on low power is valuable. On the other hand, the ability to increase the magnification of the scope is important for precision shot placement.

On my most recent wild-turkey venture, I found a flock of birds feeding alone a stream. By stalking, I closed the gap to about 100 yards, but could get no closer, having run out of cover. I jacked up the scope power and felled a tombird with a single 40-grain bullet in the pinion area, where wing and body join. No appreciable meat was lost, and the big bird was cleanly harvested. Additional magnification of the target made careful shot placement possible.

Collecting. Although I'm not a firearms collector, if I were, I would concentrate on 22-rimfire rifles. The varieties are endless and absorbingly interesting. A strong collection of 22-rimfire pump-action rifles

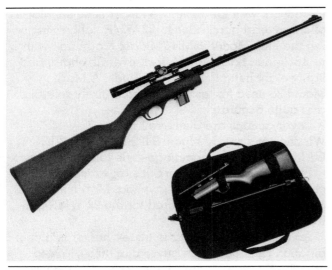

The world of 22s is replete with special models. This is the Marlin Papoose, a takedown that fits into a handy case.

would not have to entail the expense usually associated with big-bore rifles. Numerous old-time 22 rifles are for sale at modest prices. A collector would be able to find rifles of interest at gun shows, local or out of town, as well as in gun newspapers. Various "blue books" depict large numbers of different 22 rifles for study. Most of these books have suggested values attending each rifle.

The Custom 22 Rimfire Rifle. There are semi-custom, customized and full-blown customs in the 22-rimfire world of rifles. The semi-customs are those rifles that offer many features found on handmade pieces, but which are not entirely individualized. An example of the semi-custom rifle is Remington's Model 40 XR Custom Rimfire Sporter. The XR is patterned after the company's Model 700 big-game rifle. It comes in four grades with many special features. Even length of pull can be special ordered. The wood is high-grade walnut. English walnut is available on grades II, III, and IV. California Claro or American walnut is offered on all models. The stock is hand-checkered. The heart of this semi-custom is a 40-X action designed to achieve supreme accuracy in the 22-rimfire sporter rifle. A beautiful piece, this rifle has "functional aesthetics." That is, the rifle's accuracy matches its handsome features. Kimber also offers high-grade semi-custom rifles. These are bolt-action models with many distinguishing attributes.

Customized rifles include any firearms that are altered, generally by restocking the barreled action, into unique and special pieces. Winchester's Model 52 is often customized. This fine target rifle is the basis for a very handsome, extremely accurate and totally reliable rifle. The finest grade wood can be employed in any stock style. Customized metalwork is also prevalent on customized 52s. Winchester offered the Model 52 in a Sporter version, incidentally. For those who insist on it, the Model 52 Sporter can be restocked in any design, with any grade of wood. One customized 52 Sporter of note wore a full-length Mannlicher-type stock of fancy-grade English walnut.

The full-blown-custom 22-rimfire rifle differs from the customized version in that it begins life as a barrel, an action, and a blank of wood. The gunsmith usually alters much of the original metalwork, and shapes the blank into a unique stock, often with specific dimensions to match the individual shooter. Gunsmiths will also handcraft custom 22-rimfire rifles using existing rifles with original bar-

The Kimber 22-rimfire rifle is a semi-custom model of fine accuracy and mechanical excellence. This Kimber wears a Leupold 1.5X-5X variable scope sight for quick work on running rabbits, as well as longer shots.

rels. But rebarreling as well as restocking is commonplace on 22 custom rifles. These fully custom rifles often include many interesting features. The major criterion of a true custom 22 sporter is its uniqueness. There will not be another exactly like it anywhere.

THE CENTERFIRE 22 RIFLE

A major employment for the 22-centerfire rifle is informal bench shooting. This statement may be vehemently denied by the varmint shooter who fires 90 percent of his 22-centerfire missiles at farm and ranch pests. But many owners of 22-centerfire rifles do shoot most of their bullets into sand banks behind paper targets. Obtaining fine groups becomes an obsession, even though these arms enthusiasts might never enter the ranks of serious benchrest competition. The 22 centerfire offers stupendous accuracy, without the recoil and blast associated with the big-bore rifle. Therefore, hours of enjoyable range work are possible without fatigue. Nonetheless, for our purposes, there are three uses for the 22-centerfire rifle: varmint hunting (with frequent bench shooting to sight rifles in and test new loads), serious benchrest competition, and big-game hunting.

22 Centerfire Varminting. The criteria for high-performance varmint rifles are several. Accuracy is the first. Without a high degree of accuracy, delivering the projectile to a small target in the distance is futile. However, the most accurate rifle in the land will not serve for varminting if it is not flat-shooting. Therefore, the second criterion for serious centerfire varminting is flatness of trajectory. Low (flat) trajectory and high velocity go together. That's a good thing, because the varmint rifle must project a frangible bullet at high speed in order to affect self-destruction upon striking the background, and the bullet must dispense its energy immediately on the target for a humane and instantaneous dispatch. Therefore, the high-intensity varmint cartridge fires thin-skinned bullets at high velocity, simultaneously filling the requirements of flat trajectory and bullet "blowup." Another vital criterion of the centerfire varmint rifle is *repeated* fire with accuracy. This requires, generally speaking, a fairly heavy barrel. A light barrel heats up too quickly. After several shots, the rifle's accuracy may go awry. The heavy barrel heats much more slowly.

The heavy barrel aids in delivering another important varmint-rifle requirement—stability. I recently range-tested a very accurate and interesting lightweight rifle, and after sight-in, took it into the varmint field against prairie dogs. Even from the sitting position, with as solid a shooting stance as possible in the field, the rifle failed miserably. It was simply too light to hold steadily. Shots beyond 150 yards were difficult if not impossible to make, even though the potential of the cartridge was a solid 300 yards.

The centerfire varminter must have a good trigger as well, because a hard trigger pull with creep will never allow the precision of letoff required for long-range work. Lock time, considered here as the elapsed time from the breaking of the sear to the detonation of the primer, must be relatively fast too.

A seemingly minor matter, a slow lock time is, in fact, a significant detriment to pinpoint accuracy.

Finally, the precision varmint rifle must be fitted with a telescopic sight of high magnification with a clear reticle that does not obliterate a small and distant target. The scope must have high optical definition, with accurate sight adjustment capability.

Fortunately, most of these criteria are met in a large sampling of modern rifles. The single-shot varmint rifle is well-represented in Thompson/Center's model chambered for the 22 Hornet, 222 Remington, 223 Remington and 22-250 Remington. A test model in 22-250 proved very satisfactory. The T/C Contender, normally a single-shot pistol, is now available with rifle stock as a carbine. It's chambered for the 22 Hornet, 222 and 223 Remington, as well as the 22 Long Rifle. Another excellent single-shot long-range varmint rifle is Browning's Model 1885. This handsome piece is chambered for the 223 Remington and 22-250 Remington. Ruger's No. 1 Single Shot rifle is available in many different centerfire varmint calibers, including the 223 Remington, 22-250, and the speedster-class 220 Swift. Bolt-action single-shot varmint rifles are out there too. More on these in a moment.

The Ruger Mini-14 semi-auto rifle chambered in 223 Remington was tested for this book. It never failed to function perfectly, and when scoped, it proved useful for varmints. Other self-loading varmint rifles are the Valmet M-76 and Valmet Hunter, also in 223 Remington caliber. The Voere Model 2185 Auto Rifle is chambered for the hot 5.6 × 57mm, the 5.6 × 50mm, 222 Remington, 222 Remington Magnum, and 223 Remington. The semi-auto 22-centerfire rifle is well-suited to carry in a vehicle in varmint country where shots can be fast and extemporaneous. Browning's BLR lever-

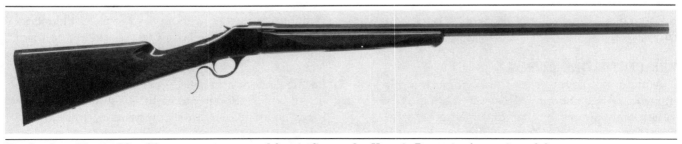

Single-shot rifles in 22 caliber are not reserved for rimfires only. Here is Browning's version of the Model 1885 single-shot, offered in 22-250 Remington.

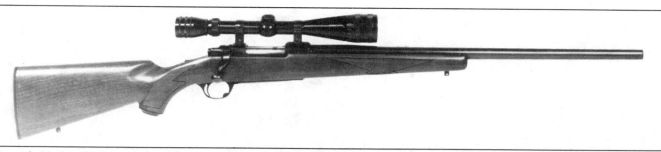

Ruger's Model 77-V varmint rifle is available in 22-250 Remington caliber. It has a heavy barrel and is fitted with Ruger's tip-off ring mounts.

action rifle—chambered in 222 Remington, 223 Remington and 22-250 Remington—also works well in varminting when opportunities are multiple and the action swift. These are specialty varmint rifles used for close, fast action.

The scope-sighted bolt-action rifle is king of the varmint class, however, with many models to choose from. Nearly every major gun company offers a bolt-action rifle in one of the hot 22-centerfire numbers. All of the bolt-action rifles chambered in 22 centerfire are suitable for varminting. However, a number of bolt-action rifles are built specifically for varmint hunting. Generally, these have barrels of heavier than sporter dimension, with medium, not light, overall weight. They "rest well," and are very accurate. Some are repeaters. Others are of single-shot design, because rapid repeated fire is seldom required for long-range varmint hunting. The single-shot style lends itself to high levels of accuracy due to the solid floor of the rifle. Such additional rigidness promotes bullet grouping.

The Beeman/Krico Model 640 Varmint Rifle is chambered only in 222 Remington caliber. It has a four-shot magazine. The rifle weighs almost nine pounds. Mossberg's Model 1500 Varmint Deluxe Rifle has a heavy barrel and weighs a stable 9½ pounds. It's chambered for the 222 Remington, 223 Remington and the 22-250 Remington. Remington's BDL Varmint Special is known for its good trigger and fast lock time. This rifle weighs about nine pounds, has a heavy 24-inch barrel and is chambered for the 222, 223, and 22-250 Remington centerfire 22 rounds. The Savage Model 110-V Varmint Rifle has a heavy 26-inch barrel in calibers 223 or 22-250 Remington. The Shilen DGA Varmint rifle is another heavy-barrel model of high accuracy potential in all of the 22-centerfire varmint calibers. Steyr-Mannlicher also has a varmint rifle with a

heavy 26-inch barrel, chambered for the 222 or 22-250 Remington. The Wichita Varmint Rifle is a very accurate model chambered in various 22-centerfire varmint rounds, including the 22 PPC. And Winchester offers its Model 70 in a varmint rifle, calibers 223 and 22-250 Remington.

By far, the most varmint shooting conducted for this work was with Sako's Vixen in 22 PPC caliber, and results were extremely gratifying. The high accuracy potential of the rifle (with its heavy barrel and stiff single-shot action), coupled with the benchrest accuracy of the hot little 22 PPC cartridge, made the Vixen a precision instrument for varminting. A handloaded 52-grain bullet achieved a muzzle velocity of close to 3600 feet per second. Groups of one-third inch at 100 yards were common as stars in a clear night sky. Oftentimes, the rifle printed groups of one-fourth inch center to center at 100 yards from the bench. In fact, when the atmosphere was clear, without undue heat waves or wind, the quarter-inch group was commonplace. It was the rifle's accuracy, coupled with the mild report and light recoil of the cartridge, that gave the Vixen the highest shot-per-hit record of our test rifles in an eight-month varminting session. Only a custom heavy-barrel rifle by Dale Storey of DGS, Inc., rivaled the day-by-day accuracy of the 22 PPC Vixen.

Bench Shooting. Competitive benchrest shooting has but one major goal: the event of each bullet flying exactly through the hole created by the bullet before it. That goal has not yet been achieved; however, previous records would scarcely qualify a rifle and its cartridge in today's competitive benchrest shooting circles. Few factory rifles can compete in serious benchrest events—although the aforementioned Vixen in caliber 22 PPC is one that could, with proper handling. Admittedly, the 6mm

The Sako heavy-barreled model chambered for the 22 PPC USA cartridge is another specialized 22 rifle (this one in centerfire). Its super accuracy makes it extremely effective in the varmint field.

PPC, not the 22 PPC, holds the lion's share of bench-rest records, but the potential for the smaller caliber to chew a tiny circle out of the paper target is decidedly there. The serious competitive benchrest shooter is seldom content with less than handmade quality, and most of his rifles are custom made. The new PPC Vixen, however, will no doubt be tuned by the bench shooter in quest of the perfect group. It will compete.

Big Game Hunting. Depending upon individual state laws, the 22-caliber centerfire cartridge may be legal for big-game hunting. The practice of taking big game, such as deer or antelope, with any 22-caliber bullet is often questioned, of course. Twenty-two caliber varmint bullets are light and not built for penetration. An exception was the wildcat 226 Barnes QT, which was used with great success on many big-game species. This wildcat fired a very long 125-grain .226-inch bullet at a muzzle velocity of about 2700 feet per second. The high sectional density and excellent ballistic coefficient of this bullet promoted long-range energy retention, as well as penetration. Dropping a big-game animal in its tracks with one well-placed projectile was common for this big 22-caliber round based on the 7 × 57 Mauser case. The 226 Barnes fired a bullet of big-game jacket thickness, however, rather than a thin-shelled missile. All doubts aside, the fact remains that every year expert hunters fill their freezers with big-game meat harvested by the 220 Swift, 22-250, and similar cartridges.

If it seems outlandish to use a 22-caliber rifle on big game such as deer, consider the fact that most states allow handguns of the 41 to 44 Magnum class. If you believe in energy figures, then you can't deny the impetus of the fast 22 centerfire. In order to give the great 44 Magnum handgun cartridge its full potential in the following derivations, a 265-grain bullet was handloaded to a muzzle velocity of 1300 fps. At 100 yards from the muzzle, remaining energy for this big missile was 818 foot-pounds (995 foot-pounds at the muzzle). Meanwhile,

a 60-grain bullet starting at 3600 fps from the 22-250 achieved a 100-yard energy level of 1359 foot-pounds. The 220 Swift drives the same bullet at 3700 fps. The 5.6 × 57mm RWS 22 centerfire pushes the same bullet at 3800 fps muzzle velocity for even more power, the latter having a 200-yard remaining energy of about 1200 foot-pounds.

I am not an advocate of a 22-caliber thin-jacketed varmint bullet for general big-game hunting—but the above energy figures are undeniable. Expert hunters using projectiles designed for big-game hunting, and not for explosive effect on varmints, can cleanly harvest big game with 22 centerfire rifles. Bullet placement is the watchword of these hunters, and only the "good shots" are attempted. Were I to go afield with a 22 centerfire for game larger than deer, however, my preference would be the 226 Barnes wildcat with its long, and comparatively heavy, projectile. Bullet weight is important in field performance on big game, and this heavier 22 caliber missile of greater mass would penetrate much better than its lighter cousins.

The right 22 rifle for you—what is it? It's the 22-rimfire model that meets your particular needs in the field or at the target range, the rifle *you like best*. You prefer the way it looks, the way it handles, and how it performs. The same can be said for the 22-centerfire rifle. If that rifle is for varmint hunting, the major employment for the vast majority of hotshot centerfire 22s, be sure to seek accuracy and shooting stability above all other attributes. The species normally hunted with the centerfire 22 are not large. They do not require great stopping power in a rifle. Streaking bullets of frangible design cleanly drop woodchucks, jackrabbits, and similar-sized game with totally humane effect out to a full 300 yards and sometimes much farther. But you have to hit 'em first. And that requires, above all else, supreme long-range precision in bullet placement.

6 WHICH 22 HANDGUN FOR YOU?

Handguns in 22 caliber are high-service firearms. They do Yeoman's work for their owners. The 22-rimfire revolver, single-shot pistol, or semi-automatic pistol is a shooting instrument of major importance in any complete battery. The 22-rimfire handgun serves many purposes, including camp gun, trail gun, competition shooting, informal target shooting, silhouette matches, small-game hunting, varminting, survival, and plinking. The 22-centerfire pistol (and revolver, in a few rare instances) is a special firearm as well. It can be used for most of the duties performed by the 22-rimfire handgun. Scope-sighted, it becomes an interesting varminting machine. There have been so many changes in the world of handgunning in the past decade or two that the old-time sidearm image is as worn as a million-year-old stream rock. All of the 22 sidearms discussed here are currently available, even though some are out of manufacture. These long-lasting arms are often sold in like-new condition in sporting stores and hock shops, or through arms newspapers. Every 22 sidearm should be selected on the basis of function—the shooting purpose that the firearm will fulfill.

THE RIMFIRE 22 HANDGUN

The first consideration is the selection of a semi-automatic pistol, double-action revolver, or single-action revolver. The single-shot 22-rimfire pistol is also in switch-barrel models that allow interchangeability for a multitude of calibers on one pistol frame. The latter is well-illustrated by the Thompson/Center single-shot pistol. One flick of an external manual firing pin selector allows the T/C pistol to handle both centerfire and rimfire barrels. Thereby, the T/C is capable of functioning as a single-shot rimfire pistol, as well as a single-shot centerfire pistol, depending upon choice of optional barrels. As noted, there are many other single-shot

rimfire pistols for competition target shooting. These are quite specialized.

What are the criteria that steer the selection of the 22-rimfire revolver or pistol? First, let's look at accuracy. Target matches are shot with 22-rimfire semi-auto pistols in high competition. All in all, the 22 pistol renders the more sparkling accuracy of these two general handgun types. This does not impune the accuracy of the revolver, however; and for trail use, plinking, small-game hunting and other 22 sidearm chores, the revolver shoots with ample precision to accomplish the job. Cartridge capacity goes in favor of the pistol. For example, the fine Charter Arms Pathfinder revolver is a

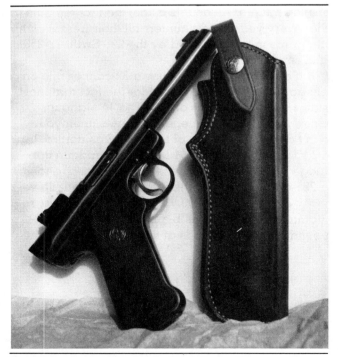

The 22 semi-auto, or simply "auto" pistol is a good choice for the rimfire fan.

The Smith & Wesson Model 650 Stainless Kit Gun is offered in 22 WMR chambering. **It makes an excellent camp sidearm and trailgun.**

sixshooter, chambered for 22 Long Rifle or 22 Winchester Magnum Rimfire (WMR), with two-, three-, or six-inch barrel. There have, however, been nine-shot 22-rimfire revolvers. Nonetheless, the 22 pistol usually carries a 10-shot clip, and my own Ruger Mark II is outfitted with Ram-Line 12-shot clips. So firepower goes in favor of the pistol. Extra clips give the pistol an edge in fast reloading too. I pack two extra clips for my 22 auto, both tucked into one Uncle Mike's carrying pouch, giving a total of 36 shots on the trail without opening a fresh box of 22 ammo.

The pistol is flat-sided. It tucks away neatly. There is no cylinder to cause a bulge. There are no pressing decisions in sight choice—both pistol and revolver are capable of wearing equally good sights. Both handle well. However, individual shooters may prefer the feel of one style over the other. Both are entirely reliable, except for cheap models, in which case neither style can be counted on. Incidentally, low-grade semi-autos are rare, but there are a number of ill-made 22-rimfire revolvers around. Avoid them. Buy a good brand.

Tradition swings in favor of the revolver, especially the single-action sixgun. Looks? That's a matter of personal preference, but there are two areas in which the revolver wins this particular comparison debate. First, a revolver may be outfitted with a convertible cylinder. This means that in one revolver, such as the Ruger Single-Six, both 22-rimfire standard ammo and 22-rimfire magnum ammo may be used by simply switching cylinders. Second, the revolver can handle 22 Short, Long

and Long Rifle ammo. The pistol cannot.

There are choices within choices, too. The 22-rimfire semi-auto pistol comes in a small pocket model or a full-scale version. Most of us will choose the latter, especially for its excellent sights, sometimes lacking on the pocket version. The barrel may be short or long, heavy or standard in weight. My trail gun has the heavy barrel. The minor additional weight is not a carrying problem, and the sidearm holds a bit steadier with the up-front mass. But the standard barrel keeps pistol weight and bulk down.

If your choice is a revolver, you'll have to decide between single-action or double-action. The single-action serves well and should not be considered a drawback. The fact that the hammer must be cocked for each shot causes no problem in small-game hunting, plinking, or target shooting. The double-action revolver offers more rapid fire, however, in that the sidearm can be activated with the pull of the trigger alone, which automatically brings the hammer back and allows it to fall forward. Choose the style of firearm you prefer, with the sights you like. Don't worry about its single-action or double-action nature. The double-action is manually cocked for serious shooting anyway, since this allows a much more refined trigger pull.

Twenty-two rimfire choice is further complicated these days, happily so, by the innovative sidearms being offered. for example, Browning's standard Buck Mark 22 Pistol is now available in optional styles—there is a Buck Mark Silhouette model and a Buck Mark Varmint model. The former has a

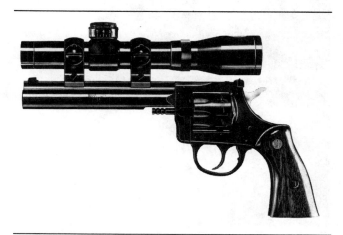

Today's 22-rimfire revolver may wear a scope sight. This H&R swing-out-cylinder model is fitted with a 3X hunting and silhouette scope sight.

heavy 9⅞-inch barrel with a .900-inch muzzle. It comes with a Millett Gold Cup target rear sight and a hooded front sight. The Silhouette also has special grips. The Varmint model has the same heavy barrel, but no sights at all. It's fitted with a full-length scope base instead. The scope fits very close to the receiver on this model. RWS target ammo in the Varmint model registered groups of only .45 inch at 25 yards. These are but two examples of today's many different 22-caliber handgun styles. There are many new competition models as well for the seeker of target shooting trophies.

The competition 22 handgun is a specialized piece of fine-tuned equipment, beautifully made and interesting. (Some of them look like the fictional Buck Rogers ray gun). Of course, they are very accurate. The competition rimfire handgun fills the needs of the serious target shooter out to win the gold, but will seldom be found in the hands of the plinker or small-game hunter. One word about that: if the marksman is very interested in high scoring in the plinking and small-game arena, there is

The author's 22-rimfire semi-auto pistol has three clips, the original 10-shot clip and two plastic 12-shot clips housed in an Uncle Mike's belt container.

nothing wrong with choosing a competition model 22-rimfire handgun—except for the cost. These fine guns are expensive. The Smith & Wesson Model 22 Heavy Match Barrel semi-auto pistol, with 10-shot clip, sells for $500. However, when the major goal of the backcountry hiker using a 22 pistol is to secure important fresh food, bullet placement is the key to success; and if you can't center 'em with the high-grade competition 22 handgun, you probably wouldn't have gotten your game with a less accurate model. Informal target shooting is also a lot of fun when the handgun is capable of match-level accuracy. It's only fair to put the author on the spot in asking what he's selected for his 22-rimfire sidearm—actually, a few different models, but on the backtrail, where most of my serious 22-shooting seems to take place, I find the semi-auto pistol ideal. Mine is a Ruger Mark II with target sights and heavy barrel.

As for sights, if you're content to whip your little 22 handgun out and splash the dirt up close to a tin can at 35 paces, choose a model with a slice in the topstrap for a back sight and a barleycorn-shaped blade front sight. The 22 sidearm is not a baseball. You don't shoot it with instinctive tossing of the bullet in the direction of the target. You aim it. And aiming requires sights. Before getting lynched by those who prefer the fixed-sight model, I admit to having a heavy-duty Charter Arms trail gun in 44 Special caliber with fixed sights. It's meant for close-range work only, should some wild beast grab my boot and not want to let go. There is no reason to outfit this rugged revolver with target sights. If very close-range work is your only 22-rimfire handgun goal, fine. Go with fixed sights. For all other duty, obtain the best adjustable sights your model choice allows.

A backwoods hunter friend of mine woke up in camp one morning announcing, "I'm going to get us some snowshoes for supper." He did—two of them—after he used up all of his 22-rimfire ammo and part of my supply. Even though the shots were close, trying to harvest rabbits cleanly with a fixed sight revolver was no easy task.

Sight choices include fixed (no easy adjustment), adjustable sights, target-type adjustable sights, and the scope. For most 22-rimfire handgun shooting, the adjustable iron sight in standard or target form is ideal.

Barrel length in the 22-rimfire handgun is more crucial to accuracy than the reader may assume.

On the trail, it's hard to beat a 22 semi-auto pistol. Because of the excellent sights, and a sturdy rest, making head shots on small game is an almost sure thing.

Some time ago, a shooter discovered that his 22 pistol was punching perfect 32-caliber holes in the target 25 yards away. He took the problem to the National Rifle Association staff. The staff duplicated the pistol, target, and ammo. Their 22 pistol also produced neat, round, 32-caliber holes in the target at 25 yards. It turned out that bullet bases were upsetting in the very short two-inch barrel of this particular semi-auto pistol. The bullets looked as though they had bell bottoms, the NRA staff explained. Accuracy was destroyed. Turning to a somewhat harder 22 Long Rifle bullet improved the condition, but accuracy was still very low from the short barrel. The test was enlarged. Using a 22

semi-auto pistol with a 5½-inch barrel, groups were carefully recorded, the barrel bobbed by one-half inch after each shooting session. Here is what happened. From 25 yards, firing Eley Tenex target ammunition, 22 Long Rifle, 40-grain bullet, the pistol grouped .70 inch with its original 5½-inch barrel.

Nothing was said of recrowning, i.e., recessing or beveling, the muzzle after each session in this test; however, muzzle crown was not a contributing factor to accuracy as the barrel was bobbed. The decline in accuracy was commensurate with the shortening of the barrel. In fact, when the barrel was cut to five inches even, the group size did not change statistically. It grew smaller, but only to .68

Practice in the varmint field improves the handgunner's chances with his favorite trailgun. Through stalking, good close shots on these prairie dogs paid off.

inch, which is not a statistically significant amount of change to call it certain improvement. But at 4½ inches the group *declined significantly* in tightness, growing to .95 inch center to center. At four inches, another group enlargement was recorded, albeit a small one, .99 inch. At 3½ inches, group size plumped up to 1.19 inches center to center. When the barrel was chopped to three inches, group size again blimped out, this time to 1.37 inches. At 2½ inches, the group became a full 1.55 inches center to center. Compare that with the original .70-inch group, and the difference is marked. Things grew even worse when the barrel was sawed off to two-inch length, the group size again increasing, this time to 1.70 inches, pretty lousy performance.

To set the record straight, short barrels are not inherently inaccurate. I tested a short-barreled revolver with good results. If your 22 pistol or revolver requirement is compactness, buy the barrel that suits that demand. Then, test various ammunition until you find the particular brand that shoots most accurately in that sidearm. However, according to present testing, medium-length to long pistol barrels show greater accuracy than shorter barrels.

The next chapter deals specifically with rimfire accuracy and further information on pistol barrel length and accuracy is revealed there. It is my contention at this point that part of the problem encountered with withered accuracy in the short pistol barrel has to do with bullet upset. A harder-based bullet may prove more accurate in these short-barreled models. Nevertheless, there is also the question of proper powder consumption to consider, and the short barrel may not allow an efficient burning of the powder charge.

As for velocity and barrel length in the 22-rimfire handgun, in one test, a 5½-inch pistol barrel achieved a muzzle velocity of 1063 fps with the 40-grain Remington 22 Long Rifle cartridge. When the same barrel was lopped off to only two inches, the velocity with the same cartridge fell to 802 fps. With the 5½-inch barrel, this pistol delivered a muzzle velocity of 1034 fps with Remington's hollow-point 22 Long Rifle ammunition. But when the same load was fired in the bobbed two-inch barrel, velocity plummeted to only 776 fps.

Obviously, barrel length in the 22 sidearm is important to achieve optimum muzzle velocity and bullet energy. The short barrel has its place. But short pistol barrels do not deliver the velocity potential of the 22-rimfire round. And until better infor-

The standby single-action 22-rimfire revolver is well-adapted to many uses, from plinking to small-game hunting. This Ruger Single-Six Convertible model is stainless steel. By switching cylinders, the shooter has a choice between 22-rimfire or 22 magnum rimfire ammo.

mation is available concerning *why* tests reveal diminished accuracy in short barrels, the data must be considered as they now stand: the longer pistol barrel delivers better accuracy than the shorter pistol barrel.

A word about the 22 WMR in the pistol or revolver—this is a good cartridge in the handgun. Information to the contrary should be viewed with suspicion. I have not found the 22 WMR a veritable powerhouse in the sidearm, but it carries considerably more authority than its smaller rimfire brother, the 22 Long Rifle. The 22 WMR may not provide match-winning accuracy in the handgun, but it delivers a level of accuracy capable of handling a great percentage of 22-rimfire sidearm work. Son John Fadala has used his Ruger single-action 22 WMR on the backwoods trail for years, collecting mountain grouse and other edibles. Winchester and Federal 22 WMR ammo was tested in a revolver with a 5½-inch barrel. The muzzle velocity was 1396 fps for the 40-grain Winchester full-metal-jacket bullet. Using Federal's 22 WMR ammo, the

40-grain bullet achieved 1336 fps muzzle velocity with a very low (excellent) standard deviation.

Federal's 50-grain 22 WMR bullet left the muzzle at 1115 fps from the 5½-inch barrel. In a Dan Wesson 22 WMR revolver, groups of about .75 inch at 25 yards were common with Federal ammunition and the 40-grain bullet. That's good rimfire performance from the handgun. The 50-grain Federal bullet proved adequate for close-range varminting in one field study. On a high-mountain hunt, the cartridge was four for four on marmots. These are very tough rodents that weigh as much as a dozen pounds or more, requiring good ballistic performance for a clean harvest. Only close shots were attempted, the longest being 39 paces from muzzle to marmot. But the 22 WMR hollow-point did the trick.

As noted, the 22 WMR is also offered in a semi-auto pistol. The aforementioned AMT semi-auto Automag Mark II chambered for the 22 magnum rimfire cartridge has a 10-shot clip. The pistol sports a six-inch barrel, weighs 23 ounces, and measures 9⅜ inches overall. Its Millett adjustable rear sight and fine blade front make a good aiming combination. This pistol is of rugged stainless steel construction. The T/C Contender has a 22 WMR barrel option, should the shooter want a single-shot 22-rimfire magnum handgun. The Wichita Hunter single-shot pistol is also available in 22 WMR. Another 22 magnum is the Anshutz Exemplar bolt-action pistol with 10-inch barrel. This is a repeater in 22 magnum that carries four rounds of ammo in its magazine. The Charter Arms Pathfinder revolver is

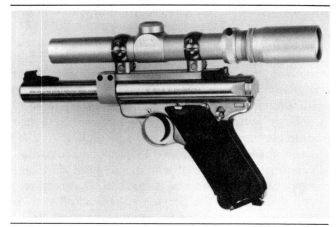

Styles of 22-caliber handguns are as diverse as their functions. And scopes, for example, are at home on the 22-rimfire sidearm as well as the centerfire models, as this Ruger demonstrates.

chambered in 22 magnum, as is the Smith & Wesson Model 650/651 Kit Gun. Freedom Arms has a well-made four-shot 22 WMR revolver, a tiny package of close-range power for the hiker or camper. Don't forget Ruger's Convertible 22 WMR sixgun. The 22 WMR is well-represented in the handgun world.

THE CENTERFIRE 22 HANDGUN

In the entire scheme of things, the 22-centerfire sidearm is a new development. Of course, in firearms it's difficult to find anything that hasn't been touched on in the past. Such is the case with the 22-centerfire handgun. In the early 1900s (around

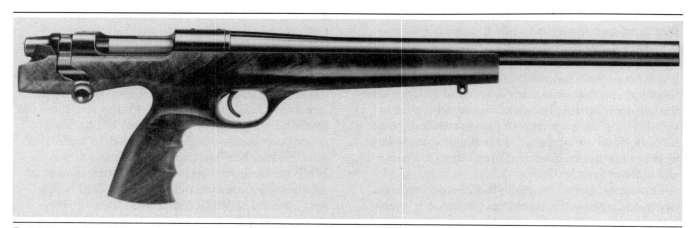

Remington's XP-100 custom pistol is chambered for the 223 Remington cartridge. This hot centerfire pistol is designed to wear a scope sight (note absence of iron sights).

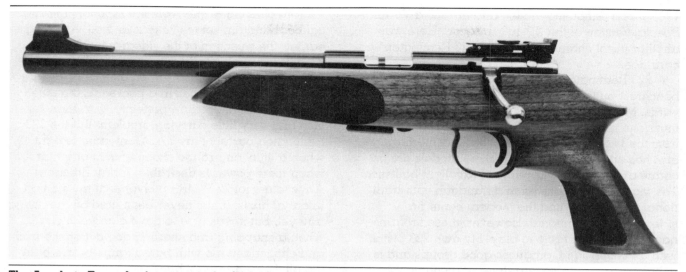

The Anschutz Exemplar is a target pistol (single-shot) used in the unlimited class of silhouette competition. Note the bolt operates from the left, which is well-suited to the right-handed shooter who is not required to switch hands when he wants to operate the action of the gun.

1914), gunmaker Fred Adolph of Genoa, N.Y., was producing a single-shot pistol chambered for a 22-caliber centerfire cartridge of his own invention. However, it was not until the late 1950s and early 1960s that work began with an interesting handgun cartridge known as the 22 Jet developed by Remington. The 22 Jet was chambered in a Smith & Wesson Model 53 22 Center-Fire Magnum revolver. The cartridge was officially called the 22 Remington Jet Center-Fire Magnum, which was developed by necking down a 357 Magnum case to 22 caliber with a fairly sloping shoulder. Advertised muzzle velocity for the 40-grain .222-inch bullet was 2460 fps from a test barrel. But in the S&W revolver, velocity was 1870 fps, still quite good. The Model 53, with its 8³⁄₈-inch barrel, had a dual firing pin arrangement. Rotation of the hammer nose pivoted the firing pins. An adapter allowed the use of 22-rimfire ammunition. So the 53 could be fired with either 22 Jet, or 22 Long Rifle ammo. The 53 was not entirely satisfactory, but it was interesting.

The Thompson/Center Contender proved a natural for centerfire 22-caliber cartridges. Barrels in 22 Hornet, 222 Remington, and 223 Remington are currently offered for the T/C. The pistol should work well with the 22 PPC, too, but there is no commercial Contender barrel chambered for that round yet. T/C barrels have also been chambered for the 22 K-Hornet, 218 Bee, and 221 Fireball. Ithaca had an X-Caliber pistol, Model 20 target model, and a

Model 30 hunting model, chambered for the 223 Remington cartridge. Interchangeable barrels of 10 or 14 inches were offered for the X-Caliber.

The 223 has found its way into several other pistols, such as the Kimber Predator. This handsome and well-made sidearm is also chambered for the 221 Fireball in 22 caliber, which size is our only interest for the 22 book, of course. The Predator is compact, but not overly light. It has stability. Kimber's Predator has a barrel of 15¼ inches. It's a bolt-action pistol bereft of sights, because it was designed to wear a scope. Built on the famous Model 84 action, this pistol has an AA Claro walnut stock and uses the Kimber scope-mounting system. Hand-checkering is available on the Super Grade Predator.

An RPM pistol is offered in caliber 225 Winchester, among others. The 225 is a semi-rimmed cartridge, a design that works well in some single-shot action styles. Although semi-rimmed, the 225 headspaces on the shoulder, as a rimless cartridge would.

Then there is the Ultra-Light Model 20 Reb Hunter's Pistol, built in 22-250 Remington. This strong bolt-action single-shot pistol, with a five-shot magazine, has a 14-inch Douglas barrel.

The famous Remington XP-100 bolt-action single-shot pistol goes back to 1963. Originally, the XP-100 was chambered for the 221 Fire Ball, which name was later changed to 221 Fireball. Following in

1980 was a Silhouette model, and in 1986 a Varmint Special version of the XP-100 surfaced. Here was another pistol chambered for the 223 Remington cartridge.

A 223 Remington handload firing a 53-grain benchrest bullet produced a .60-inch group at 50 yards. Muzzle velocity was 2961 fps 12 feet from muzzle to mid-screens on the chronograph, this from the 14.5-inch barrel. Thus, the 22-centerfire sidearm has come a long way. Today's models are accurate and generally capable of excellent ballistics. The marksman interested in a handgun with traditional styling may find the modern centerfire sidearm unconventional. However, these firearms have an important role to play. My own 223 pistol, with 3X scope sight, produces good groups and is in every way a viable varminter at a couple hundred yards.

From plinking to survival field function, the 22-caliber handgun serves its master well. As noted earlier, the selection of the sidearm in 22 caliber is predicated upon application—what will the handgun be used for? When I am on the backtrail with my "house" on my back in a packsack, the little semi-auto fills the picture perfectly, with high-service and very little carrying problem. But the 223 Remington barrel of my T/C Contender is right when a little long-range shooting is in order, or when more power is desirable. A tiny Freedom Arms four-shot 22 WMR revolver is at my side on informal hikes. It has never been fired on the hiking trail yet, but it was nice to have along one day when a snapping and snarling dog cut off the trail and challenged me with bared fangs before backing off. More on the 22 handgun in upcoming chapters. But for now, on to 22-rimfire accuracy.

7 IMPROVING YOUR 22 RIMFIRE ACCURACY

The keys to the kingdom of rimfire accuracy are many. With these keys, the shooter can open the doors to improved grouping. When Colonel Whelen made his famous statement, "Only accurate rifles are interesting," the echo of his sentiment touched upon the entire world of shooting—rimfire and centerfire, sidearm and longarm. Shooting isn't a game of horse shoes. Close doesn't count. On target does. It's interesting, and perhaps even necessary, to establish what rimfire accuracy is before launching our ship of search into this subject. If the shooter does not know what to expect, how can he be satisfied with the groups made by his 22-rimfire sidearm or rifle? Since the inception of the BB Cap, shooters have wanted to improve the accuracy potential of their rimfire shooting machines. Their goal of high-grade accuracy has been shared with manufacturers of arms and ammunition the world over. Today, we have the most precise 22-rimfire ammo ever made, along with the most advanced firearms to chamber them. The following discussion is meant to improve the level of performance with these fine guns and ammo.

Accuracy is an involved subject. During a two-year research period, accumulated data on the topic filled a small book. This and the next chapter are the strained broth from those data. Criteria for accuracy run from the design, condition, and configuration of the bore to the shape of the powder charge in the case. Maximum accuracy results when precision and consistency are secured in all areas.

THE FIREARM

Perhaps you should buy a better rifle or sidearm. Tell this to shooters and you may as well say that their kids' noses are too long, or their favorite hunting dog is ugly. But the sad fact remains: if your desire is close-clustering of bullet holes on the target, you may have to buy a firearm capable of doing the job. This advice stands taller for handguns than for rifles. Over the years, many 22-rimfire rifles have rested on my test bench. Most of them shot acceptably well. But only precision-made handguns shot with match-winning accuracy.

Sometimes you can combine both sporter and target rifle in one sleek rimfire creation, such as my Kimber rifle, which was made with specific criteria in mind, especially accuracy and stability. My Kimber is not a lightweight. I recently proved its accuracy by firing several five-shot groups into one-third-inch patterns, center to center, from 50 yards, using Lapua Long Rifle ammunition. My Ruger heavy barrel pistol outshoots an older lightweight model with short barrel too. So sometimes the best

One of Sam Fadala's favorite small-game rifles is capable of making five-shot groups like this at 75 yards. Such accuracy pays off in the field when the target is no wider than a tree squirrel's head.

way to improve accuracy is to upgrade the machinery.

22 RIMFIRE ACCURACY IN THE DAYS OF YORE

Knowing the progression of 22-rimfire accuracy is helpful in gaining a perspective on modern rifle and handgun capability. United States gallery shooting was popular in the late 1800s, and this type of shooting promoted the gallery load. Indirectly, the gallery load led to more accurate 22-rimfire field ammunition. The U.S. Cartridge Company may have offered the first good gallery ammunition. It was initially loaded with black powder, smokeless taking over in the late 1890s. Lesmok was found in gallery loads into 1911. This mixture of black and smokeless powder, sometimes called "nitro," was more accurate than the first smokeless powder 22-rimfire loads. Peters was linked with King's powder company; therefore, King's semi-smokeless powder was found in Peters 22-rimfire ammo. A semi-wadcutter bullet was also available for gallery shooting. Remington tried a semi-wadcutter missile, but later dropped it. Later still, CCI developed a semi-wadcutter bullet for the 22 Long Rifle, but the bullet never became available to the general public. Nonetheless, these developments prompted further investigation of 22-rimfire accuracy potential.

Semi-smokeless powder made sense in its time. It provided greater accuracy; besides, priming mixtures were corrosive anyway, so even if smokeless powder was used, the bore still required cleaning after each shooting session for best barrel life. Suddenly, a non-corrosive priming mixture appeared. Smokeless powder coupled with non-corrosive priming created a whole new dimension in 22-rimfire shooting. Rigorous bore cleaning was a thing of the past. Bullet lubrication grew more sophisticated as well. Bullets could be electroplated with copper, for example, to prevent leading of the bore. These bullets, it was said, created more bore wear than regular "greased" lead projectiles. Whelen stated that copper-plated bullets wore a bore out in 50,000 rounds, whereas the same bore would last 250,000 rounds with standard 22-rimfire bullets. Soon, properly lubricated 22 bullets that did not unduly wear the bore became the rule.

Accuracy was on the rise. Whelen kept records. In 1912, his tests with REM-UMC ammo and Lesmok gave an average of 1.95-inch 10-shot groups at 50 yards. Winchester's Lesmok provided the same level of accuracy, or about 2.0 inches. Peters's Lesmok was better (maybe it was the good King's powder that helped). Whelen recorded groups of 1.30 inches. The Colonel discovered that by 1914, Winchester's Lesmok was producing .78-inch groups at 50 yards for 10 shots. His test rifle in 1911 had been a Winchester Single-Shot with 26-inch No. 3 round barrel fitted with a Winchester A-5 scope sight. This was no doubt the test rifle that produced the above groups. Match-grade ammunition provided excellent results. In 1918, 100-yard groups of about one inch center to center were recorded with match-grade 22 Long Rifle ammunition. The 22 Springfield (US Rifle, Cal. 22, Model of 1922 M1 Springfield), chambered for the 22 Long Rifle cartridge, was developed for "ranges from 50 feet to 200 yards." It wore a Lyman No. 48 aperture sight coupled with a standard 1903 black front sight on a 24-inch barrel. Tests for accuracy with this rifle included 50-yard shooting in which 10 shots had to cluster into a one-inch circle. Ammo that could not achieve this level was shunned. The following ammo qualified: Remington Kleanbore, Winchester Precision 200, Remington Palma, U.S.N.R.A., Peters Tack Hole, and Western Marksman, to name some brands.

Precision 22-rimfire shooting was well underway. In 1930, Jerry Hilborn of the Roosevelt Rifle Club of New York fired a 9/10-inch group at 100 yards, with nine of the bullets cutting a 13/16-inch pattern; the 10th shot opened the group to 9/10 of an inch. He

A firearm is no more accurate than its ammunition. In gaining the most from a given 22-rimfire rifle or handgun, accurate ammo is the byword. Fadala found RWS brand to be quite accurate.

Match the ammo to the rifle for best accuracy. John Fadala tries various brands of 22 Long Rifle fodder in a Winchester Model 75 Sporter.

used U.S. 22 NRA Long Rifle ammo. While the emphasis was still on plinking and small-game hunting, 22-rimfire rifles had also become serious instruments of match competition. High-speed ammo did not perform with the accuracy of match-grade fodder, but Federal XL hunting loads printed groups in 1936 under 1.5 inches at 50 yards. Furthermore, upgraded ammo made the popular 22 hunting rifle a far more accurate shooting instrument. A Marlin Model 39 lever-action model with a Wollensak 4X scope printed a 1.35-inch group at 50 yards *for 120 shots*. Now on to modern 22-rimfire accuracy and how to improve it.

THE AMMUNITION

Grades Of Ammunition. The devotee of 22 firearms has a broad variety of ammunition to choose from. Many other products vary hardly at all from one brand to the next or one model to another. For example, a given car model costing several thousand dollars more than a lower-priced style may exemplify no dramatic difference in actual function, its extra cost lying mainly in cosmetic appointments. Twenty-two ammo is not this way. Brands do make a difference. And various grades of 22-rimfire ammunition offer significant levels of accuracy difference. In one exemplary shooting session, 22 Long

Rifle high-velocity ammo was fired alongside standard-velocity and match-grade ammunition, all of the same brand, all from the same rifle, and under the same shooting conditions. The ammunition was fired randomly, with an average compiled for four five-shot groups. Long rifle high-velocity ammo was fired first, then match-grade, then standard-velocity, then match again, high-velocity, and so forth, giving no one grade of ammo an edge in terms of bore condition or atmospheric changes. When "the smoke cleared," the high-velocity product had provided an average 1.25-inch group at 50 yards. Standard-velocity ammo printed .95-inch groups. And match ammo had built .77-inch groups. Considering that a rabbit's head is about an inch and a half wide, even the high-velocity fodder was capable of a head shot at 50 yards. But on the face of it, the match-grade ammo was more accurate. Grades of 22-rimfire ammo do make an accuracy difference.

Matching The Ammo To The Firearm. Compatibility is the key. For many reasons, some quite defined and clear, others perhaps not so easy to isolate, certain ammunition shoots better in a given firearm than others. This fact was brought to bear a short time ago when a particular scoped bolt-action rifle created better groups with Winchester T-22 ammuni-

Proper sight-in eliminates as much of the human element as possible. The well-made portable benchrest, such as this Cabella's model, offers a steady platform from which to shoot.

tion than it did with a high-class (and very expensive) match-grade ammo. As noted above, match-grade ammunition produces great accuracy, as a rule. But as in all shooting, individual rifles perform individually. Therefore, it was only a mild surprise when off-the-shelf ammo provided better groups than match-grade fodder in this one rifle. Choose ammunition on the basis of grade, to be sure. Most matches are won with match ammunition and most varmints are dropped with high-velocity 22 Long Rifle hollow-points, but a careful matching of ammunition to the firearm, rifle or handgun, is essential in order to find that level of compatibility.

All tests for this book were from a benchrest, on only windless days, and with firearms in top condition. The reader, too, must control his test-shooting when trying to match ammo with rifle or sidearm. Use a bench. Pick good days. Fifty yards makes a reasonable test distance for the 22-rimfire rifle, 25 yards for the sidearm. A scope makes a big difference when trying to sort out the significant differences among various ammo brands and grades. Since 22-rimfire ammo is reasonably priced, it is not abrasive to the wallet to buy a wide variety of test samples. Try different brands and grades and decide only after averaging *several* groups. It is invalid to fire one group and rely on that single test for your ammunition decision. That decision, by the way, is not always formulated on the basis of accuracy alone. My Kimber rifle shoots Lapua ammunition in very tight clusters, but on the cottontail trail with that rifle, something on the order of Winchester's 22 Long Rifle silhouette ammo, Remington's standard-velocity Long Rifle or Federal's Champions (all which shoot very nicely in the rifle) will go along. For varmints, Federal's Spitfires may find their way into the Kimber's chamber. That's the beauty of the 22 rimfire—ammo choices are ocean-deep.

Standard Deviation. Since the modern chronograph has become fairly common in individual ownership and at the shooting club, shooters now have standard deviation figures at their fingertips. Oehler's 33 Chronotach, for example, computes standard deviation as a readout. You no longer need your pocket calculator. Standard deviation is a measure of *variance*. The goal is to see how much variance there is in a particular box of ammo. I use five-shot strings. Detractors of standard deviation generally choose to downgrade the formula's value in shooting by using arguments from educational-psychol-

In sighting the micrometer "peep" rear sight, click adjustments are used. Each click has a definite value at the target in terms of minutes of angle.

ogy applications.

However, as Oehler Research states, standard deviation remains a good means of studying ammo variance. It is not to be used by itself, though. It is only one indication of ammo excellence. But show me ammunition with a high standard-deviation figure, over 100 fps for example, and chances are, that ammo will not deliver the full accuracy potential of your firearm. Never rely on standard deviation alone. But if you have access to a chronograph and if that machine reads out standard-deviation figures, record them and compare them with actual group sizes of your ammo. Example: a brand of imported bargain ammunition was compared with a high-grade brand. The latter always provided smaller groups. Standard deviations for the bargain brand were 41, 56 and 46 fps, while the match ammo registered numbers of 9, 11 and 13 fps.

Sorting 22 Rimfire Ammo By Weight. The practice of weighing 22-rimfire cartridges in order to place them into specific batches—light, medium and heavy, for example—has its positive and negative sides. It is true that group sizes can be shrunk by weighing ammunition. If you weigh 50 rounds of 22 Long Rifle ammo, you'll note slight variations among them. By grouping the cartridges according to weight, you'll improve uniformity, and improved uniformity aids accuracy. However, weighing cannot account for bullet condition (flat spots, for ex-

ample), amount and distribution of priming mixture, bullet uniformity, and bullet configuration (a specific bullet shape may be more compatible than another in your firearm). It is more reliable to buy match-grade ammo when you demand match-grade accuracy than to take the time to weigh each cartridge in an attempt to improve uniformity. Furthermore, remember that ammo may have to be selected in accord with the action of the firearm. My Ruger pistol and Marlin semi-auto rifle actions will not function with some milder 22 Long Rifle ammo, which does not offer the impetus to force the bolt back. But pre-weighing ammo is an economical means of improving accuracy.

OTHER KEY CONSIDERATIONS

Sights. Accuracy is obviously improved when the potential of the rifle is more fully realized through good sights. The telescopic sight is king, but good iron sights have their application too. Aperture or peep sights can produce very close grouping. The use of the peep sight optically sharpens the target. The smaller aperture further sharpens both front and back sight, although a larger aperture is best for most hunting. Shooting glasses and corrective lenses aid in seeing the target clearly. Match the sight to the rifle and its use. A silhouette rifle, for example, will carry a powerful telescopic sight. A rifle used for hunting cottontails in the brush may have open iron sights. The "peep" sight is excellent for all shooting in which the target need not be magnified. This is a chapter on accuracy, and the accuracy potential of the rifle or handgun is best served by a scope sight.

The scope sight is functional for reasons other than clear aim. A pattern of ammo behavior is far easier to establish when a scope is mounted on the firearm. For example, I've discovered brands and grades of 22-rimfire cartridges that put three of five shots into a neat cluster, with the other two going wild. The scope allows more precision of aim, hence more uniformity in ammo-grouping. In short, you can tell what's going on with your ammo when the firearm is capable of consistently good groups. Furthermore, body control can be greatly enhanced with a telescope, especially a high-power unit. The scope magnifies the degree of motion so greatly that the shooter has a graphic illustration of how he actually handles his firearm. Once he isolates body-motion problems, he can correct these negatives through mental and physical self-training. Shooters are amazed as they improve on the silhouette field, the rifle more and more under control.

Be sure that the scope matches the rifle or handgun. My own Model 75 Winchester Sporter rifle wore a scope for some time; today it a has an aperture sight. I found no scope that correctly fitted the receiver for proper eye relief without special extension rings, which I did not want on that particular arm. I fought it for a long time, missing close shots when I forgot to pull my head back on the stock in order to gain a full "sight picture" in the scope. Finally, I removed the scope and installed the aperture sight. The rifle has been more productive ever since. However, a 1.5X-5X Leupold variable scope complements my Kimber bolt-action rifle, the wide field of view at low power working perfectly in the rabbit coverts, with the higher power providing a more magnified target for longer shots. A handmate 22 rifle I carry often, a Model 70 Marlin semiauto, is equipped with a Bushnell 2.5X scope, perfect for that fast-action rifle on jackrabbit plains as well as in cottontail tangles. Remember, scopes fit 22 handguns too. Be sure to select a "pistol scope" with proper eye-relief for your favorite 22 rimfire sidearm.

Targets. Shooters may blame a poor group on the firearm or sight system, when in fact the target is at fault. If you can't clearly see the target, you can't hit it. Scopes help by making the target optically larger. But good targets increases the visibility of the aimpoint. For example, Outers offers targets punched for a three-ring binder for collection with bright orange bull's-eyes. These targets, in different dimensions, accentuate the aiming point, especially in dim light. Hoppe's has an interesting sight-in target printed on 14 × 14-inch paper. It uses red graphics for greater visibility. The Hoppe's target offers good visual contrast between the bull's-eye and the background. Targ-Dots are another option for increasing the visibility of the aiming point. These paste-on fluorescent orange circles contrast sharply with the background, offering a clear bull's-eye.

Shoot when wind and mirage are minimal, which is early morning in some areas. Watch the position of the sun. When possible, allow sunlight to illuminate your target.

Barrels. A well-made barrel in good condition is obviously required for top accuracy. Fortunately, the vast majority of today's barrels are of precision

Built-in accuracy deserves a good sight system. The author's bolt-action Kimber sports a Leupold 1.5X-5X variable scope.

manufacture. If the barrel is heavy (stout), bedding becomes less critical for accuracy, because the barrel itself controls harmonic vibration, and because the thicker walls of the barrel heat more slowly and therefore do not as readily expand against the channel in the stock. Heavy target barrels are often free-floated; that is, they do not touch the mortise in the stock from a given point in front of the receiver all the way to the muzzle. But not all barrels work best free-floated.

In attempting to improve accuracy in two of my rifles, a professional gunsmith re-bedded the barrels and actions in their stocks. Nothing else was done to them. Since both rifles were of somewhat sloppy fit to begin with, bedding the actions in fiberglass improved their performance.

This is not a catch-all cure for the 22 rifle. Not every action has to be glass-bedded for improved accuracy. However, if the action fits loosely in its mortise, then glassing may offer improvement. Free-floating a barrel is also no cure-all. Unfortunately, there is no way of knowing for certain (beginning gunsmiths sometimes fall into the trap of thinking that one process will make all rifles shoot well) whether full-length barrel bedding or free-floating will offer the greater improvement in accuracy for the 22-rimfire rifle. A compromise is initially to free-floating the barrel. If no improvement, a pressure point is placed in the barrel channel of the stock. This pressure point may be a raised bed for the barrel to rest on, created by building a small fiber-

Expect to reach the potential of your firearm's accuracy only with a proper trigger. The crisp and light (but totally safe) trigger pull disturbs aim the least. This trigger was found on a special match rifle.

glass pad in the barrel channel of the forend.

Accurate barrel life depends upon many factors. Cleaning is one of them. Improper cleaning ruins more barrels than neglect. Failure to clean the bore also ruins it eventually. Colonel Larson, an exhibition shooter, kept records on his Marlin Model 39 Mountie rifle, which fired 800,000 rounds of ammunition through one barrel before that barrel was replaced. This'll give you some idea of the longevity of a 22-rimfire rifle barrel—when proper care is exercised. More on maintenance in Chapter 29.

A filthy bore, clogged with powder residue and lead contamination, cannot deliver peak accuracy. Oddly enough, a squeaky-clean bore may not deliver consistent results, either. To demonstrate: after a rifle bore was cleaned completely, 10-shot groups were fired at 50 yards. A pattern began to emerge. It seemed that shot numbers four through 10 were clustered, whereas numbers one, two, and three were not. Later, as a continuation of the same study, the bore was cleaned thoroughly, and then three shots were fired to foul or "dress" the bore. The 10-shot group now had no fliers in it. All 10 bullets clustered in a circle. This idiosyncrasy may or may not exist in your rifle, but it is worth looking into when you want pinnacle-high precision.

Triggers. No serious shooter of the big-bore rifle would allow a poor trigger pull to destroy the accuracy potential of his firearm. Yet it is common for shooters of the 22 rimfire, sidearm or rifle, to overlook a stiff, hard trigger with creep, which averts

accurate shooting. Certainly, some triggers mechanically disallow fine pull. However, many models have triggers potentially capable of good crisp letoff. Don't work on your own trigger. Take your firearm to a gunsmith. See if that trigger can be safely improved upon. The trigger pull on a Remington 22-rimfire target rifle I have possesses a crisp letoff at under a pound. My Kimber 22 hunting rifle has a safe trigger that breaks like an icicle at 1.75 pounds.

PISTOL ACCURACY

The following data are condensed from numerous tests. Previous notes on pistol accuracy, appearing in the last chapter, are synthesized here, along with additional information. Recall that the longer pistol barrel shot better than the very short one. One of the apparent reasons for this fact is the manner and completeness of powder combustion within the bore of the barrel. However, more important reasons are increased weight up front for steady holding, and better vibration characteristics in the longer tube. Coupled with these points is another criterion—barrel stiffness. A flexible barrel is not as accurate in the pistol as a stiff barrel. Heavy barrels usually offer greater stiffness. Therefore, it may not always be the actual weight of the pistol barrel that affects accuracy, but rather the level of stiffness of that barrel.

In some tests, thinner but stiffer barrels were more accurate than heavier but more flexible barrels. Counterweights, as used on target pistols, helped in all tests because they, in effect, increased rigidness. These counterweights also aided in dampening barrel vibration. All target-grade pistols tested were very accurate, incidentally, which needs to be mentioned, because one way to secure greater accuracy in a 22 handgun is to buy an accurate model to begin with—simplistic, but factual. Further, it must be restated that the pistol is generally more accurate than the revolver in the 22 rimfire world. And remember to select match ammo for serious target work. A muzzle break, as such, is unnecessary on the 22-rimfire pistol, however. Do keep in mind that cold weather may change point of impact in the pistol. For winter shooting, check your sight-in before counting on hitting the bull's-eye. Keep the bore clean. Leaded bores work no better for pistols than for rifles. Today's 22-rimfire pistols are very accurate. Expect good results. A test of the Anschutz Exemplar, a variant of the

Model 1416 action with a left-hand bolt (meant for right-handed shooters) produced a .66-inch group at 25 yards with Ely match-grade ammo.

ACCURACY OF THE 22 SHORT AND LONG

Some of us enjoy shooting the 22 Short or Long from time to time. Does this 22-rimfire application mean loss of fine accuracy? Not necessarily. A long time ago, test firings with Federal Lesmok 22 Long ammo provided 1 11/16-inch groups at 50 yards. It is still possible to gain reasonable accuracy from the Long in some rifles. Furthermore, a Pope barrel chambered for the 22 Short on a Model 52 Winchester action provided groups as small as a half-inch at 25 yards with match ammo. Even at 50 yards, groups as stingy as 1 1/4 inches were registered. In the right firearm, the Short can shoot well. Incidentally, there are match pistols chambered for the Short cartridge, and high-grade match ammo to fit them.

FUTURE IMPROVEMENTS IN 22 RIMFIRE ACCURACY

Many improvements are yet to be realized in the world of 22-rimfire accuracy, among them bolts that "lock up" with greater precision, finer triggers on medium-priced rifles, more precise bedding of the action and barrel, plus a serious look at all criteria that pertain to accuracy in big-bore rifles.

As for ammo, several improvements are possible. The first is bullet weight. S&W (with Alcan) had an accurate experimental 53-grain cast bullet in a rimfire loading in the early 1970s. Experts feel that a heavier bullet in the 22 Long Rifle would improve accuracy and energy retention. Naturally, the problem of stabilization rears its head—rifling twist *may* have to be quickened in order to stabilize heavier (hence longer) 22 bullets fired at only 1100 fps muzzle velocity. Bullet *shape* has been studied. The alteration of test bullet configuration did not improve groups. "Nose slump" was noted with sharp test bullets, whereby the bullet's point changed shape, perhaps in the bore or at muzzle exit. A sharper profile in a soft test bullet did not improve accuracy—current bullet shape proved quite accurate, but further study of bullet shape is ongoing.

The bullet crimp has always been paramount in rimfire accuracy. This aspect of 22-ammo manufacture is quite advanced today, but continued investigation for even greater uniformity is not without

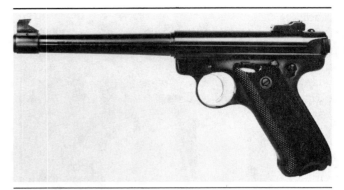

So far, studies indicate that the long, stiff barrel as that on Ruger's Mark II target model promotes accuracy with the pistol.

merit. Machines used in pulling bullets from 22 rounds indicate the pressure required to unseat each missile. The age of technology may lead to superior methods of crimp-testing, bullet crimping, and totally uniform neck friction.

Uniform case-wall thickness is another area of consideration. Concentric case walls are sought after in big-bore match ammunition, and advanced case refinement could lend greater precision to the already excellent 22-rimfire cartridge. Furthermore, a condition of 100 percent loading density (for our purposes, loading density is a "full case of powder") could elevate accuracy. Some ballisticians maintain that Lesmok 22 cartridges were more accurate than early smokeless-powder 22s due to

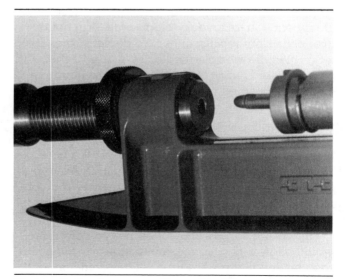

Modern technology, as evidenced in this special bullet swaging device, has helped improve bullet uniformity.

loading density: Lesmok powder *filled* the case; smokeless did not. Perhaps we need a modern 22-rimfire powder with a burn rate that will allow the case to be filled, leaving no dead-air space. A full case of powder gives the powder column a uniform shape, and powder column shape, some experts insist, is important to consistency of burning and to consequent accuracy. Bullet lubrication is another area of 22-rimfire accuracy study. Beeswax and tallow can be replaced with refined, modern lubricants. Currently, tests for new lubes and different methods of applying them to the 22 bullet are underway.

Finally, methods of installing priming mixture may be improved. When the priming mixture is introduced to the bottom of the case and consequently escorted out to the inside of the rim, some of the chemical may be deposited along the walls of the case. "Spinning" of the priming mixture also tends to apply traces of the chemical on the interior walls of the case. When this occurs, the additional priming compound becomes a part of the charge,

in effect, altering to a degree the uniformity of ignition and the effect of the powder charge from one cartridge to the next. If the priming compound could be installed as a pellet and then "squashed out" into the rim by a rod, each case would be uniformly primed and there would be no problem with additional priming mixture along the inside walls of the case.

Paraphrasing Whelen, only accurate 22-rimfire handguns and longarms are interesting. The shooter should determine the accuracy level of his 22 rimfire, improving upon it through wise ammo selection and, when necessary, the upgrading of his firearm. Ammunition companies, working tirelessly for years to ever improve their 22-rimfire product, should continue research, with strong consideration of a heavier 22 Long Rifle bullet along with the various tenets of accuracy improvement listed here. But for now, whose complaining? Not I. Not when my Kimber 22-rimfire hunting rifle can put all its bullets in smaller than a half-inch circle at 50 yards when fed a diet of match-grade ammo.

8 THE ACCURATE 22 CENTERFIRE

Many tenets contribute to 22-centerfire accuracy. We are again dealing with a subject worthy of tomes, and again the data are compressed in order to fit the format of this book. The 22-centerfire cartridge is different from its larger-caliber brothers on various counts. That must be understood. Whenever the energy of a comparatively large powder charge is funneled through the small volume of a 22-caliber bore, generated pressures, velocities, and energies escalate rapidly. To carry this further, consider the interesting 17 Remington cartridge. Increments of only one-half grain of powder develop significant velocity and pressure variations due to the small volume of the bore.

The 22 centerfire is not a cantankerous, hard-to-reload, flighty cartridge at all; however, it does command special consideration in its handling because it is a thoroughbred of the highest order. The "hot 22s" are perhaps the most interesting cartridges ever invented, with taut-bowstring trajectory, high energy (for lightweight bullets), and a capability of remarkable ballistic performance. The preface, "About the Book," promised 22-centerfire accuracy information based on shooting tests. That promise is fulfilled here.

22 CENTERFIRE AMMUNITION

The Cartridge Case. Precision-shooting experts claim that the shape of the powder charge (and powder column length) as the powder as confined within the walls of the case has much to do with consequent accuracy. I find the statement slightly overblown in light of the many accurate groups fired with the 300 H&H Magnum and other slope-shouldered cartridges (such as the 30-30 in a benchrest barrel); however, this does not imply that powder charge shape is of no consequence. *Supreme accuracy* does seem to keep company with certain case designs. The world of 22 centerfires has all

The modern 22 PPC (right) has a straight case body with sharp, 30-degree shoulder. The design is considered correct for accuracy attainment. Typical of the older slope-walled design is the 25-35 cartridge on the left.

manner of case shapes, from the exciting to the hohum. The most accurate rounds seem to be the exciting ones. Since there is an entire chapter on the 22 PPC USA cartridge, details on the round are saved for that space. However, consider for a moment the 22 PPC case. It is a squat cartridge instead of a tall and thin round. The 22 PPC USA has a small flashhole. It uses small rifle benchrest primers. Here is a model case for accuracy, and in my experience, it is the most accurate 22 centerfire cartridge.

The accurate case is dimensioned to take advantage of "100 percent loading density." Loading density is a bit more complicated than the round having a "full case of powder," but for our purposes that definition serves well. We're looking for a powder that fills the case with *safe loads*. The 22 PPC is again a good example of this condition. Most of its accuracy loads are those in which the powder charge fills the case, leaving no dead air space. There are examples that fly in the face of this accuracy fact, loads that do not fill the case, yet maintain accuracy. But the most accurate 22 centerfires seem to enjoy 100 percent loading density. For example, the famous 222 Remington, a very accurate cartridge developed by Mike Walker of Remington (and others), has 100 percent loading density in most of its tight-cluster loads.

Uniformity in a case is also important. For varminting, cases need not be weighed and sorted. In benchrest competition, cases will usually be sorted by weight. All cases must be trimmed to length. This not only improves uniformity, but also pro-

motes safety. A stretched neck can cause trouble, creating too much neck friction and raised pressures.

Accuracy devotees may wish to ream primer pockets for uniform depth (with Sinclair's Primer Pocket Uniformer). The flashhole can be deburred and smoothed (with Sinclair's flashhole deburring tool). And necks may be turned. Outside neck turning is the more popular method of turning neck dimensions these days. These rules for cartridge-case uniformity and accuracy enhancement pertain to bench shooting, in the main. Serious varminters may certainly apply these stratagems, but most of us won't, because the mythical one-hole group, while it would be nice in varminting, is not necessary to success. What accuracy should be expected? Nowadays a minute of angle is rock bottom for the serious varminter, with a minute of angle being actually 1.047 inches at 100 yards. But we're talking an inch at 100, two inches at 200, three inches at 300, and so forth, for five shots, measured between the centers of the farthest bullet holes. My personal varmint rifles better a half-minute of angle.

The above points are central to 22-centerfire cartridge case uniformity. Benchresters require far greater precision to be in the running. For example,

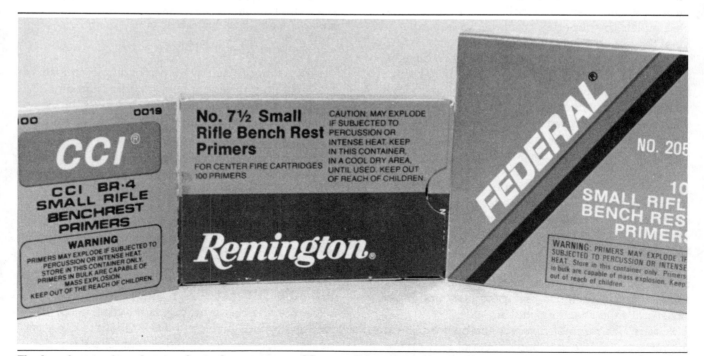

The benchrest primer is prevalent where supreme 22-centerfire accuracy is desired.

Ferris Pindell, co-creator of the 22 PPC, fired a group measuring only .138 inch center to center at 100 yards at the 16th annual meeting of the National Bench Rest Shooter's Association. He was using a 222 Remington Magnum cartridge, but in a custom-made rifle with a three-groove barrel, and he was shooting custom-made bullets.

The Jacketed 22 Bullet. The accurate bullet is concentric. It is not lopsided. It enjoys good gyroscopic effect. It tends to spin on its axis without undue wobble (but be careful—bullets that wobble can also create very close clusters). The lead core is homogeneous, the molecules of its alloy dispersed throughout. In other words, separated traces of tin or antimony will not be found in the bullet's lead core. The jacket can withstand the ravages of high velocity in the bore as well as in the atmosphere. The bullet holds up to dimensional changes in the bore as the projectile obturates, or fattens out, to fit the bore. The heel is smaller than the shank of the bullet; it enlarges to bore dimension for accuracy and stability. Furthermore, accurate bullets exhibit uniformity of diameter. For example, a micrometer will reveal an exact .224-inch diameter time and again in a sample check of good bullets from the same box. The preferred bullet nose for accuracy seems to be the hollow-point; however, for highest accuracy, the point has a rather closed hole, not a large one. Commercial 22-caliber centerfire, jacketed bullets are superbly crafted, and generally meet the above criteria.

The condition of the 22 jacketed bullet's base is essential to accuracy. Not to make too much of it, but the base is somewhat the "steering" section of the missile. Imperfections—such as dents, blemishes and other incongruities—may cause the missile to go astray. Bullet shape is also important, but accuracy has been gained with many different configurations. So far, it seems that the pointed projectile is the best choice all around. Blunt bullets give no better accuracy, no better expansion, no better brush-bucking ability. Some 22 jacketed bullets are rather blunt-nosed in order to achieve higher weight without undue projectile length, insuring stabilization in a given rifling twist. But the sharp-pointed bullet holds onto its initial velocity (hence its energy) much better than a round-nosed missile. It's the shooter's choice.

Primers. The manner in which the powder charge is ignited can have a strong effect not only on the subsequent velocity of the bullet, but also on the

To measure a three-shot cluster with calipers, gauge the group size from the center of one bullet hole to the center of the farthest bullet hole in the group.

level of accuracy achieved. For example, in testing a 257 Weatherby Magnum, switching from a mild primer to a Federal 215 lifted muzzle velocity by 200 fps. Conversely, going from a standard small-rifle primer to a benchrest small-rifle primer improved groups significantly in a 22 PPC. The shooter can safely experiment with primers in his own favorite 22 centerfire by keeping all cartridge components constant—case, powder charge, and bullet—while alternating different primers. Several groups, not one or two, will eventually prove which primer is the better one in terms of accuracy enhancement.

BUILDING THE ACCURACY LOAD

The 22-centerfire cartridge is handloaded so frequently that bullet sales in this caliber rank toward the top among most manufacturers. Great handloads are built through careful step-by-step mea-

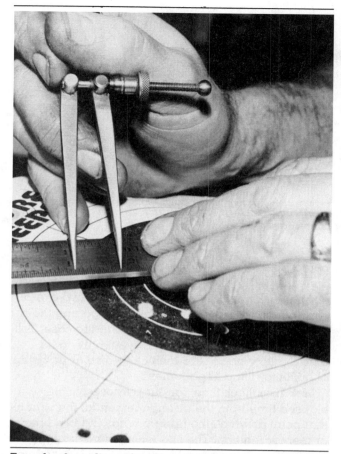

Transfer the calipers from target to ruler to determine measurement.

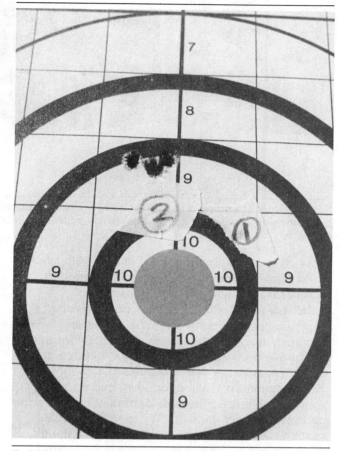

At 200 yards, this varmint rifle remains capable of bullet-hole touching accuracy.

sures. Shooting 22 centerfires is so enjoyable that building the best load is a pleasure, not a task. Juggling of components is essential. The cartridge case is component No. 1 in the process. Settle on the most uniform case you can find. Then search out the bullet your bore likes best, as well as the powder charge and correct primer. Juggling does not mean haphazard trial and error. *Use a loading manual.* Do not invent your own powder charges. Do not switch powders at will. Do follow the directives in the loading manuals, but note the plural: manuals. Ideally, you'll have several resource loading manuals in your arms library.

Rifles are individual in nature. That's why it takes bench-testing to arrive at a best load for your particular 22-centerfire rifle. Keep notes. A card file is useful, or a notebook. Write down not only the exact load and resulting group obtained with it, but also the temperature at the range. Heat can raise

pressures. Loads that work well in your rifle on a cool day may prove to be erratic on a summer varmint hunt or benchrest shoot. Preferably, conduct handload research in the summer. Then the worst that can happen is a slight loss in performance on a cold day, rather than the reverse, where a load built in winter reacts adversely to the heat.

Careful handloading involves many rules. This book is not a basic loading manual, so consult reloading texts for these rules and follow them. Initially, choose those powder types that have a burning rate conducive to 100 percent loading density. For example, when I was working up accuracy loads for the 22 PPC, I found that 26.0 grains of H-322 gave better accuracy than 23.0 grains of H-4198 *in my particular rifle.* You always have to add that.

Benchresters neck-size only when resizing brass. Varminters don't have to. Full-length sizing aids

Not long ago, obtaining a benchrest-quality bullet required custom bullet-making. Today, many bullet-making companies offer 22-caliber benchrest bullets for centerfires.

easy chambering of the round, and in tests, neck-sized brass fatigued as quickly as full-length re-sized brass. I prefer full-length resizing.

Bullet Seating Depth. In a test of bullet-seating depth, some rifles showed marked differences in accuracy as bullet depth was altered. Other rifles seemed less sensitive to the seating depth of the projectile, perhaps due to a difference in throat configuration. In seeking top-level accuracy for your 22-centerfire rifle, consider bullet depth an important aspect of the load. Try to set your bullet seating die so that there is .015 inch from the tip of the projectile to land contact. Do not seat your bullet to engage the rifling and do not seat the bullet deeply into the case. Since arriving at .015-inch gap between bullet point and rifling is very difficult to achieve without calipers, a simple method is to darken the tip of the bullet, as with a felt tip pen, and then seat it fairly long in a dummy case (no powder or primer at all) until the bullet engages the rifling. You can tell when this occurs because the lands will impress a mark on the "painted" bullet nose. Now slightly rotate the stem on the bullet seating die downward. Reseat the bullet in the dummy case and repaint its nose. Chamber the dummy cartridge again in the rifle. There should be no mark on the bullet when the dummy cartridge is withdrawn from the chamber of the rifle. Subsequent bullets will be seated in the die to the same length. Keep your dummy cartridge, for it is a gauge that will allow you to set the seater die exactly for proper bullet seating depth. Place the dummy cartridge in the reloading die box for easy location.

Leade or Throat. In having a custom rifle cham-bered, consider having the throat of the chamber dimensioned so that a bullet can be seated in a normal fashion while maintaining standard overall cartridge length, without the bullet engaging the rifling or having to be deeply seated in the case. Tell your gunsmith that ideally you would like to be able to allow about .015-inch clearance from the tip of bullet to rifling engagement.

Lock Time. Lock time, for our purposes, is the elapsed time from the disengagement of the sear to that point at which the firing pin has indented the primer for ignition. The shorter lock time is conducive to greater accuracy because there is less time allowed for rifle movement between trigger pull and actual departure of the projectile from the muzzle. Although the shooter has little control over lock time, in building a custom rifle a knowledgeable gunsmith can tell you which actions have fast lock time. Lock time can be computed, but the formula is unwieldy and for our purposes unnecessary. A gunsmith may also improve lock time.

RECOIL

Recoil is a significant factor in accuracy, mainly, but not exclusively, for indirect reasons. Directly, recoil affects accuracy because it causes barrel whip. However, barrel whip in a 22 centerfire with a fairly stiff barrel is not a big problem. Light recoil does, in this manner, aid accuracy to a small degree. Heavy recoil reduces accuracy because it disturbs the shooter. Consider recoil in two ways. First, there is the "actual" recoil of the rifle, which can be measured in foot-pounds of energy. Second, there is "felt" recoil, the effect of noise and push on the shooter. Even though rifles do not physically

Accuracy hounds try various powders before settling on the one that is just right in their own 22-centerfire rifles or pistols. Loading data abounds in the various handloading manuals.

harm us, we may flinch because our senses are violated when the firearm "goes off." Imagine you're standing on a street corner. A friend comes up suddenly and startles you. You jump. You were not hurt, not even touched, yet your body reacted to the suddenness of your friend's approach. When a firearm goes off, there is blast and some actual movement of the firearm. Our bodies react to these "offenses" by flinching, unless we learn to control our senses. The 22 centerfire generates little actual recoil, but the sharp crack can induce flinch. Control that by recognizing that the mild 22 centerfire is no threat to your well-being. Learn to follow through, so that when the rifle or pistol is fired, the body does not react to the blast, but maintains its posture.

BARREL BEDDING FOR ACCURACY

A competent gunsmith can free-float the barrel on your varminter, thereby insuring uniformity. Even with the lightweight barrels, floating can be a key to improved grouping. Changes in weather do not affect a properly free-floated barrel. Nor does minor stock warpage. Barrel heat has less effect on the group when the barrel is free-floated. And a floated barrel is free to vibrate at will, without those

vibrations dampened by contact with the barrel channel of the stock. The receiver of the free-floated rifle, however, is tightly bedded, and often glassed in.

Finally, remember that if free-floating does not improve accuracy in a particular rifle, a gunsmith can easily install a pressure point, by fitting either a small fiberglass pad or a thin piece of tanned leather near the forend.

THE ACCURATE RIFLE

The accurate 22 centerfire rifle has a properly bedded barrel, whether free-floated or pressure-pointed, depending upon the individual rifle. the action is "stiff" and has little "give" when the rifle is fired; it is firmly bedded into the stock. Lugs can be lapped in, or a PPC insert installed to insure proper "lockup" of the cartridge in the chamber. An accurate chambering job has minimal headspace and confines and controls the round within the chamber.

Magazine interruption can deter stiffness; therefore, some varmint rifles, even though bolt-action, are single-shots. The accurate Sako 22 PPC USA bolt-action rifle, for example, is a single-shot. New bolt-action designs are under investigation. One

Bullet seating depth can be very important to accuracy. The exciting 226 Barnes cartridge (left) requires "seating out" of the bullet, due to extreme length. However, even this cartridge insisted upon a specific bullet-nose-to-land distance for best accuracy.

Lack of recoil and muzzle blast indirectly aid accuracy in the 22 centerfire. Here John Fadala takes an informal rest over a boulder (forend padded with rifle sling). He can relax. The 22 PPC USA cartridge offers very little recoil.

test model has proved to be very strong, so strong that in independent tests, the barrel was literally blown away from the breech of the rifle, and yet the bolt itself was not set back.

Finally, consider barrel weight a dimension of accuracy. The heavier barrel "holds steadier." It offers stability. It heats less rapidly. It vibrates more independently of its bedding, no matter the style of bedding. And it is stiffer. Free-floated, it tends to ignore barrel whip.

Resting the Barrel in Varminting. Long-range varminting requires a rested firearm for precision of bullet placement. On a recent marmot-hunting trip, every long-range shot was accomplished by resting the rifle, generally on a flat boulder top. Perhaps it's now common knowledge, but it's worth mentioning again that for the sake of accuracy, the barrel itself should not rest against anything. The bullet tends to strike higher as the barrel rests farther and farther out towards its muzzle. In one test (and all tests gave unique results depending upon the firearm) a 22-rimfire rifle struck 10 inches high of

aimpoint a 100 yards when the barrel was rested near the muzzle on a hard surface. Rest the rifle at the forend, preferably on a surface with give, rather than a hard object. Do not rest the rifle by the barrel.

The Clean Bore. Best groups in some rifles were obtained after "dressing the bore" with a couple of shots before attempting to fire five-shot strings. However, this does not imply that a dirty bore is best for accuracy. Bores that were fouled, especially with metal, failed to obtain best groups.

Although methods of cleaning are given in the appropriate chapter, here is how to check for copper-wash (jacket-metal) fouling in your 22 varminter. First, insert a bit of clean white cotton or white cloth about and eighth of an inch into the muzzle of the rifle. Second, use a bore light to shine against the interior of the muzzle. The cotton or white cloth will reflect upon the bore and a golden coating may appear on the lands of the rifling. That golden color represents metal fouling and should be removed with Shooter's Choice or similar solvent, along with Flitz or JB Compound. Remember to get the bore dry before shooting again. An oily bore can alter point of impact, and can sometimes open group size as well.

The Accurate Scope. High-power scopes do wonders for bullet grouping. A fine rifle can be short-changed at the range if the scope lacks the definition or the magnification to refine the aimpoint. My 22 PPC wears a straight 12X Leupold scope. A 22-250 in my battery carries a 4X-12X Bushnell, the lower settings used in brush and timber, the higher power for long-range varminting. Benchrest shoot-ers use high-power scopes, the 36X being no stranger to the benchrest match. Targets are small. Magnification not only enlarges them but also teaches the shooter body control, visually revealing his physical unsteadiness so he can correct it. Choose the right reticle for your long-range scope. A fine target dot is good. Fine crosswires are also acceptable. The duplex reticle is also very good if the center wires are very narrow.

Shed some light on your shooting too. When trying to produce close groups, align the target to receive the benefit of the sun when the range al-

Twenty-two centerfire accuracy is built into a rifle like the one gunmaker Dale Storey is holding. The Douglas air-gauged barrel, plus Dale's close tolerance chambering and careful action/barrel bedding, go a long way to ensure close groups.

lows mobility of target placement. Light from the target diminishes in exact proportion to the square of the distance. A foot-candle of light equals one candle flame one foot away. But when the distance is two feet, the resulting "power" of the light falls to only one-fourth foot-candle. At 10 feet, there is only 1/100 of one foot-candle of light. Light rays scatter. Image size as perceived by the human eye's retina gets very small as distance increases. Consider an image at 50 yards. It will be seen as only 1/50 the size the eye perceived at one yard. Therefore, a well-illuminated target is important in 22-centerfire testing.

Accurizing Your 22 Centerfire. For best accuracy, the firearm must be in a peak state of repair. Ensure that your rifle is sound, with all bolts tight and no cracks in the stock. Glass-bed any action that is not firmly seated in the stock. Free-float the barrel, and if that fails to upgrade accuracy, install a pressure point. Clean the bore, removing metal as well as powder fouling. Check for throat erosion, or ask a gunsmith to do this for you.

To locate any rough spots in the bore, first attach a cleaning patch to one end of a cord; then run the other end through the barrel, out the muzzle, and attach it to a fish-weighing scale. As you grasp the scale and pull the patch through the bore, the scale will register drag if a rough spot is hit.

Recrown the muzzle if the crown looks rough. Forget about bore lapping for all general purposes, but lapping the scope rings might not be a bad idea. Lapping is accomplished with a dowel or steel rod and lapping compound, the object being to align the rings so that the scope is free of torque when it is held in the mounts.

Accurate Shooting. Start with a stable rifle. Upgrade the rifle using the accurizing methods described above. Mount a high-power scope on your varminter, a variable if some of your shooting is in tight as well as open country. Make sure your scope has a proper reticle for fine shooting. Use the benchrest methods outlined in a later chapter. Ensure that your target is truly visible, the aimpoint small and well-defined. Consider load testing on good days of high light and low wind. And work on the human elements—good eyes and steady body. If corrective lenses are necessary, buy a good pair of eyeglasses. Practice for topflight body control. Steadiness can be improved upon, especially with the game of silhouette shooting, using high-power scopes.

THE 22 CENTERFIRE PISTOL

Many of the points laid out here pertain to the 22-centerfire pistol as well as the 22-centerfire rifle. The modern 22-centerfire pistol is capable of excellent accuracy. A scoped Remington XP-100 in 221 Fireball created a group size of one inch at 100 yards for five shots. I would like to see this and other pistols chambered for the 22 PPC USA cartridge.

9 THE 22 RIMFIRE AT 200 YARDS

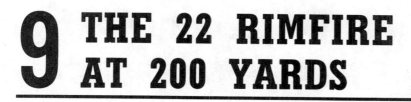

"See if you can hit that, over there, against the dirt bank." I looked across the long draw to the earthen backstop of which my partner spoke. There was something prominent in the center of it. But I didn't know what it was.

"What is that?" I asked. My companion looked through his binoculars again.

"It's a stick, a piece of lath. Not too wide, but it must be a foot long."

"O.K.," I agreed. The iron-sighted 22 rifle gave no detail of aim at that distance. The first shot was low, but in line. The second shot was closer. So was the third. On the fourth shot, the strip of wood did a flip and descended the full length of the slope. Then a miss. Miss. Hit. Hit. "How far is that?" I asked my friend. He was no more certain of the distance than I was, but we both agreed that the piece of wood had to be an honest 200 yards away.

Too far for the little 22 Long Rifle cartridge? I suppose so. But 200-yard shooting with the 22 rimfire remains one of the best practices I know of, along with considerable challenge and a lot of fun. I can't say that the 200-yard dirt-bank/wooden-stick episode got me started in 200-yard 22-rimfire shooting, but I can say that the recent event put me back into the sport.

As a young marksman with a 22-caliber Winchester Model 61 rifle fitted with a 4X scope, I had already invented an enjoyable game. Living within walking distance of a lonely chunk of real estate outside of Yuma, I frequented the sandy flats. One day I placed a tin can in a clear spot and paced off 200 long steps. To my surprise, if not amazement, I could hit the can. Every shot? No way. But sufficiently often to remain convinced that shooting the 22 Long Rifle cartridge at 200 yards was within the realm of reason. The soft earth surrounding the tin can marked the bullet's strike, precipitating changes in sight picture. Now, many years later, I

still enjoy sessions of 200-yard 22-rimfire shooting.

Every aspect of big-bore shooting is magnified in the 200-yard 22-rimfire game. Bullet drop and wind drift are enlarged measurably over the flat-shooting high-intensity cartridge. These exaggerations of 22 Long Rifle ballistics at 200 yards produce a teaching platform unlike any I've ever known. The marksman becomes a master of angles. He learns to dope the wind with uncanny accuracy. My last 200-yard rimfire session took place 24 hours before the materialization of this chapter. My friend Gene Thompson and I were in the Snowy Range, a tall Wyoming mountain chain overlooking the border into Colorado. At an estimated 200 yards was a pine cone resting in the center of a sandy clear spot perhaps three yards wide. "Hey, Gene," I said, preparing my Model 82 Kimber for action, "there's a safe and interesting target. Watch this." Gene and I both shot at the distant target with my 22 rifle. That was interesting shooting. And fun. And, as always in 200-yard 22-rimfire shooting, lessons were learned.

Quite some time ago, 200-yard rimfire shooting was more common than it is today. Even 300-yard shooting with the 22 rimfire was not unknown. H.W. Shaw described "The 'Pipsqueak' at 300" in an article for *The American Rifleman*. The target was a 12-inch bull's-eye. I tried a 12-inch bull at 300 at my own range and found that once I had the aimpoint figured out, that size mark was a solid possibility for the little 22 Long Rifle, especially with match ammo. But 200-yard work was more fruitful.

When the US Rifle Caliber 22 Model of 1922 M1 Springfield chambered for the 22 Long Rifle came out, its services were stated thusly: "It is intended for extremely accurate small-bore target-shooting at ranges from 50 feet to 200 yards . . ." (*The American Rifleman*, March 1930, p. 32). There was no hesitation in claiming 200-yard accuracy with the

Downrange, a target at 200 yards appears quite small, even when it's three empty coffee cans (within white circle). Wind makes 200-yard 22-rimfire shooting tricky business. Learning to "dope the wind" with the little 22 at 200 yards transfers to big-bore long-range shooting.

22 Long Rifle round. Two-hundred-yard shooting in the 1940s was prominent as well: " . . . we had a supplementary lesson with the .22s at 200 yards, using the .30 caliber A and D targets," reported one shooting-club member in 1941, adding, "Ping! and the paddle showed a 6 o'clock 4, close to the black. Then came four 5s, and I thought I heard a murmur of surprise. We shivered and froze, but we stayed until dusk." I can well understand the last statement. I, too, have stayed until dusk delivering 40-grain bullets to a downrange target supposedly too far away for its ballistic impetus.

A venerable Pope 22 barrel delivered 10-shot groups of four to five inches at 200 yards in one test of uncrimped 22 Long Rifle ammunition. My Kimber produced fine 200-yard groups with Eley and Lapua match-grade fodder. Numerous five-shot groups clustered into three inches center to center. When the wind was nil and conditions just right, groups were even smaller at 200 yards. Considering that this rifle consistently shoots into 4/10 of an inch at 50 yards, with frequent stingier center to center showings, the latter is no real surprise. Frank J. Haas scored 496 × 500 on a four-inch bull's-eye at 200 yards with a Model 52 and match-grade ammo.

The 22 rimfire and 200-yard shooting can make a master marksman of you. Just remember to select the right ammo for the rifle. Interior bore dimensions and nuances of ammo variation make such mating crucial when 22-rimfire accuracy must hold to 200 yards. Sight in normally—about 85 yards with the 22 Long Rifle. Then reset the sights by noting the number of clicks necessary on the micrometer rear sight or scope adjustment in order to affect a dead-center pattern at 200 yards. The elevator bar on the open sight can be cranked up for long-range work, too; but hairline precision with the open iron at 200 yards will be lacking.

Long-range 22-rimfire practice is more than interesting and rewarding. It's also downright easy on the pocketbook as compared with big-bore shooting. Furthermore, it's the lack of recoil and non-disturbance of sight picture that allow such fine practice. You can see the effect of the bullet striking a hard target, or scattering sand near that target. Naturally, you won't readily pick out 22 bullet holes in the black at 200 yards, so paper-punching is a bit less interesting than shooting at movable targets. Consequently, my own 200-yard rimfire shooting is primarily at "animated" targets. A block of soft pine, for example, will usually topple with a hit at 200. Heavy silhouette metallics won't, and they're a bit small to hit consistently at that range

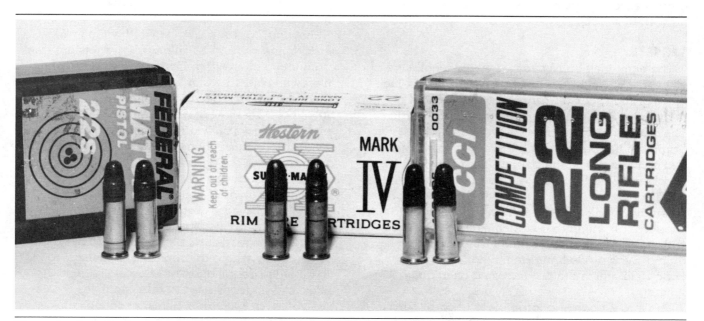

The author has used target ammunition for years in his 200-yard shooting because of its standard velocity and high accuracy. Remember that the standard-velocity 22 Long Rifle cartridge is less affected by the wind than the high-velocity round.

Two-hundred-yard shooting is enhanced with a rifle like the one above, built for stability, and wearing a powerful telescopic sight. Iron sights also work well for 200-yard rimfire shooting, especially when they are micrometer aperture sights mounted on a fine target rifle such as this Anschutz 1411 (below).

anyway, although I have used them with some degree of success (while they don't fall, they often turn when struck).

TARGETS

The eight-inch bull's-eye is a worthy challenge at 200 yards, as is the 12-inch bull. When the six-inch blaze orange stick-on Targ-Dot came along, I attached these to large target boards at 200 yards. The orange circles showed up well and offered bright aiming points. Using a rifle rest, a shooter can consistently hit the six-inch Targ-Dots, but it's nearly impossible to score on them repeatedly if the wind is blowing. From a solid benchrest position, when the wind cooperates, it's not impossible to keep 'em all within the six-inch circle at 200 yards with an accurate scope-sighted rifle and target ammo. Such a rifle firing Remington Target 22 Long Rifle ammo did just that on a calm day not long ago.

The target board—a large piece of cardboard to which the target is fastened—can be very important to all of this. Know the dimensions of that board. If you don't want to alter your sight setting,

you can use the frame of the target as your aimpoint at 200 yards, provided you know the size of the frame.

Shooting "for the black" is worthwhile in 200-yard rimfire work, but "animated" targets are generally more interesting. Cardboard milk cartons filled with colored water work well. Hits are fairly easily seen as the dark liquid streams out of the bullet hole. The flow of water animates the target in this case. Blocks of wood are animated because bullet strikes cause them to fall over. Empty food cans are large enough to hit at 200 yards, but they are difficult to budge when filled with sand, and seldom offer signs of being hit when they are empty. Balloons are great fun, and can be effortlessly picked up afterwards to avoid littering the area. Clay pigeons are also interesting, but should be used only where appropriate. It's difficult to pick up all of the debris after the shooting session. Besides, clay pigeons are just a bit small for consistent strikes at 200 yards, unless shooting commences from the bench. Animated targets for 200-yard shooting are limited only by imagination, safety, and litter considerations.

All shooting positions are acceptable in 200-yard rimfire marksmanship, but the offhand stance makes consistent hitting difficult with the average hunting rifle. The sitting position is more viable, or a sitting position coupled with a portable rest of one sort or another, such as a packframe. Prone shooting is very worthwhile. When a well-executed prone position is maintained, a remarkable degree of success is possible. Kneeling is all right, too, although not nearly so steady as a good sitting shot. The bench is also a fine platform for this work, and it does not detract from most of the ballistics lessons taught by the 200-yard rimfire-shooting game.

WIND DRIFT

Drift is the lateral deviation of the bullet's path from the plane of departure caused by the rotation of the projectile. In other words, bullet rotation forces the missile to drift over in the direction of spin. A right-hand twist forces the bullet to deviate to the right. A left-hand twist persuades the projectile to deviate left. Forward velocity is slowed greatly by the atmosphere (and gravity), but rotational velocity is not affected nearly so much. The bullet just keeps spinning on its axis all the way to its final destination. Our concern is not with drift as such, but rather with "wind drift," or "wind deflection," the bullet departing from the original line of flight due not to spin, but to the forces of moving air.

At 200 yards, the little 22 pill is badly bullied by the zephyrs. That exaggeration makes learning about wind drift all the more graphic, however. When a shooter *sees* how far his 22 Long Rifle missile is pushed aside by the wind, he gains a much greater appreciation for wind deflection in centerfire shooting. The bullet is a "flying gyroscope." Therefore, the angles of the wind alter bullet movement. There is a "free gyroscope" effect. Forces exerted upon a gyroscope are not felt at the point of exertion, but 90 degrees away in the direction of rotation. Bullets from a barrel with right-hand twist therefore lift in a crosswind coming from the right, but drop when the crosswind is coming from the left. The low ballistic coefficient of the 40-grain 22-rimfire projectile magnifies these values, offering the shooter terrific learning opportunities.

In theory, the time it would take for a bullet to go from muzzle to target is compared with the time it would take for the same bullet at the same muzzle velocity to cover the same distance if it were fired in a vacuum. The difference in time is lag (or lag time). Lag time has much to do with bullet drift. A big surprise may be in store for the 22-rimfire fan who finds that his high-velocity ammo drifts more at 200 yards than standard-velocity bullets. However, when the speed of sound is surpassed, there is greater bullet disturbance that there is below the speed of sound.

This is called the "disturbed region," and when bullets fly just below this threshold, which is very roughly in the 1100-fps realm, they aren't as badly pushed around by the wind. So guess what? The high-velocity bulllet (depending upon various other factors) could drift off-target as much as 25 percent more than the standard-velocity missile. Range tests agree with the theories of disturbance. Comparing target-velocity Federal 22 Long Rifle ammo with high-speed Long Rifle rounds, the former flew

Hits on a coffee can at 200 yards with a 22-rimfire rifle are gratifying—and good practice.

Richard Reitz demonstrates the sitting position, firing a Ruger 22-rimfire rifle topped with a Bushnell scope sight. The sitting position works well for 200-yard rimfiring.

off course by a lesser margin than the latter when fired in alternating shots from the same rifle.

Formulas that can be applied if the reader is interested are: D=R×V/250 for three and nine o'clock winds; D=R×V/300 for two, four, eight, and 10 o'clock winds; and D=R×V/500 for winds from one, five, seven, and 11 o'clock (from Edwards Brown data, *The American Rifleman*, May 1946). *R* is range in yards. *V* is the velocity of the wind in miles per hour (m.p.h.). And *D* is the horizontal deflection in minutes of angle. So it is range in yards times wind velocity divided by the corresponding constant number. Remember that a minute angle of 1.047 inches at 100 yards. Trying to prove the formula at the range is not too easy because wind velocity is seldom constant. Neither are the approaching *angles* of the wind. But you can expect a 22 Long Rifle bullet to drift over a good seven minutes of angle, or about 14 inches, at 200 yards in a crosswind of only 10 m.p.h. Of all elements in shooting, wind drift is perhaps most clearly illustrated visually for the 200-yard rimfire rifleman. Watching the splash of dust two feet off target in a wind only 20-m.p.h. strong is convincing of its effect. Turning later to the high-velocity 22-centerfire rifle, "doping the wind" is far easier than it was before becoming a fan of 200-yard rimfire shooting.

BULLET DROP

Of course, bullet drop is another well-illustrated feature of 200-yard rimfire shooting, and there are two ways to handle the problem. The first has been mentioned already—readjust the scope or iron sight to compensate directly for the falling of the missile. Then you know that so many clicks up of the scope or micrometer rear sight (or a rise of the elevator bar on the open iron sight—not very precise) will put the bullet on target at 200, right in the bull's-eye, and returning the sight to its original setting will reinstate the 85-yard "normal" sight-in of the rifle. The second method is hold-over, and it has

value because it teaches the shooter how to achieve and maintain the correct sight picture in order to "drop the bullet" into the target at long range. In the field, few of us will stop to make sight adjustments for long-range shooting. We have to know, instead, how to judge distance, and how to compensate or correct for that distance in terms of the firearm's trajectory. Compensation means holding high.

Small-game hunting with the 22 Long Rifle calls for a sight-in of about 85 yards. This is an especially propitious sight-in distance, because it puts the bullet on target first at 20 yards, which is often just right for hunting squirrels, cottontail rabbits, and other small game. So sighted, the 40-grain bullet falls a couple of feet below the line of sight at 200 yards. Trying to judge that drop gives the

Firing from the prone position with a 22-rimfire rifle makes sense in 200-yard shooting. However, all shooting positions are used in this sport.

shooter a real challenge.

You'll need a large target. Place a bull's-eye (or Targ-Dot) high on the target board, because you know that the bullet is going to drop appreciably with the 22-rimfire rifle sighted for 85 yards. Take a solid stance at the bench and fire at least 10 shots with your crosswire held dead center on the bull. (This work is possible with the iron sight, but is much more difficult because the bead will subtend a large diameter at 200 yards.) Ideally, the rifle and ammo will be capable of close grouping at 200 yards. Disregard all fliers. Consider only those bullet holes that form a group. Find the center-most part of the 10-shot group, and draw a horizontal line through it. Measure from that line to the center of the bull's-eye above it and you will have the number of inches the bullet drops on the average for 200 yards when your rifle is zeroed dead-on at 85 yards.

BEATING THE FLINCH

Recoil is a function not only of actual foot-pounds of energy, but also of invasion of the senses. Because of the latter, primarily, we may tend to flinch when the gun goes off. One way to beat the flinch is through a great deal of 22-rimfire shooting, because the mild-mannered little firearm does not offend our delicate senses to a noticeable degree. Therefore, it's easy to control flinch when firing the rimfire. By shooting over and over again, with concentration upon all tenets of good rifleman practice, the marksman eventually learns to ignore the noise of his 22 rimfire (always wear ear plugs, even though the 22 is not nearly so noisy as a centerfire), and follow-through becomes second nature.

The shooter knows he has controlled flinch when he maintains the same stance before and after firing his rifle. Even after the bullet has struck the target, the eyes do not blink. The body does not jump at the crack of the rifle. Every muscle remains poised, but relaxed. Shooting at the 200-yard range with a 22-rimfire rifle multiplies the problems of riflery, but at the same time, benefits the rimfire rifleman who has suffered the plague of flinching. Instead of a high ballistic-coefficient bullet wandering slightly off course because of impaired shooter control, a 40-grain 22-caliber projectile of low ballistic coefficient flies way off course at 200 yards. A slight infringement on the angle at the muzzle is multiplied dramatically at this distance.

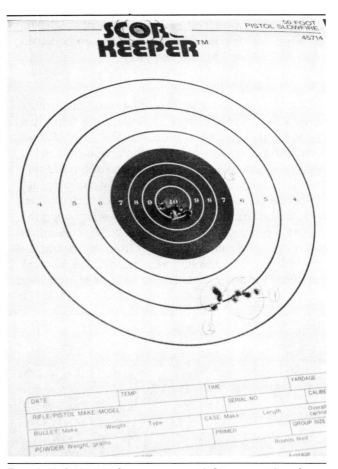

Proper sight-in is, of course, essential to squeezing the accuracy potential from your 22-rimfire rifle. The first group landed low and to the right of center. Adjustment brought the second group closer to center. Bolder adjustment was just right, bringing the group up and more to center.

Evidence of poor rifle management is clearly established when the shooter misses the wooden block at 200 yards not by an inch or two—an error he can overlook in long-range shooting with the little rimfire—but by a dramatic foot or more. Unfortunately, flinching is transferable. Look at a fellow who flinches badly when firing a 30-06, and you will see a marksman who very likely flinches with a 243 as well—and perhaps even a 22 rimfire. Break the flinch with plenty of concentrated effort firing the 22 rimfire. Two-hundred-yard 22-rimfire rifle shooting is a multifaceted shooter-enhancement program all by itself. It's also one of the best games in the entire sport of shooting. And now onto other worthwhile 22 rimfire games.

10 USING GAMES TO SHARPEN YOUR SKILLS

Annie Oakley used her Marlin 22-rimfire rifle to charm large audiences at the Buffalo Bill Wild West Show. Tom Frye fired thousands of 22-rimfire rounds through his Remington semi-auto rifle at aerial targets. Winchester's Herb Parsons delighted crowds everywhere with his amazing 22-rifle feats, including his eggs-in-the-air shooting trick. Professional marksmen have used the 22 rifle (and handgun) almost since the little rimfire came off the drawing board.

Safety is the primary command for all shooting, and safety is the watchword in 22-rimfire games. With proper backstop, many excellent 22-rimfire games, mostly with rifle, but certainly not to the exclusion of the handgun, can be enjoyed all year long, rain or shine. Games are teaching tools, whether they are played by children or adults. Skills are honed through games. Valuable experience is gained through games.

PURPOSEFUL PLINKING

When a reporter asked Omark-CCI's Dave Andrews where all the ammunition went, he replied, "Mostly into dirt banks." Be it 22-rimfire or 22-centerfire ammunition, that's exactly where the bulk of missiles end their brief flight through the atmosphere. Sighting in and target shooting use up vast quantities, to be sure, but most are fired in the game of plinking, even when it's not called that.

Ideally, plinking is purposeful. There's a big difference between emptying a rifle's cargo into a backstop mostly to hear the crack! crack! crack! of the firearm, and firing at well-conceived targets. I've said many times that a box or two of 22-rimfire ammo and a peaceful hour to shoot them in can be the best mindrest for the high-tech person. I call the 22 rimfire the poor man's therapist. In that regard, perhaps the safe, but mindless, firing of a few rounds into the backstop is all right. But planned

plinking serves the same pacifying purpose while also improving marksmanship.

The 22 rimfire can play understudy to the big-game rifle during plinking sessions. This is a "miniaturization" of the shooting scene, in a way. Consider that the 22-rimfire rifle behaves over a range of 100 yards quite like the high-speed big-game bullet behaves over 300 yards. If one sights his 22 rifle to strike the bull's-eye dead on at 20 yards, the bullet will rise briefly, striking the bull's-eye again at about 85 yards, then dropping a couple inches below the line of sight at 100 yards. Naturally, it is impossible to be exact in this regard, because there are so many different 22-rimfire loads out there; however, this trajectory pattern is a fairly decent representative of the 22 bullet's flight. Now consider a 270 Winchester properly sighted in. The 130-grain bullet is on at about 25 yards, crosses the line of sight again at 275 yards, and strikes about three inches low at 300 yards. In effect, the 22 Long Rifle's trajectory over 100 yards is a miniaturization of the 270 Winchester big-game cartridge's trajectory over 300 yards. You can see the application already.

In a very real sense, shooting the 22 rifle at the 100-yard range can offer silent transfer value for the fellow who owns and fires a high-intensity cartridge big-game rifle. The 30-06 with a 150-grain handload, the 7mm Remington Magnum, 243 Winchester, and numerous other popular flat-shooting cartridges fit the niche, all of them producing very similar trajectory patterns out to 300 yards. The miniaturizing of the big-bore rifle experience can pay off fat later on when the shooter finds himself engaged in target shooting with the centerfires, or beating a path through the hunting field, especially out west where long shots are common (although there are plenty of long-shot opportunities in many eastern settings as well). Peterson Instant

Annie Oakley was one of the finest trick shooters in the world. She used a Marlin 22-rimfire rifle for much of her shooting, and even in later years could hit small targets out of the air with her rifle.

Targets Company has produced a series of "Trophy Animal Targets." The theory behind them is stated as follows: "Scientific research tells us that if you practice a skill enough, it will be imprinted into your memory. Therefore, by using a Trophy Animal Target for practice, its kill zone will be imprinted into your memory." The Peterson targets are scaled for a range of 25 yards.

Many different game animals are represented, from deer to black bear. The peel-off self-adhering target comes with a legend relating the distance from which the target has been reduced, along with a white dot representing a proper strike zone. The pronghorn antelope target, for example, is to be fired upon from 25 yards, but it represents a reduction from 350 yards. The black bear target fired at from 25 yards represents a 300-yard shot at that big-game animal. The coyote target at 25 yards presents an example of a 260-yard shot. And so forth. The approximations make interesting practice targets and enjoyable plinking practice.

PRACTICING STANCE

The major shooting stances are perfected easily through 22-rimfire shooting during any and all of these rimfire shooting games. With 22-rimfire rifle in hand, the shooter can study standing, sitting, kneeling, and prone positions, along with the use of the sling, the hasty sling, and field rests. These stances fit well into purposeful plinking, giving the shooter solid practice in the standard shooting positions recognized over the years as best for all-around good marksmanship. This sort of practice allows repetition with enjoyment. The very word *repetition* connotes boredom, but there's no boredom here, sending 22-rimfire bullets into the backstop while practicing various means of controlling the rifle. Descriptions of shooting positions prevail in many general shooting texts, including *The Rifleman's Bible*, a title of my own. Practice is vital to shooting success. Conversely, practicing improper shooting stance is a means of reinforcing bad shooting habits. Learn and practice the correct forms.

BEATING THE FLINCH

This subtopic has surfaced before. In our look at 200-yard shooting, the practice of firing a lot of 22-rimfire ammunition at long range was broached as one means of putting the flinching gremlin to flight. The same is true of games and general plinking

Peterson's Instant reduced targets are fun for all members of the family shooting team, and from all shooting positions. From 25 yards' distance, the author's nine-year-old daughter fired on the bear, goat and sheep targets from the offhand stance, while Dad took a solid stance with his Kimber rifle and fired shots at the coyote.

with the 22 rimfire. Concentration is the key. Haphazard lead-throwing is not. Games aid concentration immensely. Everyone knows how fast the time flies when a person is involved in a fast-paced game. The spinning hands of the clock whirl ever faster when the shooter is fully devoted to producing specific results with a rimfire rifle or handgun. This level of concentration can serve to break the flinching jinx completely. There is simply no time to dwell on bad form, which is the pedestal upon which stands the flinching demon. The shooter concentrates on the rules of his game, whether the game is some sort of purposeful plinking or one of those listed below. By repeatedly observing the best possible shooting form and concentrating fully on the task at hand—rim-smacking a tin can to make it fly from a circle, for example—the flinching remedy is painlessly internalized.

Practice from any shooting stance is accomplished with 22-rimfire games. Richard Reitz shows one style of offhand shooting, with left elbow resting on hip.

DRY FIRING

Dry firing is an entirely safe practice when safety precautions are faithfully observed, as they must be. It is also an excellent means of learning firearm control, rifle or handgun. First, and of absolute necessity, the rifle or sidearm is checked to insure that it is completely free of ammunition, not only in the chamber, but also in the magazine. This totally empty firearm is then employed in dry firing. Second, dry firing is conducted only toward a safe backstop. Even though the firearm is unloaded, it is treated as a loaded gun and aimed only in a safe direction. Dry firing works so well because the absence of ammunition allows the shooter to see precisely where sight alignment was positioned when the rifle or handgun went "click." There is no dis-

turbance of aim from a fired bullet to lure the attention away.

In dry firing, the shooter aims at a precise target with his empty firearm. He follows the tenets of good marksmanship, including the careful squeezing of the trigger. When the trigger is pulled, the click is matched with the sight picture. Ideally, follow-through will be so precise that the two will coincide perfectly—the sear will disengage; the firing pin will fall, and yet the crosswire or iron sight will remain glued to the target like wood laminated to wood. That's successful dry firing—being able to *call the shot* perfectly. Proper dry-firing technique follows a shooter onto the target range and into the game field. Incidentally, concern for dry-firing damage to the rifle can be greatly alleviated by using a defunct 22-rimfire case to stop the forward thrust of the firing pin. Dry firing is very worthwhile practice, as long as the rules of safety are strictly observed.

HANDGUN PRACTICE

The 22 handgun will serve for most of the games mentioned in this chapter. In using the handgun, practice various methods that will transfer to the target range and hunting field. The one-hand hold, two-hand hold, even the use of a field rest will pay off in later "real life" 22-rimfire handgunning. Grip the handgun with the same hold every time. Consider the index or trigger finger an independent part of the hand. Grasp the sidearm in a safe, com-

In plinking and shooting games, practice proper methods. Here the trigger finger is treated as an independent part of the shooter's hand.

The common tin can has been a plinker's target for a long time. Colt 22-rimfire handguns and a couple of cans add up to an enjoyable shooting session, one that can help you beat the flinch.

fortable manner for the revolver, but relax the index finger; then bring it into the picture independently, sort of sneaking that finger into the trigger guard. That way, trigger squeeze is mastered with the sights optically pasted on the target, the handgun going off without notice.

THE INDOOR RANGE

When unfriendly weather—the cold, hot, snowy, or wet variety—enshrouds the land, most shooters take up other activities. Those who have an indoor range, however, can continue with their sport. The indoor or basement range need not be an elaborate affair. Nor does the shooter require a great distance. The firearm fan fortunate enough to have a 30-foot basement area free of furniture or family activity has a wonderful setup, but 20 feet or less will also do the trick. Obviously, the backstop must be foolproof. My friend John Doyle and I used to shoot every day at his indoor range. We kept in sharp form that way. The ready availability of 22 CB Long ammo from Federal and CCI and 22 CB Shorts from Winchester make indoor shooting a comparatively quiet affair, too. NRA-affiliated clubs

"Tin Cans in a Circle" makes an excellent 22-rimfire shooting game. Nicole Fadala has plinked each tin can out of the circle with her 22-rimfire rifle.

can offer consultation concerning the correct type of backstop, target, and ammunition for a specific indoor-range location. Build your indoor range correctly and you will have a wonderful and safe place to practice with both rifle and sidearm.

SOME 22 RIMFIRE GAMES

Tin Cans in a Circle. The rules of this 22-rimfire game are simple. A circle is drawn on the ground in front of a good backstop. The object of the game is to shoot the cans out of the circle. The cans must completely clear the perimeter, not merely touch the line. The shooter who masters the rim shot stands to win this little game. By driving a 22 bullet into the rim of the can, the metal container is made

to leap away. Sometimes, one shot will send a can sailing well out of the circle. The winner is the person who has fired the least number of shots in propelling the greatest number of cans from the circle. Usually shooters take turns, but since the competitors are on a firing line, it is safe to play the game with simultaneous shooting. The first person to drive the most tin cans from the circle wins. The marksman with the semi-auto rifle or sidearm has an edge, so turn-taking makes more sense unless all participants have similar firearms.

Tin Cans on the Line. This is a variation of the circle game. Draw a straight line on the ground in front of the backstop, and place tin cans upon that line. The shooter gets one shot at each can and no more. The

Matches lined up on a dirt bank make excellent close-range 22-rimfire targets. The major objective is to strike the match head without hitting the wooden shaft. Use a point system: 3 for a head-strike; 1 point for hitting the matchstick.

winner is he who propels the greatest number of cans off the line with the fewest shots. When the marksmen are so good that each competitor always knocks all of his cans off the line, the rules can be adapted to include the total distance in feet that each can flies. The shooter whose combined distance is greatest wins. For example, if five cans are propelled three, four, five, five, and six feet off the line, that score is 23. Highest score wins.

Striking the Match. Aligned in front of a backstop are several kitchen matches supported with their tips upward. This contest is for close-range shooting only, with the winner igniting the greatest number of matches with the least number of shots. The contest requires very close holding and an under-

standing of the close-range bullet path. The way to win is with a little session of pre-sighting. Place an ordinary target with small bull's-eye at the same distance occupied by the matches. Then insure that you know exactly where your firearm is hitting at that distance. When you know that, striking a kitchen match becomes less of a problem, although the challenge never seems to dwindle. This is an interesting little match, if you'll excuse the feeble pun.

Draw a Picture. A sheet of scrap tin or a chunk of cardboard placed in front of the backstop is the only hardware necessary for this little game, which is stolen from Annie Oakley's (and others') demonstrations of marksmanship. The plan is to draw, with bullet holes, any picture or outline the shooter is capable of producing. Keeping the bullet holes "on line" is the problem. Making an image of a bird or early 20th-century touring car isn't that complicated, except for those holes that don't stay in line.

Charcoal on a String. Stretch a section of twine between two stakes driven into the ground in front of a backstop. Attach charcoal briquets to the twine by tying them on with string. The slightest breeze upgrades the challenge of this little game exponentially. Hitting charcoal briquets dangling from a line is not so tough, but hitting those same chunks of charcoal as they sway in the breeze is another matter.

Bottle Cap Shoot. There are many variations of this game. The simplest method is to align bottle caps on the ground all in a row, and the shooter who centers the most with his rifle or handgun is the winner. But the bottle caps can also be suspended, as with the above charcoal briquets, or stuck in the earth in an irregular pattern. Bottle caps often register a hit by sailing into the air, but even when they don't, the clear bullet hole shows the result of good marksmanship every time. The winner of this match is the one who hits the most bottle caps with the fewest shots—simple enough, and pretty darn good practice.

Suspended or Swinging Gong. Some commercial targets have swing-away metal disks; however, a hunk of metal suspended in front of a backstop is the only target required for this 22-rimfire game. You can place the metal at any agreed-upon distance. Two hundred yards calls for a fairly large chunk, but you can erect smaller ones at 100, 50, even 25 yards. The shooters agree on allowable shooting postures—offhand, prone, sitting, whatever, with or without a rest—and he who pings the most bullets on metal wins. As a safety measure, the suspended gong is always placed directly in front of the earthen backstop so that bullets cannot ricochet away, but will be trapped every time. A breeze turns this game into the "swinging gong" target.

Field Plinking. Field plinking is perhaps king of the 22 games, for it allows the marksman a healthful walk in the outdoors, and it offers excellent practice. The targets are not pre-set for range. You don't know how far away each target is. Therefore, skills in distance judgment and bullet placement are stropped to a keen edge.

Roving in the field can produce some of the most worthwhile plinking of all. Be sure of your backstop. Many out-of-the-way areas are perfect for this shooting game.

Field plinking requires a vacant area with backstops. *Consider no target without a backstop.* Bits of old wood, an abandoned beverage can (which you pick up after shooting to rid the area of litter), or a stump are some of the target possibilities. Picking up that discarded can, by the way, is part of the game. You pace off the distance from shooting point to can, then see how close your guesstimate of range actually was. Identify each target carefully before firing, not only to determine what it is, but also to ensure that it has a solid dirt-bank backstop. Field plinking may be played alone or with a partner. It's best played with a partner who watches the results of each shot through field glasses.

Games in 22 rimfire are as limitless as the shooter's imagination, provided safe range conditions prevail. Snipping the ash from a cigarette was one of Annie Oakley's little tricks, and the cigarettes

The young shooter can learn a great deal from 22-rimfire shooting games. But do not allow sloppy stance or haphazard shooting. Insist that the shooter follow all rules of good marksmanship and safety.

were often protruding from the lips of some trusting soul. Only a fool would attempt such a trick today. However, snicking an ash from a cigarette placed on the ground in front of a backstop poses no problem. As long as the 22-rimfire game is safe and non-littering, it will prove to be a positive experience for shooters.

Twenty-two rimfire shooting games are fun, but they are much more than that. They are teaching tools that hold the interest of the veteran marksman as well as the beginning shooter. These games have terrific transfer value. The shooter who can light matches at 10 paces is equally capable of putting squirrels and rabbits in the pot with meat-saving bullet placement. Play these games for the enjoyment. But remember that they are fairly serious business, too, because they offer the kind of practice that makes great marksmen, and they also give

a person some quiet concentration time and restful relaxation.

Most of us will never achieve the Annie Oakley level of competence in 22-rimfire shooting games. But that's all right. We will probably not break the records set over the years by 22-rimfire exhibition shooters, either. Many of these records would be difficult to shatter. Tom Frye, shooting for Remington, spent two weeks firing 22 Long Rifle ammo at little wooden blocks tossed into the air. He missed six of them in that time span. However, he hit a staggering 100,004 out of 100,010 blocks flipped up before him. That any one of us will put holes in that many 2¾-inch wooden blocks whirled in the air is doubtful. However, there can be no doubt that those of us who play 22-rimfire games will set our own records—personal records of improved marksmanship and great enjoyment.

11 PROFICIENCY THROUGH TARGET SHOOTING

Games are valuable for training, practice, construction of good shooting habits, restful relaxation, and the pure joy of the sport. Serious target work also offers most of these advantages, although stringent competition can bring stress to marksmanship. Match events are formal, with strict rules, and have national and international uniformity. Match shooting is not a major topic of this book, nor is the book intended expressly for trophy-winning targetmasters, although competitive 22-rimfire marksmen might do well to read our data on accuracy enhancement and 22-rimfire ballistics. But any interested 22-rimfire fan will expand his understanding of shooting with a fingertip touch on the world of formal targeting. As Aleksandr Yur'yev, the dedicated Russian target shooter, preached: theoretical knowledge is as important as shooting experience. (Read Yur'yev's book, *Competitive Shooting*, which has been translated by Gary Anderson for the National Rifle Association.) As with other sidetrails along the main route of shooting, target work with the 22 is growing more sophisticated, with ever-increasing accuracy in both firearm and ammunition.

Anyone with a budding interest in competitive 22-rimfire shooting should study the many materials the NRA has available on the subject. Pamphlets, books, and booklets explain various events, their objectives, rules, and appropriate firearms. After this introductory level of interest, an incubation period is recommended. First, read all you can; visit the range; watch various matches; then "rest on it." Allow yourself some time to decide whether or not serious match shooting is for you. There is usually a substantial investment in the sport, depending upon the chosen event or events, including travel to matches and incidental expenses. More important, however, is the expenditure of time. Sincere and dedicated target shooters have been known to practice for hours each day in order to perfect their form. Yur'yev often practiced without ammunition, using "dry fire" techniques similar to those mentioned in the previous chapter. When he could not get to the range, dry firing was his substitute for shooting live ammo. He credited much of his consequent success to the practice of "shooting" without ammunition. But even in dry firing, improvement comes with the investment of time.

THE TARGET SHOOTER

Dedication is certainly the prime mover in serious match shooting. Fine equipment, knowledge of ballistics, and physical ability are necessary for success (the target shooter is known for his steady nerves and a high level of mental concentration). However, great talent has emerged from the ranks of mediocrity through supreme dedication. The target shooter has an understanding not only of his rifle or handgun, but also of theory. He combines that knowledge with the "ultimate hardware" that brings success, from the accurate firearm to the properly made shooting jacket. I do not want to leave the impression that all competitive target shooting is of death-grip seriousness. You can compete for the fun of it in events that interest you. Newcomers to the ranks of target shooting should investigate the NRA's many programs, including classes in marksmanship qualification, conducted with the 22-rimfire rifle or pistol at 50 feet with scaled-down targets, fired indoors or outdoors. There are also outdoor courses at longer range, 25 to 50 yards, with 22-rimfire pistol or rifle, with all rifle shooting from the prone potion over the Dewar Course.

Pistol shooting includes slow-fire, rapid-fire and, timed segments at 25 or 50 yards. The Light Rifle Course employs the 22-rimfire rifle of weight no more that 7½ pounds, including sights. Some

Many young shooters receive their initial training on the target range. Under adult supervision, this is the sort of beginning that makes great marksmen. The National Rifle Association is the guardian of target shooting in this country. Funds are carefully allocated and well-spent on the kinds of facilities necessary to the sport. *(Photos, courtesy NRA)*

Some shooters will reach world-competition levels of target marksmanship. These shooters are athletes, physically and mentally capable of producing world-class scores on the range. *(Photo, courtesy NRA)*

events are more for enjoyment than heavy competition. Too many pages of this book could be covered with information pertaining to the many year-round, local target matches and programs for the fan of the 22-rimfire pistol or rifle. Check with the NRA or your local sanctioned shooting club for details on these close-to-home events.

THE TARGET FIREARM

Even a steady diet of dedication will not win the match for the serious target shooter if his firearm is not of top-drawer quality; therefore, the firearm draws our attention in this primer on match shooting. What is a proper target handgun or rifle? It is the correct rifle or pistol as demanded by the rules of the event. A "free rifle" fits those competitions it serves; a biathlon rifle is the obvious choice for the biathlon match, a running-boar rifle for the running-boar match, and so forth. Most of us are fascinated with 22-rimfire target firearms because of

Serious competition demands athletic perfection. Even the shooting coat becomes an important tool, aiding the marksman in obtaining excellence on the target range. *(Photo, courtesy NRA)*

Indoor target-shooting ranges offer year-round shooting. The competition can be keen, and only the most practiced and gifted shooters stand a chance of winning the match. *(Photo, courtesy NRA)*

their precision. They are created for accuracy and repeated performance. Consequently, many of them are absolutely wrong for the type of grass-roots shooting most of us do—I'd certainly not want to be saddled with a 10-pound match rifle on my next squirrel hunt. Consider the Anschutz Improved 1907 Match Rifle for prone and position shooting, boasting a trigger with nine points of adjustment, removable cheekpiece with up/down adjustment, and a buttplate that is also fully adjustable to match the personal demands of the shooter. A beautiful rifle, but specialized, as are some, but not all, target pistols, which, by the way, now dominate revolvers in competition.

SOME SHOOTING EVENTS

The Olympics honors the 22-rimfire target devotee with various competitions, not only the biathlon of winter meets, but also various "standard" events. One competition calls for firing from 50 me-

ters at a target with a bull's-eye smaller than a dime, from the prone, standing, or kneeling posture. Dozens of different matches exist in national and international competition outside the Olympics as well. Each has its own significant brand of challenge. One smallbore event in three-position rifle competition calls for the firing of 120 shots from three positions, using the 22-rimfire rifle from 50 meters distance. It is a free rifle match. The running-boar match is carried out at 50 meters with a 22-rimfire rifle. The target is a reproduction of a boar on a light-colored background. It appears from behind a concealment, runs across a 10-meter opening called a "run window," in five seconds for slow-run and 2.5 seconds for fast-run. This competition is clearly for the marksman who has mastered his rifle, for he must hold with precision, yet keep the muzzle in motion for proper lead on the target. The smallbore sport pistol event calls for 60 shots fired, 30 of them on the bull's-eye and 30 at silhouette targets. Part I includes shooting at the 25-meter and 50-meter free-pistol target. Part II consists of shooting silhouettes at 25 meters. This is a timed match.

WHAT WE GAIN FROM TARGET SHOOTING

Higher Performance Firearms. I like to compare competitive 22-rimfire target shooting with professional race-car driving. Few of us will ever crawl behind the wheel of a Formula One race car. Yet no modern driver remains untouched by the sport of race-car driving, because many facts about cars and improved driving techniques have been discovered at the race track. These developments are often interjected into the design and management of the commercial road car. Competition shooting is, as these words are penned, bringing about the study of more accurate firearms and ammunition. As target rifles and ammunition improve, some of the innovations slip into the mainstream of rifle and ammo building. Take a look at the Anschutz sporting 22 rifle and you will find several features born of competition shooting. Shoot match ammo and your cluster shrinks before your eyes.

But there is an even bigger picture—anyone who learns at least the basics of target shooting will improve every aspect of his own 22 rimfiring (and all marksmanship), from simple plinking to providing small-game protein for himself and his family. There is profit in such escalation of personal talent, increased enjoyment through greater success. I was also reminded of the "green" profit in shooting better—the bag of cottontails I brought home compared with pen-raised rabbits selling at the super market for three dollars a pound. So target shooting teaches us better style. But even when we do not participate directly in matches, betterment of arms and ammo filters into the world of standard shooting.

Improvement is ongoing. For example, a team of riflemakers in Texas, working under the banner of Kleingunther's Distinctive Firearms, has developed a special target rifle of meritorious accuracy. This 22-rimfire Olympic-model target rifle includes a very fast lock time registered in the 1.5 millisecond realm. The barrel comes from the Shilen Company, famous for accuracy. This barrel is unique because of the acceptance tolerances that range between .0001 and .0002 inches within the bore. All other aspects of barrel accuracy are equally attended to. The action of the rifle is essentially glued in place

The running boar match has steadily gained in popularity, with special running-boar rifles built for the match. *(Photo, courtesy NRA)*

Practice and dedication, along with skill, are required to compete in the running-boar match. The winner's circle holds only those shooters who deliver excellent groups on target. *(Photo, courtesy NRA)*

(reminiscent of some benchrest rifles). The action is short and stiff. All of the fine points surrounding this and many other target rifles engineered to "win the gold" eventually filter into the building of high-grade rifles for us—the "us" who go forth to shoot at paper targets for fun, gather small game for food, and plink away stress.

Improved Shooting Methods. The mental conditioning that goes into competitive shooting serves all of us well, no matter which branch of 22 rimfiring (or any other shooting) interests us most. We can learn to gain a "shooter's mind" through practicing tenets that shine in the universe of the target shooter. We can enjoy these fine points of marksmanship without undergoing the strain of competition, just as we might enjoy a better road tire without having been in the race that proved the tire's merit. In preparing for a shooting session, especially when plinking as a pressure-release valve is the object of shooting, clear the mind first as a target shooter might, with calming thoughts. Observe a moment of silence. Close your eyes. Breathe with a nice, steady rhythm. Then partake of the plinking fun. If you have a partner along, agree to speak in low tones. Don't let tenseness be part of your shooting program any more than a pro would allow tenseness to detour his bullets from the bull's-eye.

How To Control Match "Nerves." Fear of poor performance does not have to enter our realm of shooting. There is no loss of self-esteem. If you miss the target, so you miss the target. Our heart rates should remain as steady as the ticking of the grandfather clock in the hall. There is no need for competition pressure to enter. However, knowing about competition pressure and its effects is important to those of us who want to hit an empty bean can at 200 yards or cleanly bag a brace of squirrels for supper. Confidence is built through understanding that there can be pressures in shooting, and that these pressures can be controlled. Confidence is also built through the use of good equipment. Nothing ensures a hit more than faith in the accuracy and superb state of repair of a fine personal 22 firearm. Faith is also built through practice with that firearm. The more we practice, the "luckier" we get. We approach shooting as the targetmaster does—with positiveness. Be positive. Instead of telling yourself, "Don't jerk that trigger!" say instead, "OK, remember to squeeze that trigger." Learn rhythm. Howard Hill, the great archer, had rhythm. If he drew an arrow rapidly from his quiver, he completed the shooting sequence quickly. If he withdrew the arrow slowly, he completed the sequence slowly.

Better Physical Conditioning. Staying in relatively good shape leads to a higher level of marksmanship. Feeling physically well promotes putting 'em through the bull's-eye. Target shooting provides

The target rifle can be simple or elaborate. Many modern competitions call for specific "shooting machines" designed expressly for the event. *(Photo, courtesy NRA)*

some excellent lessons applicable to every facet of sport shooting, to include not only our 22-rimfire and centerfire enjoyment, but big-bore and shotgun as well.

Many of the following measures are coupled with good physical self-control. Timing is an important element of good shooting, for example. From target shooting we learn not to "overhold" the shot. Practice getting the shot away, at a tin can or a coyote, within six to nine seconds. After 12 to 15 seconds of holding time, or aiming, visual acuity begins to fade. The shooter's eye concentrating on the target becomes less perceptive. He may also begin to experience the beginning of natural body tremor.

You can even control heartbeat, and you needn't be a yogi to do it, although simple self-calming practices have an effect on heart rate through "mindpower."

Breathing style also helps control heartbeat. In shooting, we exhale, draw in a full breath, let half of it out, hold the rest, and then fire our shot. We don't touch the shot off as we are in the process of inhaling and exhaling, with the chest expanding and the body in motion. This method of breath control is not the only one. Some shooters find better control of body tremor through taking a full breath, holding almost all of it in, and then firing. It is an individual matter that must be practiced.

Trigger Management. This is another big part of serious target shooting. Study target shooters, their triggers and methods of using them, and you'll know a lot more about your own 22's trigger management.

Dealing With Mirage. And then there's mirage, which plagues not only target shooters, but all of us. These rising currents of hot air make the image

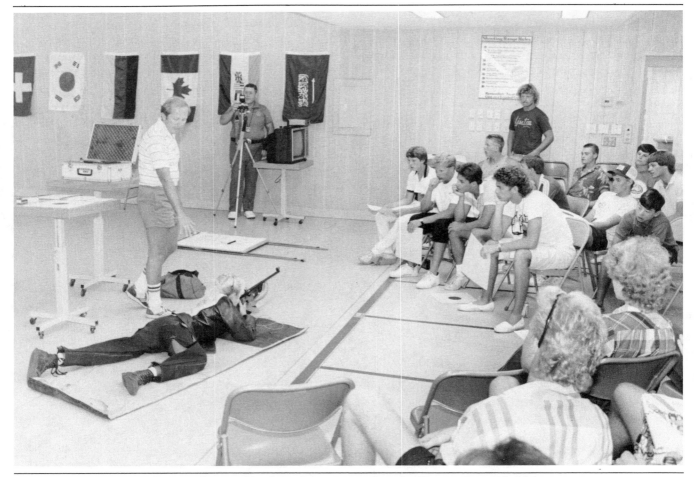

Target shooting is more than marksmanship. It is also a game of study. Here a class is held for young people who aspire to great things on the target range. *(Photo, courtesy NRA)*

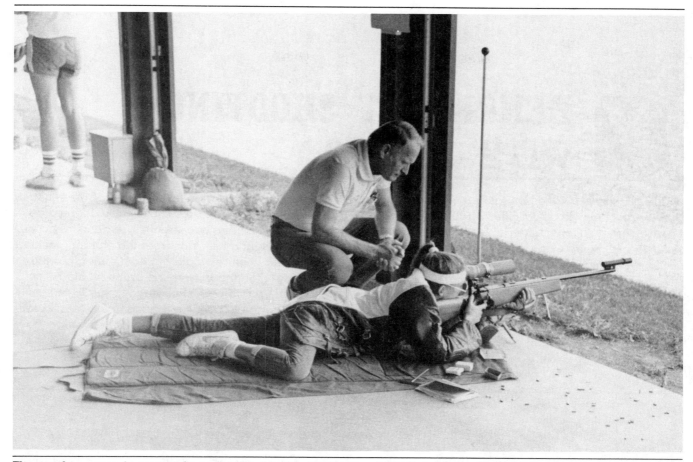

The coach—a very important figure on the shooting range. Formal target shooting is an intricate sport and one that requires coaching, just as Olympic events require coaching. *(Photo, courtesy NRA)*

before us appear as a shimmering picture. A hot barrel can also produce a certain type of mirage. Control mirage by firing when the sights are aligned and the firearm is under control. Don't wait in hope of the mirage coming under control, because it generally will not do so within the time allotted to getting a round off. Blowing on the barrel dissipates some of the heat that emanates from the steel. So when a target shooter blows across the top of his barrel, he is not doing so for good luck. These are a few of the points passed on to us from the world of target shooting. Study the sport of competition marksmanship—do some target shooting of your own—and you will become a better shot.

Many library materials are available on the sport of target shooting. As mentioned, the NRA stands ready to promote serious 22 competition all over the country. For example, the booklet *NRA Smallbore Rifle Rules* is available to members. It con-

tains the "Official Rules and Regulations to govern the conduct of all Conventional Smallbore Rifle competition." The booklet *NRA Pistol Rules* governs pistol and revolver competition. These booklets are up to date and very valuable for the person contemplating entry into the world of serious target-shooting competition. Your local library also might have several titles on target shooting. At the beginning of this chapter, I mentioned Dr. Yur'yev's book. His translator, Gary Anderson, has also written on the topic of target shooting in his fine book, *Marksmanship*, published by Simon and Schuster, 1972.

You need not be in quest of Olympic gold to gain greatly from the sport of 22-rimfire target shooting. I can think of no shooter who would not benefit from the study of, as well as the practice of, match competition, even if the only person he competes with is himself.

12 BENCHREST SHOOTING WITH THE 22

The benchrest is an essential platform of operation for all of us who shoot rifles and handguns. The entire sport of shooting sidearms and longarms takes the upsweep when the marksman learns how to use the bench correctly. Benchresting has many levels of involvement. Here are the major operational plateaus for the 22 rimfire and centerfire fan.

Sight-in, practice, rifle testing, ammunition and handload experimentation—all require the use of the bench. The benchrest was designed to eliminate, as far as possible, some of the human elements that detract from firearm control. Wise benchrest management reduces, to a large degree, the human factors that cause bullets to go astray. You wouldn't sight a new rifle from the offhand position. The sitting posture would not do it either, nor the kneeling. Sighting in from the prone would be acceptable up to a point, but when trying to remove those human elements in an attempt to gain better control over the firearm, the bench is the place to go. *The bench is the laboratory for the serious shooter.* There is no substitute for it today.

Basic benchshooting is essential for all marksmen, from hunters to elite target shooters. Sight-in of rifle, study of loads, accuracy checks of both firearm and ammo—all of these, and much more, are accomplished from the bench. *(Photo, courtesy NRA)*

A portable benchrest can be very sturdy. It allows the shooter to set up in a field situation, with most of the advantages of a permanent benchrest.

BENCHREST PROCEDURE

The prize-winning benchrester will have developed his own style of managing rifles from the bench. Our interest is the same as his—to control the firearm by eliminating as many human elements from shooting as possible. First, you need a good bench. Portable benchrests work, and they can work well. Never will they offer the rock-solid stability of the heavy bench (perhaps bedded in concrete), but my Cabela folding bench has provided a stable laboratory for shooting when the range was not accessible. A good bench is any level table-top that is firmly secured to prevent wobble. Integral to that bench is the shooter's seat. It must be aligned so that the individual can shoot in comfort. Since we are not built from a standard mould, we may have to adjust the bench seat to suit our size and body configuration.

This brings us to the first rule of informal benchshooting: get comfortable. Trying to control the firearm when your body is not under control is nearly impossible. Teachers know that students sitting at their desks must have their feet touch the ground for comfort. At the benchseat, the shooter must be able to plant his feet firmly, flat upon the ground, far enough apart for solid stability of the body. Resting on the toes thwarts stability.

Use a proper rifle rest. My own is an adjustable

Outers Pistol Perch offers a high-quality handgun-shooting aid to be used from the bench. Handguns are sighted from the bench, and some of the best handgun practice takes place at the bench as well.

model from Hoppe's. This heavy metal unit firmly supports the forend of the rifle. (There are also rests suited particularly to handguns.) The buttstock of the rifle is rested upon a sandbag. In short, the rifle must be secured front and back, and not by the forend only. The sandbag, which supports the toe of the buttstock, is vital to firearm control.

Point the rifle rest and sandbag in the direction of the target so that the least jockeying of the firearm will align it with the target. Do not place rest and bag on the benchtop haphazardly, trying to align the rifle by moving it and its rest simultaneously. Point the rests first. Then aligning the rifle will require less movement. Never place the rifle's barrel on the rest. As covered earlier, this can cause the bullet to go astray. Instead, rest the forend and toe of the rifle stock only. Allow the barrel its freedom. Refrain from shooting with your chest pressed down onto the edge of the bench; the pressure inhibits easy breathing. The 22-caliber rifle delivers so little recoil that the right elbow (for a right-handed shooter) moves back very little at the shot. Even so, get in the habit of placing a pad of some sort beneath that elbow. When firing a big bore, this pad will prevent scraping the elbow across the

It is essential to have the body under control during benchshooting. Note that the feet are flat upon the ground here, and spaced properly for steadiness.

bench during recoil. When shooting the 22s, the pad offers a little added comfort and stability.

Follow all of the rules of good benchshooting and your sight-in, practice, rifle testing, and ammo discoveries will run smoothly. Use all of the precepts of good shooting at the bench. Control breathing, for example, as you would from any other shooting posture. Apply even pressure to the trigger so that the rifle goes off without disturbance of aim. Use the proper target—one that fits the sights. A big black bull's-eye is all right for iron sights; however, refine that aimpoint when trying to test the accuracy of your scoped firearm and its ammunition. The higher scope powers call for very small aimpoints. Use the benchrest as your laboratory. Know what your 22s are doing. Eliminate as much of the human factor as possible from your tests. Initial sighting-in, resighting, and testing are not the only values of benchshooting for the everyday marksman. He learns much about all aspects of shooting from benchresting. So don't forget to practice from the bench. Such practice is invaluable for improving marksmanship.

22 RIMFIRE BENCHREST SHOOTING

Rifle Magazine No. 115 carried a piece by L.W. Brown describing an upcoming 22-rimfire sport: BR-50, shooting for best group at a distance of 50

The elbow is not only rested here, but also padded. Padding is not as important in 22-shooting as in big-bore work. The high-recoil firearm tends to skid the elbow across the bench, while the 22s do not. But the rest aids shooter comfort, even in 22-rifle work.

The Hoppe's rest, shown beneath the forend of the Sako varmint rifle, offers not only steadiness, but also considerable adjustability. It is backed up by a Hoppe's shot-filled bag for buttstock support.

yards. This event is a scaled-down version of the interesting, sometimes intense, and now almost worldwide, game of benchrest shooting for the "Great Quest"—all of the bullets going through the same hole, the "zero group," where center-to-center measurement for the string is actually zero. In other words, all of the bullets have occupied the same little hole in the paper target as they passed through. But the benchrest game played with a 22 rimfire is, at this stage, a bit less stringent of rules and certainly less demanding of the pocketbook; at the moment you do not need a custom (handmade) rifle to enjoy the challenge. Shooting at 50 yards is just about right for the 22 Long Rifle cartridge. Wind bullies the small and comparatively slow-moving bullet. Nevertheless, there are already competitions at 100 yards as well as 50.

Fifty yards was selected not only for the obvious reason of 22 Long Rifle ballistics, but also because of range space. Building a range requiring only 50 yards' distance saves money, time, and space. Of course, 22-rimfire benchrest matches will become increasingly demanding of precision, as regular benchrest matches have. Yesterday's first-place groups would not even qualify for last place today among the high priests of accuracy. That's how far precision shooting has come in the past decade or

All aspects of rifle handling are observed at the bench, including careful trigger squeeze and control of the rifle. Note hearing protection.

two. Already ¼-inch group sizes at 50 yards are setting the trend in 22-rimfire benchresting, with hopes of consistent half-inchers at 100.

Another beauty of the BR-50 game is its comparative quietness. In areas where the booming of big bores could disturb nearby residents, those same people might not even hear the mild crack of the 22 rimfire.

Rimfire benchresting is also less demanding of the shooter's time. Cleaning is recommended after 200 to 300 shots, for example. And then before continuing the pursuit for tight groups, the shooter sends a few fouling shots downrange to dress the bore again.

Barrels last a long time in top accuracy form too. "In the Remington proof shop, they once put 80,000 rounds through a match rimfire barrel without cleaning it and found less than .0005 inch of wear and no loss of accuracy after the last round was fired," according to *Rifle Magazine No. 115*, p. 34.

The same accouterments are used in rimfire benchresting as in standard benchshooting—a solid table-top bench with proper rifle rests. No new range setup is called for.

The rifles fall into three major classes, although I feel these classes are subject to change in substance. However, for now there are the Sporter, Target, and Unrestricted groups—depending upon who is setting up the shoot. The last category, also known as the Unlimited group, may include custom rifles, such as one with a Remington 40X action, Hart barrel, fiberglass stock, and Leupold 24X target scope, prepared to shoot that ¼-inch group at 50 yards. In one set of rules for 22-rimfire bench-resting, the Sporter class allows a rifle up to 8.5 pounds in weight with a maximum scope power of 12X. Many rifles fall into this category, including the Remington 541-S or 541-T, various Anschutz models, and the Kimber 82. The Target class allows rifles up to 14 pounds weight with any scope sight. Most of the 22s in this class are silhouette models. These two classes must be factory only; no specialty rifles allowed. However, the Unrestricted or Unlimited class has no limitation on rifle weight or scope power. Bull barrels are OK.

The Unrestricted class allows the imagination to run wild. This type of freewheeling piques the interest of the experimenter. The Unlimited class is to shooting what the Formula One car represents in racing. In due time, most of us "grassroots" shooters will benefit from knowledge gathered by those 22-rimfire devotees interested in the one-hole group. Shooting methods will also improve, and those improvements will be passed on to the rest of us. Rifle technique is already demanding for anyone who wants to win a BR-50 match. Masterful doping of the wind is also essential to winning, as is the rifle's inherent accuracy level, proper bench-rest style, the shooter's talent, and the compatability of rifle and ammo. That last criterion continues to run true for all branches of 22-rimfire shooting.

Twenty-two rimfire benchresters have learned to test many different brands of ammunition in an attempt to reach a match made in heaven, the type of ammo their particular bench rifle likes best. Once they have located that ammo, these shooters have been known to run out and buy large quantities of the given lot or run the ammo came from, ensuring that they will have captured a good supply of the exact fodder their rifles shoot best.

Shooters apparently prefer the short leade or throat of the match-type rifle for best results in BR-50 accuracy. Short throats have been common in target rifles for many years. The chambers of these rifles, and some single-shot match pistols, are not only on the short side, but also of minimal head-space and diameter. The 22-rimfire round, in other words, fits these chambers very tightly. Seated bullets are engraved. That is, a round inserted into the chamber and withdrawn without firing will bear the marks of the rifling. In seating a round, the cartridge will glide into the chamber smoothly, but will be felt as the bullet engages the rifling toward the

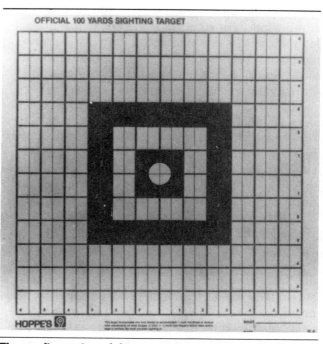

The configuration of the target is very important in benchshooting. This Hoppe's target offers a clear and precise aimpoint, essential for learning the most about a firearm.

end of the bolt-closing stroke. Sporting rifle chambers do not have this setup. There is clearance in front of the bullet, the sporting chamber being about .175 inch longer than a match chamber.

WIND DEFLECTION AND WIND FLAGS

In firing the 40 required shots in 22-rimfire bench-resting, wind doping is essential to good grouping. The 22-rimfire expert learns early on that wind diverts the little bullet from its appointment with the bull's-eye. He also learns that there is less wind drift in standard velocity ammo due to lag time (discussed earlier). The coefficient of drag peaks in that region of disturbance, at around the speed of sound and up to about 1500 fps, then tapers off at about Mach II. Of course, the 22 Long Rifle does not reach Mach II in any current loading, so standard-velocity ammo gives about a 20-percent wind-drift advantage over high-velocity 22 Long Rifle ammunition. A 10 m.p.h. crosswind drifts the high-velocity bullet more than 1½ inches off course at 50 yards, and from 5½ to 6 inches at 100 yards. The 40-grain bullet from a standard-velocity 22 Long Rifle will drift just a bit more than an inch off target in the same 10 m.p.h. wind at 50 yards, and a little less than 4½ inches off course at 100 yards in the same wind. A downrange wind will cause the bullet to hit a little low. An uprange wind will cause the bullet to strike a little high on the target. These latter "facts" are not chiseled in concrete yet, by the way. More study is needed. But shooting experience tends to support the high/low bullet print as stated here.

Reading wind flags properly improves the odds for a close group at the target. Important are the speed and the direction of the wind. Together, these factors force bullets away from their intended destinations. The worst is the crosswind, blowing directly against the shank of the bullet. Experience brings more conjecture (and conjecture could be right) concerning high/low hits at the target. Again, it seems that wind striking the right-hand side of the bullet causes the missile to rise, while wind striking the left-hand side of the bullet causes the projectile to drop. These data are for a right-hand twist, and the directional rotation of the bullet could help account for the phenomenon. Further study is needed on the matter. The tail wind, as noted above, depressed the bullet, while a head wind lifted it. Remember to check the wind flags *downrange*. The same goes for hunting or rimfire shooting at 200 yards. While the wind may be blowing from a certain direction near the shooter, it could be blowing differently around the target. Sometimes wind and mirage combine to bring even greater doping problems. A lot of experience shooting rimfires in the wind and in mirage management bring greater success. Keep shooting. A lot.

22 CENTERFIRE BENCHREST SHOOTING

There can be no doubt that the current king of the benchrest match is the 6 PPC USA cartridge, and not a 22-caliber round. At the same time, many 22s, including the 222 Remington and 22 PPC, have won titles in the past, and are still capable of supremely accurate groups. Furthermore, a good deal of local benchrest shooting continues with the 22 centerfire. Although I shoot both 6 PPC USA and 22 PPC USA rifles, I do far more with the latter because my benchresting is for enjoyment and learning, not competition, and my 22 PPC finds its way to the varminting field most often. Serious precision shooting is much like serious Olympic-type match shooting—those engaged in these branches of marksmanship don't need a lot of help from the rest of us. Their sport is set. But I see 22-rimfire bench-

Factory-ammo accuracy has been vastly improved in recent times, as witnessed by Winchester's Supreme line. Supreme 22-250 ammo made this group at 100 yards. Later shooting with the same ammo provided even closer clusters.

shooting as an upcoming event for the reasons stated above, and because we can all become involved close to home, at just about any range, and without unloading the contents of our wallets in order to join the fun. Twenty-two centerfire bench-resting is also going to continue in popularity among those of us who are not out to win prizes, because it is at the bench that we sight our rifles, re-sight them, check for accuracy, work up various handloads, and determine just which factory ammos are best suited to our particular needs. While serious competition benchshooting is for that unique marksman who revels in controlling every facet of ballistics, 22-centerfire benchshooting of the "everyday" kind is very valuable to all of us who enjoy firing the fast 22s.

Ultimate rifle accuracy is the goal of centerfire benchresting. A bull's-eye is generally meaningless. The group is everything. The one-hole group, in essence, had been achieved a very long time ago. There are many examples of one ragged hole in the target. Now the quest is for the zero group, with the bullets not only creating one hole, but making that hole the same caliber as the projectile. When the bullets literally fly through the same hole, Mecca will have been reached. The 22 centerfire would thereby produce a 22-caliber hole. The distance between the farthest-apart shots on the paper would be nil—zero—zip—nothing. That achievement still lies a few centimeters beyond the grasp of the precision shooting fan. But it seems to be getting closer to reality all the time. Groups are certainly getting smaller. More on this later when the 22 PPC is discussed in its own chapter.

The classes for precision benchrest shooting are Sporter (maximum weight 10.5 pounds, 6mm or larger), Light Varmint (maximum rifle weight 10.5 pounds, any caliber), Heavy Varmint (13.5 pounds maximum weight, any caliber), and Benchrest Rifle or Unlimited (no restriction on rifle weight or caliber). All of these rifle classes have brought innovation to the ranks of everyday shooting. The expert, event-winning, benchrest shooter knows every thread in the tapestry of his game. He is a handloader of the highest order, can tune a rifle like a fine violin, and can read the wind as a scholar reads his books. If you have a desire to get into the fantastic sport of precision shooting, begin by going to a match. Check with local shooting clubs to determine who is working with precision shooting in the area. Also, find a copy of *The Accurate Rifle* by Warren Page. It will clarify many points on benchresting. The late gunwriter discussed accuracy, the quarter-minute rifle, use of the bench, testing, actions, barrels, the supremely accurate match bullet, scopes for accuracy, mirage, wind, bedding secrets, accuracy cartridges, handloading techniques, cleaning methods for accuracy, and much more. It's a readable text on a subject that can be quite complicated. And you don't have to become an all-out competitor to enjoy the book, or the sport. I'll always appreciate those quarter-inch 22 PPC groups my Sako rifle produces for me when I do my part. So small a cluster will bring a smile to any shooter.

THE ULTIMATE HANDLOAD

You can't talk about precision benchrest 22-centerfire shooting without bringing handloading into the conversation, although recently tested Winchester Supreme ammunition in 22-250 Remington produced handload accuracy from a Dale Storey custom rifle. Tenets of 22-rimfire accuracy were broached in Chapter 7. Accuracy results when precision and consistency are secured. Cartridge components must be precise and nearly identical time after time. The case itself must be correct from primer pocket to neck. The firearm is a machine. It must be a machine that functions with precision and definite repeatability for accuracy to reproduce itself over and over. The human machine must also

The bench allows for a close cluster of bullet holes in the target. From this initial point of impact, the shooter can determine with confidence the correct sight changes necessary to put succeeding groups on target.

be in shape and under control, and shooting conditions have to be reasonable for achievement of success in terms of accuracy. The shooter must also know how to overcome various elements of the atmosphere in order to bring in the small group repeatedly. Cartridge/rifle/shooter: the triumverate of precision shooting.

The first part of the trio is generally a handloaded proposition for the ultimate in precision. Cases are properly prepared, as touched on in Chapter 8. Powder charges are thrown with care from a measure by those who strive for the one-hole group, with a scale to verify the charge weight. Components are juggled until the perfect combination is reached. Accuracy tricks are employed—for example, the powder measure is kept at the full stage for uniformity by inserting a powder funnel at the top of the cylinder. The powder funnel is recharged as the level of powder falls. By keeping powder in the funnel, the level in the powder measure itself is always constant. The height of powder in the measure maintains the same level in this manner. How important is this? The method seems to help with some powders far more than with others. But no statistically reliable test has been run that proves this.

This has been a glimpse at the world of bench-resting. Match-level competiton, such as the Super Shoot, in which the challenge for the one-hole group is presented to all who are interested in achieving it, looks like no other form of shooting. The rifles are handmade examples of art, yet not the art one associates with fine custom sporters wearing beautiful English walnut stocks. These stocks may be of composite manmade materials, brightly colored. Shooters take along a set of cases to the match, and reload them right on the spot, us-ing powder measures to throw charges. Most of the accouterments are crafted in small specialty shops, and loading dies are often cut with the same reamer that cut the chamber of the rifle, so very lit-tle sizing of the fired brass is necessary—fascinat-ing, but not a sport for everyone. It is essential as our laboratory. In benchresting, we sight-in new firearms and keep them on target through periodic resighting. We also test 22-centerfire handloads and factory ammo from the bench. We carefully wed 22-rimfire ammunition to the individual rifle or handgun, and we also practice firearm manage-ment from this stable shooting platform, improving shooter control and the understanding of wind and what it does to bullets.

13 RIMFIRE SILHOUETTE SHOOTING

From over the border came this interesting shooting game, originally intended to offer the big-game hunter a shooting contest, not unlike the turkey shoots of our American forefathers. I was introduced to the game by two friends from Nogales, Sonora, Mexico—Señor Victor Ruiz and Señor Milo Martinez, both of whom were active in this shooting sport early in the game's beginning. Then on assignment for *Gun World* magazine, I covered the first big meet in America, held in Tucson, Arizona. The big draw in *silueta*, or silhouette shooting, was the animated target with four different species of game represented.

Big-bore rifles were used. Initially, only "hunting" rifles were allowed. I recall eight pounds with scope being the weight limit. But as in all competition, when the interest grew, so did the desire to create special firearms to better meet the challenge of the event. As the sport matured in America, the NRA came to the rescue, as it were, by establishing standards for the game. These rules helped to promote silhouette shooting all over the U.S., as did the inception of two dedicated groups, The United States Silueta Association and the International Handgun Metallic Silhouette Association. The sport was just too interesting to remain limited to big-bore rifle shooting, as is evidenced by the latter organization mentioned above, a handgunning body.

RULES OF METALLIC SILHOUETTE SHOOTING

Silhouette shooting has been fired from only one rifle position since the beginning: offhand, no sling allowed. This posture is maintained today (except in handgunning). Many years ago, while visiting Mexico, I learned that the offhand rule was installed as a device to aid hunters who wanted to improve their ability in that stance. Rules were always simple, but not necessarily relaxed, as some have suggested. True, there were and still are only three range commands: *Listo!* (Ready), *Fuego!* (fire), and *Alto!* (Cease Fire). *Listo* calls the shooters to the line. They may prepare their firearms. *Fuego* starts the match. The shooter has two minutes and 30 seconds to complete the round, shooting at five targets. *Alto* calls for a cease-fire. Time is up. Naturally, a cease-fire may be called at any time during the match as well as at the end of a shooting session. What really caught the eye of the shooter, and some of the non-shooting public as well, was the target itself—four targets, actually. These were, and still are: the *gallina* or chicken, the *javelina* or "pig," a musk hog if you insist on accuracy, *guajolote*—the turkey (shades of the old turkey shoot), and finally the *borrego* or bighorn sheep.

Five targets are set on each stand (rail). These targets must be fired on from left to right only. Any target struck out of sequence is a no-count, as is

Targets for *silueta* include a *borrego*, the bighorn sheep. Note the bullet splash from a 22 Long Rifle projectile.

The silhouette match is a group sport during competition, but can be enjoyed individually and informally as well. Here serious competition is underway.

any target that does not topple from its perch. No matter how much the metallic silhouette whirls around, this does not count as a score. The target must fall. In the 22-rimfire rifle version of the game, the chicken is placed at 40 meters distance (44 yards), the pig at 60 meters (66 yards), the turkey at 77 meters (84.7 yards), and the sheep at 100 meters (110 yards). Coaching is OK. A person standing behind the shooter may relate where the bullet struck in relation to the target, giving helpful advice for the next shot. Because there is a raised earthen berm behind the targets, misses can be accurately accounted for. Each shooter fires a total of 40 shots. The shooter with the most hits wins. Simple. As for a tie, that's dealt with simply too—a shoot-off determines the winner. Sixty seconds are allotted to fire at the sheep, and if all shots hit again, then the sheep is replaced with a turkey. The booklet *NRA Silhouette Rules* details these and other rules of the sport (currently available for a half-dollar from NRA headquarters).

SMALLBORE RIFLE SILHOUETTE: A FAST-GROWING GAME

The inclusion of a 22-rifle event was a natural outcome of the match's popularity. Twenty-two rifle metallic silhouette games were an inevitable and natural progression for many reasons. It was simple to scale the game down. Whereas the farthest target in big-bore silhouette had been the sheep at 500 meters, now it was a sheep at 100 meters, one-fifth the distance. Every target was reduced in range to one-fifth the original distance. The targets were in turn reduced in size to correlate with the reduction of range—one-fifth the size for each cutout. The 22 was quiet. It could be used on ranges close to town. The 22 silhouette range required a distance of only 100 meters to the farthest target butts. A high-power-rifle range was not needed. The little 22 rimfire did not ruin the metal targets, which were previously battered by the big bores. Further aiding the economy of the sport was the availability of suitable rifles at a modest cost. And ammo

The four metallic targets of the 22-rimfire *silueta* game are (from left) the *borrego* (ram), *guajolote* (turkey), *javelina* (wild pig), and the *gallina* (chicken). The metallic targets are placed on a rail. In order to score a hit, they must fall completely over. Turning one around is not considered a hit.

Joe King of Yuma, Ariz., takes aim with his silhouette rifle, a Remington 513-S with a 6X-20X Leupold scope sight. Joe has found that the high-magnification scope aids in improving shooter stability by magnifying body motion.

Ideal for silhouette shooting is this Leupold 6X-20X scope sight. The turrets are marked "BULLET IMPACT" with indicator arrow designed to aid the shooter in changing his sight setting for the various metallic targets and also for range condition.

was also inexpensive. No wonder 22-rimfire silhouette shooting became the fastest-growing aspect of the *silueta* sport. The low investment of the sport continued with modest accessories: a spotting scope and a shooting vest. The 22 match was fun, easy to get started in, gentle on the wallet, and it didn't take all day to complete a round, with only 40 shots doing the job.

Rifles. The NRA established a maximum weight of 10 pounds 2 ounces for the 22-rimfire rifle silhouette game. Many 22 rifles qualified, of course, and as certain as sun on the Sahara, shooters began to crave specialized shooting instruments for better efficiency. Thus was born the Anschutz 54.18 MS Silhouette Rifle, built to meet all of the requirements of the NRA rule book. Customized rifles were also inevitable. Shooters could modify existing target rifles for good balance and steady offhand holding, while meeting weight limitations. The maximum criteria could not be surpassed. However, shooters could elect to build or use rifles that were well under the limitations of the match. It was further all right to reduce range if targets were reduced commensurately in size. The end result has been a wide range of *silueta* games, including matches for the air rifle.

Scopes. Telescopic sights have been around for a long time. Many of the more astute "buffalo runners" used sophisticated scope sights, some of them 20X in magnification with stadia wires for

range judgment. These men shot hundreds of animals in response to the U.S. Army plan of reducing the Plains Indian by attacking the source of his livelihood (that's why Army wagons were on the range giving away free ammunition, and that's why each bison tongue was worth one dollar). However, in spite of the antiquity of the scope, many modern sportsmen balked when glass sights finally reached the sporting-goods shop for the average shooter to buy. Some of them, intelligent shooters otherwise, claimed that rifle telescopes made their shooting unsteady. I was amazed to hear of modern shooters who insisted on lower power scopes for silhouette shooting because they did not want to see the degree of their own body

Designed especially for the silhouette match, these Winchester Super Silhouette 22 Long Rifle cartridges carry a 42-grain truncated cone bullet with a blunt nose. (They are also excellent for small-game hunting.)

motion through a high-power scope sight. It is true that the high-power scope can cause trouble for the beginner, but not by magnifying the target too much. The trouble comes in locating the target in the small field of view. I had this problem myself in using a 24X scope. However, the high-power scope has distinct advantages over lower-powered units.

As Joe King, a dedicated silhouette shooter, tutored me, the strong scope revealed my own body tremor, which helped by showing me that I had to be steadier to create more hits. I benefited from Joe's training as I coaxed my body to respond to the motion revealed by the high magnification of the 24X scope. A variable scope is allowed, and since we now have excellent variables in the 6X-24X realm, 6.5X-20X range and other units, there is no reason to select a low-powered scope for silhouette work. Joe King is going to the 36X next, because he has trained himself to make use of the extra magnification. These big scopes resting upon smallish 22-rimfire rifles may seem incongruous at first, but they work very well and offer a great deal of training potential for the shooter. Also, the powerful scope sight allows the shooter to select a specific aiming point on the metal cutout. By aiming at a minute portion of the target, a "miss" might still be a hit. The specific part of the silhouette aimed at might be missed, but the bullet may still make contact with the metal target at some other point. The target scope offers precise and repeatable adjustment—the shooter can make instant on-the-range settings for the various metallics and their specific ranges (as well as wind conditions, if he chooses to do so).

Ammunition. We know that standard-velocity ammunition drifts a bit less upon the wind than high-velocity 22 ammo. However, when the wind is not causing a problem, high-velocity ammo may be the choice for silhouette shooting because, as noted above, the metal cutout must be knocked down, not merely tipped, shoved, plinked or pinged. A bullet of higher delivered energy is therefore not a bad idea. And wouldn't you know it? The ammo companies deferred, Federal bringing out a Silhouette ammo in 1982 with a 40-grain bullet at 1150 fps. Winchester followed with its Super Silhouette load in 1983, firing a 42-grain blunt-nosed projectile at 1220 fps. I never had the chance to test Federal's silhouette load. However, my Kimber rifle with 22-inch barrel delivered an average muzzle velocity of 1226 fps with a standard deviation of only 15 fps

Handgunners now enjoy their own version of the silhouette sport, and this Thompson/Center Contender in 22 Long Rifle chambering is a very good silhouette model.

with Winchester's silhouette load. This ammo shot so well in my hunting rifles that I have used it in the field in a Model 75 Winchester Sporter and a Kimber Model 82. It is very accurate in both.

THE SHORT-RANGE PISTOL

The 22 rimfire was also allowed in the short-range pistol silhouette shooting match. Here, the chicken was placed at 25 meters, the pig at 50 meters, the turkey at 75, and the sheep a full 100 meters away. The shooter was not limited to the off-

Browning's Buck Mark 22 pistol in the silhouette model offers a 9⁷⁄₈-inch barrel with a .900-inch muzzle diameter. Precision sights include a Millet Gold Cup No. 360 with interchangeable front posts.

This is a pistol stance used in the sport of 22-rimfire silhouette shooting.

hand position now. Here was a brand-new match with some fantastic possibilities. Big-game hunting, as well as small-game hunting, with the handgun had grown immensely over the years. Now, fans of the one-hand gun could practice at the range with a game, the same fine game of *silueta*, but geared for sidearms. Enjoyment plus practice plus challenge. It all added up to another winning target shooting event.

The 22-rimfire silhouette shooting game is a great teacher, as well as a fine pastime for the shooter to enjoy. Moreover, the challenge is there for anyone who wants to respond, with the best rifle and matched ammo, plus plenty of practice until he owns a trophy or room full of them. If you can hit a *gallina* at 44 yards, you can cleanly take a cottontail that far. The transfer value is supreme. Show me a fellow who can knock the metal targets down with regularity, and I'll show you a hunter who can cleanly bag a limit of small game for his larder.

14 THE HUMBLE SAFARI: SMALL-GAME RIMFIRING

The airplane dipped a wing. Below me was the border. I was flying from my home in Wyoming to a neighboring state to speak to members of a sportsman's club. The arbitrary divider between states was invisible, yet quite dramatic in impact. Wyoming, blessed with poor soil (a blessing for those of us who desire to keep some of the land in its original form), offered few crops, but many antelope and deer. The other state had game, too, and a nice amount of it, but what had been antelope and plains-deer habitat was now a succession of wheat fields. An ear of corn, an apple, a watermelon, an orange, a potato, all are grown on *former* wildlife habitat. That's fine. We need the good food raised on our wonderful American farms, and farms can also provide superb small-game niches. However, let he who looks askance at the hunter remember as he partakes of crop foods that they all derive from reduced wildlife habitat. Vegetables and fruits constitute a harvest. Hunters, too, are involved in a harvest. Hunting is the honorable procurement of food and trophy in an act of self-reliance and acceptance of responsibility, along with a respect for wildlife and the laws that govern huntable animals. The "humble safari," as I call it, is going forth with 22 rifle into field and hill to harvest the natural protein gift of the land: rabbits, squirrels, even bullfrogs and 'possum, depending upon where you live. This chapter is about small-game hunting with the 22.

Small-game hunting means finding your quarry, dropping it cleanly, field dressing it with care, processing it further at home for freezer or fry pan, and finally cooking the meat correctly so that the end result is a succulent meal. Most small game is cyclic in its population dynamics. Never hunt rabbits and they still cycle. Many studies have proved this. In the winter of 1983-84, thousands of rabbits died in the Rocky Mountains as Dame Nature

wielded her icy scythe. Even without that hard winter, though, the rabbit population would have fluctuated. No one is certain of the exact cause. A virus that surfaces from time to time? The rabbit is a "replacement species." It matures quickly. And its life cycle is comparatively short. Seasons and limits are set by biologists in accord with these facts. Go ahead and hunt small game. These animals are a renewable resource that can be harvested annually with no detriment to the species. Small-game hunting is the least expensive of the hunting sports, requiring minimal gear. Enjoy it.

ADVANTAGES OF THE 22 RIMFIRE

Shotguns are fine for small game, but the 22 rifle (and sometimes handgun) offers a unique harvesting tool for the littler edibles of forest, desert, and swamp. If we set out to invent a perfect cartridge for small-game hunting, I doubt that we could surpass the 22-rimfire round. I've hunted with the 32 rimfire—it was good. I've used the 25-20—it served well. But head shots were still the rule with these cartridges, in deference to the meat; therefore, these larger rounds were no more satisfactory with head shots than the ordinary 22 rimfire. Besides, the limitation of range and power of the 22 rimfire is welcomed in the small-game field. The report of the 22 rimfire is mild and inoffensive. The cartridge offers a real challenge of marksmanship. It is effective, yet not too powerful. It shoots far enough, yet not too far. The 22 demands only a small initial investment. Used 22 rifles can still be found for $75, even less, and 22-rimfire ammo is about as cheap as factory "shootin' fodder" comes. In short, the 22 rimfire is accurate, amply powerful for small game, of sufficient "reach," and its rifles are trim, handy, and inexpensive.

The small-game season is long. Even when winter has closed like a white cloak around the home-

The cottontail rabbit's life cycle is up and down, whether hunted or not. The rabbit offers high-protein, low-fat meat and is an important resource in many areas.

stead, you can pick up a 22 rifle and follow the trail of the cottontail, snowshoe, or squirrel. I can think of no better exercise when the hills are white and the sky deep blue on a December day. A Minnesota hunter reported taking a coyote, a ruffed grouse, and a snowshoe hare in a single outing with his 22 rifle. The 22 is a hunter's delight and hundreds of thousands know it. Using data from the U.S. Department of the Interior, *Shooting Sports Retailer* magazine took a look at hunter breakdown for the USA. Only hunters 16 years of age or older were included. The state of Missouri had almost a quarter-million rabbit hunters. Texas was closer to a half-million, and Pennsylvania wrote over 600,000 rabbit licenses. Little (and beautiful) Rhode Island reported more than 10,000 rabbit hunters. Out West, numbers decline with overall lower population, but Arizona has more than 120,000 rabbit hunters. California is home to more than a quarter-million too.

Squirrel hunters are also well represented. Alabama's bushytail devotees number more than 260,000. Arkansas approaches a quarter-million squirrel hunters. Ohio has over more than a quarter-million, as does North Carolina. The American hunter knows the joys of the humble safari. Those joys redouble when the tool of the harvest is the 22-rimfire rifle.

WHICH RIFLE?

A good rule of thumb is to select the rifle you like. I've bagged limits with bolt-action single-shots not worth two farthings on the used-gun rack, single-shot hammerguns dating back to the Stanley Steamer, a Kimber semi-custom beauty, a handsome Winchester 75 Sporter, a faithful Marlin Model 70 semi-auto, and old Remington Model 12 pumpgun, a Savage target rifle, and too many others to lift to the surface of memory. You may wish to choose your small-game hunting rifle by matching the action style with that of your big-game rifle. If you're a lever-action fan, look at lever guns by Marlin and Winchester. If you like a pump-action, check the trombone-style 22s, especially on the used-gun rack. But don't shortchange yourself. The little 22 rifle is a workhorse, but it's just as important as—maybe more important than—your big-game rifle. Wally Taber summed it up when he said, "Unbeatable, Even in Africa," the title of an article in *The American Rifleman* of September 1952. Taber added (p. 37), ". . . bar none, it is the most utilitarian of all rifles on safari." It is also the most utilitarian rifle off safari.

Sights For The Hunting Rifle. The open iron sight is as useful today as it was 100 or more years ago. I still like this sight system, and find it far more useful than others who condemn it. Primitive? Open irons sights are to rifle scopes what the Neanderthal axe is to the guided missile. I can't argue otherwise. And yet, they work, especially for young eyes with good visual accommodation. The open iron requires focus on three planes: rear sight, front sight, and target. Older eyes don't always do well at this. These basic sights are fast. And aligned properly, they serve in guiding bullets to the mark. But that's it. Laying further bouquets at the feet of the old iron sight would be overpraise. They're good. They work. And if you're making head shots with your open irons, stick with 'em.

But the aperture sight is more refined. I've fired very stingy groups with micrometer sights. Furthermore, while the open iron sight generally sports an elevator bar for elevation, with windage handled by drifting the rear sight (and sometimes the front as well) in a dovetail notch, the micrometer sight generally has precise "click" adjustments for fine-tuning. Quarter-minute clicks mean a quarter-minute of angle. My Model 75 Sporter, after failing to wear a scope well, has served exceptionally with a "peep sight." The peep seems almost too easy to use for some shooters. They want to consciously align the front sight in the circle of the rear sight's aperture, when all they have to do is look through

A brace of bunnies. Good food. Good hunting. A fine mid-winter break for John Fadala, the author's son. Note scoped bolt-action rifle with carrying strap.

the disc, put the front sight on the target, and fire when the rifle is stable. Period. The eye will automatically seek the point of greatest light, which is dead center in the "peep hole." Don't complicate things by trying to center the front sight. The peep sight has only two planes of focus—front sight and target—which eliminates the necessity to focus the eye on the rear sight, as with open irons. Also, the bottom of the target is not blotted out with the peep sight.

While I like and use both open irons and receiver, or peep, sights, there's no doubt that the scope is supreme commander of sighting instruments on the 22-rimfire rifle. The little "22 scope" is very reasonably priced and offers a magnified target and clear aiming point. If the budget screams when you try to wrestle another dollar out of the kitty, look into the economy 22 scope (but don't mount one on your spring-piston air rifle, because the double-recoil effect can scramble this scope's innards). Reason has to outrun respect for the 22 scope, however. I have to admit that the little $20 unit is a dismal aiming device compared with its larger and more expensive brothers. There is nothing wrong with a fixed power, full-scale scope on a 22 rifle, something in the 2.5X to 3X range for close work, perhaps a 4X or even a 6X for longer shots. I like a variable. My Kimber small-game rifle wears a Leupold 1.5X-5X (not a compact), crystal clear, fast as a rattler on lower power, sufficient of magnification for longer shots on 5X. A scope sight is a paid-up insurance policy for head shots on small edibles. The full-size scope belongs on a 22-rimfire rifle. The 22 deserves it. Any reticle you like is OK with me, dot, simple crosswire, duplex—the last is hard to beat. But be certain that the reticle offers a fine aiming point—no big posts or super-thick crosswires to blot out small targets (head shots) on small game.

Sighting In. Any rifle deserves to be sighted for optimum ballistic impetus. For example, those who sight a 270 for 100 yards are destroying that round's trajectory potential. It should be sighted for 275 yards instead. The 22-rimfire rifle should be sighted for its potential too. Some shooters prefer to print the 22 Long Rifle bullet dead on at 75 yards. I have no argument with this. Francis Sell, well-known hunter and writer, advised this method, which puts the 40-grain bullet an inch high at 25 yards, 1½ inches high at 50, on at 75 of course, and about three inches low at 100 yards. My sighting

dead-on for 20 yards, as I mentioned earlier, places the 22 Long Rifle high-velocity projectile on target at about 85 yards. The bullet strikes about an inch high at 50, but only about two inches low at 100 yards. A bullet describes an arc known as a parabola, so it crosses the line of sight twice; therefore, you get a nice close on-target group for small game (20 yards), plus a second on-target crossover of the bullet at 85 yards, and at 100 you wouldn't miss a rabbit with a head-on sight picture.

Each scope has sight-in instructions that need not be restated here. Basically, ensure that you understand the value of your scope's adjustment. If each click is worth a quarter-inch at 100 yards, then it takes four clicks to move the point of impact an inch at 100 yards. Arrows show which way to rotate the adjustment dial. Meanwhile, if you're sighting in at 50 yards, you must double the value of clicks. At 50 yards it will take eight clicks to provide an inch of movement on the target. My initial sight-in transpires at 20 yards, so the value of clicks is roughly 18 to the inch, which is close enough for this first step. I then move the target to 85 yards for zero refinement.

Uphill and downhill shooting can be puzzling. At severe angles, even with a high-intensity big-game cartridge, a steeply angled shot at 300 yards will go quite high, whether the angle is down or up. That the shot is uphill or downhill matters less than the angle of the shot. A shot at 300 yards on a steep slope may have to be held as if the target were only a bit over 200 yards away. The 22 rimfire is not employed over very long range compared with the high-speed centerfire rifle. So just remind yourself to hold a bit low when the shot is steeply angled. This applies more in the varmint field where shots are longer. Most small-game hunting takes place at close range. Angles are seldom important. But be aware of uphill and downhill angles and what happens to trajectory should the situation arise.

The Carrying Strap. The 22 rifle is usually light as a leaf, but even so, a carrying strap makes sense. The strap is good for two things: ease of rifle-toting, and steadying your aim. My most-used 22-rifle strap is an Uncle Mike's inch-wide model with QD swivels. Being able to remove the strap quickly is nice for benchshooting, where it only gets in the way. The narrow strap offers plenty of support, and it serves also in the "hasty sling" mode for steadier holding. The hasty sling, whereby the hunter wraps

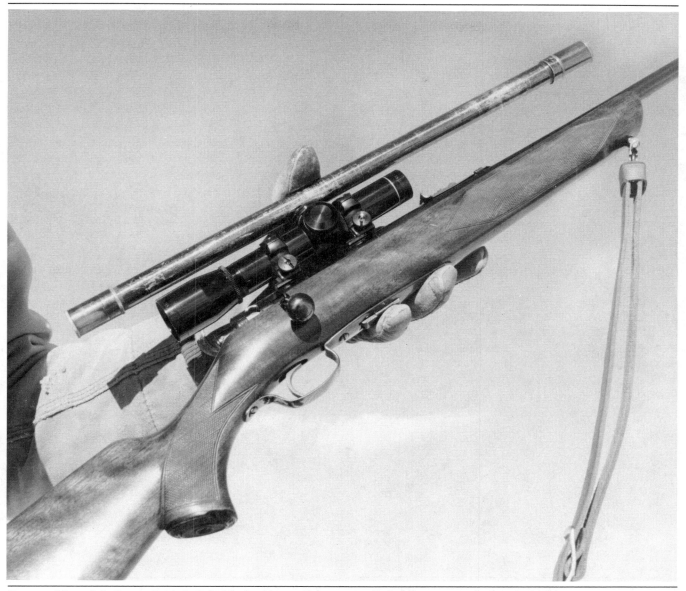

A very old model telescopic sight is held above a modern scope. Today's compact scope nicely fits the slim lines of the 22-rimfire rifle. Such a scope-sighted 22 rifle is ideal for small-game hunting.

his arm through the strap once to "clinch up," is considered by many shooters a band-aid approach to true sling support. Perhaps so, but I have found the method decidedly worthwhile. The additional support helps steady the rifle from the sitting and kneeling as well as offhand positions. It works for me and has promoted many successful head shots I might have easily missed. So consider a carrying strap—a true sling can be a bit large and out of place on a 22-rimfire rifle. You will use that strap continually in the field.

AMMO FOR SMALL GAME

The 22 Short hollow-point has accounted for a great many rabbits from the firearms in my home. My family and I often use the 22 Short hollow-point because of its quiet nature and positive results at the ranges we usually take cottontails—about 20 yards. I have no compunction against shooting out to 50 yards with this ammunition. These days, I'm using fewer Shorts because the manufacturers of my current small-game rifles recommend Long Rifle only. However, when my slide-action Model 12

Note the carrying strap on the 22-rimfire hunting rifle. The strap is ideal for carrying and steadying the rifle in the field. Obviously, hunter and rifle worked together successfully on this outing.

goes afield for rabbits, she's fed a diet of 22 Short hollow-points. Having used these on squirrels as well, I have found no problem with shots up to 20 or perhaps 25 yards, which is as far as my squirrel opportunities generally present themselves.

The 22 Long catches it from all quarters. If you want to become a gunwriter in America you have to sign an oath agreeing to condemn the 22 Long at every opportunity. But I have one particular rifle that happens to feed 22 Longs best. And I've used the orphan cartridge on many outings with perfect

satisfaction, generally for head shots on cottontails and snowshoe rabbits at ranges up to 50 yards. However, enter my two bolt-action gametakers, center stage, and the little Long takes to the wings. Since head shots only are the rule, I've found no reason to employ the 22 Long Rifle hollow-point for cottontails. Squirrel hunters seem to prefer the hollow-point because these tough cookies are able to carry more lead than Mr. Cottontail, so if the preferred head shot is missed, then let the strike be made with a 22 Long Rifle hollow-point. More on this below.

The hollow-point has always been a good idea, a way of coaxing more impact from the 22 bullet. The cavity-nosed missile came out sometime in the late 1800s, if you take to heart a notice in an August 1904 issue of *Shooting and Fishing* magazine, that said the Union Metallic Cartridge Company had been offering 22 Long Rifle hollow-points "for several years." Furthermore, the announcement claimed the cartridge had been invented for rabbit control in Australia. The U.M.C. Company soon offered the hollow-point to the American shooter.

Not to be a broken record, but, yes, you guessed it—the best bet once again is to try several brands and types of 22-rimfire ammo in your 22 hunting rifle in order to tailor a proper matchup. I often use target ammunition when hunting nearby in a particularly broken badlands area that happens to house many cottontails. The shots can be tricky. They are not long shots, but seldom is the rabbit in clear view. Usually, it settles in the brush with only a small portion of the head showing. Close-grouping means a lot here, and cost of ammo is not important. Careful shooting usually takes a limit of 10 rabbits with 10 to 12 rounds of ammo. One of my 22-rimfire hunting machines, the oft-mentioned Kimber, likes Eley Tenex ammo. Expensive, sure, but a box will last me four trips and 50 rounds will bring 40 or more rabbits to the freezer. Noting a standard group size for this rifle is difficult because groups vary with range condition; however, on my most recent test shoot I was pleasantly surprised (maybe stunned is not too strong a term) when RWS R-50 ammo produced the glory group of the day—1/3 inch for five shots at 50 yards, not once, but several times during the test run. That brand of accuracy easily puts its signature on the 1 1/2-inch-wide aiming point of the smallish western cottontail rabbit out to 50 yards.

As for shot cartridges, see the discussion of grouse hunting below. And what about a flat-nosed 22 Long Rifle round, something like Winchester's offering of the 22 WRF? The idea of a wadcutter, or at least semi-wadcutter, to make neat round holes in paper has been taken to the hunting field. Some hunters believe that the flattened nose of a soft 22 Long Rifle bullet will do a much better job of dropping game than the conventional contour. Remington had a run of wadcutters from 1933 to 1939. The 40-grain bullet was advertised at 1275 fps, pushed by 2.25 grains of smokeless powder. The round was

called the Kleanbore .22 Long Rifle Indoor Target Cartridge; now it's a collector's item. However, in recent times a small tool has been offered to support the 22 Long Rifle so that the rounded nose can be truncated to resemble a semi-wadcutter. I have used, with good effect, Winchester's Super Silhouette ammo, which does have a rather blunt nose. The blunt nose may indeed offer more impact than a round profile. Proving such a point is difficult at best. Winchester's Silhouette load appeared to have more impact than round-nose ammo fired in the field test. However, the slightly heavier bullet and good ballistics of the Super Silhouette were probably responsible for the results.

GET YOUR 22 RIFLE IN SHAPE

Before hunting, make sure your 22-rimfire rifle is ready to go. If it's a used model, clean the bore as described in Chapter 29. Do the same thing if you have not treated your faithful 22 to a good bore scrub in a long while. If you have any doubts about your rifle's state of repair, the gun doctor should take a look. A professional gunsmith can strip your rifle, giving it a good inspection. Have him tighten or replace stock screws and bolts. If your rifle's group is not too shiny with any brand of ammo, tighten the major stock screw, then back it off just a crack. Sometimes this bedding trick aids accuracy. If the trigger can be safely improved, have the gunsmith work on it. Now your 22 gamegetting machine is ready for action.

THE 22 RIMFIRE HUNTING PISTOL

The subject of the 22 pistol/revolver was given attention earlier. Remember, however, that in choosing your small-game sidearm, accuracy is the watchword. Consider only accurate 22 sidearms with adequate sights. I carry a Ruger heavy-barrel semi-auto on the big-game trail. It has brought to bag a number of delicious meals. It has also become the main firearm in camp after the big-game tags have been canceled.

GETTING THE GAME

The Cottontail Rabbit. Number One in the land. The cottontail is the most-hunted small-game animal of all. It abounds in many areas, providing at least marginal shooting in every state. Most rabbit seasons are long, with generous bag limits. After all, whether rabbits are hunted or not, their numbers are going to cycle dramatically. The resource may as well be used for human consumption. Cottontail rabbit meat is easy to care for and cook. Dress soon in the field. A rimfire-harvested (head shot) rabbit won't have internal juices mingled with the meat. However, remove vicera soon anyway, skin the animal (that takes all of one minute), and rinse the carcass if you carry water, as I do. Deposit the cleaned and cooled meat in a plastic bag. At home, soak your rabbits in brine plus a half-cup of white vinegar. Rinse. Package (first in plastic wrap, then regular freezer paper for a long-lasting seal).

My book, *The Complete Guide to Game Care and Cookery*, shows how to section a rabbit neatly and quickly with knife or small cleaver. These pieces then go into a pressure cooker, along with a dash of paprika, a sprinkling of garlic powder, and a pinch or two of tarragon. If you like other spices, use them. After 20 minutes of pressure cooking, cool the cooker; remove and drain the meat. Then fry your rabbit nice and brown. You can use any coating you like—flour or cracker crumbs—or none at all (latter preferred by calorie-counters). Fry in light grease, medium heat. I use olive oil, just enough to keep the meat from burning in the Silverstone fry pan. Olive oil, nutritionists say, is good for you. A splash of sherry is nice. A great meal, and you harvested the meat yourself—with a 22-rimfire rifle.

Many methods are used in bunny hunting. Out West, our rabbits never had a chance to attend Harvard. They are not terribly intellectual, or hunter-tutored. Slow-pacing a good area usually brings ample opportunity for shots. When winter snow covers the landscape, that's my favorite time for rabbits. The big-game season is over. But I don't mind. The "lowly rabbit" is good enough for me. The "king of protein" lures us out of the house for crisp fresh air and healthful exercise; I'm grateful for it. A warm coat, such as my favorite Browning down parka, chases away the cold. It's comfortable hunting.

If the rabbits are "brushed up" on the hillsides, my compact Bausch & Lomb 10x28 binoculars search 'em out—something like a big-game hunt for deer. Then I make a stalk. I said these rabbits aren't too sophisticated, but that does not mean you can tramp right up to them point blank. Plinking and silhouette shooting have upgraded my faith in the offhand shot, and I harvest some rabbits from this shooting posture. But if I can get a rest, I'll take

it, and if not, a sitting shot will do. Even a kneeling shot, with hasty sling intact, offers a steadier sight picture than the offhand stance. There are numerous articles and plenty of books, too, describing regional rabbit hunting. If you're new to the game, study the subject; then apply your "booklearning" where it counts: in the field.

Your way of 22 rimfiring for rabbits is no doubt as good as any other, and if your plan for the harvest has not yet jelled, it will. The most unusual way I have pursued the cottontail is by bicycle. The mountain bike is a two-wheeled peddling machine that is fit for tough trails and rugged country. I can pump from my dooryard to a small ranch not far away and be on the rabbit trail in 20 minutes. "Bicycles and walking are the best exercise for your heart," a cardiologist told a friend of mine who had bypass surgery. "Get out and walk. Or ride a bike." My buddy did both. He hunted small game to make his touring interesting. There isn't anything wrong with my ticker, but I took up walking and bicycling anyway, as exercise modes. I just happened to spice the workouts by carrying a 22-rimfire rifle along for rabbits.

Habitat varies widely in cottontail country, for rabbits dwell in many kinds of territory. An interesting survey listed prime locations for rabbits in various states—here they are: river bottom land (Colorado), lake shores (Kansas), rock piles (Wyoming), creek bottoms (Nebraska), cholla cacti patches (Arizona), lava fields (Idaho), badlands (North Dakota), deserted farmlands (South Dakota), and swamps (Oklahoma). Naturally, these sites are not exclusive to the states specified. I've seen cottontails in marshy country in Arizona and on deserted farmlands in Colorado. All 50 states are home to Mr. Rabbit. Seasons are generous—no closed season in Arizona or New Mexico—with ample hunting in Montana, Oregon, Ohio, New York—just about everywhere. Find your own rabbit niche. Look for sign. Autumn trails, winter snow paths, pellets sprinkled on the ground; these lead to rabbits. There's probably a rabbit-hunting area not too far from your own home.

The Snowshoe Hare. Dense cover generally marks the territory of the snowshoe hare. He is frequently hunted with dogs, or by breaking through the thick country with shotgun in hand, ready for the flush and run of this white-furred game animal. But he can certainly be hunted with the 22. Snowshoes don't "hole up." And they are found over a wide

The tree squirrel, second in small-game popularity in this country, and Number 1 in the hearts of thousands of hunters.

cales—the finest small-game trophy in the world in the minds of many hunters. In his book, *Hunting With The Twenty Two*, C.S. Landis wrote: "Though he live a thousand years, there are few things a man will accept in trade for good squirrel hunting with a small-bore rifle, once he has become really expert at that sport." Furthermore, squirrel hunting is a lifelong activity. You can begin squirrel hunting in your youth and continue bagging the prince of the treetops well into the golden years of life. You don't have to be a mountain climber, swamp guide, or long-range hiker to bag a limit of bushytails. Landis summed it up this way: ". . . there is no substitute and no improvement upon good squirrel hunting!"

The Treetop Prince's way of life varies not only by virtue of biological difference, but also in accord with environment. Writing a definitive piece on squirrel hunting is like relating what it's like to live in America. Hunting squirrels in Alabama is one thing; hunting squirrels in Arizona can be quite another matter. My base of experience comes from the West. Sift the data presented here. Separate the granules of fact into particles that fit your domain: East, West, the swamp, farmlands, high mountain forest—whatever. That's the way all hunting information should be handled anyway. There are, however, some generalized squirrel facts worth knowing.

Bushytails have good vision for rodents, quickly detecting movement, rather than finite sedentary detail. I've had a squirrel eat lunch with me without knowing I was there. I simply sat still. One twitch

area, from forested Canada, New York, Pennsylvania, to Washington and Oregon. He lives in the wilderness, or at least the wilds, and he cycles in population just as other game does. Solitary and mostly nocturnal, he can be trailed in the snow. Snowshoes are usually stillhunted. The rifleman tries to locate his quarry by checking ahead with binoculars to distinguish its outline in the brush. Once the hunter locates the hare, he can dispatch it with a preferred head shot. But use 22 Long Rifle hollow-point ammo here. Running snowshoes can be tagged, but trying for a head shot at this darting target is asking for a lot.

The Tree Squirrel. He may rank second by hunter numbers, but those figures are still extremely high. Also, the bushytail is *Numero Uno* in many lo-

There are many varieties of tree squirrels to be hunted. The gray on the left is compared here with the Abert's squirrel on the right, both taken on the San Carlos Indian Reservation in Arizona.

later, my visitor was gone. A good sense of smell, yes, but the squirrel is not always in a position to take advantage of that ability. I doubt that we lose many opportunities because of being scented. Hearing is bell-tone clear and razor precise, however. Make the wrong noise and Mr. Bottlebrush Tail is gone. Make a lot of noise and he may only flatten out on a limb, resuming his business in about 15 minutes or even less. His magnificent tail is used as sunshade, blanket, aerial counterbalance rudder for treetop acrobatics, and almost as a parachute. He also expresses emotion with his tail, especially "anger." (Giving human characteristics to wild creatures is a dangerous thing to do.) But the tail, be it flagged east or west, in swamp or near farmfield, can be a giveaway. I've located grooming squirrels a number of times. One more thing—a squirrel can survive almost any fall. Mark that fact when we talk about quick and humane harvesting. Nicking one off a branch is not going to keep him down.

The squirrels I hunt hate rain, cold, and wind. On the other hand, a buddy of mine back East says that squirrel hunting on windy and even rainy days is quite promising. My squirrels get up early, but they don't necessarily stay out all day. They love coming out after a storm, and may respond to falling barometers by taking shelter—I've noted fairly poor hunting when the weather was about to turn sour. Give me a bright morning on a clear day without wind and I'll take it every time in preference to any other kind of weather for squirrel hunting. Squirrels are masters at hiding (bear that fact in mind), and use cover with soldier-like expertise. They are diurnal; that is, they are active by day, sleeping by night. They do not hibernate. They are quite solitary, except for the mating season, and they do build nests (sometimes in people's attics). There are five major groups of tree squirrels in America: tassel-eared, fox, gray, red, and flying squirrels. And which state has the most variety? Arizona, with three races of tassel-eared squirrels, four of the fox variety, and two reds. Where I hunt, winter is the absolute ruler of squirrel numbers. Bad winter, few squirrels. Good winter, good squirrel hunting. Man has precious little effect. Finally, unlike Mr. Cottontail, the squirrel can be long-lived.

Habitat. Coast to coast, habitat varies. Although farming removes much big-game habitat, farming can also provide tremendous small-game niches, sometimes for squirrels. There are areas where

Gene Thompson searches for squirrel sign at the base of this tree. In squirrel hunting, the rifle is carried without a round in the chamber. There is plenty of time to bolt a round home if a squirrel is sighted.

squirrels would not make it without crops. I was told of a good squirrel-hunting place once. But when I got there, "Darn," said I, "this spot doesn't look so good." But it was, because over the hill was a stand of corn. The unlikely looking micro-environment yielded good hunting. The area's scant trees provided sufficient cover for the squirrel, and the corn, along with a little natural forage, made a good living for him.

Mainly, know your area. Check it out before season if possible. An old logging road, drained swamp, abandoned farmstead, dry waterway, all can be good habitat for Mr. Chatterbox. Go look for yourself. Check out the food supply, not only farmfield chow, but acorns, various nuts, Russian olive trees. Find out what the squirrels in your area dine on; then see if you can find these foods. Try to "cut sign." Look for evidence of feeding, and digging.

Hunting Methods. Since squirrel habitat and lifestyles vary widely in North America, so must hunting methods. Squirrel hunters have plied their sport from tree stands, stumps, and canoes. They use squirrel calls and even predator calls when looking for a scolding response from Mr. Bushytail. In the high mountains of the Southwest (I hunted squirrels on Mt. Lemmon outside of Tucson at an elevation of well over 8,000 feet above sea level), I prefer *still-hunting*. That does not mean staying still, as C.S. Van Dyke states in the great old book, *Still Hunter*, again available through Gunnerman Books. It means moving with care and planning over the landscape. That's how I hunt my squirrels, by still-hunting for them. If I see one up ahead ground-walking, I dash for him, because he will "tree" like a hound-chased cougar. Then the "look-see" happens. You might convince me to leave home without a hat and coat, but you'd never get me to leave my binoculars behind. I might carry smaller models, such as the B&L 10x28, but I shall have my

Fadala uses binoculars to find a bushy-tail in a tall tree. Note author's Kimber 22 rifle with its carrying strap, which frees the hunter's hands.

magnification one way or another. My self-treed bushytails are, almost to a squirrel, located with the glass. And I have no count of squirrels located initially by finding them among the trees with the binocular. Hunt squirrels as you will, or must, in your locale. I shall stillhunt, with binoculars showing the way.

The Squirrel Rifle. Sometimes the squirrel rifle isn't a rifle. Pistoleers with expertise do well on squirrels. Of course, modern sidearms can be scoped for more precise aim. Any 22 rifle is fine, from single-shot to semi-auto. But if you want a truly great 22 rimfire for squirrels, do two things: buy an accurate rifle, and scope it. If you really measured your shots on squirrels, 20 to 40 yards would probably be a fair estimate of normal harvesting range. Just about any 22 rifle is accurate that close, you say. However, you don't always get a whole squirrel to shoot at. The head is the best target anyway, but sometimes you don't even get to see the whole head. Now that super-accurate rifle becomes your best friend, its scope pinpointing the squirrel amidst a camouflage of branches and bark. Get a good scope. Light levels are usually low among the trees. A cheap scope simply does not have the light-gathering ability of a more sophisticated model; nor does it always have the quality of definition afforded by the better glass.

Squirrel Ammo. The 22-rimfire cartridge is ideal for squirrels. More power would ruin more meat. The Long Rifle hollow-point dominates because of its laudable performance on body shots, but the dedicated squirrel hunter should be going for the head anyway. I won't buck the consensus by saying the 22 Long Rifle hollow-point is wrong. I've fired many at squirrels, but I'm leaning more and more toward the most accurate 22 Long Rifle ammunition for the given rifle. My last batch of squirrel ammo turned out to be RWS R-50 fodder, because I found it to be very accurate in my Kimber (and I just happened to have a modest supply on hand left over from testing). Lapua has a hollow-point match ammo, by the way, for those who want both match accuracy and the cavity nose.

What about "barking" your squirrel? I've barked squirrels with my 32 caliber Hatfield muzzleloader, and I've heard of many hunters who directed their bullets to strike the tree branch just below a squirrel's chin, delivering a knockout blow. The leather-stocking trailblazers of our Early American seaboard were noted for this trick of marksmanship,

Hug a tree—one method of getting that steady shot, especially in squirrel hunting.

but I'll put my bet on the clean head shot. Get a rest when you can. When there's a small tree nearby, "hug" it, wrapping an arm around it for a rest (*see* illustration).

Limbs make good rests too. Be sure to cushion the forend with a hand, and avoid resting the barrel directly on a hard surface. An accurate scope-sighted rifle loaded with precise ammo is the best squirrel hunting tool. Squirrel recipes abound in cookbooks—the rabbit recipe noted above works well for fried squirrel. Squirrel stew is a famous dish too. Squirrels offer a wonderful hunt, and also great transfer value to the big-game field, even for elephants, according to one hunter. "The best possible training one can have for stalking and shooting elephant in close cover, using the brain shot, is squirrel hunting with a good .22. The same qualities

of hunter patience, rifle-accuracy, and visual alertness are required in both" ("Hunting the African Elephant," by John B. George in *The American Rifleman*, November 1955).

Mountain Grouse. Seldom hunted independently, the mountain grouse of the West is a fine 22-rimfire quarry. Big blues or smaller ruffed grouse, these mountain birds are legal fare for the 22 and downright delicious in the fry pan. They can be quite unwary. My most-used firearm for grouse is the sidearm. My sons use their revolvers with 22 WMR CCI shot cartridges. This plastic-domed ammo carries an 1/8 ounce of No. 11 shot, for about 170 pellets per round. Muzzle velocity is about a 1000 fps from the handgun—good for close range only, but grouse are often taken at 10 to 15 feet from the muzzle. A pattern at 15 feet will see about 90 percent of the shot on target in a 12-inch circle. The 22 Long Rifle shot cartridge (about 125 No. 12 shot) is also good for grouse at very close range only—a maximum distance of 20, perhaps 25 feet.

Other Small Edibles. The 22 rimfire is used on many other small-game edibles, not only in North America, but just about everywhere. One of the more enjoyable 22-rimfire hunts is for bullfrogs. Luckily, this hunting was mine in youth. We fired on frogs straight down into the water only, and I never saw a bullet ricochet. But no shot should be taken if the bullet has any chance of glancing off the surface of the water. The banks of the canal ditches we hunted were very steep. A bullet could never climb them even if it had skipped from the water. Quiet water—creeks, ponds, or irrigation ditches—is home to the bullfrog. The head shot is the only shot, lest the slippery fellow kick his way into a murky hideout after being hit. The 22 Short is ample. I like the hollow-point Short for its greater impact, but also for its propensity to flatten out quickly, dissipating its energy rapidly. Frog legs, coated with seasoned flour and deep-fried, are a delicacy commanding folding money in fine restaurants. Bullfrogs are a game species, so check your game laws for seasons and limits.

Raccoons are often dispatched by the 22 bullet, and opposums are sometimes brought to table with the same missile. Mention snake meat and people shudder, "Oh, how could you eat a snake?" And yet, these same dainty diners think nothing of devouring chicken embryos, especially when they are disguised in a two-tier chocolate cake. The delicately flavored white meat of a large diamondback rattlesnake is good food. End of sermon. Armadillos I have not eaten, but some consider your woodchucks and rockchucks good fare when broiled over coals. Turtles are small game of edible perspective too. A full complement of small-game food harvested by the grand 22 rimfire could unravel itself like a ball of yarn. Suffice it to say that the basic 22-rimfire cartridge is the grand provider, collecting delicious food for the delight of the palate in

Author uses tree stump for a rest. Taking a rest with an accurate 22-rimfire rifle, such as this Kimber model, greatly increases the odds of placing that bullet just right for a meat-saving shot.

a vast outdoor field of honest exercise and true enjoyment.

Long seasons are the rule—Colorado has a 5½-month squirrel season. Oklahoma opens its squirrel-hunting season on May 15 at present and it runs for several months. Arizona has a 12-month cottontail hunt. Other states are equally generous in allowing the small-game sportsman time afield. Out-of-state small-game licenses are readily available and reasonably priced, while big-game tags are often on a drawing-only (lottery) basis and quite expensive. My "someday soon" plan is to pack the camping trailer with provisions and set out on a pilgrimage, making a humble safari to contiguous states for the thrill and fulfillment of small-game hunting. My implement of the harvest will be a 22-rimfire rifle, backed by a pistol. My motive will be great joy in the outdoors, and some very fine tablefare when the shooting day is done.

15 SUCCESSFUL RIMFIRE VARMINTING

Everybody has a varmint. The most gentle granny will fling a tea cup at a tiny inquisitive mouse that dares to examine her kitchen floor in pursuit of a bread crumb. The fact came home to me one day when I was visiting two friends. The couple is sanctioned by the game department to care for injured birds. Kinder people never drew breath. As I was observing a kestral the "bird saviors" were trying to salvage—it had gotten into an argument with a barbed-wire fence and lost—I noticed something peering up at me from outside of the bird cage. It was a large spring-loaded trap. Cocked. A bit of enticement was tied with dental floss to the release mechanism. Any hapless rodent that touched the bait would have its neck configuration altered permanently. "Problem with rodents?," I queried. "Trap looks pretty big for mice."

"Rats," the man replied. He shook his head with disgust when he said the word. "Tired of them eating all the bird food."

"Oh," I said.

The current trend toward varmints is to remove the word from game management circles. The new term is "non-game animal." Many game departments have been on a push to interest non-hunters in wildlife. "Non-game animal" gives the varmint more class, especially if the game department is asking for revenue from individuals who don't hunt. The term is a euphemism; it sounds more refined than varmint. But as with all euphemisms, the word changes, but the facts don't. If one of the old gang "passes away" in the night, you can bet he's not going to be at the next poker game any more than if he had died. Varmints have no malice whatsoever. They are simply going about their business as nature planned. A varmint is any animal that destroys or degrades something precious to man. When the Anderson Mesa study in Arizona was completed, the consensus was that coyotes were

eating as high as 90 percent of the antelope fawns in the area. A coyote program prevailed. Antelope numbers grew. The coyote was not eliminated, of course. But a different *balance* resulted from the control program.

The balance of nature is not a straight line as taught in grade school. It is a jagged up-down affair, with populations rising and falling, whether man is there or not. The great dinosaurs were not eliminated by men. They were gone long before man was prevalent on the planet. Nature took care of them, every one. Varminting is a control mea-

Prairie dogs are small targets compared with woodchucks, but are often quite numerous. They have been known to "mine" thousands of acres of pasture and are therefore classified as varmints with a year-long season and no bag limit.

sure. The animals cause problems for mankind, and in the laws determining hunting seasons and limits, these animals are given little or no protection. While that seems pompous on the part of man, and it may be, it is no different from the fellow who sprays his house for termites or rids the basement of mice. The varmint is generally not protected with seasons because it must be controlled.

Varmint hunting is the least noxious of the controlling devices used to thin varmints. In fact, hunting will seldom generate the necessary inroads on a varmint species required to keep that group under control. Hunting, however, can offer a modest population reduction. A rancher had decided to control the prairie dogs that were destroying his pastureland. His method was poison. When my son and I got there, the poisoning program was about to commence. "If we can keep 'em thinned back, will you still put the poison grain out?" we asked. No. He hadn't wanted to use poison in the first place. My son employed his 22-rimfire rifle for the close shots, I used a 22 PPC for the long ones, and by summer's end the spreading of the village was slowed if not stopped. We had made a realistic impact; the remaining prairie dogs were not poisoned. The carcasses were easy food for predators, such as eagles and hawks, although admittedly they were also food for other prairie dogs, which eat their own kind in a second.

THE 22 RIMFIRE ON VARMINTS

The 22 Long Rifle hollow-point and 22 Long Rifle hyper-velocity load will take any predator on the continent. Even a mountain lion in a tree will succumb to one well-placed shot from the little 22. However, long-range shooting is out of the question for clean kills, which is the demand every hunter places upon himself whatever the quarry. Mount a careful stalk and get within 75 yards of a large woodchuck. Aim your accurate 22-rimfire rifle for the head shot. Deliver the bullet with precision. The chuck will drop instantly. We have put coyotes down with one shot at ranges up to 50 or 60 yards, with 75 yards being a long shot on these larger varmints. The next chapter deals with long-range precision shooting of varmints. The centerfire is the goat's glands of that work. Rimfire varminting is for the stalker.

As with plinking, rimfire varminting is a miniaturization of the big-bore scene. Employing the 22 Long Rifle at ranges not to exceed 100 yards

closely matches the trajectory pattern of the high-speed big-bore out to 300 yards. A handloaded 30-06 Springfield using the 150-grain bullet will deliver its missile three inches high at 100 and about three inches low at 300 yards. The 22 Long Rifle sighted for 85 yards will put its 40-grain bullet about two inches low at 100 yards. Energy patterns are an interesting trade-off too. Striking a 300-pound big-game animal with a ton of remaining energy equates somewhat to the 40-grain Long Rifle hollow-point hitting a small varmint. There is a certain match-up of energy per animal size in both rounds.

Varmints are hunted for modest control, but this author is not trying to sidestep any part of the issue—varmint hunting is challenging and interesting, and the sport has great transfer value. A shooter who is expert in making head shots on

Bill Fadala poses with a scope-sighted Weatherby Mark II semi-automatic. The semi-auto 22-rimfire rifle is very accurate and makes a fine rimfire varminter.

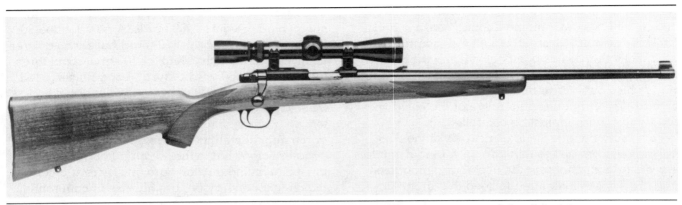

The 22-rimfire varmint rifle is any rifle the shooter happens to own. However, a scope-sighted model like this Ruger Model 77/22 comes highly recommended.

chucks at 75 yards is certainly better prepared to put his big-game bullet on target when deer or elk season arrives. In the varmint field, a hunter can improve his stalking arts, perfect the running shot (as on jackrabbits), and enhance his abilities to dope the wind, compensate for bullet drop, and determine actual range. The hunter who makes a habit of pacing the distances of his shots soon learns how to judge the range of his varmints better. While afield, he can also test hunting equipment and sharpen his skills in finding game with binoculars.

USE THE APPROPRIATE RIFLE

Match the rifle to the hunting style. Reducing the ground squirrel population around the garden does not require match accuracy. Placing a bullet directly on target when a prairie dog is 75 to 100 yards away does. A friend wanted a 22-rimfire rifle for jackrabbit hunting. He preferred a bolt-action model and ended up with the Browning A-Bolt with its fast 60-degree bolt throw and high-grade accuracy. He especially liked the 15-shot clip option on the A-Bolt, and the positive feed and good ejection qualities of the rifle. In short, here was a fast-action rifle with high-capacity clip and easy large-diameter scope mounting. Just right for jackrabbits in the hands of its owner. That's the way to choose your 22 rimfire varmint rifle—pick the one that fills the bill for you.

My own lifelong love affair with the 22 has prompted the inclusion of several rimfire varminters in my gun rack. None is a showpiece. All are rugged field pieces. You soon learn, when you own more than one model, which arm you prefer in ac-

tual practice. It's the one you reach for most often. My little Remington Model 12 pump gun comes off the rack for close-range work. Its iron sights are ample for such shooting, which means ranges seldom exceeding 50 paces. It's a fast-action rifle with reasonable magazine capacity, and it reloads easily. Reliable, sufficiently accurate for short-range work, well-balanced, the little rifle is a pleasure to use in rimfire varminting—under some circumstances. But one of my rabbit or squirrel rifles generally gets the nod for more serious work. On marmots, which may weigh 10 pounds or more, bullet placement isn't the only thing—it's everything. I know I can get a perfect head shot with the high-accuracy bolt-action rifle. Dispatch is 100 percent. Not a single big rodent has made it to his den. All have been dropped on the spot with one shot. As with all hunting, match the rifle to the game (or "non-game" in this case). Match your 22-rimfire varmint rifle to the conditions presented by the specific varmint to be hunted. And put a sling or carrying strap on that rifle.

VARMINTS TO HUNT

Hare Professor. Jackrabbits were my early tutors. Jacks have played the role of professor to many youthful riflemen. The 22 Long Rifle hollow-point is entirely adequate on jackrabbits up to 100 yards from the muzzle. On my last outing, I carried a bolt-action 22 rifle loaded with Federal Spitfires, firing the 33-grain hollow-point bullet at an advertised 1500 fps, and dropped a half-dozen hares. Four of them were on the run, but the range was close. The impact of the high-speed bullets stopped these jacks in their tracks at close range. Federal high-

John Fadala takes a jackrabbit with his well-used Model 69A Winchester 22-rimfire rifle, fitted with a ³/₄-inch tube Redfield scope.

This young yellow-bellied marmot will grow up to be about the same size as his eastern cousin, the woodchuck.

velocity hollow-points had also proved more than adequate on previous jackrabbit safaris. Choosing between the hyper-velocity 22 Long Rifle hollow-point for jacks is difficult since both work so well with good bullet placement at modest range.

Canal jacks taught me how to make running shots. From them, I learned a lot about hold-over and wind deflection. Because the environment of my youth included vast sandy reaches (the dunes of Yuma), I probably fired farther at jacks under those conditions than I would ever think of doing where I hunt today. Here, a hare might go over a hill, being lost though hit. There, one wasn't likely to get away. In those days, I followed the 75-yard sight-in. This put the bullet seven inches low at 125 yards and 14 inches low at 150 yards.

I wasn't the only one to find success on jacks at 150 yards in such open country. Percy Brown, writing in *The American Rifleman* (May 1951, p. 15), said, "... for jack rabbit shooting, a good .22 is hard to beat. And the .22 long rifle cartridge is a potent little package up to 150 yards, especially with the hollow-point bullet." When there is any kind of cover, however, make 100 yards maximum for Hare Professor. The 22 WMR stretches that to 150 yards. Using Federal 22 WMR ammo with the 50 grain-bullet, I dropped eight for eight a while ago.

Woodchucks and Rockchucks. The rockchuck in my region is the yellow-bellied marmot, a woodchuck that took Horace Greeley's advice about going west. The eastern variety is *monax*, from the Indian word signifying "digger." The 'chuck is a tough rodent. Although hunters boast of 25-pounders, and I am sure there have been some, the largest of the clan officially weighed 17.5 pounds, this one from the Northwest. I have hunted the marmot in Alaska, Canada, Idaho, and Wyoming, with various 22-centerfire rounds, the 22 WMR, and the 22 Long Rifle hollow-point. I have never lost one with any caliber. The reason is not my uncanny world-winning shooting ability. Rather, the record stems from a feeling of inadequacy. I shoot within the confines of the individual cartridge's ballistic potential and no

Hunting marmots with a 22-rimfire rifle (next two pages) means stalking for the close shot. The bullet must be well-paced for success, and when it is, the little 22 rimfire drops marmots cleanly. John Fadala hikes a big Rocky Mountain canyon in search of marmots. In the second photo, it is evident that he has placed his bullets well.

farther. Using the 22 Long Rifle hollow-point, the preferred maximum range is, with me behind the scope, about 75 yards. Given perfect circumstances, I have no doubt that the 22 Long Rifle could cleanly drop 'chucks at 125 yards with head shots. When only the head protrudes from behind the rock or from the den, it's head shot or miss. Under such circumstances, 100 yards with a well-sighted, accurate rifle—and rifleman to match—is probably a reasonable maximum yardage for the 22 rimfire on "meadow monks."

My faithful binoculars have gotten more chucks for me than any other hunting tool, aside from the rifle itself. Rockchucks, as western woodchucks are called, can be spotted from great distances with optics. The rocky terrain allows close stalking. It does take great care to get really close, but you can do it. And once you do, the little rimfire is plenty of gun for the job.

I've also hunted marmots along logging roads. The animals may still dwell in isolated rockpiles scattered among the timber, but they also live within fallen tree slash. By simply pacing along with an alert eye, getting close to these often wary animals is not so difficult.

The 22 WMR is even more potent medicine for chucks. The hollow-point jacketed bullet offers plenty of force up to 125 yards. Personal experience with the 22 WMR on chucks does not not surpass this distance. Perhaps 150 yards is a reasonable maximum range with the powerful 22 magnum and its 40-or 50-grain jacketed pill. While the 22 WMR is no doubt the preferred chuckster of the rimfire clan, it remains a fact that a good stalker with a 22 rifle loaded with Long Rifle ammo need not feel inadequate. Wally Taber said it well:

"While strictly speaking the old reliable .22 isn't a chuck cartridge, it will stop 'em cold in their tracks with a properly placed head shot."

Prairie Dogs. "Oats laced with strychnine. That's what I'm going to use." Strychnine was still in vogue at the time and the rancher was prepared to use that or any other method to save his fields—and livelihood—from ruination. "At 10 pups a litter, it's no time at all until you're up to your boot tops in these things," he went on. I could see his point. One horse down with a broken leg. The rancher himself under the horse, with medical bills from the hospital to prove his plight. He was fed up. His bull pasture looked as if a thousand little bombs had fallen in it—craters everywhere.

The fast-action Charter Arms AR-7 rifle, put to work on prairie dogs at close range, proved more than capable.

By far, most of our prairie-dog hunting has been with the 22 Long Rifle hollow-point and 22 Long Rifle hyper-velocity ammo. Either will do the job up to 100 yards, especially with head shots. At very close range, a shot through the shoulders will also put the prairie dog out, but if you're that close, go for the head shot. Following successful bowhunts, I found that I could stalk prairie dogs with total success using the 22 rimfire. It took care, but close-range shots were possible.

Our last shoot occurred in a dry stretch of terrain in northern Wyoming near Arvada. My son and I were hunting in tandem, a system that works well. I was using the 22 PPC for the long shots. John was taking care of the close-range or readily stalkable dogs with his 22 rifle packing 22 Long Rifle Fiocchi hyper-velocity ammo. John's a good shot with his Winchester bolt-action, scope-sighted 22 rifle, and using the potent Fiocchi ammo he was able to drop dogs cleanly out to 100 yards and a trifle farther. While I've not always found the lighter-weight hyper-velocity bullet ideal on 'chucks, the smaller prairie dog is better dispatched with them. The explosive nature of the hyper-velocity 22 Long Rifle hollow-point delivers a considerable blow. It is to be recommended.

Cats. The mountain lion is far too large for any 22-rimfire cartridge when the animal is encountered in canyon country where shots must be taken at ranges past point-blank. On the other hand, the 22 rimfire is adequate (and often preferred) when the cat is treed. Mountain lions have been given a promotion from the ranks of varmint to big-game status in some locales. Although I've had the good fortune of seeing several free-roaming lions in my lifetime of outdoor involvement from Arizona to Canada, I've not bagged one. However, my amigo John Kane, Colorado professional hunter, has taken many. He's found the 22 rimfire adequate for treed

Although not a first-line coyote rifle, the 22 rimfire works quite well from close range only. This coyote was dropped with one shot.

lions, but uses a 30-30 or 44 Magnum rifle whenever he feels there is the smallest chance of the cat tumbling among the dogs with the fire of life still coursing through its body.

Given a close opportunity on a bobcat, the 22 Long Rifle with a head shot will drop the cat cleanly. Personal experience runs small. One bobcat. One shot. Range, 50 paces. Head shot. Twenty-two Long Rifle solid point. That was it. I've seen others, one recently at 20 paces, but the bobcat is a furbearing animal. It was summer. The pelt would have no value anyway, and it would have been illegal to fire even had I a spark of interest in the cat, which I did not. Dedicated bobcat hunters running dogs will find the 22 Long Rifle more than adequate for this quarry.

Coyotes. As interesting a varmint as one will find, the coyote is doing well for himself everywhere. In fact, his range is expanding. Coyotes have recently been spotted within the city limits of Los Angeles. Dwellers in the foothills surrounding Tucson can also expect to hear the yodel of the prairie wolf any night of the week. In my last high-mountain camp in Wyoming, the serenade of God's Dog was with us when we went to sleep at night; it awoke us during the night, and the plaintive cries said "good morning" to us at every sunrise. I like the little excuses for a real wolf. But they definitely need control. Their numbers are at peak in many areas. The coyote is best hunted on the open range with a long-range varmint rifle and high-power scope; however, just in passing we have bagged a few close-range specimens with the 22 Long Rifle hollow-point. A solid chest hit will put the coyote down when he's 50 yards away. The Long Rifle round will also work at 75 and even 85 yards, but it's not ideal for farther ranges. The 22 WMR is better, with a range of effectiveness out to 150 yards or so.

Foxes. The fox is really a small fellow, and can be cleanly harvested with the 22 Long Rifle hollow-point at close range. Depending upon the habitat, foxes can be encountered at very close range. Our own foxing is along lonely roads. Encounters are of the accidental kind. If the fur is of value, you may wish to drop Reynard. If not, you may wish to wave a goodbye as he sneaks off through the foliage. Foxes are supposed to be . . . "foxy." Trappers I know say otherwise. I have encountered this predator in various outdoor settings and have often gotten easy shots just for the taking.

CALLING

Then there is calling. In territory not overworked by the call, coyotes, foxes, bobcats, and many other predators can be lured in so close that the 22 Long Rifle hollow-point bullet will quickly drop them with one shot. Murray Burnham could call Lucifer out of Hades with one of his predator units. Burnham Brothers calls have been field-tested by the company for years. They work. My last use of the call produced a camp friend. An owl came in, took a long look at the "predator" blowing the call, and decided to hang around the area. I had been calling from my nearby camp. The bird flew closer to the campsite and there it remained as a guest for a while, waiting for me to turn into a rabbit, I suppose. As well as luring protected species, such as the owl, calls can attract many varmints. Because the call serves to bring 'em in close (Murray Burnham has photos of coyotes, foxes, bobcats and other predators lured to rock-tossing distance), a good shot with a 22 rimfire can do a splendid job of harvesting these animals. Since the calls come with written instructions, be sure to buy the calling record or tape, too, so you can actually hear what the calls should sound like.

Personal experience leads to several conclusions. First, don't expect the call to work every time, even if the predator you're trying to lure is actually in sight across a canyon. For reasons known only to the predator itself, even a very well-executed session of imitating a rabbit in distress may have nil effect on a coyote, fox, or any other animal that usually preys on the cottontail or jackrabbit. Never be discouraged by such failures. I once saw a coyote across a draw, perhaps 200 yards distant. Waughhhh! Waughhhhh! Waughhhh! Nothing. It may as well have been an anti-call I was blowing. Two hours later, I was still bleating plaintive cries from my call when two coyotes almost ran over each other trying to reach my location. In fact, they frightened each other away and I got no shot at all.

There are vast materials on the art of calling, as well as the aforementioned written methods and instructional cassette tapes and recordings. Try to imitate the expert sounds you hear on the cassette or record. But even if you're not that great, don't worry too much. My dear friend Max Wilson of Tucson was giving a one-man demonstration on his newly acquired predator call to a one-man audience: me. It sounded so funny that I was soon doubled over on the ground with laughter, only to look

Late afternoon found hunter and fox on the same ground at very close range. The Marlin lever-action 22-rimfire rifle was adequate for the task. Foxes are not generally hunted with the 22-rimfire rifle, but can be if the hunter will take only the close, clear shots for perfect bullet placement.

up suddenly to see a fox stalking us. I was the gunner and dropped the fox, but the last laugh was on me.

Just don't give it up too soon. Call for 10 minutes. Wait. Call again. Give a locale 30 minutes or so before pulling out, and be sure to remain hidden on a good viewpoint. Sometimes the caller doesn't even know he's lured predators close because he can't see around him well enough to tell. And other times, the chosen hideout is so flimsy that the incoming predator sees or smells the caller.

FURBEARERS

Furbearing animals are sometimes of the predator class, sometimes not. Where I live, the badger is a furbearer, but he is not a predator. There is a season to abide by, and the hunter must possess a trapper's license to hunt a badger. There are numerous furbearing animals of considerable value that are properly hunted with the 22 Long Rifle or 22 WMR rimfires. From a trapline, the handgun suffices with low-powered ammo, including the Short. On the trail, the stronger loads prevail—fur damage is undesirable, but losing the animal is even less acceptable. Coyotes, foxes, raccoons, muskrats, beavers, martins, mink, wolverine, weasels, and other furbearers may be taken with the 22 rimfire, but proper licensing is essential—some species might not require a license (coyotes and foxes require none where I live), others might require a trapper's license. Check with your local game department before taking to the trail of furbearers.

The entire business of fur hunting and trapping is a science in its own right. Wilf Pyle, expert outdoorsman, biologist (with much knowledge of the coyote), and seasoned hunter/trapper has written a guidebook on the subject. It is entitled *Hunting Predators for Hides and Profit*, a Stoeger publication. It is recommended reading for those interested in a good inside look at the right way to call, track, and care for furbearers. Wild animal status changes with time, public opinion, and the decisions of the various game departments. Crows (and ravens) were varmints not that long ago. Now they are protected (there may be certain open seasons in your area—check carefully with the game department before hunting). Hawks and owls were once considered varmints, with no closed season on them. So were golden eagles. The decision was made that the numbers of game animals taken by these birds was a good trade-off for the pests they also hunted, and all hawks, owls and eagles are protected now. The magpie is also protected. A varmint is only a varmint by decree, not by predisposition. When the law declares that it is no longer a varmint, its status immediately changes.

Varmint hunting with the 22 rimfire requires dedication to selecting the correct rifle for the job (and sometimes a pistol or revolver for specific work, such as ground-squirrel shooting at short range). The rifle must be capable of good grouping, because varmints are tough; head shots are the rule. The 22 Long Rifle hollow-point is the usual choice of ammo, except when more rimfire power is needed, at which point the 22 WMR is called upon, either with 40- or 50-grain jacketed hollow-point bullets. Stalking skill is a definite asset in 22-rimfire varminting. The dedicated hunter who uses his 22-rimfire rifle with skill and care is not undergunned. He is carrying an instrument of precision and effectiveness, a firearm to be counted on.

16 PRECISION CENTERFIRE VARMINTING

Centerfire varminting takes place in a field of precision. Varminting may be, and often is, accomplished with just about every cartridge under the sun. I have carried a 30-30 as a varmint rifle when traveling in backcountry where a light, short, rugged rifle for incidental varmint shooting was useful. Remington's Accelerator loads in 30-30, 308 and 30-06 have served many varmint hunters who use the

big-bore rifle. These cartridges fire high-speed 22-caliber jacketed bullets held in 30 caliber sabots (pronounced SAH-bows). However, this chapter is not about incidental varmint shooting. It is about the precision varminting machine, a 22-caliber hotshot, firing frangible bullets at high velocity for flat trajectory, coupled with long-range accuracy. You can shoot varmints with any rifle you like. But the centerfire varmint cartridge is a unique and interesting package. Its particular traits are shared by no other cartridge group. Varmint rifles come in various calibers, such as 6mm, but we are concerned only with the 22-centerfire varmint cartridge chambered in a true varmint rifle.

THE 22 VARMINT RIFLE

The criteria for the type of varmint rifle of our interest are few, but important. Many rifles will meet some of them and serve well in the varmint field, but that does not qualify them for our purposes. I have, for example, a lightweight bolt-action repeater that has taken many varmints, but that rifle proves constantly that it is not on a par with the instruments discussed here. On one prairie dog hunt, I used the little repeater for a half-day, a 22 PPC USA varminter the other half. In terms of hits and misses, the 22 PPC's record was twice as good as the little rifle's. No surprise here. These criteria pertain.

Accuracy. No matter what the velocity of a cartridge, it will not qualify in the long-range arena unless it and the rifle that chambers it are both very accurate. What accuracy? The byword is one minute of angle. Most of the literature on the subject of varminting calls for this basic degree of accuracy. I have found, however, that the truly efficient varmint rifle exhibits much better than minute-of-angle accuracy. My own rifles shoot in a half-minute or less. This means, for our purposes, half-inch groups at

The centerfire varmint cartridge differs from the big-game round in several respects. It shoots a lighter bullet. Although the muzzle velocity of the varmint round is not always higher than its big-game counterpart, it often is. The bullet is frangible, designed to break up, whereas a big-game bullet should hold together for penetration. The 222 Remington rounds shown here use a light-jacketed 50-grain bullet at 3200 fps muzzle velocity. The 30-06 (center) cartridge has a 180-grain heavy-jacketed bullet at 2700 fps.

The Sako varmint rifle exhibits all the traits necessary for high-scoring: an accurate and heavy barrel, stiff action, good weight for steadiness, and chambering for a flat-shooting cartridge.

100 yards. In theory, this should carry out to one-inch groups at 200 and 1½-inch groups at 300 yards. However, due to atmospheric conditions, human variables, and many other factors, the half-minute rifle indeed prints half-inch groups at 100 yards, but out to 300 yards, two-inch clusters are considered more than acceptable.

As an example of supreme long-range accuracy, my Sako 22 PPC USA heavy-barrel varmint rifle has printed numerous ⅓-inch groups at 100 yards, and a number of ¼-inch groups. This master level of precision proves itself over and over in the varmint field. Up against a particular 22-250 (which is a superb varmint cartridge), the 22 PPC USA, with ballistics a full 300 fps below the 22-250 rifle, pro-

duced more hits, even out to ranges estimated at 400 yards. Although there was a little more bullet drop to cope with in the 22 PPC, the extra accuracy of the 22 PPC helped to account for its better record. This does not mean that the great 22-250 isn't accurate. These facts pertain to one particular 22-250 rifle only.

Trajectory. Regardless of how accurate the cartridge is, it will not qualify as a true long-range varmint round unless it has flat trajectory. How flat? There are four levels (my invention) of 22-caliber centerfire varmint cartridge—the 22 Hornet class, the 222 Remington class, the 22 PPC class, and the 220 Swift class. Trajectory levels vary among these, as noted below in sight-in suggestions. Each class

Fadala used a Sako varmint rifle in 22 PPC USA caliber to drop this marmot from long range. The scope is a Leupold 12X.

has its own merits. The 22 Hornet and 218 Bee are very mild, comparatively quiet, gentle, and supremely good for varminting at 200 to 225 yards. The cartridge, in part, dictates the configuration of the rifle. The little Hornet, which chambers nicely in a short action, allows the construction of a very pretty little rifle. Actual trajectories are discussed under sight-in measures below. Suffice it here to note that 22 centerfire varmint cartridges, in general, must be flat-shooting. If not, the hold-over required for long ranges becomes hit and miss, es-

The Kimber Ultra-Varminter is a highly accurate rifle. Accuracy is paramount in varminting, where the targets are small and the distances often great. Note the heavy barrel of this rifle.

pecially miss.

Recoil. Lack of recoil is a blessing to the shooter, especially in the realm of "felt recoil." Remember that felt recoil is the violation of our senses when a firearm goes off. It is not the actual foot-pounds of energy generated through recoil. The first three classes of 22-centerfire varmint cartridges are sufficiently mild-mannered to give the shooter a strong sense of confidence, because they do not "bark loudly." The 220 Swift class, which includes many 4,000-fps hotrock rounds, can render enough muzzle blast to make some shooters blink—until they realize that the actual recoil of all the Swift class is innocuous.

Barrel and Overall Weight. A heavy barrel offers several advantages. It heats slowly, offering sustained accuracy in continuous shooting, whereas a pencil-weight barrel heats quickly. The heavier barrel is stiffer, and is generally more accurate. On the one hand, it is less sensitive to contact with the barrel channel, and on the other, because it is heavy, it often reacts quite well to free-floating. This sort of barrel is more independent, you might say, than a lighter tube. Also, stability comes in part through rifle weight. Nobody enjoys packing a rifle that hefts like a sack of grain, but when it comes time to shoot, decent weight pays off. The heavier rifle offers better control. This is a fact borne out by *silueta* matches, where the rules limit rifle weight, because the fellow who can master a heavier rifle would have an edge.

Light rifles are enjoyable to carry; they have a place. Heavy rifles shoot great, and they have their place. My precision varminters are hefty, except for one "rover" piece which goes where I go, but it is not called upon for precision long-range shooting.

About barrel length, there are two major factors to consider. The longer barrel may have more whip, and barrel whip is not conducive to improved accuracy. The shorter barrel is stiffer than a long one—less barrel whip. Therefore, a long barrel on a benchrest rifle is a rarity. On the other hand, reduced barrel length means reduced velocity. For example, one particular 22-250 lost about 100 fps when the barrel was cut from 24 to 22 inches. The loss of only 100 fps may seem meaningless, but shooting is a game of pounds and inches, foot-

Varminting can provide excellent exercise. The author enjoys a summertime high-country hike for marmots while carrying his Sako 22 PPC varminter along.

A varmint rifle is no better than its sights. The Sako varminter is considered the most accurate factory rifle of all, and yet it could not deliver long-range accuracy without a good scope sight. Here a 10X Bushnell scope is used for jackrabbit hunting on the open plains.

pounds of energy and inches of trajectory. If the shooter does not mind a modest velocity loss, then a shorter barrel on the 22-centerfire varminter is acceptable. If he desires to strain all of the velocity possible from his cartridge, then a shorter-than-usual barrel may not be acceptable. Furthermore, the shorter barrel yields greater muzzle blast. A long barrel is quieter.

Triggers. The precision centerfire 22 varminter has a good trigger, which means the trigger pull is clean and crisp and light (but, of course, entirely safe). Look again to the benchrest boys—there are no five-pound trigger pulls on any of their winning rifles. My own varmint rifles are taken to a profes-

sional gunsmith for trigger adjustment. The triggers are set for lightness and crispness, but also for *safety*.

Sights. Simply, the true 22-centerfire precision long-range varmint machine wears a scope. That's the bottom line. Below, details on varmint scopes are enumerated.

Sling. I want a sling on my varmint rifles. While some varmint shooting takes place from a sedentary post (I've remained in one location for an hour near prairie dog villages), roaming for varmints is also quite enjoyable and often necessary. Walking several miles on marmot hunts in the West is commonplace.

OTHER VARMINT RIFLES

The 22-centerfire varmint rifle described above is a bolt-action model, repeater or single-shot. However, there are other 22-centerfire rifles that serve their owners admirably, especially under specific circumstances. Ruger's single-shot is offered in various 22-centerfire varmint calibers, as is Browning's modern version of the old Winchester Single-Shot.

Ruger's Ranch Rifle in 223 Remington caliber is another non-bolt-action rifle that finds itself in the varminting field. The rancher or farmer may carry it in the pickup truck, for example, as he makes his rounds. Under these circumstances, long-range shooting might not be the rule—fast-action might. The little Ruger semi-auto comes into play quickly and is designed for easy scope mounting. The Ranch Rifle is about three feet overall length and fits into pretty tight places.

GLASSWARE FOR VARMINTING

Glassware plays an important role in 22-centerfire varminting. My field optics include a Bausch & Lomb 10x50 Discoverer binocular, which helps locate distant varmints, from prairie dogs to coyotes. When I'm less serious about the day's tally, a handy 10x28 B&L glass fills the bill. A spotting scope is valuable, but not essential, in the varmint field. It can be used for finding varmints. I like a strong binocular for taking note of a partner's shot. Varmint hunting glassware is of high magnification because the quarry is often small and far away, but also for the important reason of coaching.

We tallied some tremendously long-range shots on a recent prairie dog safari through coaching. Watching with a 10X binocular, the coach marked the strike of the bullet. "OK. That was just a little low and a few inches to the left." With that sort of information, the marksman adjusted his next shot, holding a little higher on the target and a bit to the right for wind deflection of the bullet. Quite often the very next shot was a hit. The uninitiated shooter may scoff at 300- and 400-yard shots, believing them to be exaggerations. They are not. But such long-range shooting may require coaching, and that's where good optics help. It is OK to coach a shot while looking through your own rifle scope, but the field of view may be limited and it may not always be possible to relate the exact strike of your partner's bullet. The 10X binocular is better.

The Varmint Scope. The varmint scope is essentially a target sight, a "benchrest" telescope resting atop a flat-shooting, long-distance 22-centerfire varmint

Long-range varminting requires optical aid not only in the telescopic rifle sight, but also with varmint-finding tools, such as these Bausch & Lomb binoculars.

A winter coyote taken at long range. It is easy to see that the varmint rifle used under these conditions must possess long-range accuracy and sufficient remaining energy to get the job done.

rifle. Best bet is to install the scope that matches the rifle, its cartridge potential, the specific type of varminting to be done, and the personal preference of the shooter. I had a beautiful 24X Leupold scope mounted atop my 22 PPC USA rifle initially. Of course it worked well. However, even on prairie dogs, the full 24X magnification did not seem necessary for my particular shooting with that particular rifle. Plus, summer varminting on the flatlands meant heavy-duty mirage. I switched that scope for a Leupold 12X unit and continued making excellent long-range scores with the 22 PPC rifle, finding that the scope's lesser magnification was sufficient, and mirage no so much a problem at 12X as it had been at 24X. However, there is no substitute for high magnification, not only due to the obvious size

increase of the target, but also because of enhancement of the aimpoint.

So don't go too low in power. If you want the best of both worlds, go variable. The high-power variable has come to the fore. Apparent reticle size increased with amplified magnification on some early variable scopes. This condition made them unsuited for long-range varminting. The reticle blotted out too much target. Today, the reticle retains its optical dimension throughout the range of magnification. Therefore, the reticle size appears to be smaller, as it were, as the target grows large in the image of the scope. The reticle dimension covers less of the target on high magnification, which is exactly the desired condition. So today's high-power variables make excellent varmint scopes.

On lower power, finding the target is easy in the larger field of view. Should a coyote burst from cover at close range, it can be picked up in the view of the scope. On high power, size increase of the target is a real boon, along with increased precision of aimpoint. A 6X-24X Bausch & Lomb scope installed on a 22-250 heavy-barrel varminter proved its worth time and again, from medium to very long-range shots. A variable makes sense on today's 22-centerfire varmint rifle.

Reticle choice is extremely important. The heavy crosswire or dot has no place on a varmint scope. The reverse is required, a fine crosswire or very small dot. Either reticle functions admirably. Choosing between the two is difficult. The duplex crosswire works well, too, especially on the variable, because close-range targets can be picked up nicely with the heavier main wires, while the fine center wires offer a precise aimpoint for long-range shooting. Reticle choice rests with shooter prefer-

The Sako 22 PPC rifle is rested across a rock shelf for a long shot. Note, however, that the forend of the rifle does not make contact with the hard shelf. The shooter's left hand is under it.

ence, as long as the heavy wire or dot is excluded. Obviously, big posts and other esoteric and large reticles are unsuitable in a varmint scope.

Bright, powerful, with fine aimpoint—that is the varmint scope. High-quality optics really pay off big when the target is small and far away. About the adjustable objective—scopes that have them are excellent for clear focus of target, but the scope may be out of focus at any given time should a target present itself at a range for which the scope was not previously adjusted. Adjustment takes only a few seconds, however. The adjustable objective is worthwhile on a varmint scope, but not essential to success. Precision adjustment is important on any scope, of course. These days, that's not much of a worry. Scope adjustment is accurate and foolproof on all of the good brands. When a scope is adjusted, it stays that way. Backlash, as it was called, meant that after you made an adjustment on the scope it might not hold. Today's high-quality scopes have remedied that problem.

Sighting In. Specific sight-in will be broached later when individual cartridges are discussed. However, the four classes of 22-centerfire varmint cartridge listed above do sight in categorically. The 22 Hornet and 218 Bee with the 50-grain bullet at 2800 fps muzzle velocity sight nicely at about 175 yards. Sight them in with the center of impact about two inches high at 100 yards. This puts the bullet back on the target at roughly 175 yards, an inch or so low at 200, with an assured striking distance, even on smaller varmints, of 225 yards. The 222 Remington class with a 50-grain bullet at 3300 fps, including the 222 Remington Magnum and 223 Remington, sights well at about 250 yards. Again, the bullet's point of impact is about two inches high at 100 yards. The 222 bullet's trajectory so sighted allows for 300-yard shots even on smaller varmints, such as prairie dogs. The 22 PPC with a 50-grain bullet at 3600 fps sighted to strike two inches high at 100 yards prints the bullet about three inches low at 300 yards; hits to 350 yards are not uncommon with this cartridge, in part due to its excellent accuracy, but also commensurate with its flat trajectory.

The 220 Swift, 22-250 Remington, 224 Weatherby, 5.6 × 57mm RWS and other rounds capable of squirting that 50-grain pill out of the muzzle at over 3900 fps may be sighted for 300 yards on the button. This puts the bullet's center of impact just a shade over two inches high at 100 yards. With an accurate rifle (just before this was written, a Dale

Storey heavy-barrel 22-250 was fired with under two-inch groups at 300 yards), hits out to 400 yards are possible with this sight-in method. As far as power is concerned, the 22 PPC class and 220 Swift class can deck a prairie dog or similar varmint at ranges beyond 400 yards. It is *hitting*, not retained energy, that challenges such long-range shooting with the 22 varminter. We have come full circle to the two initial criteria for long-range varminting success: accuracy and flat trajectory. Without the first, hitting becomes more accident than intention. Without the second, bullet-drop guesswork grows unwieldy and impractical.

EFFECTS OF WIND DEFLECTION

Over and over we hear how the little 22 centerfire is shoved out of the way by wind. Of course, this is true. But what cartridge is not kicked around by wind? None. The beloved 30-06 with a hand-loaded 180-grain bullet beginning at 2800 fps muzzle velocity is drifted off-target by about seven inches at 300 yards in a 10 mile-per-hour crosswind. The 220 Swift firing a 50-grain bullet at 4100 fps drifts 8¼ inches off course, same distance, same crosswind. The 30-06 wins, but the difference is minuscule.

SHOOTING POSITIONS

The finest long-range 22-centerfire varmint rifle in the world will not pan out if the shooter does not handle it correctly, and that means getting the rifle steady enough to allow proper bullet placement. Consider first the offhand shot. Can you hit varmints from this shooting position? Of course you can, but seldom at long range. I watched a silhouette champ down prairie dogs out to a couple-hundred yards from the offhand posture, and that's fine shooting. But when the range increased beyond 200, this fellow sought a rest. Any steadying object will help. In marmot hunting, in high mountains generally loaded with huge rocks, the top of a boulder offers a platform for shooting. Stout tree limbs can offer an outdoor benchrest as well. When no rest is available, the prone shot is often the best alternative—try pulling your right leg forward to lift your body slightly off the ground to avoid shake from breathing as the lungs expands and contract. A portable rest is also useful. The Harris bipod attaches to the rifle, for example, and comes in sizes that allow sitting or prone shooting postures.

HANDLOADING

Serious 22-centerfire varmint shooters are handloaders. Handloads are less costly, more powerful, and more accurate than factory loads. The last part of the trio is less true today since Sako has brought out its 22 PPC USA ammo and Winchester its Supreme line. Groups with either of these rival and often surpass handloads. Supreme ammo, used in testing a Dale Storey 22-250 custom rifle, registered 3/8-inch groups and commonly grouped under a half-inch. However, handrolled fodder still saves money and it is generally more powerful than factory ammo. Generally. Sako's 22 PPC USA ammunition with 52-grain bullet provided a muzzle velocity of 3460 fps. Handloads with the same bullet gave 3600 fps with Norma N201 powder, but with powders more readily available muzzle velocity was closer to 3500 fps. The other advantage of reloading is versatility. It is possible to produce small-game or turkey-hunting ballistics with any of the hotrock 22s when you are a handloader. For example, look at the reduced loads for the 223 Remington (in its own chapter). With such loads, small-game hunting is possible without undue meat destruction.

No loads listed in this book come from personal testing. The bullet companies and powder companies have provided reams of valuable loading data, well-tested and reliable. The loads presented here are from these sources. As with all shooting, however, personal testing in the individual rifle is necessary to find that hospitable combination where powder, bullet, primer and case join blissfully for greatest performance.

Such testing is easy and safe. Always begin with *suggested* starter loads, never with maximum loads. Then work the load up gradually. Half-grain increments can pay off in smaller capacity cartridges because each additional half-grain weight of powder makes a significant pressure difference within the case. Remember that there are 7,000 grains weight in one pound, so when speaking of a half-grain of weight, we are talking about a very tiny mass. Accuracy is the major goal, but not the only goal. Often I read of individuals who are aglow because their varmint rifle has achieved a high level of accuracy. But the chronograph shows the load to be sub-par in velocity, meaning that trajectory and downrange ballistics suffer. I contend that one does not buy a 220 Swift in order to have 222 Remington ballistics. Load with great care, but find the right combination for good accuracy along with the ballistic potential of your cartridge.

Power was one of the criteria listed for handloading. While we do not often think in terms of delivered energy in varminting, because the cartridges used seem oversized compared with the mass of the varmint, remember that increased power through full-throttle muzzle velocity delivers the flattest trajectory. However, along with the flatter trajectory comes the potential to quickly and humanely drop the intended quarry. The ballistics of the 22 Hornet compared with the 220 Swift instantly reveal the value of increased velocity in terms of Newtonian energy levels.

The best Hornet loads of my knowledge push the 50-grain bullet at 2800 fps muzzle velocity from a 26-inch barrel. The 220 Swift's 50-grain pill from the same barrel length can be coaxed to leave the muzzle at 4100 fps. The Hornet load develops a muzzle energy of 870 foot-pounds. The Swift load develops a muzzle energy of 1866 foot-pounds. At 300 yards, the Hornet's 50-grain bullet is down to about 1740 fps for a retained energy of 336 foot-pounds, while the Swift bullet has fallen off to 2726 fps for a retained 300-yard energy of 825 foot-pounds. Look at it this way, by increasing the velocity of the same 22-caliber 50-grain bullet, the Swift has roughly the same energy at 300 yards as

The Harris Bipod greatly enhances field steadiness. These bipods attach to the rifle and can be swung into place swiftly. Some models work from the sitting as well as prone position. This Harris bipod has been installed on a 22-250 rifle.

the Hornet has at the muzzle. This does not mean that the Hornet is a lesser cartridge in the eyes of the hunter—the little Hornet has its place and is far preferred over the Swift in some applications. But one cannot argue with the difference of ballistics noted here.

Reloading is a natural for the 22-centerfire cartridge. One bullet company spokesman told me that while the 150-grain 30-caliber projectile remained No. 1 in sales, three of the top five bullets with the company were 22 caliber. Another company spokesman provided similar figures. One more thing about 22-centerfire handloading—yes, reloading saves money; provides a high-energy, low trajectory product; oftentimes yields the more accurate cartridge; and allows the shooter to turn his firebreathing 22-250 ballistically into a 22 Long Rifle if he so desires. However, these pluses leave out a very important factor—the joy of handloading. Handloading is its own pastime. There are many of us who relax with handloading. It is a very interesting activity within the realm of shooting, and by handloading one learns a great deal more about firearms and ballistics. For those who wish to load in quantity, there are new presses available that offer greater speed, such as the RCBS Auto 4 × 4. For those who are not interested in volume, there are many standard reloading outfits worthy of consideration.

THE NATURE OF THE BEAST

Big cases holding small bullets carry the intrigue of screaming velocity and table-top flat trajectory. But it is knowledge of varmints that hones the hunter's skills. This is why I study the "nature of the beast" in many sources, from biological papers to popular books. Learn more about your varmints. Such knowledge will add immeasurably to varminting with the 22 centerfire. I recently learned more about the local prairie dog when I read the work of zoologist John Hoogland, who discovered infanticide among these little creatures. It took six years for the zoologist to realize what was happening when a lady prairie dog slipped into the burrow of its sister. Eventually, Hoogland had proof that the trip was rather macabre—the devouring of young from the neighbor's litter. While this bit of knowledge falls only into the realm of interesting fact, much other information directly aids the hunter as he applies the precision 22-centerfire rifle in the varmint field. Varmints are unique within the ecosystem. They are fascinating, from the close encounter of bobcat or cougar, to the distant reachout for a 400-yard marmot.

17 THE 22 MAGNUM RIMFIRE

No other cartridge in the world fits exactly into the niche occupied by the 22 Winchester Magnum Rimfire, known popularly as the 22 WMR or simply 22 magnum. That absolute uniqueness qualifies the round for its own chapter. The 22 WMR also qualifies because there is nothing in cartridgedom that works exactly like it. Ballistically, it falls somewhere between the 22 Long Rifle and the 22 Hornet. You can handload a number of 22-centerfire rounds to behave just like the 22 WMR, of course, and I have. A friend had me concoct turkey-hunting loads for his 22-250 Remington. My handcrafted ammo cooled the hot 22-250 down to turkey-taking temperature, firing a hard 50-grain jacketed bullet at about 1800 fps, which fairly well duplicated 22 WMR performance.

But you won't go into a gunshop and buy any other round that turns up 22 WMR ballistics. This rimifre magnum cartridge is to the 22 Long Rifle what the 30-06 Springfield is to the 30-30 Winchester round. The 22 WMR does indeed "magnumfy" the 22 Long Rifle, just as the 30-06 boosts 30-30 ballistics. I arrived at the altar of 22 WMR worship a comparatively short time ago. Bad notice had steered me away from the round. I failed to see any just cause for its existence. Not powerful enough for bigger varmints. Not sufficiently far-shooting to stand alongside the 22 centerfires. Too powerful for small game. What good was it? It turns out that the 22 WMR is the king of wild-turkey rifle cartridges; works quite well on the javelina (peccary or musk hog) of the Southwest; is an excellent varminter up to about 125 and even 150 yards, depending upon the varmint and the conditions; and can serve for hide hunting with solid bullets.

Not accurate, some say. To the contrary. Two rifles I tested in 22 WMR— one a Marlin Model 25, the other an Anschutz Bavarian—were quite accurate. These scoped rifles proved capable of better

accuracy than I can hold.

The uniqueness of the cartridge is furthered by its various loadings. Winchester and CCI offer a 40-grain jacketed hollow-point bullet and a 40-grain full-patch full-metal-jacket bullet. The former is considered the varmint hunter's choice. The latter may be used for small-game hunting and wild turkeys, if shots can be picked and placed. The "solid" tears up little meat, but it can do a good job of dropping Ben's Bird with careful bullet placement. Federal offers the same two loads, plus another: the 50-grain hollow-point bullet. This may be the best turkey taker of the clan. RWS has a 40-grain jacketed bullet in 22 WMR, and a soft-point hollow-point bullet

The 22 Winchester Magnum Rimfire (WMR) cartridge (second from right) is shown with a 32 Long rimfire (far right), an early attempt to boost rimfire power; the 22 Winchester Rim Fire (WRF), a round that fires a 45-grain bullet; and the 22 Long Rifle (far left). Note that the 22 WMR is the only one of the four that has a jacketed bullet.

The peccary, a fierce breed of wild pig found in southern Texas and hunted with hounds: a drawing by Audubon

This rather preposterous rendition of the Southwestern *javelina* or peccary, an Audubon creation, depicts one of the big-game animals currently hunted with the 22 WMR. Arizona has allowed the cartridge on peccary for a number of years.

as well. I did not have faith in the 22 WMR as a javelina cartridge until I saw two of these little "wild pigs" dropped with one shot each. A fellow writer, Bob Hirsch, prefers the 22 WMR for peccaries and has had high success with the cartridge. His daughter employed the little rimfire round last season, dropping a boar with one shot.

Javelina are tough. Good shot placement is paramount to clean harvesting. So it takes a careful marksman to put these pigs down cleanly with the 22 WMR, but the round can do the job. I was no longer surprised when a couple of coyotes fell to the cartridge at ranges of about 125 yards and 60 yards (the latter in the timber). On prairie dogs, strikes to 150 yards were not impossible to make, and the round was effective on these rodents up to that distance, especially with the RWS soft-point hollow-point bullet.

About the only legitimate complaint that seemed pertinent concerning the 22 WMR was its overly abundant force on small game. I cannot recommend it for such use. Nor is it a plinking round. Its ballistics are not necessary for either chore, and I will stick with the standard 22-rimfire round for such work.

My first turkey with the 22 WMR came to me as I

enjoyed what I call a busman's holiday, going hunting without all the paraphernalia of my business, especially cameras hanging about the neck. I was supposed to go into the area early, set up camp and wait for a friend to join me.

I was waiting for my friend, sort of, resting back against a creekbed bank when a "gobble-gobble" reached my ear, floating on a gentle and propitious zephyr. "Hmmm," I said, "sounds like the birds are looking for me." I had decided I would harvest a cottontail supper with the 22 WMR, using the full-metal-jacket bullet. So when the turkeys showed up I aligned the crosswires, held, and fired. One wild turkey tag canceled at 20 paces. I explained to my partner how I had intended to wait, but was forced by hunter instinct to reach deeply into my bag of turkey-taking tactics to bag that wiley bird. After a long search and painstaking stalk, I had my chance. My buddy listened to the whole story then

Ann Hirsch, daughter of well-known Arizona outdoor writer Bob Hirsch, poses with field-dressed javelina on packframe. She got the little "wild pig" with a 22 WMR rifle. *(Photo, courtesy Bob Hirsch)*

asked, "Did the hunt spoil your noonday nap?"

Winchester engineers dreamed up the 22 WMR during the enjoyably dull Eisenhower years. By 1959, the cartridge was off the drawing board and on the gunshop shelf. "Announcing the all-new 22 Winchester Magnum Rimfire," an early advertisement read. "There's been a basic change in the entire concept of rim fire shooting—the first major break through in two generation," said Winchester. It was true. Winchester touted the round as better for small game and varmints, with "extra smashing power and a flatter trajectory." Printed ballistics were a bit optimistic, with claims of 2000 fps muzzle velocity with the 40-grain bullet, 1660 fps remaining at 50 yards, 1390 at 100, and 1180 fps left over at 150 yards. That would make the 22 WMR at 150 yards the near equal of the 22 Long Rifle at the muzzle. Its muzzle energy would be 355 foot-pounds. Even from a handgun, muzzle energy would be over 200 foot-pounds. Although actual ballistics did not turn up quite so much snort, they were very good all the same.

To understand the 22 WMR, you should know a bit about the 22 Winchester Rim Fire (WRF). The WRF was developed for the same reason that prompted the newer 22 magnum—more 22-rimfire power, but a very long time ago. It was chambered at first in the Winchester Model 1890 pump-action rifle. For a while, it was called the 22-7-45, which is blackpowder nomenclature for 22 caliber, seven grains of black powder and a 45-grain bullet. The 22 WRF was made in the usual fashion. That is, the bullet fit inside of the cartridge case, unlike the 22 Short, Long, and Long Rifle, in which the bullet is the *same diameter* as the cartridge case, requiring that the projectile's base be beveled to fit into the mouth of the case. The 22 WRF had a flat point, which was credited by some for its success in the small-game/small-varmint field. Remington loaded a nearly identical cartridge, calling it the 22 Special, but with a round-nose bullet. An initial muzzle velocity of about 1110 fps was noted. W.W. Greener got 1137 fps muzzle velocity from a 24-inch barrel in actual test. At that time, the 22 Long Rifle fired a 40-grain round-nose bullet at 1070 fps using Lesmok Powder. The 22 WRF was accurate enough for hunting purposes. The bullet was inside-lubricated, unlike the exterior bullet lube on the 22 Short, Long and Long Rifle.

When the 22 WMR was in the sunrise of its span, the 22 WRF was in the sunset of its longevity. So dimensionally close is the 22 WMR to the 22 WRF that the latter can be fired in guns chambered for the former. Naturally, the 22 WMR will not fit the chamber of the shorter 22 WRF. The 22 WMR's case length is 1.350 inches, while the 22 WRF has a case length of 1.17 inches, and the 22 Long Rifle's case is 1.00 inch long. Bullet diameter for the 22

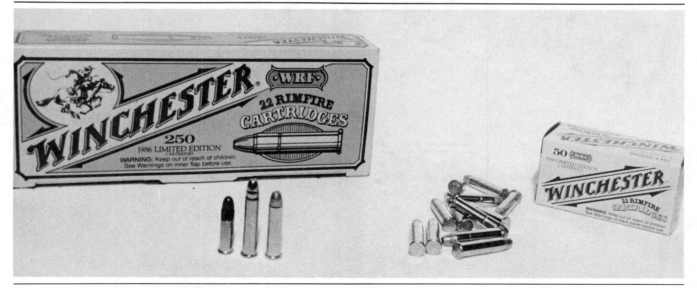

The 22 Winchester Rim Fire (WRF) is the forefather of the 22 WMR round. The two are so similar that the 22 WRF will work in rifles chambered for the 22 WMR, although the reverse is not true for reasons of chamber dimension.

WMR is not the same as the 22 Long Rifle. The Long Rifle's bullet diameter is .223 inch, while the 22 WMR fired a .2245-inch bullet, the same bullet diameter as 22-centerfire cartridges. Disagreement has arisen concerning chamber pressures with the 22 WMR. The best shows 24,000 pounds per square inch (psi) maximum, which matches the maximum chamber pressure for the 22 Long Rifle high-velocity cartridge. Both rounds stabilize their bullets with a 1:16 rate of twist. Winchester was not first to offer a firearm for its new hotshot 22-rimfire cartridge. When the NRA ran 22 WMR tests in 1959, its staff shooters used a Savage Model 24 over/under, 22 magnum up top, .410 shotgun barrel below. The NRA also tested two handguns: Ruger's Single-Six and Smith & Wesson's Model K-22 Masterpiece. Winchester 22 WMR rifles were not yet ready.

Remington's answer to the 22 WMR rifles was a very interesting one, and quite workable, but the cartridge never gained a sizable following. It was the 5mm Remington Magnum, a fine little rimfire of 20 caliber, not 22. Today, a box of 5mm ammo commands collector prices and no firearm has been made for the little rimfire for years. Using a bottleneck case (not actually a new idea—there were rim-

Federal Cartridge Company developed a 50-grain hollow-point bullet for the 22 WMR cartridge. The heavier bullet is recommended where greater bullet penetration is desirable.

Two offerings in 22 WMR: Marlin's Model 1894M lever-action rifle (above); and the Anschutz Bavarian bolt-action rifle, built on the Match 54 action. The latter is offered in a host of other calibers as well.

fire bottlenecks in the 19th Century), the 38-grain bullet zipped away from the muzzle at an advertised velocity of 2100 fps. A 38-grain 20-caliber (.2045-inch) bullet was somewhat ahead of a 40-grain 22-caliber bullet in sectional density; therefore, on paper at least, the little Remington 20-caliber rimfire was an all-right cartridge. But it languished while the 22 WMR flourished. The only factor that prevents the 22 WMR from even wider use today is money. The ammo costs considerably more than 22 Long Rifle fodder, and the latter is so good in its ballistic niche that shooters continue to use it, not by the millions of rounds, but by the billions.

Knowing the reader would be interested in chronographed figures for 22 WMR ammo, my machine went to work on four brands of ammo: Winchester, CCI, Federal, and RWS. Chronographing was accomplished with a 22-inch, not 24-inch, barrel. Bear that in mind. Also, the figures noted here were taken at 12 feet from midscreens, so muzzle velocity would be a bit higher. Winchester's 40-grain hollow-point bullet averaged 1853 fps, while the same brand using the 40-grain solid-point bullet averaged 1823 fps—an insignificant difference. CCI's 40-grain hollow-point earned 1859 fps in one string and 1836 fps in another. CCI's solid-nose 22 WMR ammo registered 1818 fps.

Federal ammo chronographed at 1885 fps for the 40-grain hollow-point, and 1550 fps with the 50-grain hollow-point bullet. Federal's 40-grain solid was not chronographed. RWS ammo showed 2025 fps with the 40-grain full-metal-jacket bullet and 2097 fps with the 40-grain soft-point hollow-point bullet. Meanwhile, a test of a new run of Winchester's 22 WRF ammo gave 1300 fps with a 45-grain bullet. From a Ruger Single-Six revolver with 5½-inch barrel, Winchester's 40-grain solid earned 1396 fps. Federal's 40-grain hollow-point achieved 1336 fps and Federal's 50-grain hollow-point 1115 fps. As with the 22 WRF, there is a 22 WMR shot load. At ten feet, from the regular 22-inch rifled barrel, the pattern dispersed over a foot. On a rattler poised at the end of your bedroll, the shot load would be quite effective.

Accuracy was also considered. All four brands of ammunition proved quite accurate from the Marlin rifle and the fine Anschutz Bavarian. The Bavarian, a new model as this is written, uses the 1700 Match 54 action. It's stock of "old world configuration" is cut full; the trigger is adjustable, the barrel free-

floating. Fifty-yard groups of an inch were common. Three-quarter-inch groups were frequent. The Bavarian was still so new that I had not yet fit it with the right scope for testing, having only a 2.5X compact available at the time. Today, that rifle wears a 6X scope and the extra magnification has helped realize its accuracy potential. Groups of 1½ inches at 100 yards are no problem to achieve with the Anschutz. Range conditions were never ideal, either, when the 22 magnums were tested. The same step-by-step approach to finding the best combination of rifle and ammo for the 22 Long Rifle should be applied with the 22 WMR. Shoot enough to gain a good average accuracy statement for each ammo brand and bullet style.

VARMINTING WITH THE 22 WMR

Sighting in for the full potential of the 22 WMR's trajectory pattern means putting the bullet about 2½ to 3 inches high at 50 yards. The groups will cluster a finger-width low at 150 yards with this sight-in arrangement. I found this sight-in useful, because the cartridge was effective on prairie dogs and jackrabbits that far away. A sight-in of two inches high at 50 yards put the bullet a little lower at 150 yards, but still within the dimensions encompassed by the jackrabbit and stand-up prairie dog. The only marmots hunted with the 22 WMR were

The 22 WMR makes a fine medium-range varmint round. John Fadala uses a Marlin 25M bolt-action 22 WMR on a prairie dog hunt.

stalked as if the 22 Long Rifle were in use. I doubt that 75 yards separated shooter and marmot at the longest. The 22 WMR with 40-grain RWS hollow-point dropped each marmot with one shot. Bushnell Banner 6X scopes were excellent on both of the 22 WMR test rifles for varminting because they offered adequate target magnification out to 150 yards, my self-imposed limit for jacks and prairie dogs. The scopes were also fine for marmoting at much closer range. A 4X scope adorned my first 22 WMR, but I found the rifle ballistically worthy of more optical power than that.

Originally, I kept my range down to 125 yards on prairie dogs and jackrabbits. More work with the 22 WMR and the hotter RWS ammo extended that range by 25 yards. Learning the two rifles also aided in better shot placement beyond 125 yards. But 150 was the max. The 22-WMR fan should stalk rockchucks and woodchucks. Long-range varminting is for the long-range varmint rifle chambered for high-energy cartridges. But the 22 WMR proved that it was a worthy varminter when used within its realm of ballistic potency.

THE WILD TURKEY

With any new endeavor, I study up on the subject to arm myself with knowledge before striking out. I read a good deal about hunting wild turkeys with the 22 WMR that resulted in knowledge—plus confusion. Some writers loved the solid bullet. Others said it was a wounder. My first bird fell to a 40-grain solid, but that was less plan than design. At merely 20 yards, it was no trick to place the pill just right. With only two more harvests under my belt, qualification as resident wild-turkey expert on the 22 WMR is still pending; however, the last bird was felled with the 50 grain hollow-point and it seemed to offer a little bit more authority without undue meat spoilage. Naturally, conditions dictate the ammo for any sort of hunting.

I hunt birds more by glassing for them from ridges than by traditional methods. Find a roost. Know the birds are using it. Look for a waterhole. Check for fresh sign. And when assured of activity, look for the turkey by taking the high ground and glassing. When the hunter locates them, he stalks, or more appropriately sneaks, into the path of the feeding birds, waiting for their arrival. Shots at 20 to 50 yards are the rule. I'm convinced that at such close range, the 40-grain solid will continue to work

Large for a javelina, this boar weighed 45 pounds field-dressed. The 40-grain bullet, however, did the job.

as well as it did on my first bird. And, remember, a bullet through the pinion area, where wing joins body, drops turkeys without too much meat loss.

The 50-grain hollow-point, however, which was brought out at the request of pistol silhouette shooters who wanted more momentum to knock their targets down, has less blow-up with more impact. A low body hit, aiming to strike the spine, will not destroy much edible meat, and yet the 50-grain hollow-point offers good penetration and power. In the old days, "real" turkey rifles were the 25-20, 32-20 and even the 32 rimfire. These slow-movers were not terribly explosive; they hit hard enough for wild turkeys, and they ruined little meat. Today, the 22 WMR, perhaps with the 50-grain bullet instead of the 40, may well be the best wild-turkey rifle cartridge off the gunstore shelf. I can't think of a better one offhand, not when meat destruction is compared with cartridge authority. The combination of a 50-grain, 22-caliber, jacketed hollow-point bullet in the mid-1500-fps range seems to be a good one.

THE JAVELINA HUNT

The Arizona Game & Fish Department installed a rule governing the use of the 22 WMR on javelina: it would be allowed. At the time, I was not sufficiently familiar with the cartridge's impetus, and must admit to misgiving. Now, however, I recognize the 22 WMR as adequate for these little musk hogs with appropriate hunting style and consequent proper bullet placement. Javelina may not be that difficult to hunt. I've succeeded on all but one outing in my lifetime, and I've hunted them since boyhood in Arizona and Sonora, Mexico. However, the hunter success rate is rather low (30 percent is considered good) because these animals can be difficult to locate.

I advocate hunting them by first locating the telltale sign to insure that the "hogs" frequent the area. They leave plenty of notice, chewed agave plants, nips out of prickly pear pads, and little bomb craters dug into the earth in search of roots and wild onions. The second phase of the system is hiking the terrain, but not in headlong ground-covering rapidity. Rather, the idea is to gain good vantage points from which to search for your quarry with binoculars. My favorite pig optics are now a pair of Bausch & Lomb 10x50s. Such magnification and good light-gathering ability are useful in locating these smallish and squat animals as they feed on the hillsides. Look for a series of black dots in the distance. Sometimes the black dots are used-up cacti known as *sotos* where I hunt. But when the black dots change position on the hillside, you either have mobile cacti or wild pigs.

Then you stalk. Mr. Magoo was a sharp-eyed cookie compared with your average javelina. These little porkers can, however, detect your aftershave a mile away. So in stalking, keep the wind in your face. Don't let your boots cry out a warning by stepping on things that go crack! Stay low as you stalk. Even Mr. Magoo can see you if you break the outline of the horizon or tramp along in plain sight. If the wind does not change, a shot of 20 to 50 yards is no big trick. Although the 40-grain hollowpoints have served well on porkers, the 50-grain bullet might be even better. Also, try a box of RWS ammo with the 40-grain soft-point hollow-point bullet. Slip one of these high-speed missiles between the ribs and your tag is canceled. Or, since the range is going to be so close, consider a head shot. Remember to watch the wind. Use a "wind bag" to

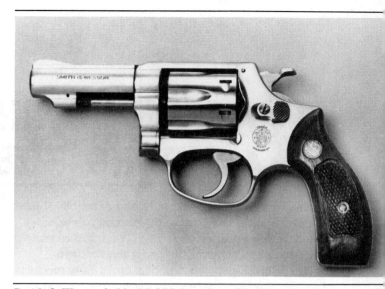

Smith & Wesson's Model 650 Stainless Steel Kit Gun is a well-made revolver offered in 22 WMR chambering. This is a rugged firearm and well-suited to trail and camp.

detect changes in the air currents. This is a small pourous cloth sack half-filled with fine white ash from the fireplace. One snap of the bag and a puff of white dust filters to the ground, revealing the air currents with great accuracy.

THE HANDGUN

Already mentioned, the handgun in 22 WMR is useful for camp protection, close-range pest control, small game, and of course the silhouette shoot. Remember that there is now a 22 WMR semi-auto pistol as well as the fine Ruger convertible revolver (with 22 Long Rifle and 22 WMR cylinders). This semi-auto pistol is the AMT Automag II, a gas-operated model.

The 22 WMR stands alone in its division. It will never take the place of the 22 Long Rifle, nor was it ever meant to. However, it has been chambered in some very interesting and worthwhile rifles and handguns, and it deserves the attention of the 22 fan who wants to fill a specific gap in his battery. That gap seem to lie between the 22 Long Rifle and the 22 Hornet. While 22 WMR ammo is too costly for plinking and too powerful for most small-game work, it is just right for wild turkeys, javelina and modest-range varmints in the hands of the careful shot. The big brother of the old 22 WRF is here to stay.

18 SEEKING AND BUYING THE USED 22

The 22 fan seldom owns only one example of the caliber. Rimfire rifle, rimfire pistol or revolver, 22-centerfire rifle, and nowadays a 22-centerfire pistol may comprise a basic battery for the modern shooter. The 22 devotee has numerous new models to select from. But there is an even larger world of used 22s to consider, hundreds of them, some quite exciting and interesting, even though they did not withstand the buffets of new manufacturing methods, changes in the economy, or even the whims of buyers. These golden oldies are gone, and yet not gone. No longer manufactured, they are still available for he who searches for them. Buying a used 22 may be a measure of budgeting—there are fine examples at modest prices. Although it's nice to find a shiny new 22 rifle under the Christmas tree, it's also great when a beginner's first rifle is a previously owned classic, a rifle no longer made. Reasons other than financial propel the 22 buyer into the used market also. "They don't make 'em like they used to" is a fact when it comes to many 22s. If you want a Winchester Model 61 pump-action 22 in standard or magnum chambering, you have to buy a used one. That fine rifle has not been manufactured for years. If you enjoy the nostalgia surrounding the old-time single-shot 22 rifle, you may want to look for a Remington Model 4 or Model 7, because you aren't going to find a new Remington-made rolling-block 22 rimfire at your local gunshop.

DON'T BE FOOLED—KNOW WHAT YOU REALLY WANT

Age does not guarantee value or excellence. While there were many truly fine 22s manufactured over the years, mainly rimfire rifles and handguns, many new models are as good, and in some cases better, than the oldies. Don't be fooled. Know what you really want and why you want it. Romance plays a big role in 22 shopping and guided my

search for a Model 75 Winchester Sporter. Eventually, I found the discontinued model and bought it. I'm happy I did, but to say it surpasses the workmanship or accuracy of my much newer bolt-action Kimber would be to speak from a platform of nostalgia, for it's not true. The Kimber is more accurate, and I believe mechanically superior to the older rifle. I wouldn't trade the Model 75 for anything, but neither am I fooled—it's a great old rifle, but it's not better than my new one. If you are looking for historical significance, a special grace and class, something no longer made and most likely never to be built again, seek out that fine out-of-manufacture 22. But don't expect it to necessarily outperform a modern firearm. If you want a bargain-priced 22, a used model may be perfect, but look first to see what you can find on the new gun rack.

COLLECTING

My firearms are for shooting, not collecting, but if I were a collector, the 22 rifle would be my goal.

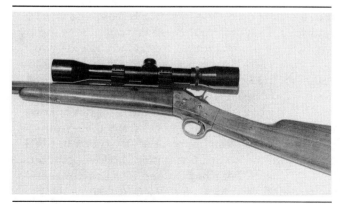

A Remington Model 4 rifle can still be found in excellent condition, even though the rifle has not been manufactured for decades.

There were so many interesting models that a lifetime could be spent looking for favorites. Specialization would be possible. Single-shots alone would make a collection. Since firearms are so long-lasting, many examples from the past remain intact. For example, you may still find a Stevens Model 80 Repeater somewhere. It was produced from about 1906 (exact date unknown) into 1911, chambered for the 22 Long and 22 WRF. The 22 Long version had an adjustable cartridge stop, which allowed for reliable feeding of 22 Long Rifle or 22 Short cartridges. This was a slide-action rifle, typically light and small, as were most 22s in the earlier days of manufacture.

Speaking of old, examples of Flobert rifles are not impossible to find. A Warnant-action Flobert single-shot made in Belgium and chambered for the 22 Long cartridge might be stumbled on, for example. Many Flobert rifles were produced in Belgium and imported into the USA until about 1910. These were chambered for the 22 BB Cap, Short, or Long. Three examples of actions were available: the original Flobert style with combined hammer and breechblock, rifles with the Remington-type of pivoted breechblock design, and the aforementioned Warnant action with a rotating breechblock. Names you and I have never heard of were attached to many 22 rifles. The Detroit Rifle Company built a 22 rifle from 1905 to 1906. It weighed but two pounds and had a loading port in the bottom of the barrel. Actual length of the rifled portion of the barrel was barely 12 inches. There were various versions of this rifle. The Savage Favorite was introduced in 1894. It sold for six dollars. Incidentally, this rifle was reintroduced by Savage in the 1970s with a price tag in the $40 range. The Stevens Visible Loader is another interesting 22 rifle of bygone days, introduced in 1908. I saw one at the last gun show I attended. Tubular magazine, pump-action, you could see the ammo fed from the tubular magazine into the chamber. The rifle had no extractor. The fresh cartridge on the way up pushed the spent case out, until the last shot, which case was removed by hand.

Four versions of the Stevens Crack Shot rifle were produced. These were single-shots. The first Model 16 used the tip-up action devised by Joshua Stevens in 1864. A later Model 16 was a side-lever rifle. The Models 26 and 72 (modern version) wore the underlever design, which is more familiar than the first two. The Springfield Model of 1922

bolt-action 22 rifle had a five-shot box magazine and weighed nine pounds. The rifle was modeled after the Springfield Model 1903 service piece, and it had a full-throw bolt, requiring the same pullback as the 30-caliber rifle. Some of the earlier autoloaders are interesting collector's models too. The Winchester Model 1903 appeared in Jack London's *Mutiny of the Elsinore*, and was mentioned by Stewart Edward White in *The Outing Magazine*. It had a blowback action with free-floating barrel, and it fired only the 22 Winchester Auto cartridge, not the 22 Short, Long, or Long Rifle. Remington's Model 24 is another example of an early collectible autoloader, a Browning design that was updated into the Model 241. Browning Arms still makes a version of this rifle in its famous 22 Autoloader. Marlin has offered its famous Model 39 in various versions. It's quite collectible. By the middle 1980s, Marlin had produced and sold over two million 39s in one version or another, beginning with the Model 1891, into the Model 1892, the Model 1897, and eventually from the 39 to 39A in many different styles. There's seemingly no end to the 22 rifles one could collect. Some are exotic and different; others are just strange.

WHERE TO FIND THEM

Gun shows abound countrywide. There is no American town entirely removed from proximity to

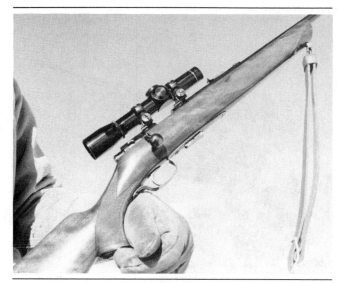

Fadala found a Model 75 Winchester Sporter in excellent condition at a good price. With scope sight added, the rifle became a first-line small-game/varmint outfit.

Some 22s, such as this Remington Model 582, carry a relatively low used price tag, but are very good service pieces. Rifles like these can be found through various outlets, including *The Gun List* newspaper.

a gun show. If you're the horsetrader type, the gun show is your cup of tea. Prices are usually negotiable, resting between the seller's asking figure and the buyer's idea of a bargain. The local newspaper's classified section is also an excellent place to locate that 22-caliber rifle or handgun of your dreams. Try the gunshop too. Sometimes garage sales are worth a look, as are hock shops and even junk shops, which may occasionally have a nice 22 on hand at a good price. I found a fine little 22 rifle at a flea market. There are two far-reaching newspaper clearing houses for used guns. These are the *Gun List* and *Shotgun News*. Thousands of 22-caliber rimfires and centerfires are listed in both.

The author feels that some rifles of the past, although well-made and desirable, can be over priced. The Winchester Model 62 slide-action rimfire rifle can cost $400 on today's market.

THE COOLING-OFF PERIOD

Old guns aren't always great guns. Used guns aren't always bargains. That's why the cooling-off period is recommended. After locating that 22 of a lifetime, give it one last day or two of consideration: What, actually, do you want it for? I thought I couldn't live without a Model 63 Winchester 22 semi-auto. I finally found one that wasn't entirely overpriced, bought it, and liked it, but soon found that while plinking with the fine little 63 was enjoyable, the rifle served no better on tin cans than an old standby I owned that had not cost $65 a pound. I didn't need it for small game, either, so the 63 got sold. Ask yourself: What real service will this piece see? Do I really need this firearm for my collection? Cool off a day or two. Then decide for or against the purchase. One problem—the "hot" items don't last. If, for example, you covet a Winchester Model 52 Sporter and one pops up at a bargain price, you'd best grab it. If you don't, I will.

If possible, try the firearm before you buy it. Often, that's impossible, but if you're dealing with a friend or the local gunshop, take the rifle out and shoot it before purchasing. Or at least agree on a trial period; three days is common. The 22 of your dreams may be a pretty ordinary shooting iron in the cold light of day. Also, a trial gives you a chance to find functional fault with the piece, such as "spitting lead" from a revolver, or feeding, ejection, or even accuracy problems with pistol or rifle.

HOW MUCH TO PAY

Old cars and old guns command their prices based on how many were made, how fine the product was and still is, and also upon an intangible, a sort of phantom desire that enters the airwaves like an atomized love potion. The Model 62 Winchester slide-action rifle, for example, is a honey of a shooter, but it fires no truer than hundreds of other 22s. Yet, you might have to pay 400 bucks for one in prime condition. I said *you* might have to. I wouldn't. Several guidelines should be considered first. Start with gauging the cost by inflation. In the early 1950s, a brand new Winchester Model 52 Sporting Rifle with aperture sight sold for about $150. Today, parting with $1,000 for one in good shape means you found a bargain. In the early 1950s, a new passenger car might run $3,000. Today, you'd pay seven times more for a similar vehicle. Seven times $150 is $1,050, so the Model 52 Sporter at 1,000 is in keeping with inflation. Not all things have inflated in like fashion, of course, but I did buy a nickel soft drink yesterday for 50¢.

Second, compare the price of that used rifle to its modern counterpart. There are rifles made today that resemble in function and purpose the 22s of yesteryear, be they rimfire or centerfire models. When looking at a pre-64 Model 70 Winchester in 220 Swift, compare it with modern rifles of the same caliber. Unless you desire the pre-64 Model 70 for its singular merits, you may find that a new model will serve your purposes as well and perhaps better than the old. Besides, new means all of the barrel wear belongs to you, not you and the previous owner(s). Third, check a blue book of gun values, such as Flayderman's or *Gun Trader's Guide*. Fourth, look into *Gun List* or *Shotgun News*—the first is arranged alphabetically and according to models—and see what price the 22 firearm you want is commanding at the moment.

BUYING USED 22 FIREARMS

The Enduring 22-Rimfire Rifle. Many wonderful 22-rimfire rifles have been built throughout the history of gunmaking. For many reasons, most of these fine firearms have been discontinued. Sako's Model 72 bolt-action rifle is an example. So is the Winchester Model 52 Sporter, Winchester Model 75 Sporter, Savage Model 23, Springfield Armory 22, H&R Targeteer, Remington Model 12, Winchester Model 61, BSA No. 12, Remington Model 4—the list seems endless.

A search for a specific used rifle can be great fun, with many sources to consult beforehand. When I was looking for my Model 75 Sporter, I first learned more of the piece through *Firearms Assembly 3*, an NRA book by James Triggs. I found it had

a fine reputation, was chambered in 22 Long Rifle only, with a 24-inch barrel, speed-lock action, modest checkering, 5.75 pounds weight; and it had a good trigger pull of about 2.75 pounds (adjusted weight). The rifle came with a five-shot clip, but a 10-shot clip was optional.

Old *American Rifleman* magazines carried advertisements for the rifle. Madis's *The Winchester Handbook* revealed further information. Madis noted 1938 as the year of introduction. The margin of profit for the Winchester Model 75 Sporter was listed as 40 percent higher than comparable lower-grade Winchester 22s. The 75 cost only 20 percent more to produce than the excellent, albeit plain, Model 72 bolt-action 22, but it sold for twice the price. In 1938 only 1,198 Model 75 rifles were produced. Madis notes the speed lock to have a mere .2-inch firing-pin travel. I learned something else

A used 22 rifle may have years of remaining service in it. This Model 12 Remington was treated to a barrel liner, which restored the rifle's accuracy and life.

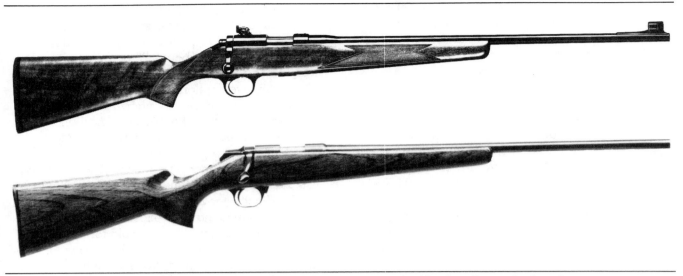

Various factors may contribute to the high demand (and price) of certain 22 rifles. One is the fact that a model is discontinued, such as the H&R Model 5200 (above), an accurate and all-around excellent firearm. Another factor is the production of a particular arm in limited quantity. For example, only about 2,000 of Browning's A-Bolt 22-rimfire rifle (below) with laminated stock were made. These firearms often become collector's items.

after buying my used 75 Sporter—it was made in 1948. A list of serial numbers and year of manufacture in the Madis book held that information. Knowing that there was a 10-shot clip available for the 75 Sporter, I contacted Walter Lodewick, 2816 N.E. Halsey St., Portland, OR 07232 and purchased an original clip in new condition.

Search for that 22 rifle that's no longer manufactured. But don't miss out on half the fun. Read about your dream rifle first. There will be information available in firearms texts, "blue books" listing features and prices, and old magazines. Check for information in outdated editions of *Shooter's Bible* (Stoeger) and *Gun Digest* (DBI Books). And once more—temper your buying decision with rationality. I've bought and later sold a number of had-to-have-'em firearms because in "real life" they were not quite what I'd expected. On the other hand, some of the oldies remain forever in my personal battery because they are more than I ever hoped for.

The Used 22-Centerfire Rifle. The 22-rimfire rifle is a pretty safe buy because it does not wear quickly. Thousands upon thousands of rounds fly downbore before the barrel is worn out. But the 22 centerfires can be quite another story. Putting comparatively heavy doses of powder through their bores may indeed bring wear sooner than later. But the used 22

centerfire can be as much a bargain as the rimfire rifle. You just have to watch a little closer for wear. Various criteria for sensibly buying 22s are listed below. There are vast numbers of excellent 22 centerfire rifles in the used marketplace. A friend bought a Savage 112-V single-shot varmint rifle. This rifle—with its 26-inch heavy, free-floated barrel ($13/16$ inch at the muzzle) and stout stock—shot better than its new owner dreamed it would. The bore was like new, and the price was quite reasonable. The Savage 112-V was chambered for the 222 Remington, 223 Remington, 22-250 and 220 Swift. Your favorite 22-centerfire varminter may well emanate from the ranks of the used. While it's true that these hot 22s may be subject to comparatively rapid bore wear, it is also true that some marksmen buy varmint rifles, but do not fire them often, finally deciding to sell them in nearly new condition.

The 22 Handgun. Rimfire and centerfire handguns are sold far and wide, used but in excellent shape. Below, a list of tips on what to look for will help the reader buy a good used 22 sidearm. But first a few general pointers. Avoid old, light-frame models. These extra-light arms are all right if they have seen little use, but some of the ultra-light models exhibit a lot of wear. Avoid modern low-quality used handguns, whether imported or homegrown. Low price does not always equate with junk, however. There are many low-priced H&R and Iver Johnson handguns that cost little, but serve well. Be careful of obscure brands. But don't think of chain-store arms as necessarily poor grade. Sears sold a number of very sound firearms made by major arms factories, for example.

Tips On Buying A Used 22.

1. Check to see that the firearm is unloaded before studying it for purchase. Do not be satisfied by working the action. Actually look into the chamber area or at least feel with a pinky finger to ensure that there is no cartridge stuck in the chamber. Check the magazine as well. A round could be hung up there.

2. Check for missing parts.

3. Check for broken parts, especially the safety.

4. Look at the serial number. It should be clear and untampered with. The serial number may be used to identify year of manufacture.

5. Look for alterations. Some alterations diminish the value of a firearm. The collector value is usually reduced by stock refinishing, and metalwork rebluing, and holes drilled in the receiver for scope mounts. Of course, a well-mounted telescope on a previously untapped receiver does not always spell degradation of value.

6. Check for heavy use and undue wear. With a bore light, study the chamber of the 22 centerfire. A dark throat indicates wear. Rifling should be sharp. Lands should not appear rounded. Erosion is sometimes quite obvious. There may be a "rusty" ap-

Remington's Model 37 Rangemaster rifle is still offered in rather abundant numbers at reasonable used prices. It makes a nice firearm for the shooter who wants to try his hand at targets before going into a more expensive model.

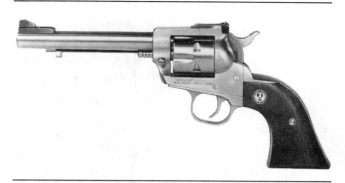

Bargains in used 22-rimfire handguns also abound. A well-made revolver, such as this stainless-steel Ruger New Model Single-Six, will last many lifetimes.

pearance. Insert a bit of cotton or white cloth into the muzzle. Push it down an eighth-inch. Then use the bore light to reflect illumination from the cotton. This will clearly reveal the rifling at the muzzle, showing possible muzzle damage, rifling wear, or both. *Remove the cotton or cloth immediately after checking for wear.* Do not leave an obstruction in the muzzle.

7. Look for loose sights. Remember that any broken or loose part may require gunsmithing time and expense. Consider that expense as part of the firearm's real cost.

8. Revolver—check for a loose cylinder with hammer down, holding the trigger rearward. Check for timing; with the hammer cocked, the locking bolt should simultaneously engage the notch in the cylinder. See that the cylinder aligns with the barrel—a dowel can be pushed down the muzzle. The dowel should align with the mouth of the chamber in the cylinder. Edges of the chamber should be clean, not battered from dry firing. Look for undue wear of the locking-bolt notch; there should be no burrs or nicks here. Spin the cylinder and observe rotation of the ejector rod; if the rod wobbles elliptically instead of spinning true, it's bent.

9. Pistol—see that the magazine fits. Check safety features. Put the safety on and pull the trigger firmly. The pistol's firing pin should not fall. The magazine should work freely. The barrel face of the semi-auto pistol may reveal dry firing marks and consequent battering and damage.

These are some clues useful in separating the good buy from the unwise buy in a used 22. If in doubt after employing these guidelines, have your gunsmith check the firearm. Good gunsmiths are

Starting out with a used rifle, especially a 22, makes sense.

busy people whose time is valuable. You will pay a reasonable fee for this service. But a trained eye can spot a flaw in a firearm in a wink. If the gunsmith steers you away from a used 22, he's earned his fee. If he says, "Go ahead; this is a good one," you will be buying with confidence. Either way, his services have paid off.

THAT FIRST 22

Maturity and overall readiness more than chronological age dictate when the beginner should have his or her first 22 rifle. However, age is also important, especially as it relates to size and strength of the individual. A youth too small or weak to handle the rifle is a hazard to himself and those around him. The rifle must be under control, and keeping it under control requires a certain level of physical ability. One point bears repeating, however: a young shooter may be strong enough to hold and aim a rifle and manage the direction of the muzzle, and yet not be able to cock the plunger of those single-shots that have one. There are grown women who are wonderful marksmen and excellent handlers of firearms; yet they find these plungers uncomfortable to use. Hand-eye coordination is another point of readiness. The shooter must be in command of his coordination in order to handle and aim a rifle. Readiness also means accep-

tance of responsibility. If the child cannot accept and carry out minor house chores, he's not ready for a firearm. If he cannot obey home rules, he's not ready for a firearm. If he shows lack of respect for the rights of others, he's not ready to own a rifle.

A used rifle makes sense in early training, not because the firearm will be abused, but because of the simple fact that no matter how much we, as parents, love to shoot, perhaps not all of our offspring will enthusiastically share the same desire.

I have always advocated the single-shot 22 rifle for beginners. However, there are compromises. The Anschutz Achiever is such a compromise. Its length of pull is adjustable. As the shooter grows, the stock can be lengthened. The bolt-action is smooth, easy to operate, and has no plunger to pull back. Although the rifle has a single-shot clip adapter, once the adapter is removed, the Achiever becomes a clip-fed repeater. In that way, when the shooter advances beyond the beginner stage, he can enjoy the advantages of a repeater.

The Anschutz Woodchuck rifle is designed for young shooters. It, too, is a bolt-action repeater and may be found new or in good used condition. It is easily scoped, but comes equipped with iron sights. The little single-shots of days gone by were nice starter rifles, too, and may be found in good condition today. Many excellent falling-breech action designs were available in the old days, such as the Remington rolling block and the Savage singles.

AFTER YOU BUY

Once you have found and purchased your used 22 firearm, treat it to a good cleaning. The suggestions laid out in Chapter 29 for rimfire and centerfire 22s make the job easy and foolproof. Be certain to remove metal fouling from the 22-centerfire rifle. High-speed jacketed bullets tend to leave traces of themselves in the bore. If you need instructions for field stripping, check the guides that deal with this subject. For example, *Firearms Assembly/Disassembly Part III: Rimfire Rifles* by J.B. Wood relates to taking apart (and putting back together) a number of 22-rimfire rifles. The used 22, rimfire or centerfire, rifle or handgun, can be purchased in conditions from new-in-the-box—which of course are not really used guns at all—to like new or excellent, as well as workable but scuffed. Bought with care, many of these 22s are bargains that offer an economical avenue to building a nice battery for the modern shooter.

19 THE 22 BACKCOUNTRY GUN

Haven't you ever wanted to toss a few essentials into a backpack, grab a sleeping bag, some rope, a lean-to tarp, a few condiments, a little grain, some cook gear, and a partner and "head to the hills" for a little while? An old friend and I used to make such "constitutionals" every year. We did not call them constitutionals at first. We called them survival trips, but there was never any do-or-die attached to these retreats, so the name was changed. The best trek of all lasted more than two weeks. It took place on a remote backdrop in Sonora, Mexico. My partner and I had already hunted in Sonora during the big-game season and we had in-

cluded our 22 rifles on the gun permits. Now we had hunting license and gun permit in hand, a lot of open season for small game in front of us, and an annual stream of cold water to guide us into (and back from) the high country, and to provide our liquid needs. Since that long-ago time, I've hunted east and west, north to Alaska and Canada, and I've experienced the mecca of gamelands, Africa. But no mental pry bar could unseat the wonderful memory of the little "22 constitutional" to Mexico and the dozens more like it that followed.

The 22-rimfire rifle was always our only provider

Author and friend Gene Thompson set up a camp in the badlands. Should the need arise, it's good to know basic survival skills. But don't forget your gear; carry with you the necessary hardware for living off the land, including the proper firearm.

of food as we "made it on our own" on our back-trail constitutionals. Over the years, though, our gear changed. We traded the large tarp for a five-pound Peak 1 mountain tent, and old sleeping bags for modern lightweight models. We tossed a few instant foods into the modern packsack for backup. But the firearm remained the same: the 22-rimfire rifle—but with an addition. We learned that the 22 pistol was also useful in out-of-the-way places. This challenge is self-imposed and non-dangerous. It is a matter of mental and physical rejuvenation. And all it takes is a little time, an open season for small game, and a trusty rimfire.

THE RIFLE

Your favorite 22 rimfire: That's the rifle to take on the backland constitutional. The rifle with which you can shoot straight. The rifle in which you have confidence. And perhaps, most of all, the one you like best. For me, that's a bolt-action, clip-fed repeater, certainly one of the more reliable models around. And it's scoped. Even though this is not a serious venture, it's nice to have the main course in the bag by the end of the day, and the scoped rifle may be that slight edge that puts the meat in the pot. Also, the rifle should "pack well." Hiking and exploring can lead the outdoorsman on long trails. A rifle that fits the occasion is desirable. I don't mean a lightweight by necessity. Balance is more

Fadala backpacking a piece of high-country real estate in the Rocky Mountains. His rifle is the Kimber bolt-action with 22 Long Rifle chambering.

Fadala takes aim with his Model 75 Winchester, fitted with aperture sight. Although this rifle is considered a collector's piece, it is also highly reliable and very much at home in the backcountry.

The 22 rifle is not the only 22-caliber firearm at home in the backcountry. Ruger's rugged 22 pistol is put into service here.

important. Some rifles simply pack well. Others don't.

THE HANDGUN

One more time, it's sights that make the difference, along with the inherent accuracy of the one-hand firearm. No matter how nice the little 22 handgun packs, or how handsome its lines, hitting is the key to success when you're counting on the gun to bring meat into your camp. While ammo for the rifle is the 22 Long Rifle, there's nothing wrong with thinking 22 WMR for the sidearm. At handgun velocities, bullet fragmentation is held to a minimum. If you have an accurate 22-magnum revolver or semi-auto pistol, there's no reason to leave it home on this trip.

THE GAME

Cottontail rabbits of badland and forest have fed us more than any other small-game edible on the

constitutional trail, but along river bottoms tree squirrels may be in season too. Some states, as noted earlier, have long tree-squirrel seasons. If you know how to cook it, the young marmot makes for good fare over the coals. Bullfrogs are good. All of the edibles listed in the small game chapter serve up fine in the backcountry camp.

THE AMMO

The 22-rimfire round offers compactness and comparative light weight. If you don't think so, place five in your left hand and five 30-06 rounds in your right. A 50-pack of 22s fits into any pocket on the pack. Take plenty with you. The Long Rifle is certainly the rimfire of choice for the constitutional. But which one? The same conflict of choice always arises. The high-speed round may not offer the accuracy of the standard-velocity cartridge. On the other hand, the Long Rifle hollow-point will serve better when the hit isn't perfect. But you're going for the head shot anyway, so you don't need a hollow-point. I gave up on this conundrum a long time ago. The major criterion is: the backtrail ammo must be accurate in the specific rifle. The rifle I carry likes standard-velocity fodder. If a mountain

John Fadala carries his favorite Model 69A Winchester 22 rifle while exploring the backcountry. A story unfolds in tracks as he examines the soft earth.

grouse is hit a little low, meat loss is minimal with the standard velocity solid-point bullet.

PACK STYLE

Hunting with a pack offers freedom and safety. The full-sized pack is the obvious choice for longer hikes. These may be used in conjunction with a packframe or as a frameless unit. The packframe is my choice for the big-game season, but it's only necessary on the 22 constitutional if your pack is too small to accommodate your sleeping bag. Then the bag can be tied onto the frame. Otherwise, a

Another option for the backcountry wanderer is a soft or frameless pack, such as this L.L. Bean® Model 518WL.

The backcountry fan may wish to employ a pack and frame, such as this one offered by L.L. Bean® company of Freeport, Me. It's the Moose Bag packsack coupled with the Freighter frame.

soft pack makes more sense. It's comfortable and easy to carry, because you don't need the kitchen sink on these little trips. You need only the basics. The pack should contain, however, many important items:

1. Compact raingear or poncho
2. Flashlight
3. Cooking pot or pan (Silverstone for cleaning ease)
4. Matches
5. Eating utensils
6. Your sleeping bag if it fits in the bag
7. Compact first-aid kit
8. Compact 22 takedown cleaning rod
9. Nylon rope, quarter-inch, 50 feet
10. Small nylon tarp (folded flat against back of pack)
11. Personal hygiene items, soap, toiletries
12. Emergency food (a couple cans of sardines?)
13. Fire starter (visit your local sport shop)
14. Lightweight broiling grill
15. Cooking oil

John Fadala prepares the coals for supper, igniting them in a cookie tin (for safety's sake). On this backcountry day-hike, a Marlin Model 25M in 22 WMR was the major rifle carried.

A fishing kit is a welcome addition in the outback. This Daiwa Minispin II was used to catch mountain trout for supper.

My backpack includes the five-pound Peak 1 mountain tent tied on. This little tent affords sufficient shelter, in concert with the down-filled sleeping bag, to weather a severe storm, let alone the mild ones encountered on the 22 constitutional outing, which usually takes place in the early fall, prior to big-game season. My outfit includes a belt kit. This is an Uncle Mike's unit that slips on the belt. It holds a pocket knife, a couple of plastic bags for dressed game, and loaded 22 clips. The small tarp with rope makes a shelter for gear or day hiking. One more thing to take along—a friend. This for-fun sort of 22 hunt is enjoyed best as a shared experience.

For short day trips, the appropriate daypack is best. This style of 22 constitutional operates from a base camp. The little daypack and belt kit contain the essentials for one day of hiking. By evening, the adventurer is back in his camp. In truly vast, but roaded, territory a ''grate-and-grill mobile camp,'' as I have named it, works fine. This means living out of a station wagon or pickup truck with a camper shell. Cooking is done by grate (over coals) or flat grill (over any heat source). The 22 fan is mobile here, using his vehicle as home in the field. Sometimes charcoal briquettes are packed in cookie tins, which provide an immediate and safe ''stove''. You need only apply charcoal-lighter fluid to the coals and ignite them. Then place the small grate over the top of the cookie tin when the coals are ready. To snuff the coals, simply snap the cookie can lid back on. Coals will often last for a couple of meals or more when used in this fashion. Many good books on backpacking fill in the details left out here. The 22 constitutional is a personal outing, best handled by the individual.

THE FISHKIT

The story would not be complete without mention of the fishkit, which for our 22 constitutional is a Daiwa Minispin II outfit—extremely light and compact, yet complete with a high-grade open-face spinning reel and a good breakdown rod. There's room in the kit for a few lures and even a little bait, but bait is often gathered on the trail, including grasshoppers (use a small leafy limb as a swatter), insects found under rocks or rotten trees, berries of various colors and sizes, and worms dug from along the stream or lake shore. The aforementioned cookie tin cooker and grate cook the fish. Use lemon and pepper seasoning.

The 22 constitutional is no trophy chase, but it has its own reward. It is a quiet outing, taking place when there are few other activities going on in the outdoors. It requires woodsmanship and hunting ability, along with marksmanship for taking game. But ultimate success lies not so much in the harvest as it does in the experience itself. Exploration, camping, hiking, and relaxation rank high here. But so do the 22 rifle and handgun that go along on the trip. The 22 constitutional is one more viable function for the most versatile of all firearms.

20 THE 22 SURVIVAL GUN

A number of years ago, a family was traveling the Southwestern desert in summer. Their car broke down. Because they were on a remote road, they decided no one would come for them. Although they were situated where shade was handy and small game was in every arroyo, or gully, they struck out. None made it. The number of survival situations in these modern times is surprisingly large. In many cases, remaining near the vehicle (or downed airplane) is the best way to survive. To say that a 22 survival gun, or any firearm, will decidedly make a difference in a survival situation is not entirely accurate. In many cases, it wouldn't have mattered. However, in many others, such a tool may have provided the margin of difference, not only for gathering small-game edibles, but also for signaling, using the three-spaced-shot method with a waiting period between volleys to call for help.

Earl Stanley Gardner, the famous author of Perry Mason novels, proved that he could "live off the land" within a hundred miles of Los Angeles, taking edibles with a 22-rimfire pistol. He managed to keep himself well-fed with the little rimfire. He was 70 years old at the time.

A modern family deciding to go "back to the land" chose a 22 rifle to help them harvest edibles. The members of the family found the 22 totally reliable and adequate for their needs. A rancher friend keeps a little "survival 22" in his pickup truck, should he break down on the back 40, which in his case is the back 20,000.

Detractors of the survival-gun idea point out that the real danger from being lost, broken down, or airplane-stranded in the outback does not come from starvation. A person can live weeks without food. However, that's not the point. Being well-fed keeps the body and mind working properly, and allows continued strength if walking out becomes the only way to make it. So the 22 survival gun is for real. Rarely will it be used for its intended purpose, and that's just the way we want it. But when it is needed, few things will take its place.

THE MILITARY SURVIVAL GUN

Thanks to the military, there is at least one standby survival 22 rifle still being built and sold these days. Early in World War II it was clear that our military men needed a relatively quiet and effective survival rifle. Bomber pilots and aircrews, as well as fighter pilots, were shot down behind

In the wild, food comes in many forms. The Ruger 22 pistol collected this hare.

The Charter Arms AR-7 rifle is a prime example of the survival gun. Here it is shown in its own floating case, which is the buttstock of the rifle.

Opening the AR-7 at the buttstock reveals the barrel, action, and clip of the rifle, all housed in compartments.

enemy lines. Continued combat was not the problem. Survival was. The Army Air Force commanders knew that the men needed food in order to sustain themselves, stay strong and alert, and find their way out of the enemy zone. Survival courses taught military personnel how to get along in a backcountry setting. But these men needed a true survival gun. The firearm finally adopted was a Stevens 22 rimfire/.410 shotgun over and under. The rugged little gun with Tenite (tough plastic) stock was quite functional. But there was a problem with the ammunition.

The trouble centered mainly around the 22 Long Rifle hollow-point, jacketless lead bullet, and also with the .410 lead shotgun slug. A *Record of Army Ordnance Research and Development* document stated the problem. Army leaders reasoned that since the ammo for the Stevens survival gun was not intended for fighting enemy troops, but rather for "killing game and for protection against attack

from animals," the hollow-point ammunition did not violate the rules of warfare. However, nobody could deny that there might be a confrontation in which the ammunition was used against the enemy. Furthermore, hollow-point bullets did violate the agreement set down in Article 23e of the Hague Regulations, which forbade "arms, projectiles, or materials calculated to cause unnecessary injury." The US Army concluded that "The Japanese would impose brutalities more severe than those inflicted upon other captured American air personnel" if they discovered the hollow-point ammunition on American prisoners of war.

Metal-jacketed ammunition would meet the requirement regarding proper projectiles. The Army Air Force commissioned Remington to develop what would be known as T-42 22 Long Rifle ammunition. The Army told Remington engineers to build a jacketed 22 Long Rifle bullet. Furthermore, there should be a 10-pound minimum bullet pull (neck

The major parts of the AR-7 are the buttstock housing, action, clip, and barrel, as shown above.

friction) for this load, a minimum mean muzzle velocity of 1100 fps at 25.5 feet, a maximum breech pressure of 22,000 psi, and a mean radius of accuracy falling within 1.25 inches at 100 yards. T-42 22 Long Rifle ammo with jacketed bullet was intended for use in single-shot fashion only, and not in any magazine.

At the close of World War II, and not so much for wartime use, the military looked at a number of drawing-board survival firearms. Various prototypes were tried. Firing a jacketed bullet was not a critical issue now. One rifle design caught on, and it is still with us today. The military called it the AR-7. We know it as the Charter Arms AR-7 Explorer. One has ridden in the back of my four-wheel-drive vehicle for years. It has provided many tasty meals.

The AR-7 is compact, with a barrel length of only 16 inches. Assembled, the AR-7 is 34.75 inches long, but when the action, barrel and magazine are inserted into the buttstock, the overall length of the rifle is 16.5 inches. Chambered for the 22 Long Rifle, the AR-7 weighs under three pounds with loaded eight-shot clip. It will not sink if dropped into lake or stream. With action, magazine, and barrel stored in the Cycolac buttstock, a tightly fitted snap-on plastic buttcap seals the package. This semi-automatic rifle was fired in the field at blocks

The Charter Arms AR-7 Explorer assembled for action. The semi-auto rifle was put through rugged tests, which it passed superbly.

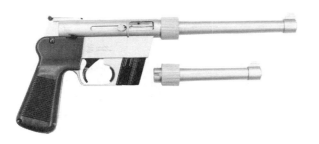

The Charter Arms Explorer SII Pistol is a scaled-down version of the rifle. It comes in 22 Long Rifle caliber, with barrel options of six or 10 inches.

of wood about an inch square. Its peep sight was good enough to support consistent hitting at 25 yards.

SURVIVAL AMMO

The 22 Long Rifle round is adequate for taking edibles at close range, as we all know, and the variety of toothsome small game in most backcountry settings is gratifying. Food prejudice would be more a problem than procuring something to eat. A snake to one culture is food, to another a repulsive serpent. Again, it is the size and weight of the 22-rimfire round that makes it worthy of its position as top-rated survival ammo. Arguments in favor of the 22 magnum, however, would hold plenty of merit. If need be, the 22 magnum would offer more harvest-

Another rifle capable of heavy-duty survival service is the Marlin Model 25M in 22 WMR chambering. Here, Fadala shows how to use the packframe as a field rest.

The Savage Model 24-V is a combination gun that serves well on the survival trail. It's a rifle and a shotgun in one unit.

ing power on larger edibles, especially in the hands of a cool shot. But for the needs of most, the 22 Long Rifle has been designated the proper choice for survival ammo.

THE SURVIVAL HANDGUN

More compact yet, the handgun would fill the bill as a survival firearm, especially in 22 Long Rifle or 22 WMR chamberings. However, most of us shoot a rifle better than we shoot a handgun. Compelled to find, stalk, and dispatch edibles with a handgun, some of us might wish we had a rifle. But for the expert sidearm fans who have accurate firearms with good sights, the handgun would have to be considered a viable survival instrument.

THE SURVIVAL PACKAGE

Those of us who move about in harsh winter country have learned that you go prepared or you don't go at all. A survival package is more than a firearm, although the AR-7 is certainly the heart of my kit. A hundred rounds of 22 Long Rifle ammo in a sealed container (a plastic map carrier) ride with the rifle. Also part of the package is a Browning Wasatch Goose Down Parka, which is worn throughout the winter and is therefore found resting on the back seat of the vehicle or placed in a plastic sack in the same location. Extra clothing is kept

dry in a plastic sack. The sleeping bag, which is never removed from the vehicle, makes this package effective. It is encased in a ripstop nylon container. The key to winter survival for anyone caught in a blizzard is to remain with the vehicle, but people get tired, cold, and hungry and decide to strike out. That's inviting disaster. So my package includes a Coleman one-burner propane stove, a pot, water container, dehydrated food and packaged drink, granola bars, and other goodies. Use a small trunk or ice chest to hold these survival items. In the trunk of a car, or back of a pickup truck or station wagon, such a survival package is more than worth what little trouble and expense it takes to assemble it.

The 22 survival gun is for real. It is a firearm with broader use than meets the eye. My AR-7 has not yet served to provide food under dire circumstance, but it certainly has come in handy. A number of times the little rifle was fit together for incidental small-game hunting that I didn't know was coming up. And should the unwanted occasion present itself, that little rifle may be called upon to provide a meal or signal for help. The rest of the time, it will, as the famous poem goes, "stand and wait," which, as the scholars have shown, does not mean standing around doing nothing, but rather standing by to serve its master as the need arises.

21 THE 22 HOUSE AND CAMP GUN

The 22 handgun or rifle has served the camper for a century, whether he's been a weekend wanderer, fisherman, hunter, or explorer. By the same token, the 22 rimfire has often been not the gun of choice, but the firearm of availability in the home. Recently, on the long-running Phil Donahue television talk show, a young boy gave an account of saving his family from personal harm as he thwarted two would-be assailants who broke into

The neat, light, trim Winchester Model 9422 rimfire rifle is at home in camp or field.

the home. He used a 22-rimfire rifle. Do not select a 22-rimfire rifle or handgun to defend your home and loved ones. There shall be nothing here to suggest that choice. However, know what your 22-rimfire firearm can do to save your life, and the lives of your family, if it must be put into self-defense service.

There are many experts in the area of self-defense who agree that the 22 rimfire is not the ideal choice in a self-defensive situation. Common sense plus experience leads to the following point of view. If you live in an area threatened by break-in and violence to you and your family, buy a dog: not an animal dangerous to people, but rather one of any size that will bark and act as an early-warning alarm system for your home. In many instances, the bark alone will be enough to persuade the would-be housebreaker to leave. When the bark does not work, and the intruder persists in entering your domicile, you are then forced to employ the second part of the plan for home self-defense: a short-barreled shotgun you can maneuver quickly and easily in tight quarters, loaded with No. 4 Buckshot. A convicted housebreaker and habitual criminal was asked, "What deterred you from breaking into certain homes?"

He answered, "Bow, wow—snick, snick. And an NRA emblem in the window." "What does that mean?," the prisoner was further questioned.

"The bark of a dog and the loading of a shotgun," he replied. "And the NRA sticker on the window means somebody inside has a gun. That's a good place to stay away from."

The shotgun is a better home-defense tool than a 22-rimfire rifle or handgun. While this advice stands firmly, the fact is, a firearm that often turns up in defense of the home is the 22 rimfire. In the event that it must be employed, what will it do? And what will it not do?

The "not do" is perhaps the more important part of the question. You cannot expect the 22 rimfire to deliver the blow associated with the big-bore handgun. A 357 Magnum, for example, is entirely elevated above any 22 rimfire in the world of self-defense. Its larger bullet penetrates far more and delivers a much greater stopping blow. An assailant bent upon injury to homeowner can be stopped far more effectively with the larger sidearm—better still with the shotgun. However, in terms of energy, the 357 Magnum loaded with a 158-grain bullet at 1200 fps muzzle velocity earns a muzzle energy of more than 500 foot-pounds. The 38 Special firing the same bullet at 950 fps muzzle velocity gains more than 300 foot-pounds of muzzle energy. The 22 Long Rifle, 40-grain bullet, leaving a handgun muzzle at about the speed of sound will turn up around 100 foot-pounds of muzzle energy.

In comparing penetration, a 22 Long Rifle high-velocity solid-nose bullet and 38 Special with 158-grain soft-nose bullet were fired into soft pine blocks. The 38 Special won with about 25 percent more penetration in this one informal demonstration. A 22 Long Rifle hollow-point bullet penetrated only a couple of inches, but did open up to 38-caliber diameter, leaving a rather large hole in the wooden block. Incidentally, a 22 WMR 40-grain bullet at about 1400 fps muzzle velocity from a handgun provided a muzzle energy of 175 foot-pounds.

The greatest penetration for the 22 Long Rifle in one wooden block demonstration was with silhouette ammunition, in this case Winchester brand with 42-grain bullet. Interestingly, expansion was also improved over the standard lead solid-point bullet in this single demonstration. Nonetheless, no 22 ammo penetrated as well as the 38 Special, which in the minds of many police experts is a minimum-power self-protection handgun. Penetration is not, of course, the only criterion for bullet performance in self-defense. But the assailant may be better stopped by a bullet of greater penetration under some circumstances. The initial premise, however, is upheld.

Firepower is another factor to consider when a 22 rimfire is forced into a life-saving situation. While a single 22-caliber 40-grain bullet is not of itself a powerhouse, a semi-automatic pistol or rifle capable of delivering multiple strikes on target can be devastating. In one examination of 22-rimfire repeated-fire performance, Freedom Arms Company

used a prototype fully automatic 22-caliber rifle firing the 22 WMR bullet. The rifle destroyed a brick wall in quick order. While the full-scale rifle is hard to wield in tight places, such as in the home, a tubular-magazine semi-automatic model can deliver a dozen or more rounds in seconds. It is questionable that any intruder would continue his course of action if he encountered such firepower.

If the 22 rimfire must be used defensively in a home, the first choice would be a semi-automatic rifle. It would be chambered for the 22 WMR cartridge. Possibly, ammo would be alternated in the magazine, with a hollow-point or RWS soft-point hollow-point first in line, backed by one full-metal-jacket round for penetration, with the remaining ammo in the magazine of hollow-point design. A second choice would be the 22 WMR sidearm, semi-auto or revolver, with similar ammo selection. Next in line would probably be the 22-rimfire semi-auto rifle, followed by any repeating action, and then the pistol or revolver. Ammo would probably be alternated here, too, with one hollow-point bullet up first, followed by solids, perhaps of the slightly heavier silhouette design.

IN THE RURAL HOME

Pressed into service in defense of life, the 22 rimfire, standard or magnum, has served better than its paper figures would suggest. But there are many around-the-grounds uses for the 22 rimfire that are not so sinister. The 22 rimfire is perhaps the best house gun when these non-life-threatening uses are considered.

One rural dweller found that his attic had been

Stainless steel has found greater acceptance among arms makers. This Ruger 22/22-magnum revolver is of stainless steel construction, very rugged and well-suited to camp or home.

A handy and powerful "miniaturized" magnum is this Marlin Midget Magnum in 22 WMR caliber, a fine rifle for the camp or home.

literally broken into by tree squirrels. He solved that problem with screen and general reinforcement of the upper part of the house. But the squirrels then gnawed on his telephone wire, finally disrupting service. They destroyed several bird feeders and wreaked havoc on birds' nests. When open season on tree squirrels arrived, the house gun went to work, not in removing the entire population of mischief-makers, but in selection of a few that were recognizable as the major destroyers of property (and birds' nests).

The BB Cap was used exclusively. The property owner's squirrel problems were kept in check with annual harvesting from that point on. The house gun was also called upon to take a few rabbits that were invading the garden. The rabbits, as the squirrels before them, were not wasted, but were used as food. These are but two examples of uses for the 22-rimfire house gun in a rural setting.

Shot cartridges have also been used to discourage small close-range pests. One farmer stated that he had removed a number of mice from the premises with 22 Long Rifle shot ammo. However, the use of safety glasses in close-range shot-shooting is imperative. The little shot may rebound. Safety glasses are called for in all shooting. But in firing shot cartridges in close quarters, they are absolutely essential. The range of effectiveness is probably 15 feet on barn mice (an approximation only) and perhaps 20 to 25 feet with the 22 WMR shot round. Rats at a near-the-house dump site were put away regularly with a 22 rimfire by one farmer, another use for the 22 house gun. The rancher, farmer or rural homeowner will find that having a 22 rimfire around is a worthwhile idea. Its employment is varied and valuable.

One rancher friend of mine began to unravel the uses of a particular 22-rimfire rifle on his spread. The list was too unwieldy to present here. However, within the time frame of two years, the rancher had used the little rifle to dispatch four trapped skunks, a number of prairie dogs that were destroying a particularly valuable piece of pastureland, and two coyotes that had returned to kill sheep. He also used the 22 rimfire to "put down" a cow that had fallen from a bank and was too severely injured to be saved, and humanely dispatched a steer and hog for butchering. He also used the rifle for the sad task of putting a ranch dog out of its misery following an accident. A 22 rimfire on ranch or farm is a house gun of immeasurable duty.

THE CAMP GUN

When I lived in Alaska, I quickly learned that a number of trappers and guides carried, or kept in camp, a 22 handgun. I wasn't surprised. The 22 rimfire has been the choice camp gun for decades. I was, however, a little shocked to learn that the camp gun of choice in the African bushveldt was a 22 rifle, or as it was called in Zimbabwe, a two-two. A newcomer to the bush would think of bigger artillery for standby, and, of course, there was always a 458 Winchester or 416 Rigby within reach. But it was the 22 rifle that provided literally all of the services detailed for a camp gun anywhere, including bringing in incidental food. Although the camp setting is a generally safe environment, the little 22 camp gun can be big medicine against small, but dangerous, animals.

Russell Annabel used a 22 rimfire against a rabid coyote. The animal entered camp with biting on its mind and Russell detoured the wild dog with good marksmanship from a 22. In one of my own camps, we encountered a rabid skunk. The unfortunate animal had lost all sense of fear and discretion, and it moved into camp in broad daylight, going straight for a tethered dog. Oddly, the animal never released its quintessential perfume. The skunk went for the dog with open mouth, leaving no doubt of its intention. When a member of the camping party interceded, the animal went straight for her. A single bullet from the 22 camp gun (a rifle) dropped the skunk.

I cannot imagine a big-game camp without a 22 rimfire gun in it, especially, but not exclusively, a rifle. The 22 is the woodsman's utility firearm. Too few big-game hunters recognize the fact that there is quite often small game in the area. When the big-game tag is canceled, the hunt is over. Many of the more remote big-game regions have little to almost no small-game hunting harvest; therefore, these transitory animals succumb only to Dame Nature and old age. Such is as much a part of the grand plan as harvesting these same wild animals; however, there is nothing wrong with putting some of this meat resource into human use as food. The big-game camp without a small-game rifle or handgun is an incomplete camp. Which camp gun for

One cottontail dinner coming up. A serviceable camp gun can also be a 22 pistol.

small game? Which ammo? In fact, it's much more a question of marksmanship than it is ballistic force.

In one high-country elk camp, our party put cottontail rabbits in the pot, plus small (but quite tasty when you know how to cook them) red squirrels, and a couple of mountain grouse. The particular camp rifle was an old H&R Targeteer, an accurate and rugged piece purchased for $35 in used but not abused condition.

This particular rifle always did its best with standard velocity fodder. Two types of rimfire ammo were kept in camp that season: RWS Target and Federal Champions. Both of these had long before proved capable of tight clusters at small-game ranges in the Targeteer. No one needed hollowpoints in this camp because 22 solid-points were adequate for one-shot kills on the small game and mountain grouse (the 22 rimfire is allowed on mountain grouse).

A camp rifle need not be a roughneck firearm. Gene Thompson tries the author's Kimber. His search for a camp rifle settled on the Kimber or Model 75 Sporter, carried in a case when not in use.

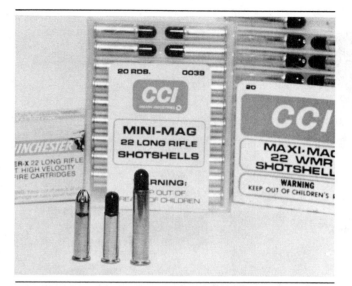

The 22-rimfire shotshell is a useful close-range cartridge. The round on the far left is the conventional 22-Long Rifle shotshell. The one in the middle is another 22 Long Rifle shotshell, but with the plastic dome shot container, and the shell on the right is the same style, but in 22 WMR caliber.

One of the gentlemen in camp said he had never seen a jackrabbit dropped with only one bullet from a 22 Long Rifle, even a hollow-point. On the way off the mountain, we encountered a jackrabbit on the lower part of the ranch. One shot later, the rabbit was in the truck, destined for skillet.

Marksmanship is the key to camp-gun success. Hit the south end of a northbound hare and you've got trouble. Put the bullet through the shoulder region or head and there's no problem. That's why an accurate 22-rimfire rifle with the ammo it likes best is the choice for camp.

But you don't have to use a rifle if you are a good and practiced marksman with a sidearm. The same old advice applies, as always: the pistol should be accurate and it must wear adjustable sights. Rifle type? Any. The semi-auto does offer that firepower mentioned earlier. There are also other types of camp guns. One is the Savage over/under, which has been offered in various chamberings over the years. The 22 rimfire/.410 shotgun combination is usually quite adequate as a camp gun. Its value is obvious—the shotgun is employed in close-range wing-shooting and the 22 rimfire performs its usual service.

The 22-rimfire magnum is another excellent camp gun caliber. It offers greater power if needed,

but it can be used for putting small game into the larder. Marksmanship is again the key to success. A 22 WMR 40- or 50- grain hollow-point or soft-point hollow-point bullet is simply more than what's necessary for small game. But that old chicken-and-egg puzzle arises again—make head shots and meat destruction doesn't matter; so use a hollow-point. Or, make head shots, and you don't need a hollow-point or a 22 magnum. My camp rifle is a 22 rimfire for that reason, firing 22 Long Rifle ammo. My camp pistol is the same oft-mentioned Ruger with heavy barrel. Charter Arms has offered its Explorer rifle in a pistol version called the Explorer II Target Pistol. This semi-auto handgun has the same eight-shot clip, but there's a wrinkle—another eight-shot clip is inserted into the handle of the Explorer II for 16 shots without bothering with clip reloading. The pistol's receiver is fitted with a dovetail notch for scope mounts. Here is a rugged semi-auto pistol that makes a good camp gun.

About snakes. I've lived with rattlers all my life, capturing them in youth for adventure and sharing camps with them in the desert of Arizona and the

Exploring around the campsite, John Fadala takes along a 22-rimfire Marlin Model 39 rifle. A reliable 22 rifle is welcomed in camp for many reasons, including procurement of food.

Another excellent camp rifle is the Marlin Model 70P "Papoose."
It breaks down and fits into a neat and small carrying case.

high badlands of Wyoming. I like the little darlin's and will not bother one without provocation. In my many years of snake experience, however, there have been a few provocations. One rattler poised itself at the toe of my wife's boot just outside of camp. The snake was within striking distance and yet it offered no buzzing warning. It reared back and I moved to Nancy's side to distract the reptile. It uncoiled, moved, and coiled once more. My 22 rimfire sidearm was in action by that time. Had the snake been remote from our camp, we would have backed off. However, with wife and little daughter in that camp for three more days, I dispatched the rattler. But it wasn't wasted; we had overcome food prejudice toward rattler meat more than two decades ago.

That rattlesnake we'd met in Wyoming. A much larger one decided to camp with us on a family outing in Arizona. We tried to evict the fellow from our camp. It was pitch dark and this particular snake was kind enough to buzz. We wanted to repay the favor, so we captured the snake, transported it downhill to an arroyo, and turned it loose. When you have lived a lifetime with rattlers, you learn that they are somewhat individual in specific size, coloration and pattern of rosettes. I'm convinced that the same buzzing reptile revisited that Arizona camp two hours later. With three children and a dog in camp, it was time to act. The snake was put away with a 22-rimfire rifle.

You don't need a gun to kill a snake. A rancher friend from Kaycee, Wyoming, carries a shovel with him as he works his summer range. So if the object were snakes alone, no firearm would be needed. But I learned a little something about shovels and snakes one year. Again, it was in Arizona.

This fellow was huge, large enough to pose a real threat. His striking distance was surprisingly long. I know, because he hit the shovel twice from quite a distance. I decided that the camp was not big enough for the two of us. But by the time I lifted the shovel, Mr. Buzztail was in the brush. I worked the blade of the shovel into the brush, but try as I might, I never managed to sever the snake's head.

The rattler began to work through the dense undergrowth away from camp. "Good enough for me, amigo," I said out loud, but at that the old boy took a turn and headed right back our way. "This shovel can go back to ditch-digging," I told my fellow campers. One shot later that reptile had a 22-caliber hole in the center of his head. Then the shovel was put to use.

Always sever the head and bury it or place it beneath a heavy rock. A small boy in Tucson died when venom from a dead snake entered the lad's bloodstream as he and another youth played catch with the carcass. That head is a repository of deadly poison, alive or dead. Get rid of it.

A shovel is fine, but I'll take the camp gun for snake dispatch. The most important aspect of shooting a dangerous snake is to watch out for bullet deflection or ricochet from the earth. Hardpan—dry, hard earth—may well bring such deflection. There are two easy ways of overcoming the problem. The first is to move in a circle around the snake until a safe angle presents itself. There will be one. You just have to look for it. The second way to overcome the problem of ricochet is with a shot cartridge in your 22 rimfire, standard or magnum. Shot will bounce and rebound from a hard surface, too, but its journey is short. This does not mean to shoot without regard for the destination of the shot charge. Not at all. However, the tiny shot from a 22-rimfire round will not travel far, not nearly as far as a 22 bullet.

How effective is shot against snakes? Very. The reason is range. We are speaking in terms of a few feet from muzzle to target. In fact, you can sway the muzzle in front of the snake's head. The snake's eyes will generally follow that motion, and when its head is in rhythm with the muzzle, pull the trigger.

Naturally, there will be differences of opinion regarding the "snake gun." A Wyoming rabies-control official, in having to work daily in skunk habitat, also a perfect place for rattlers, combined one firearm for killing rabid animals and rattlers. He chose the 22 WMR revolver, the first two chambers carrying shot cartridges, followed by CCI Maxi-Mag hollow-points. He reported that the fine shot deterred a snake strike. The snake is not tough-hided. Twenty-two WMR shotshells used at 10 to 15 feet distance killed rattlers quite well for the officer. He also killed rabid skunks with the shot charge, although he counted on the backup rounds in the cylinder to administer the coup de grâce on these animals. This outdoorsman found that the plastic container for the 22 WMR shotshell prevented the shot charge from scattering at close range; therefore, multiple pellet strikes on the snake's head were the rule. Such tightly clustered pellets were also responsible for effectiveness on rabid skunks.

The ever-useful 22 rimfire proves itself valuable in the home, especially in a rural setting. The 22 is well-employed on ranch or farm as well. And it serves a wide range of valuable jobs at the campsite. While it is not the self-defense gun of choice, it may be the first defense firearm that is there when needed. In semi-auto form, it can be quite effective. With reasonable bullet placement, the 22 rimfire, especially the 22 WMR, can deter attacks from many sources. The 22 is a big-game camp's small-game procurer, and a dispatcher of dangerous snakes when there's no clear alternative choice in the matter. The camp without a 22 is incomplete.

22 THE FEISTY 22 HORNET

The 22 Hornet has seen fame, decline, and comeback. The little cartridge provided the fuel for a blast-off into the world of high-velocity 22 centerfires. But in the 1950s, it was shot down by the advent of the 222 Remington. The Hornet burned for a while, then rose from its ashes like the mythical Phoenix. The 22 Hornet embodied the early dreams of shooters who wanted a small-caliber cartridge capable of medium-range varmint hunting. The round was also touted for small game. And it became one of the premier turkey-hunting numbers of all time. Handloaders gave it versatility with cast lead bullets and jacketed missiles. Today, the Hornet still exhibits that versatility. Its chameleon character changes from small-game cartridge to varminter at its owner's whim. It can play the role of 22 Long Rifle, 22 WMR, or itself with the adjustment of a powder measure. Hornet-chambered rifles from used to new, utility grade to showpiece, abound.

THE BIRTH OF HARWOOD'S HORNET

The sire of the 22 Hornet was Reuben Harwood. In a March 22, 1894, issue of *Shooting and Fishing* magazine, the forerunner of *The American Rifleman* journal, the Massachusetts gunsmith was credited with a 22-centerfire cartridge "for small game shooting." It was the 25-20 Winchester Single Shot round (not the later 25-20 Winchester) necked down to accept 22-caliber bullets. Harwood used black powder in his cartridge, 16 to 20 grains weight of it, behind lead bullets of from 55 to 63 grains heavy. The story goes that an observer made a remark to the effect that the Harwood in-

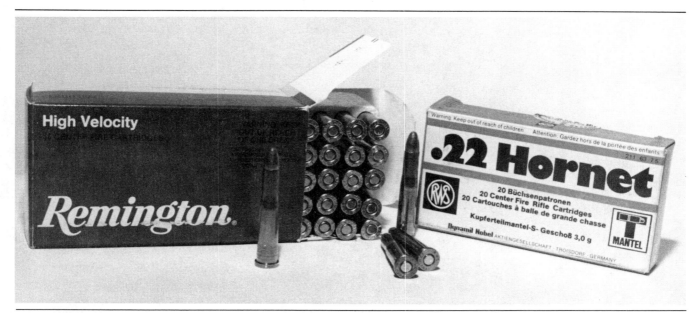

The 22 Hornet is still going strong. Ammunition is made by many companies, including Remington and RWS. The little cartridge fills a niche of its own, and many shooters call it ideal in that niche.

vention was a regular hornet, thereby naming the cartridge. The new cartridge was baptized by J. Stevens Arms & Tool Company in March 1894 with an announcement of a commercial example. There may have been J. Stevens Hornets; however, collectors don't seem to have either Stevens round or rifle in their holdings. Did the Ideal Manufacturing Company (later to be Lyman) offer a bullet mould for Harwood's baby? That, too, was announced, but perhaps never transpired. However, these announcements piqued interest in the round all the same.

Harwood's Hornet was no barn burner with black powder. The cartridge would fail for the time being. In late 1894 its inventor fell ill, and though he did not die, his work declined. He was known to continue writing for *Shooting and Fishing* magazine under the names of Iron Ramrod and Aberdeen for some time to come, but little more of his 22-centerfire cartridge was heard. The round, however, was reborn later as the 22 Lovell (*see* Chapter 27, "The 22 Wildcat"). The original concept of the 22 Hornet post-dated its inventor by many years. In June of 1930, US Army ordnance captain, Grosvenor L. Wotkyns, provided a two-page manuscript describing experiments with a necked-down 22 WCF cartridge firing bullets of .223-inch diameter. Colonel Townsend Whelen would be the voice for this cartridge, telling the world about it. Whelen would write of the cartridge in *The American Rifleman* magazine many times. In late 1930 he spoke of it, and then in September of 1931 he used its name, the "22 Hornet." This cartridge was, of course, the second 22 Hornet, following Harwood's original.

Whelen was responsible for organizing a three-member 22 Hornet fan club: Al Woodworth of the Springfield Armory, Captain George Woody, and himself. Woodworth was a designer, Woody a tool-and-die man, and Whelen an innovator and spokesman for the trio, disseminating information on the cartridge and coordinating efforts for its development and eventual manufacture. The "Three Ws" had test rifles built for the Hornet in its early configuration. Bullets for test-firing were provided by using metal-cased missiles designed for the 5.5mm Velo Dog revolver round. These bullets were also turned backwards and run through forming dies, resulting in a 45-grain flat-based soft-point jacketed bullet for the Hornet. Through the Spring of 1930, the Three Ws continued their efforts, using du Pont 1204 powder with 40- to 45-grain bullets

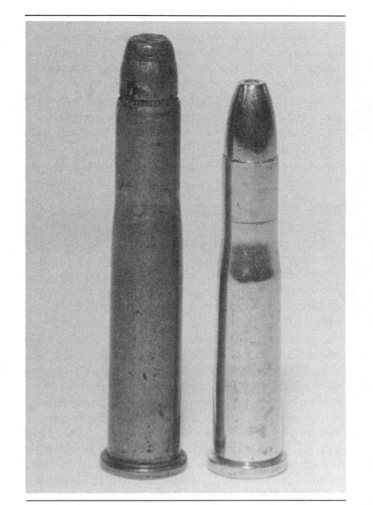

The 25-20 Single Shot cartridge (left) was used by many experimenters in the early days of wildcatting. The 22 Hornet's shape (right) is not so dissimilar to the old round.

with a muzzle velocity of about 2400 fps. Woody made a new bullet for the round as well, using the 22 Short case for a jacket by cutting the head off and incorporating a lead core.

The Three Ws named the cartridge the Wotkyns Hornet, continuing the suggestion that it stung like the insect. It did not take long for this Hornet to buzz off the ground. In October 1930, Edwin Pugsley, vice president and general manager of Winchester, made a decision to produce the cartridge. Winchester made ammo, but did not offer a rifle until 1933, when the excellent Model 54 was chambered for the 22 Hornet round. Incidentally, the Hornet would become known in Europe as the 5.6mm R (rimmed). The 5.6mm × 35 R Vierling was used in Germany for many years. It was essentially a modern loading for the 22 WCF, using smokeless powder and producing Hornet-like ballistics with bullets of 38.6 grains, 40.0 grains and 46.3 grains weight, in full-metal-jacket, lead, soft-point flat-nose, soft-point round-nose, and soft-point hollow-point styles. These bullet types reveal the varied employment of the Vierling, from lead practice and small-game bullet to hollow-point for varmints. The Hornet would exhibit the same multi-talented versatility.

GUNS FOR THE HORNET

Griffin & Hobbs, later to be the famous rifle-making firm of Griffin & Howe, produced a 22 Hornet chambering early in the game, advertising it in July of 1930 as the ".22 Cal. express rifle." Savage proved its early interest in the cartridge by offering its Model 23D bolt-action. The 23D was available from 1931 to 1947, and is still found for sale at gun shows and in arms newspapers today. Savage also offered a Model 219 break-action rifle in 22 Hornet, from 1948 into 1965. The Savage Model 340, a sturdy if not handsome rifle, was also chambered for the Hornet. Its tenure ran from 1948 into 1986. Winchester's Model 54 bolt-action 22 Hornet was followed by the Model 70's chambering of the cartridge. The little Hornet in that full-scale rifle was like imprisoning a fly in a gorilla cage, but the end result was a "sweet-shooting" outfit. If 22 Hornet recoil was nil in the smaller Savage 23D, imagine how mild the round was in the bigger Model 70 rifle. In 1957, Winchester decided to discontinue the Model 70 Hornet. The Model 43 bolt-action rifle, sized much more appropriately for the cartridge, and far less expensive than the 70, was offered in two grades in 22 Hornet.

The cartridge caught on quickly. The 1932 Stoeger catalogue offered the expensive Webley & Scott magazine rifle, as well as the Scott Martini rifle, which cost almost $200 at a time when Winchester's Model 54 was selling for about half a hundred. The Martini could be ordered in 22 Hornet in 1932—"On special order this rifle will be made up, at no extra charge, for the new .22 W.C.F. 'Hornet' cartridge," the advertisement read. The same 1932 catalogue spoke of "THE SENSATIONAL HORNET CARTRIDGE" in connection with the Savage 23D, which sold for $32.95 that year. The Hornet was hot. A Luna Target Rifle, selling for $120, was also offered in "Winchester C.F. Hornet" in 1932. This was a falling-block single-shot rifle with Lyman target iron sights. The Luna was made by Ernst Friederich Buechel, designer of world-class target sidearms. Furthermore, a No. 956 single-shot bolt-action Hornet could be purchased for $18.50. It weighed only 4 pounds, 14 ounces with its 24-inch barrel, and was called the Light Precision Rifle. When the military looked for a survival rifle larger than 22 rimfire, they gave the nod to the 22 Hornet. The Harrington & Richardson (H&R) Model M-4 bolt-action, takedown barrel, collapsible-stock rifle was chambered in 22 Hornet. Ithaca Gun Company made a Model M-6 survival gun for the Air Force. It was an over/under, top-break rifle with chambers for 22 Hornet and .410 shotgun.

The Hornet fell into decline for a while with the introduction of the 222 Remington cartridge; however, the interest of a large body of shooters brought the round back, not only in utility-type rifles, but in several high-quality models as well. Both Sako and Walther had been offering fine 22 Hornet rifles. Brno's 22 bolt-action Hornet was another top-drawer model. Anschutz gave the rifleman an exceptional rifle chambered for the Hornet. Ruger's No. 3 provided a well-made 22 Hornet for the single-shot fan. Thompson/Center's Contender pistol could be ordered with a 22 Hornet barrel. T/C's Single-Shot rifle was also a Hornet offering. The pretty Beeman/Krico could be ordered in 22 Hornet if the shooter so desired. And Kimber's superb rifle made another 22 Hornet chambering.

HANDLOADING THE HORNET TODAY

Original Hornet ballistics have been greatly outdistanced because of modern powders better-suited to its small case capacity. In the early 1930s, the 22 Hornet round was offered with a 45-grain jacketed soft-point bullet (at $3.25 per 100 rounds). In the early 1940s, the Hornet was still available with a 45-grain jacketed bullet, soft-point, advertised at 2,650 fps muzzle velocity. However, a 46-grain jacketed hollow-point bullet had been added at the same muzzle velocity. Today, factory ammunition runs with the same advertised velocity. But the handloader can push the 45-grain bullet at 2875 fps muzzle velocity, which represents the velocity obtained in a 22-inch barrel using 12.0 grains of W-296 powder. That raises muzzle energy to 826 foot-pounds. A 50-grain bullet from the same barrel achieved a muzzle velocity of 2690 fps using 11.5 grains of W-296 powder (matching advertised ve-

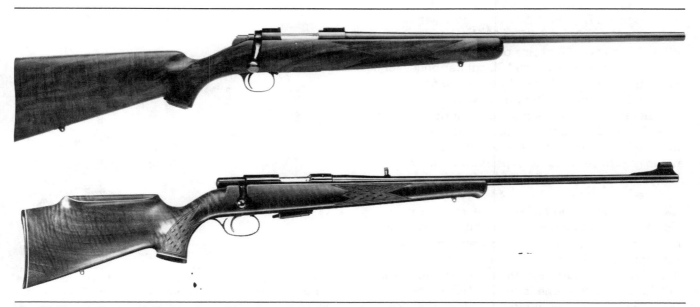

The 22 Hornet is currently chambered in some of the finest rifles of any era, including the excellent Kimber (above) and the Anschutz Model 1432 rifle (below). The small cartridge allows a petite rifle built around a short action.

locity with a 45-grain bullet) for a muzzle energy of 803 foot-pounds.

As with handloading for all cartridges, results vary among individual rifles. The particular test rifle for this work liked W-296 powder, but also did well with No. 2400. However, 9.0 grains of 2400 proved to be about maximum in the test rifle, at least in terms of good case life. That charge provided a muzzle velocity in the test rifle of 2513 fps with the 45-grain bullet. The same 9.0-grain charge using H-4227 powder yielded 2375 fps muzzle velocity. Handloading the 22 Hornet gives it that wide range of utility. One of the most accurate test loads for this work came with a cast bullet, for example. Lyman's No. 225415 Alloy No. 2 cast 49-grain projectile and 3.0 grains of Unique gave a muzzle velocity of 1334 fps. Here we have a strong 22 Long Rifle load. It's an ideal small-game taker, allowing the shooter to use his fine little Hornet just as he would a 22 rimfire in the small-game field. A bit stronger load with the same 49-grain cast bullet was 4.5 grains of Unique for a muzzle velocity of 1777 fps from the 22-inch barrel. However, Hornady's full-metal-jacket 55-grain bullet flew from the Hornet's muzzle at 2386 fps using 10.0 grains of W-296 powder. Where the full-metal-jacket bullet is allowed for turkey hunting, a good shot could employ the 22 Hornet and this 55-grain projectile in fine

fashion. The Contender also gave good ballistics. For example, a 45-grain pill pushed off at 2365 fps using 12.5 grains of IMR-4227 powder.

The promised three-way loading versatility of the 22 Hornet is easily delivered. The above cast-bullet load is a glorified 22 Long Rifle load (or 22 WRF). The 45- to 50-grain bullets at muzzle velocities nearing 2900 fps offer varminting to ranges of approximately 200 yards. And the full-metal-jacket bullet, or any tougher jacketed missile, can be used on wild turkeys. The 22 Hornet is also a javelina cartridge. After all, it surpasses the energy delivered by the 22 WMR, a "pig" round. Of course, the 22 Hornet has been used on big game, especially by the Eskimos of the northlands. More on this in Chapter 28. The 22 Hornet was not devised for big-game hunting and is disallowed in many regions.

That it has been used for big game attests to two facts: shooters will try anything, and expert hunters and marksmen can do with small calibers what persons with less woods education cannot. Bullets for the Hornet are now .224-inch diameter. However, Sierra offers a .223-inch bullet in 40 or 45 grains. These bullets are especially matched to older rifles. Remember that original 22 Hornets fired bullets of .223-inch diameter, a diminishment in size over the .228-inch bullets commonly used in the 22 Savage Imp or 22 Hi-Power and the 22 Niedner Magnum. Bullets of .228-inch diameter often weighed 60 to 80 grains. The 22 Hornet was better off with bullets of 50 grains or less. In 1933, RB Sisk of Iowa Park, Texas, offered 22-caliber bullets of 36 to 40 grains for the Hornet. These bullets worked well in the Hornet's 1:16 rate of twist.

Bullet selection is essential to 22 Hornet field success. The bullet-making companies have seen to it that we have thin-skinned bullets for the little Hornet to guarantee reliable expansion at modest velocity. This is why Sierra offers a Blitz bullet, a thin-jacketed projectile for the Hornet. Hornady has an SX (Super Explosive) bullet for the same reason. Nosler also offers proper Hornet bullets, as does Speer. However, bullet selection goes beyond blow-up capability. Since the Hornet is also considered a fine wild-turkey cartridge, the explosive missile is not the only proper one to feed it. Harder bullets offering less expansion at modest velocity are also valuable in this cartridge. These harder bullets are also more correct for javelina hunting, since penetration of hide and hair is vital to a successful harvest. The range of bullet choice for the Hornet is wonderfully varied, then, from the cast lead projectile for practice and small game to the harder (even full-metal-jacketed) bullet, where allowed, for wild turkey.

ACCURACY

Until much work with the 22 PPC USA, my own belief in accurate vs. non-accurate cartridges was not established. The 22 PPC USA round convinced me that one cartridge could be inherently more accurate than another similar cartridge. Too many fine groups had been registered with the slope-shouldered 300 H&H Magnum (even at 1,000 yards) for me to buy the accurate cartridge theory. However, certain aspects of cartridge design do lend themselves to improved levels of accuracy potential. The 22 Hornet is entirely adequate in accuracy for its intended task. It is not a benchrest cartridge, however. Tests with three different models, two of them very fine pieces, produced no startling results at 200 yards. The majority of 100-yard groups averaged about 1.25 inches. At 200 yards, these groups sizes "held steady" with 2.5-inch clusters. Of course, there were some larger groups and a number of smaller ones. A cast-bullet load provided .75-inch 100-yard groups in one rifle, for example. In brief, the 22 Hornet, while not a benchrest round, is

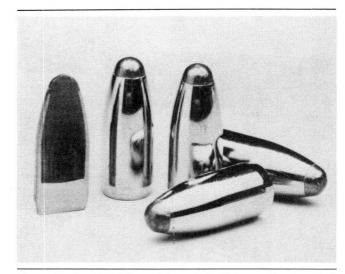

These Nosler Solid Base 45-grain bullets are engineered for the Hornet cartridge (and the 218 Bee). Jackets are thin for quick expansion at Hornet velocities.

more than sufficiently accurate for its intended service.

SIGHT-IN

In tests, the best sight-in for potential of trajectory was with a 45-grain bullet at about 2900 fps muzzle velocity. With the rifle sighted two inches high at 100 yards, the group centered about 1.5 inches high at 150 yards and about an inch low at 200. The test rifle was shot to 250 yards and printed about a half-foot low at that distance. Call it a 200-yard cartridge. At that range, energy with the 45-grain bullet is down to about 400 foot-pounds. In a shootout with a 50-grain bullet at about 2800 fps muzzle velocity, a sight-in of two inches high at 100 yards put the bullet back on track at about 175 yards and a couple of inches low at 200.

THE HORNET ON WILD TURKEYS AND JAVELINA

The little Hornet came into my life off a side-trail. I had purchased my first hunting dog, bought with dollars and traded labor. The pup was in the back of my car, and I wanted to show her to a friend. Jim Martin admired the dog and then said, "Now let me show you what I've got." His show-and-tell was a rifle, Winchester Model 43 deluxe, caliber 22 Hornet. I admitted that I would like to shoot that rifle, and we wasted no time getting to the desert, which was in those days a couple minutes from the heart of Tucson, where Jim and I lived. Jackrabbits were easily located and the quick dispatch of the first one we found left an India ink impression on the ledger of my memory. "Wow!," we both said, for Jim had not yet done much varminting with the little rifle and he was as impressed as I with the results. Soft-point factory ammo was quite explosive. That explosiveness is what originally turned me away from the 22 Hornet as a premium wild-turkey cartridge. In spite of the interest created by Jim's little rifle, I did not run out and buy one for myself.

But I did run across my second Hornet while on a wild turkey hunt in central Arizona. The big Merriams bird put to bag with the Hornet was very badly chewed up. It might be a heck of a jackrabbit rifle, I told myself, but it certainly was all wrong for gobblers. Of course, the fault lay not in the Hornet, but in the loads, which were intended for fast annihilation of varmints. They were not right for wild turkeys—not then, not now. However, several dedicated wild-turkey hunters have taken the 22 Hornet as their prince of all gobbler rifles. My own turkey favorite, the 22-rimfire magnum, is outreached by the Hornet, and the latter would be better where longer range shooting of the bearded bird is encountered. Where I hunt gobblers, ranges are short and the 22 WMR is entirely adequate. In fact, I'd want no greater power. The Hornet is considered the best wild-turkey round by a number of experts because it will do the job not only at close range, but also across Black Hills canyons and to the center of western parks or meadows where the big birds are often found.

In the hands of a careful marksman and practiced hunter, the 22 WMR is also a valid javelina rifle. If that's true, then the 22 Hornet must be considered as good as, or better than, the rimfire number. It's a matter of raw ballistics that cannot be denied.

The Anschutz Exemplar pistol is also chambered for the 22 Hornet cartridge. The varminter or wild-turkey hunter would consider this pistol a challenging firearm in the field.

Select the harder missiles. Bullets intended to come unglued on 150-yard 10-pound woodchucks are not suitable for a mature musk hog that might dress out at 35 pounds, 50 pounds on the hoof. Sufficient penetration is required for the bullet to reach the vitals. A "wild pig" bagged with the Hornet and Nosler's 50-grain Spitzer Solid-Base bullet simply flopped down immediately to move no more. A cleaner harvest you could not ask for. Basic methods of javelina hunting have been discussed elsewhere and will not be repeated here. However, the idea is to get close, putting the little 22 Hornet bullet right on target.

CURRENT USE

On the face of it, several small 22-centerfire cartridges have outclassed the 22 Hornet. The 222 Remington is certainly one of them. If accuracy is indeed more than a matter of good bullets from good barrels, and at least in part a matter of cartridge-case design, surely the 222 eclipses the Hor-

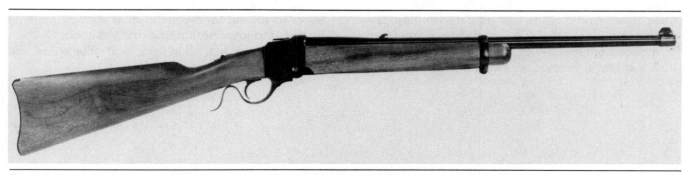

Ruger's No. 3 Carbine is another interesting rifle chambered in 22 Hornet. This handy single-shot model would be excellent in wild-turkey coverts.

net. A number of benchrest events have been won by 222s, but 22 Hornets are as scarce in benchrest rifles as snakes in Ireland. But the little Hornet is "spot on" for many shooting events. For instance, the comparatively quiet Hornet can be the ticket for shooting up to 200 yards, especially in the eastern United States, and anywhere else varmints dwell amidst dense human population. The mild-mannered Hornet, with soft-shelled bullets, does a real job on 'chucks and other varmints at such ranges. It will do the same on a coyote at that distance.

The Hornet's tiny size allows equally petite rifles to be built around it, sleek as combed cats. These rifles are trim and light in the hand. Furthermore, the Hornet is economical to shoot. Cartridge cases last 10 shots and more—one case was loaded 15 times to test it, and the primer pocket held its primer to the end of the run, but there is no sense in being greedy about it. Any time you can get 10 reloads from a cartridge case, economy is assured. Also, powder charges are small. A single pound of powder will load up to 700 rounds, depending upon the load and powder type, of course. Barrel life is long too. The mild Hornet is not hard on anything. Period. It doesn't even require "hot" primers. All loads described here were worked up with standard small rifle primers only.

THE 218 BEE

This chapter is the notch for the 218 Bee, because the good little cartridge is really no more than a 22 Hornet. Yes, the 218 will gather up a few more feet per second, and as noted in this text elsewhere, shooting is a matter of inches and feet, inches of trajectory and foot-pounds of energy. However, the little 218 does not really surpass the Hornet by enough margin to crow about. Shooters know it. The 218 Bee is not currently chambered widely. The fine Kimber Model 82 Sporter is available in this caliber, and anyone choosing it over the Hornet has my blessings; however, expect Hornet performance from the Bee and not a lot more. In a 24-inch test barrel (remember that the Hornet was tested with the 22-inch tube), a 45-grain bullet departed the muzzle at 2912 fps using 14.5 grains of H-4198. Stronger than the Hornet? Sure. How much stronger? A little.

Winchester brought the 218 Bee to market in 1938. The Winchester Model 65 lever-action rifle, a modified Model 94, was chambered for the cartridge, as was the Winchester Model 43, mentioned earlier. The cartridge was built by necking down a 32-20 Winchester to 22 caliber. It's always dangerous to advise for or against a certain cartridge. But the 218 Bee, despite ballistics that slightly surpass the Hornet (such as a 45-grain bullet with 12.0 grains of 2400 for 2911 fps muzzle velocity), is not given its own chapter because it does not currently enjoy wide popularity. It remains a favorite of some shooters, of course. Don Randall, who used to guide for big game near Dubois, Wyoming, believed strongly in his 218 Bee. You couldn't trade him out of it. When something works for you, keep it. The 218 works for Don, and a number of others. It's a fine cartridge in its own little niche, but that niche is occupied more fully by the 22 Hornet's popularity.

The waters of 22 Hornet invention are muddied because so many shooters seemed to crave a hot 22 centerfire at about the same time. The Vierling is certainly an example of this. The great gunman Adolph Niedner's 22 Magnum, a necked down 32-20 Winchester, is in line with the 22 Hornet. So were other rounds. Its factual conception, however, is not as important as two other things—the Hornet was indeed the catalyst that helped to generate other 22 centerfire cartridges, and the Hornet still works. It works very well. What it won't do is just as important as what it will do. It won't break the bank in ammo cost. It won't rattle the ears off a wooden jackass. It won't frighten the livestock into the next county. And it won't ricochet a bullet into Farmer Jones's lower 40 two miles away. What it will do is serve its master for medium-range varminting, wild turkey, and javelina hunting and just plain 22-centerfire shooting fun, all in trim, neat rifles enjoyable to own and shoot.

23 THE 222 REMINGTON AND ITS CENTERFIRE COUSINS

Mike Walker, Remington's great gun mind, was instrumental in bringing this stand-by-itself cartridge to life in 1950, a development unique on several counts. The 222 Remington was a new design. It was not derived by altering an existing cartridge case, as was the 22-250 Remington, for example. Nor was the cartridge related to predecessors, such as the Hornet's kinship with the 25-20 Winchester Single Shot. The 222 was the first entirely new cartridge to leave the drawing board following World War II. It was also the first 22 centerfire cartridge that was rimless—not semi-rimmed—but as rimless as the 30-06. In fact, if you were describing the 222 Remington to someone who had never seen one, you would do well to draw a mental picture suggesting a scaled-down 30-06 round. Third, the 222 filled a ballistic pigeonhole between the 22 Hornet and the 220 Swift. Several wildcats had previously occupied that ballistic territory, but the 222 Remington was the first factory cartridge to claim that ground. The name was catchy, two-two-two, but it related to no particular aspect of the cartridge. With its land-to-land measurement of .219 inch and its groove diameter of .224 inch, there was nothing "two-two-two" about the 222. The standard rate of twist was decided at 1:14, one turn in 14 inches, and this has remained so, except for Sears offering a 222 rifle with 1:16 twist. Currently, the 222's brother cartridge, the 223 Remington, may be found with a very fast rate of twist geared to stabilize the heavier, streamlined 22-caliber jacketed bullet.

In Remington's bolt-action Model 722 rifle, the 222 produced fine accuracy from the start. Its reputation did not have to suffer in an early utility rifle, as have other rounds that later proved their merit only after being chambered in precision arms. Furthermore, good factory ammunition was available immediately. Remington insisted on it. Today, one finds 222 factory ammo from all of the companies a cut above many other rounds. Therefore, the shooter had an accurate cartridge in an accurate rifle, with accurate ammunition from Day One of 222 availability. It is no wonder that the reputation of the round grew amazingly fast. The 222 Remington remains atop the heap of 22 centerfires today. If it is deposed, it will fall to its cousin, the 223 Remington, which seems destined to catch and pass it in popularity.

THE BENCHREST BOYS

The 222 Remington gained fame rapidly among the worshipers of accuracy. The cartridge was made to order, with a small capacity case, the use

The 222 family includes the 222 Remington (left), 223 Remington (center), and 222 Remington Magnum cartridges.

A very accurate 222 Remington was built on the Sako L-461 action with Hart barrel and PPC insert. The 222 family of cartridges has proved very effective in the varmint field as well as at the benchrest match.

of a small rifle primer, good case design with proper powder-burning features, 100 percent loading density—the small case worked well when filled to capacity with certain powders—nil felt recoil, and mild report. The round went on to win many benchrest matches. Unseating it has been terrifically difficult. When the 22 PPC was making itself felt at the benchrest matches, 222 devotees said that the only reason the little PPC was whipping the 222 was availability of high-precision match cases for the PPC. In short, the 222 would be just as accurate, or more so, if it enjoyed such precision brass. Dr. Lou Palmisano, co-inventor of the 22 PPC, had some high-grade 222 brass brought into the country, which he sold at cost to the benchresters. But the 222 did not prove more accurate than the 22 PPC, even with match-grade cases. Nonetheless, 222 Remington accuracy remains her-

alded far and wide—deservedly so. A slight alteration in the configuration of the 222 Remington case became known as the 222$\frac{1}{2}$ Remington. This mildly different round won many matches and was considered by some benchresters the best of the high-accuracy cartridges.

The 222 had also established itself as a fine intermediate-range varmint cartridge. The applause here was also deserved. Certainly it was good up to 250 yards, and the experts were doing just fine with it on varmints up to 300 yards from the muzzle. Ballistics centered around a 50-grain projectile at 3200 fps muzzle velocity. As shown below, this gave a very flat trajectory out to 250 yards, and allowed precise bullet placement as far as 300 yards from the muzzle when the shooter was expert at range determination and at figuring bullet drop and wind drift. The 222 was a dream come true for all the varminters who wanted a commercial round matching one of the middle-ground 22-centerfire wildcats. Mild-mannered, with long barrel and case life, economical to shoot, you might say that the 222 Remington was so good that developing any other cartridge to occupy the same ballistic slot would be ludicrous. But that's just what happened, not once, but twice in succession.

THE 222'S COUSINS

Shortly after 222 Remington ammo was on the gunstore shelf, Remington was at work drawing up another cartridge very much like it, not for sporting use (at the time), but for the military. The Army wanted a small cartridge of high velocity, flat trajectory, and reasonably good penetration powers for the battlefield. Such a cartridge would result in low recoil. It would allow a lighter rifle. And the soldier could carry a great deal of ammo, especially as compared with the larger 30-06 round or even the newer and smaller 308. By 1957 the military gave a nod to this cartridge. It would be chambered in an Armalite AR-15 automatic rifle. We would come to know it as the 223 Remington. The military would call it a 5.56 × 45mm NATO. By 1964, the U.S. Armed Forces adopted the 223 widely, with a 55-grain full-metal-jacket bullet at about 3200 fps muzzle velocity (5.56 × 45mm Ball M193). By 1981, NATO had its 5.56 × 45mm, with a

The more powerful 22-250 Remington cartridge (center) did not put the skids under the 222 Remington because the smaller cartridge filled a specific ballistic niche in which it prevailed for many years.

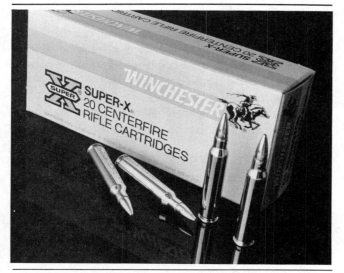

The 223 Remington has become the most popular of the 222 family trio. Factory loads abound. Surplus military ammo is available. Here is a Winchester varmint load for the 223, firing a 53-grain hollow-point bullet.

Belgian FN-designed 68-grain (SS109) projectile, a semi-armor-piercing bullet fired in rifles with a 1:7 rate of twist for stabilization. Other alterations took place, including a 5.6 × 45mm KY IWK German load with a 77-grain flat-based bullet at just over 2700 fps muzzle velocity. This ammo was stabilized in 1:7⅞ rate of twist.

The other cartridge to spin off from the original 222 Remington was called the 222 Remington Magnum. It, too, was originally thought up as a development for the military, but it became instead a sporting round. The 222 Magnum was not a magnum in any sense of the term—no belted case, no outlandish muzzle velocity, no extra-heavy projectile, or any other attribute to suggest a bigger-than-average cartridge. It was then, and is now, one fine round. Developed by Remington in 1958, this experimental military design never gained great popularity. Thus, the two offshoots of the 222 shared different fates, one becoming a military round of worldwide fame, now crowding the 222 in popularity as a sporting cartridge, while the other lounged in the shade, in spite of good ballistics and high accuracy potential. Perhaps there simply was not enough additional thrust in the 222 Magnum to rec-

John Fadala tries a 222 in the varmint field, using a carrying bag as a rest. The 222 Remington has proved itself one of the best 300-yard varmint cartridges of all time.

ommend it. All three rounds offered long cartridge-case and barrel life, plus a wide range of loads. But similarity among the three was also undeniable—the 222 Remington case is 1.700 inches long; the 223 Remington case is 1.760 inches in length; and the 222 Remington Magnum case is 1.850 inches from base to neck.

Of course, all three have devoted followers. A relative of mine owns a 222 Remington Magnum and has declared in diamond-hard terms that it surpasses the range of the standard 222 Remington by 75 to perhaps 100 yards in varminting performance. When his loads were run across the screens of the chronograph, however, they proved to offer fewer than 100 fps jump on the smaller 222. The reverse is every bit as true—222 Remington fans insist that the 223 or 222 Magnum could never compete on the accuracy range. But that is not so. Both are highly accurate. Chamber the 222, 223, or 222 Magnum in identical rifles and accuracy differences are going to be inconsequential. In fact, one benchrest match not long ago was won by a rifle chambered for the 222 Magnum cartridge. Com-

parison of the trio is like arguing the benefits of automobile engines in 300, 305, or 310 horsepower. On the highway, such horsepower differences are going to be difficult to distinguish. Likewise with these three 22 centerfires. They are all accurate. They are all effective. Rather than nitpicking at minor differences, all three are treated simultaneously under each heading below. Incidentally, for the sake of uniformity, every load listed below was built around a Remington R-P (new) case, with Remington No. 7½ benchrest primers only.

THE 222 FAMILY IN THE VARMINT FIELD

Those who wish to call the 222 Remington a 250-yard varmint cartridge, the 223 a 275-yard varmint round, and the 222 Magnum a full 300-yard harvester of varmints are welcome to the distinction. Owning a rifle chambered for the 222 Remington cartridge and having tested several 223s and 222 Magnums, the difference in potential is minuscule up to 300 yards. The 222 Magnum has an inch or so less drop in its favor at 300. And that's about it. Firing a 50-grain bullet, the straight 222 Remington developed a muzzle velocity of 3266 fps in a 24-inch barrel in the tests run for this work. This velocity was earned with 20.0 grains of H-4198 powder. Accuracy was splendid in the test rifle, a custom-made piece, with a 24-inch heavy Hart barrel free-floated on a Sako L-461 action, single-shot, with heavy stock and a PPC insert (for very close tolerance lockup of cartridge in the chamber). This rifle currently wears a Bushnell 4X-12X scope for field versatility (prairie dogs to coyotes), but was topped with a 24X scope for these tests. Considering the accuracy and the fact that 350 cartridges could be loaded with one pound of powder, H-4198 powder and a 50-grain bullet remained a standard throughout field testing. Another excellent 222 Remington varmint load was concocted with either 52- or 53-grain match bullets in front of 23.0 grains of H-4895 powder. Velocity proved to be only 3010 fps in the test rifle, but accuracy was very good out to 300 yards.

A "hot one" for the 223 Remington drove the 60-grain bullet at 3166 fps muzzle velocity with 27.0 grains of W-748 powder. Out of the 24-inch barrel, a 50-grain bullet was shoved away at 3400 fps. The fastest 222 Remington load with the same 50-grain bullet cut the airways at about 3300 fps. There's your difference in plain figures—100 fps. Nothing? No, it's 100 fps. But it takes no Tibetan thinker to figure that these two rounds are in the same varminting arena. The better loads for the 222 Remington Magnum drove the 50-grain pill at essentially the same muzzle velocity derived from the 223 Remington. The two test rifles, both with 24-inch barrels, proved just about equal in a meeting with the chronograph. In devising a sight-in system for the 222 clan, groups were clustered two inches high at 100 yards. The 222 Remington was used, firing a 50-grain bullet at a chronographed muzzle velocity of 3250 fps. The tight group centered about 1.25 inches high at 150 yards, right about on at 200 (perhaps a scant bit low—it's not always easy to discern minor differences in bullet drop when interpreting the center of impact of the group), about 3.5 inches low at 250 yards, and a half-foot low at 300.

Naturally, each rifle would have to be carefully sighted with its own particular best varmint load. The above figures, however, serve as a close approximation of expected trajectory pattern. Sight in about two inches high at 100 yards with a strong varmint load in the 222 Remington, 223, or 222 Magnum, and you can expect a hold-right-on dis-

tance of 250 to 260 yards, with 300 yard hits commensurate with the shooter's ability to judge the range accurately and dope the bullet's path to the target. Remaining energy at 300 yards, when the 50-grain bullet begins at about 3300 fps, is in the neighborhood of 450 to 475 foot-pounds. That about matches the arrival energy of the 22 Hornet's 50-grain bullet at 200 yards. If the 22 Hornet is acceptable at 200 yards, the 222 brothers are all good for 300-yard varminting. Or to look at it another way: the 222, 223, and 222 Magnum are more powerful at 300 yards than the 22 WMR is at the muzzle with its 40-grain bullet starting at 1850 fps. Even when that same bullet exits from the 22 WMR at 2100 fps, it develops just below 400 foot-pounds. Yet, the 22 WMR at point-blank range is quite adequate for varmints. Naturally, there are considerations other than bullet energy, especially bullet performance at various ranges. Nonetheless, the 222 Remington and its near-alikes do deliver the goods as far as 300 yards from the muzzle in the varminting field.

ACCURACY LOADS

Since the 222 Remington has been considered a prime benchrest cartridge since its inception, it is appropriate to talk about expected accuracy. The 222 was the only cartridge in the trio to undergo a full-scale accuracy checkout. This decision was based on the fact that the test rifle chambering this cartridge was a highly accurate model (the rifle with the Hart barrel). However, firing a couple of varmint rifles chambered in 223 and 222 Magnum followed in a rather informal way. Their performance was convincing. The original statement concerning like accuracy potential among the three rounds stands. The 222 provided 1/2-inch groups at 100 yards for five shots over and over again. It did not reach this apex with every load tried, but neither did it require a single special recipe to bring out its potential in bullet grouping. For example, 52-grain custom bullets (made for benchrest shooting) ritually grouped under a half-inch at 100 yards. Some of the groups were a third-inch center to center, but these groups were, admittedly, superior to the norm. The load was 20.0 grains of Hercules Reloader-7 powder (remember, all cases are Remington R-P, new, and all primers Remington 7½ benchrest). Almost identical groups were developed with a 52-grain Sierra bullet and 24.5 grains of IMR-4320 powder.

I built another good load around Remington's 50-

grain Power-Lokt Hollow-Point bullet after I bought a quantity of these from Midway Arms, a supply house dealing in reloading components that are out of the ordinary. Norma's N-201 powder was available at the time, and with 22.5 grains of this fuel, velocity was only a bit over 3000 fps; however, groups regularly hovered between one-third and one-half inch from the 24-inch Hart barrel. Listing all of the loads that proved worthy in the Sako-actioned Hart barrel would take unwarranted space. However, talking about how to achieve high levels of accuracy with each of the three 22 centerfires—222, 223, and 222 Magnum—is important. Standardization of components is vital, but only *after* settling upon the best loads for your particular rifle or handgun.

The only general recommendation is for the benchrest primer. It proved best in accuracy with no loss in muzzle velocity. Not to say that there was a tremendous jump from fair to wonderful groups because of the primer. But after considerable compilation of group sizes, it became clear that the benchrest primer was a factor. As for powders, several developed fine accuracy. The first 222 Remington tested was not the custom Hart-barreled model already mentioned. It was an older Sako heavy-

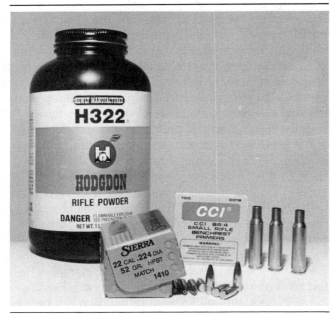

Accuracy loads for the 222 family are built through consulting various reloading manuals. There are numerous combinations to try. One will be just right for your 222, 223 or 222 Remington Magnum.

barrel L-461 factory model. Over a three-year period, that rifle never fired a group larger than an inch, center to center, at 100 yards from the bench with 10-shot, not five-shot, strings. It's mentioned here because several of the loads that were so good in that old rifle proved very accurate in the custom 222 Remington as well. The reader may wish to test the accuracy loads listed here. One or more of them could be just right for a particular 222 rifle. Today, match bullets are widespread. Several companies offer them. The match bullet is a beauty, and it must be included in accuracy tests, but not to the exclusion of regular bullets. In one 223 test rifle (an Ultra Light Arms hunting model), the regular Speer 52-grain hollow-point bullet proved as accurate as any projectile.

Cases for the 222 clan are all good. However, they are not all the same. The point is: pick the cartridge-case brand you like, buy a whole supply of them, and stick with that case. Then you never have to keep your cases separated by brand. On the other hand, if you already have a supply of cases, and they are mixed, do keep them sorted for best accuracy. In varminting, this advice is less important. For gaining benchrest accuracy levels, it is quite important. There are capacity differences, however slight, among the various case brands. These differences can show up when the cases are mixed. Pressures change. Performance is altered. That is why all tests with the 222 family of cartridges were conducted with new Remington brass only. Find your accuracy load for your rifle and *standardize* it—case, bullet, powder, and primer.

RIFLES AND PISTOLS FOR THE 222 CLAN

A Thompson/Center pistol in 223 Remington proved very enjoyable to shoot, and quite effective on varmints to 200 yards. Barrel length is an important factor in the ballistic impetus of the 222 family. Bob Milek worked with barrel length/velocity by reducing the barrel with consecutive shots in his 223 pistol. At 14 inches, the 223 cooked up a muzzle velocity of 2893 fps. When the barrel was reduced to 10-inch length, muzzle velocity fell to 2550 fps. At six inches, velocity was down to 2027 fps. Clearly, barrel-length reduction had a significant effect upon ballistics. Energy at the muzzle was literally cut in half as the barrel length was shortened from 14 to six inches—at 14 inches, muzzle energy was about 1,000 foot-pounds. At six inches, muzzle energy plummeted to about 500 foot-pounds. There-

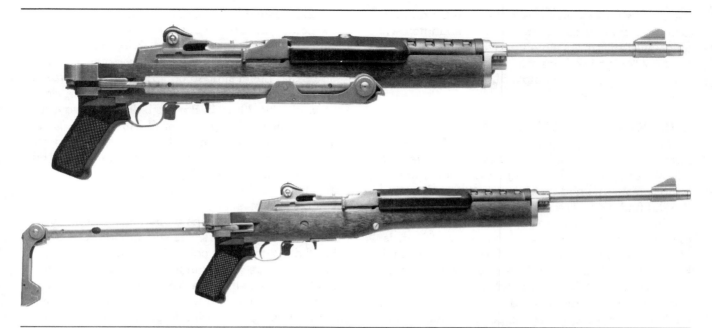

The 223 Remington has gained a great following due to its chambering in semi-automatic rifles such as the popular Ruger Mini-14. This versatile rifle is available in a folding stock model shown closed (above) and open (below).

fore, the pistoleer must decide what he wants—a shorter barrel for portability, or a longer barrel for performance in the 222 family of cartridges.

Rifles for the 222 clan are so numerous in brand and style that any attempt at compiling all of them would surely come up short. On one end of the spectrum, you can buy a Ruger Mini-14 semi-auto rifle in 223 Remington chambering. This little gem works extremely well for its intended purpose— rapid fire with low recoil and high velocity. The tests conducted for this work proved the Ruger a very worthy shooting machine. Reduced loads with a 55-grain bullet worked very well in the Ruger semi-automatic rifle, incidentally, but when the powder charge was dropped too low, the rifle finally failed to reload itself. This occurred in one test with a 55-grain bullet and 18.0 grains of IMR-4198 powder. Muzzle velocity was below 2600 fps, which seems to be (at least in the test rifle) a minimum for function of the action. In the test rifle, a jump to 19.5 grains of IMR-4198 powder with the 55-grain bullet brought the action back into service. The hardy Ruger semi-auto 223 makes an enjoyable range rifle. It is also handy in the pickup truck for the rancher or farmer who is not interested in a bulkier varmint rifle. Jackrabbit hunters, especially, find the Ruger semi-auto very effective, not only on the run-

ning shots, but also at longer ranges. The Ruger scopes easily. When it sports a variable, such as a 2.5X-8X, it serves for both up-close fast action, and longer shots where greater magnification of target is desirable.

The Kimber Model 84B is pretty enough to make a combat sergeant weep. This light bolt-action rifle (6¼ pounds as a sporter, 7¼ pounds as a varminter) has the Mini-Mauser action developed by Kimber. The Mini-Mauser uses a claw-extractor and it has a three-position wing safety, like that of the Model 70 Winchester. The scaled-down action allows equally small overall rifle dimensions, providing the Kimber 84B with not only light weight, but also a trim appearance. It looks and handles like the Model 82B 22-rimfire rifle. Two of the 222 family are chambered in the Kimber 84B: the 222 Remington itself and the 223 Remington round. With the winds of popularity blowing in favor of the 223, it's quite possibly the right choice of cartridge in this sporter.

Numerous bolt-action rifles are chambered for the 222 family of cartridges, especially the 222 and 223. The Mini-Mark X is a short-throw bolt-action offered in 223 Remington, with a 20-inch barrel. The beautiful and accurate Sako rifle chambers the 222 clan. Remington's fine Model 7 is chambered for the 223. As these words are written, an Ultra Light is being made for me in caliber 223 Remington with quick-twist rifling. As stated above, the list of rifles for the 222 clan is a long one. It even includes a lever-action model, Browning's BLR, in 222 or 223 Remington calibers.

JAVELINA AND THE 222 FAMILY

The first morning of javelina season a good many years ago found us perched on the side of a hill. My partner and I were "glassing" for wild pigs, a most useful method of finding the little fellows. We did find them. The stalk went easy—stalking javelina does not require commando expertise—and in a short while the band was within 50 yards of us. My partner fired. I fired. Then I fired again. I knew I couldn't miss from 50 yards, not with a Sako heavy-barrel 222 Remington capable of putting 10 shots into an inch at 100 yards. At the second shot, the boar dropped over. On inspection, I found two holes not an inch apart. Yet the first strike landed without visible effect. The problem was the bullet—too hard. This short story is mentioned because it is possible to select a bullet that is too hard to expand reliably at 222 velocities. The excellent Jordan 60-grain pill used on the boar was such a bullet—accurate, and capable of good penetration on a pig-sized target—but a bit too tough for 222 velocities.

My forthcoming rapid-rate-of-twist 223 Ultra Light rifle will be on the javelina trail somewhere in the future, but it will not be firing super-hard bullets. Rather, it will use one of the excellent heavyweight 22 jacketed missiles (heavy by comparison) that have surfaced in the past few years. While these larger bullets do not exit the muzzle at scintillating speed, they hold onto what they start out with. At 100 yards or so, the usual javelina range for the stalking hunter, these long bullets carry up well (retain velocity), offering good penetration and sufficient energy for game of wild-pig size. The 68-grain Hornady, 69-grain Sierra, 70-grain Speer Semi-Spitzer, and 70-grain Barnes 22-caliber bullets require more revolutions per second to stabilize them. Fast-twist rifling has been introduced to keep them spinning on their axes, point-on, rather than tumbling.

The rate of twist in the Ultra Light rifle is 1:7.5. That will stabilize any of the longer-than-usual 22-caliber jacketed projectiles offered today. Velocities, as mentioned above, are not going to run terribly high with these long bullets from the 222 clan.

The 223 pushed the 68-grain Hornady boattail hollow-point match bullet out of the muzzle at close to 2800 fps (23-inch barrel), using 23.0 grains of H-335 powder. The 69-grain Sierra hollow-point boattail Matchking bullet slipped out of the muzzle at about 2850 fps with 25.5 grains of IMR-4320 powder doing the work. The 70-grain Barnes bullet got away at 2750 fps, using 26.5 grains of W-748 powder. Those 222, 223, and 222 Magnum fans who do not possess a rifle with quick twist might want to look into a 60- to 63-grain bullet. The 60-grain Barnes took off at 3000 fps from the 23-inch test barrel when the bullet was backed by 27.0 grains of W-760 powder. While javelina hunting remains a sport enjoyed by comparatively few hunters, it is still important to note that the 222 family of cartridges using loads mentioned here, as well as many others, proves excellent for game of this size. The last porker dropped by my 222 Remington was cleanly harvested with one shot using the Nosler 60-grain BT solid-base spitzer bullet backed by 23.5 grains of H-335 powder. Muzzle velocity was about three grand.

THE WILD TURKEY AND THE 222 CLAN

If the 22 Hornet is the turkey-takingest cartridge going, then the 222 family can also lay claim to turkey-hunting rounds because duplication of 22 Hornet ballistics in the 222, 223, or 222 Remington is very simple to accomplish. However, this is not to take away from the 22 Hornet in any way. Not all 222-family cartridges are chambered in petite rifles of enjoyable packing weight and size. Given a varminter in 222 Remington or a sporter in 22 Hornet for gobblers, I'd pick the latter every time. On the other hand, a Kimber sporter, Sako, or the cloud-weight Ultra Light in any of the 222 clan would make superior wild-turkey rifles. The wild-turkey cartridge faces a serious problem—it must deliver sufficient power to drop Ben's bird cold, on the spot, and yet it must not destroy a lot of good meat. Essentially, the animal, or in this case, the wild bird, is dispatched either by interruption of the spinal cord activity, to include not only the spinal hit, but also a brain or neck shot, or by disruption of tissue and the function of that tissue (lung shot, for example). There is also a shock factor, but this trail leads to some unscientific pathways.

How do you go about delivering a knockout blow on the one hand, without too much destruction of edible meat on the other? Some shooters like the full-metal-jacket bullet; other turkey hunters claim it

Kimber's Model 84B rifle is available in two of the 222 family: the 222 Remington and 223 Remington calibers.

is a curse, wounding birds. My experience is limited to a couple of birds that dropped instantly when hit in the wing/body area. But would a bird struck in the body drop from a solid bullet? A compromise may be in order—neither a full-metal-jacket bullet, nor a very fragile missile, but a *hard* projectile at medium velocity. The 222 clan offers a myriad of possibilities here. Those old Jordan 60-grain bullets that proved too hard on wild pigs delivered quite a blow to the "softer" wild turkey, dispatching without too much destruction. The new heavy 22 bullets at medium speed should work as well or better. On one hunt, two wild turkeys fell to two shots from 223 rifles and 55-grain bullets backed by 8.0 grains of Hercules Unique powder, muzzle velocity about 2000 fps. With this load, the 223 was a beefed-up 22 WMR in performance. For more bullet expansion, the 45-grain Sierra Semi-Pointed bullet from the 223, backed by only 6.0 grains of Unique, delivers about 1900 fps muzzle velocity. At 50 yards, groups were about a third-inch center to center with this load.

SMALL GAME WITH THE 222 FAMILY

The beauty of handloading for the 222 clan, as well as many other 22 centerfires, is the ability of the shooter to tame his firebreathers with reduced loads that emulate the 22 rimfire. The only catch, if indeed it is one, is sensitivity of these loads. In developing the best reduced load for 22 centerfires, it is wise to work in one-tenth grain increments. A tenth of a grain is an extremely small weight. There are 7,000 grains weight in one pound, 437.5 grains in one ounce. However, in using very light charges of fast-burning powder, a mere tenth of one grain weight can matter. Once again, the explosive force desired on varmints is not correct here any more

than it was for wild-turkey hunting. The idea is to harvest the small-game animal cleanly without undue meat loss. Sierra's Semi-Pointed 40-grain bullet proved very accurate in the 223 with 6.0 grains weight of Hercules Unique powder. Muzzle velocity was about 2000 fps. Groups of about a half-inch at 50 yards were common. The Sierra 45-grain Semi-Pointed bullet (load given above) was also excellent on small game from the 223.

The 222 Remington, using a 50-grain bullet and 11.0 grains of IMR-4227 powder, was quite accurate. For small game, a 45-grain cast bullet, Lyman's No. 225415, left the muzzle at only 1700 fps, using 5.0 grains of Red Dot powder. The same load in the 222 Remington Magnum resulted in approximately the same muzzle velocity. Hercules Unique powder in a 5.0-grain charge with a 50-grain bullet developed 1700 fps, also in the 222 Remington test barrel. The shooter should consult his loading manual, or better yet several of them, in order to build the best reduced load for his 222, 223, or 222 Magnum. The 22 rimfire is my preferred small-game rifle caliber. However, for those shooters who have a pet rifle chambered for one of the 222 family of cartridges, the reduced load is the answer in turning the 22-centerfire varmint cartridge into a small-game round. The lightweight 222-centerfire sporters in these calibers carry nicely and are quite accurate in the small-game field.

BIG GAME

In spite of the point of view that many of us do not consider the 222 clan right for big-game hunting, thousands of big-game animals have fallen to the cartridge, especially up north by the native Alaskan and Canadian hunter. Today, at least one company recognizes the 223 Remington as a deer cartridge in that a controlled expansion factory-loaded bullet is offered in that caliber. No one can argue that the 222 class of centerfire cartridge has enough remaining energy at 100 yards, for example, to drop deer-sized game. That there are better big-game cartridges, however, is fairly clear. The 222 Remington and its offshoots have been and will remain high in popularity, not only as varmint cartridges, but also as general-shooting rounds of great accuracy and light recoil. From benchrest to varmint hunt, the 222s are at home.

24 THE AMAZING 22 PPC USA

The destiny of great wildcat cartridges is to "go factory." There are numerous examples of this truism, including the 22-250 Remington, 243 Winchester, 6mm Remington, 7mm-08, and 25-06, to name a few. In 1988, another wildcat left the ranks of do-it-yourself cartridges to become an over-the-counter number: the amazing 22 PPC USA. Its equally famous counterpart, the 6 PPC USA, also joined the ranks of factory rounds, but concentration here, in keeping with this book's direction, is on the 22-caliber version of the cartridge. A paraphrasing of Ralph Waldo Emerson goes: "Build a better mousetrap and the world will make a beaten path to your door." If you applied the adage to the 22 PPC, it would go: "Build a better cartridge and the ammo companies will tell you to go bury it." Both PPCs were treated as illegitimate offspring for well over a decade following their inception. Even after conclusive proof of their worth, no American ammo company offered to make factory fodder for the PPCs. Finally, Sako of Finland capitulated, offering both rifles and ammunition to the American shooting public and the world.

The 22 PPC USA suffered from the fact that the original wildcat round had to be made from 220 Russian brass. There were no easily located commercial cartridge cases to work with, and certainly no factory-loaded ammunition. Oddly enough, both PPCs also failed to catch the eye of the public because they were labeled "benchrest rounds." Shooters thought that was all they were good for. But the PPCs were much more than precision-shooting cartridges. The 22 PPC, our major focus here, exhibited excellent ballistics. Was it not a superior varmint cartridge, as well as a pearl of accuracy? The test goal was to answer that question.

When somebody says that a given mousetrap is best, it is the field-tester's job to match other good mousetraps against it to see just how great the

"best" one really is. A head-on-head battle ensued. A custom Sako Vixen Varmint rifle, a prototype of the current commercial Sako Varminter rifle, was

The 22 PPC USA cartridge (left) looks to the Russian 7.62mm for parentage. The little cartridge began as a wildcat and remained so for a long while, but is now available in factory form from Sako.

the control firearm to test the new 22 PPC USA and its Sako rifle. The control rifle was no off-the-shelf model. It wore a heavy Hart barrel and a PPC Insert (a device used to develop very close locking lug fit to the breech), and it represented handmade quality throughout. At the time, the rifle was topped with a 24X target scope, although in the name of versatility it now has a Bushnell 4X-12X scope. With the rifle chambered for one of the most accurate cartridges, the 222 Remington, the test was acid. The goal—to shoot this fine custom 222 against a factory Sako rifle chambered in 22 PPC. If anything, the deck was stacked in favor of the custom 222. The 22 PPC USA test rifle wore a 12X scope, not a 24X scope, which further favored the 222. No cartridge test is complete using only two sample rifles; however, the data gathered during benchrest sessions were significant.

Everything was kept as constant as possible for non-laboratory testing. Variables were at work—the rifles were fired from a benchrest, not a machine rest—but the variables were equally present for both rifles. Each firearm was given the same consideration, using the best combinations of excellent bullets, powders, and benchrest primers, in order to give each rifle and cartridge an equal chance at performance. New 222 cases were weighed for uniformity and sorted. After a thousand bullets had pierced paper targets downrange, an obvious conclusion surfaced. The 22 PPC was

The 222 has taken a back seat to the 22 PPC USA cartridge (center). The latter has set many records, and its larger sister, the 6 PPC USA has set even more.

the winner. It won every time. Perhaps nothing was proved. The guardians of precision shooting, those nitpicking experts who outside-turn neck cases, spin bullets, and drop powder charges from special measures that equal scale-weighed loads we mortals put together, had already proved that the PPCs were currently the most accurate cartridges in the world.

Before relating the interesting details of the 22 PPC birthing and nurturing, establishing briefly what both cartridges have done is valuable. It reveals what all the excitement is about. They have, or at least the 6 PPC has, supplanted the grand wizards of benchrest-accuracy cartridges: the 222 Remington, 222½Remington (wildcat), the 219 Donaldson Wasp, 6 × 47, 308, and many other fine rounds. The PPCs are the goat's glands of the winner's circle. For a while, the 219 Wasp was the cartridge to beat, then the 222 Remington in its original or slightly altered form, the 222½. Now it's the PPCs, especially the 6mm version, but the 22 PPC also showed its winning colors by capturing the 100-yard benchrest accuracy contest at the Nationals prior to 1975. Little notice was given. The 22 PPC produced the smallest 10-shot group fired at the Speer Match in the Unlimited Class, again in its infancy. The group was .204 inch center to center. At the 1975 Super Shoot, Lou Palmisano, co-inventor of the cartridge, won the 100-yard Heavy Varmint Class Aggregate with the 22 PPC. Five-shot groups totaled .265 inch center to center, .050 inch better than second place that year, which in benchrest competition is significant.

A 14-year old boy emerged victorious over 80 grown men in 1976 when he won a 200-yard Benchrest Shooters National Championship event for a 25-shot aggregate, firing a group measuring .3280 inch. That lad was David Palmisano, Lou's boy, and what was he was shooting? A 22 PPC. From 1981 to 1985 there were 116 International Benchrest Shooters (IBS) records broken, every one by a PPC. In under a decade, 179 IBS records were bettered, 149 of them with a PPC. Although ammo factories seemed uninterested, the benchrest boys were not complacent about the PPCs. By 1981, of the 60 competitors at the IBS match, 59 were using the PPC. At Super Shoot III, a 22 PPC won the Heavy Varmint Aggregate with a .264-inch group for 25 shots. At this time, the PPCs have taken several hundred first places in various competitions. When, in 1987, various IBS records were set, the 6 PPC set

Dr. Lou Palmisano, a vascular surgeon, co-developed the now famous PPC cartridges that hold the numerous records described in the text.

'em all. In 1987, several National Bench Rest Shooters Association (NBRSA) records were set. All but one was captured by the 6 PPC, and that one was taken by a 6 PPC with a shortened neck. In spite of all of this, neither the 22 PPC nor 6 PPC was factory-recognized until 1988.

PPC. What does it mean? It means Palmisano-Pindell-Cartridge, named for its co-inventors, Lou Palmisano, a vascular surgeon, and Ferris Pindell, a diemaker/gunsmith genius. At the 1974 Super Shoot, the men got together. They had a uni-goal: each wanted to see a leap forward in precision shooting. The two men had no idea (I wonder if the impact has yet struck) that they were going to invent not only the most accurate cartridges in the world, but also two supremely fine hunting cartridges—the 22 PPC for varmints and the 6 PPC for varmints and medium-sized game.

The men sifted through the criteria of excellence in bullet grouping and decided they wanted the following: a 52- to 53-grain 22-caliber, match-grade bullet, fired at modest velocity from a case designed to give the powder charge the most advantageous shape for best combustion characteristics. The case should be short, since short, fat cases seemed to present the best powder charge shape for accuracy. And the case should offer a capacity that would allow the complete combustion of the charge during bore time. In other words, there would be, in theory, no unburned powder to add to the "ejecta," which is the sum total of the mass (bullet, powder gas, unburned powder, primer chemicals, etc.) fired through the bore of the rifle.

Palmisano began to cogitate on the matter. Lou had already invented medical instruments of merit. His father, a mechanical wizard himself, had put his son to work in the garage at an early date. Lou learned the workings of things. He became a highly successful surgeon, but his talents did not end there. He studied all manner of shooting instruments as well as medical instruments. Lou took a look at the 7.92 Kurz, a German round of small case capacity, boxy nature, and good accuracy. He worked with, and is still working with, altered 220 Swift brass. Then the 220 Russian caught his eye. He and Pindell agreed that here was the raw material for their new ultra-accuracy round. The cartridge had been used successfully in Russia and Finland by sportsmen and shooters. The 1962 World Shooting Championship in Cairo saw Russian team members using a necked-down

The stubby 22 PPC USA round being inserted into the single-shot bolt-action Sako varmint rifle. Super accuracy, plus fine ballistics, combine to make the 22 PPC in the Sako the most efficient varminting combination the author has used.

7.62 × 39mm cartridge, which would later be known as the 220 Russian. The 7.62 × 39 was chambered in the Russian AK-47 and AKM assault rifles, as well as RPK and RPD machine guns and the SK45 semi-auto carbine.

The 22 PPC was born of 220 Russian brass. Palmisano liked the fact that 220 cases were very uniform. Therefore, the 220 Russian case was fire-formed to create a 30-degree shoulder with a body taper of only .010 inch from base to shoulder. In time, Palmisano convinced Sako to manufacture a batch of cases. The flash holes had to be drilled, not punched, for better uniformity. These flash holes, by the way, were undersized—.066 inch, instead of the usual .081- to .082-inch dimension. (I believe the current flash hole size of the PPC cartridge is .061 inch to .062 inch). The small rifle primer had already been touted as correct for the most efficient type of ignition for high-grade accuracy, and the PPC rounds would use the very uniform benchrest primer in this size. The cartridge case length would be 1.515 inches, with a head size of .445 inch, as compared with the 30-06 head size of .473-inch diameter.

Pindell's Precision Tooling began to chamber rifles. An August 1974 issue of *Precision Shooting Magazine* advertised the round as the "Pindell Palm Cartridge." Both 22 PPC and 6mm PPC were offered. Cartridge cases were imported. The late Dan Pawlak was called upon to run many sophisticated tests on the new cartridges. His conclusions were extremely gratifying. Although many engineers still maintain that time/pressure curves mean little to performance of a cartridge, Dan felt otherwise. He used such figures to conclude that the inherent accuracy potential of the PPCs was high.

"This cartridge is very interesting," said Dan, "It has good pressure capability in spite of its short length. . . ." Pawlak later stated, "After completing more testing of your .220 PPc [sic] we have made some striking observations." Pawlak found, using time vs. pressure curves, that the bullet was exiting the barrel (with the test load) 640 microseconds after peak pressure had been reached, leaving only 8,000 psi muzzle pressure. In short, the cartridge was efficient, burning its powder charge quite completely, and giving minimal disturbance at the muzzle. Roland Franzen, once head of instrumentation at Diehl in Nuremburg, West Germany, noted that these results were well ahead of the 7.62 NATO, often used as a standard, which had considerably more muzzle pressure by comparison.

Later, Pawlak further concluded that by compari-

Compared with the 30-06 cartridge, the 22 PPC USA is a small package indeed. However, it is also a very efficient package, developing as high as 3600 fps muzzle velocity with bullets in the 50-grain class.

son with the parent cartridge, the 220 Russian, the 22 PPC was far superior in every department. Another factor surfaced during testing. The harmonics—vibrations—when firing the cartridge were conducive to uniformity and consequent high accuracy. Pawlak was impressed. He said, "The significance of this cartridge is surely underestimated." The larger capacity of the cartridge as compared with the 222 or the original 220 Russian was important not only to powder/bullet balance, but also to performance, as this happy varminter was later to discover when the pipsqueak case pushed a 52-grain hollow-point out of the muzzle at about 3600 feet per second. Capacity of the 22 PPC USA proved to be 33.8 grains weight of water, 2.1 grains weight over the 222 Remington Magnum. In engineering talk, the short length-to-diameter ratio of the case improved the ignition-transfer capability, not just from primer to primer, but from granule to granule of powder. These points helped move the PPC ahead of the similar-capacity 222 Magnum, with its longer body style, in spite of the fact that the 222 Magnum also used the small rifle primer (albeit with a larger flash hole).

The precision-shooting boys outside neck-turned their 220 Russian brass so that the resulting PPC

The 22 PPC USA cartridge (center) has a head size in between the 30-06 and the 222 Remington.

rounds were very uniform (there is a Forster turning tool for this operation). Cases were neck-sized only, and then just the forward portion of the neck. Neck friction was maintained in this fashion. If the bullet has to escape inertia A one time and inertia B the next, premium accuracy is denied. However, benchrest techniques were not used for my initial testing, and yet the 22 PPC USA proved extremely accurate. These first reloading efforts were for shooters like you and me who want to enjoy both rounds in the everyday sense, some passive bench-shooting, a little bit of target work, but also varminting. The 22 PPC proved a varminter's dream, because it captured that major criterion for success—supreme accuracy.

RCBS loading dies were soon available for the 22 PPC and an RCBS Auto 4 × 4 press was put into operation, turning out large quantities of ammunition in order to give the 22 PPC a broad base of data for study. As stated above, all initial handloading techniques for testing the 22 PPC were "standard" in nature. Cases were full-length resized, not neck-only sized. Cases were neither weighed nor sorted. Necks were not turned. The question was: Would a shooter have to go through a religious reloading ceremony in order to gain what has come to be known as PPC accuracy? Or could he handload in the usual fashion to obtain excellent groups? The goal: to find out what the 22 PPC would do under careful, but not esoteric, reloading and shooting circumstances. The records compiled by the benchrest shooters already proved how the PPCs worked in their hands. But what would the 22 PPC do for varmint shooters?

Factory ammunition proved to be carefully manufactured and extremely accurate. Handloads tailored to match the particular idiosyncrasies of the test rifle were slightly in the lead for group size, but 22 PPC factory ammo grouped steadily at a startling 3/8 of an inch center to center at 100 yards. A few five-shot groups were even smaller than that. Of course, ammunition can be only as accurate as the firearm that chambers it. The PPC rifle, imported by Stoeger Industries of South Hackensack, N.J., proved to be matched to the ammunition, meeting the criteria set down earlier for a true 22 centerfire varminter. The stiff single-shot action guaranteed stability. The precision heavyweight barrel, free-floated, helped to maintain uniformity shot to shot. The semi-beavertail forend also enhanced the rifle's steadiness. The heart of the Sako

PPC Varmint Rifle is the long-familiar and excellent A-1 short action, the L-461. Specifics include a heavy barrel 23.75 inches long. This is not a bull barrel, but muzzle diameter is a full .865 inch. The barrel is free-floated; it has six lands and grooves, hammer-forged rifling, a twist of 1:14, and a concave crown.

Overall length of the rifle is 43 inches. The Varminter weighs about 8½ pounds. No sights. The receiver is dovetailed in Sako fashion for the Sako scope mount. This is a single-shot rifle that encourages rigidity. There is no magazine box cutout. The action's rigidness is further insured through a steel-supported flat-bottomed receiver.

I noticed a different "feeling" when shooting these rifles, a vibration not generally encountered. A fellow shooter benchtested the rifles and said, "This rifle feels different when it shoots, but I don't know why." When I suggested that the vibration was unusual, he agreed. The unique vibration quality of the PPC rifles may have contributed to the excellent group developed at the test range.

The stock is plain walnut, tight-grained. The Monte Carlo design is superfluous, but many shooters prefer that buttstock configuration. The forend seemed bulky at first, but proved its merit both at the range and in the varmint field. The rubber buttpad is for slippage, not recoil. There's not enough "kick" in either of the 22 PPC or 6 PPC to knock a soda cracker over. Checkering of the wood is very nice, in panels at the forend and wrist. The triggers on both test rifles were acceptable as they came from the factory, but not entirely crisp and light. Dale Storey, a gunsmith who specializes in accurate rifles, fine-tuned them. They were much crisper after his expert service. For further refinement, he installed new trigger springs. The triggers may be adjusted for two-stage or single-stage mode. Most non-target shooters prefer the latter. Overall cosmetics are very good, with a pleasingly dull oil stock finish. The rifles lived up to the potential of PPC ammunition accuracy. In fact, the title "most accurate" was conferred by *The American Rifleman* magazine in a quote from the NRA staff: "The 6mm PPC and .22 PPC ammunition and rifles received for testing proved capable of accuracy levels not previously encountered in shooting tests of factory ammunition/rifle combinations."

PPC Ammunition is initially expensive, with loaded rounds advertised at about a buck each. That's a lot of green to lay out for one pop. How-

Although designed as a benchrest round, the 22 PPC USA in the highly accurate Sako rifle is a supremely fine varminter. This marmot was dropped from long range with the combination.

ever, unloaded/unprimed cases are also available, and a batch of test brass was reloaded 27 times. After the 27th loading, the cases still proved functional. That considerably reduces the overall high cost of ammo. So the 22 PPC ends up no more expensive to reload than other rounds, and even less costly than cartridges with short case life. A word of caution to owners of custom PPC benchrest rifles hand-built for competition. These rifles were supplied with very tight chambers. Precision shooters, as noted above, neck-turn their cases to gain close tolerances between cartridge and chamber. Clymer, a leading reamer shop, reported that its reamers were ground to deliver extremely close tolerances. Sako factory PPC USA ammunition is very precise, but the ammunition is geared to match the factory rifle's chamber. For safety reasons: **do not use factory 22 PPC USA (or factory 6mm PPC) ammunition in custom-made tight-necked chambers without first making sure that they fit properly.** High pressures could result. Clymer is offering reamers that will enlarge the neck sections of custom PPC rifles to accept Sako factory ammo and brass.

The PPCs continue to delight shooters because of

their accuracy. Lou Palmisano shot an amazing target, witnessed by his shooting club, measuring .303 inch center to center for five shots, unofficial score. It was fired at 300 yards. Lou's goal is to reproduce that group under official conditions. The PPCs spoil you. The shooter gets used to accuracy levels that were previously elusive. Following a shooting session, I was asked by an interested bystander, who was sighting his rifle at the gun range, "How did she do?" I shook my head in disappointment.

"Not so good," I said. "Wrong loads. She only made half-inch groups."

The fellow studied my target. Then he shook his head. "Yeah, so I see," he mumbled, taking another look at the target and then a longer look at me. He walked back to his shooting bench without further comment.

The criteria laid down for precision long-range varmint shooting listed accuracy as a major contributor to success. However, it was boldly stated that accuracy is not enough. Comparatively high delivered energy is also important. So is a flat trajectory. The first day in the varmint field, the 22 PPC USA proved its mettle—in spades.

A prairie dog is a small target, especially beyond 200 yards. But the 22 PPC dropped seven rodents in a row, five past 250 paces, two at more than 350 paces (probably 275 to 300 yards as the bullet flies). The ground was flat. If anything, distance guesstimations were conservative. Get a good rest, center the little varmints in the crosswire, hold a steady picture in the scope, dope distance and wind, squeeze the trigger, and zap! At all ranges, dispatch was fast and humane.

Passing up no tough shots in favor of good scores we took them as they came. We "glassed out" two of the little rodents well away and below in a damp draw. Exact distance was a question mark. Two shots to get the range, then one varmint zeroed. He plopped over like a bowling pin. Next shot was a miss. Then another toppled over. Range? It took 512 long paces to reach the site where the varmints lay. True, we fired five shots for two hits. And the angle helped reduce holdover. But the targets were almost invisible to the naked eye—two fly specks on a distant green carpet. Even through a 12X scope, they looked tiny. After getting the range, we enjoyed an impressive number of long-range strikes that day with the Sako Varminter. Hits greatly outnumbered misses.

John Fadala quickly learned that high-grade accuracy paid off in the varmint field. He cleanly dropped these prairie dogs from well over 300 yards.

Dr. Palmisano enjoying success on prairie dogs with his own 22 PPC USA cartridge and the Sako rifle.

Varminting with the 22 PPC was not to the exclusion of range-testing. We continued working from a solid benchrest under fairly decent shooting conditions. Choosing calm days, we accomplished some shooting in the precision style—with weighed cases, carefully prepared powder charges, and variables held in check. Each test bullet was a custom missile of match-grade quality. The particular test rifle in 22 PPC proved as accurate as the 6 PPC in these tests. Both rifles produced 3/8-inch groups at 100 yards from the bench. We shot a great deal. No powder was spared. No bullets. No primers. Groups sizes of only a quarter-inch center to center occurred frequently when there was no wind.

Chronographing sessions followed the workup of accurate loads. First, however, the most accurate loads for the test rifle, in terms of accuracy, were constructed. Let the velocity chips fall where they may. Fortunately, the hotter recipes proved very accurate, which was pleasing. Velocity did not have to be sacrificed for accuracy. Terminal energy was high. Long-range bullet grouping was superlative. Chronographings with Sako factory ammo showed the 22 PPC's 52-grain hollow-point boattail bullet departing the muzzle at an average velocity of 3459 fps, this figure taken at 12 feet to center screens, and not mathematically worked back to the muzzle. The standard deviation for the 22 PPC factory ammo achieved an excellent low figure of 17 fps, with a high figure of only 23 fps from the mean (average) velocity. These standard-deviation figures and velocities were recorded with the Sako PPC Varminter from its 23.75-inch barrel. Elevation was 6,000 feet above sea level at the test site. Temperatures ran from 75 to 85 degrees F.

We tried many handloads in the 22 PPC, guided by data from the current Speer loading manual. Speer's results and those achieved with the 22 PPC test rifles were almost identical. The CCI BR-4 primer was excellent. I obtained a shell holder in PPC head size and used the RCBS Big Max press for seating primers. I also employed a Lee hand unit for priming. A 28.0-grain charge of accurate MR2460 powder duplicated the ballistics of the Sako factory 22 PPC. However, a 52-grain Speer bullet split the airways at 3561 fps at 12 feet using 28.5 grains of N-201 powder (not easy to find). That's pretty close to 3600 fps at the muzzle.

A 53-grain Sierra Benchrest bullet with 28.0 grains of B1-C-2 cut ragged one-holers at a

hundred yards, but velocity was only 3142 fps. The same bullet with 23.0 grains of H-4198 earned 3214 fps. Standard deviations were low, with 10s and 12s common. The 53-grain Sierra Benchrest bullet coupled with 28.5 grains of Accurate MR2460 powder developed 3400 fps with a standard deviation of 10 to 16 fps in my tests. Accuracy was sterling. This combination nailed many long-range varmints. Accuracy was the key to field success with the PPCs, but flat trajectory through high velocity was also responsible for the cartridges' high-scoring record. I liked the 22 PPC best for varmints.

The 22 PPC was sighted with 52- and 53-grain bullets at about 3500 fps muzzle velocity to strike two inches high at 100 yards from the muzzle. At 200 yards, the group printed about three inches high. The bullets punched home on the money at 250 yards and fell about three inches below line of sight at 300 yards. Hits to 300 yards were readily possible with the two-inch-high sight-in at 100 yards. However, the 22 PPC USA cartridge was surprising beyond 300 yards, with remarkable bullet placement managed by doping wind drift and bullet drop with a "sighter shot." At 350 yards, the group printed about five inches low (although bullet clustering was still quite fine at this range, the variable of group size did affect estimation of bullet drop). As familiarity with the 22 PPC grows, gauging shots beyond 300 yards becomes second nature.

The PPC's trajectory was flat enough for serious varmint-shooting to 350 yards. Mild report and very low recoil were partially responsible for the best record of hits vs. misses I've yet compiled in long-range pest control. But I had a problem deciding on the right scope for the 22 PPC—a balance between power and ease of use—so I played the game of "musical scopes" for quite a while. Many different scopes rested briefly atop the 22 PPC rifle. Originally it wore a 24X Leupold target scope once used on the heavy-barreled 222 Remington rifle mentioned above. But even to 300 yards and beyond, shooting at prairie dogs and marmots, a 12X sufficed, and mirage was less a problem. Many days in the field were warm, with targets that danced on the field of view. I didn't pick a variable (my favorite) because I used the 22 PPC strictly for long-range work. The heavy barrel was very effective for repeated fire. The 22 PPC was tested with 30 consecutive shots from the bench without a cooling period, shooting at six different bull's-eyes in

Fadala took this open-country jackrabbit with the 22 PPC USA Sako rifle. Sam found that the low-recoil, high-accuracy cartridge insured hits at very long range.

succession. The last group was nearly identical to the first group, making repeated fire, at target or varmint, very precise.

The 22 PPC sparkled in the varmint field. Ballistically, it seemed to fit that notch supposedly occupied by the 222 Remington and its brothers, in between the 22 Hornet and 220 Swift. However, longer association with the round put it closer to the Swift in long-range varminting. Perhaps the 22 PPC fits best between the 222 Remington and the 220 Swift, if we must pigeonhole it. Anyone who prizes accuracy above all will enjoy the 22 PPC Sako Varminter rifle regardless of the ballistic domain it actually occupies.

A few basic laws strain the potential from the 22 PPC and its rifle. First, the shooter should work up specific accuracy loads for his personal rifle. Noth-

ing changes here. Rifles are individuals, no two exactly alike. The best loads in the test 22 PPC Sako Varminter may not prove to be the most virtuous in another rifle. Second, although a tad more velocity can be realized with regular small-rifle primers, every indication seems to point to benchrest primers for best results in the PPC, even for varminting. Third, sufficient scope power should be mounted on the 22 PPC to take advantage of long-range accuracy potential. The cartridge has ample terminal energy and trajectory, allowing 300-yard, even 350-yard shooting of varmints.

The dream of moving a notch higher on the scale of accuracy was realized when the PPC cartridges were first envisioned, finally developed, and then made available to the general public of shooters. Although designed for benchrest accuracy, the 22

PPC USA and the 6 PPC USA are no more confined to the target range than any other good cartridge. For many marksmen, these rounds will be shooting delights to be enjoyed solely at the range, where the joy of clustering bullet holes in ever-tighter groups will be appreciated. For the rest of us, the PPCs, and especially the 22 PPC, are going to serve a much broader function. Target range accuracy? Sure. But also hunting. The 22 PPC is an excellent varmint cartridge. Supreme accuracy and good ballistics make it so.

The best loads for the 22 PPC transpired with bullets in the 52- to 53-grain class. N-201 powder gave pinnacle-high accuracy with 28.5 grains and either 52- or 53-grain missile. Velocity for this load was 3561 fps 12 feet from muzzle to midscreens. In a later test, the same set of components, except for a change to a Remington 7½ benchrest primer, yielded 3594 fps at 12 feet, which would be a solid 3600 fps at the muzzle. Accuracy remained tophat high. Another good load, this one with a 52-grain hollow-point bullet, was 28.5 grains of Accurate No. 2460 powder for 3460 fps. An accurate load with a 53-grain benchrest bullet found 23.0 grains of H-4198 providing 3214 fps. The 22 PPC proved itself with several different powders and bullets. It also proved itself to be a fantastic cartridge/rifle combination for long-range varminting.

25 THE HIGH-SPEED 220 SWIFT CARTRIDGE

The 220 Swift has taken a pounding from the gun press over the years. Not every writer condemned the cartridge, but many have, and on numerous fronts. It's been called inaccurate and difficult to load for, and labeled a barrel burner and cartridge-case eater, along with many other epithets. When the 220 Swift hit the street, some hunters simply had to try it on everything from mice to moose. Reports of performance varied widely. In the main, excellent woodsmen and marksmen had no trouble bringing down deer-sized game with one shot from the Swift's 22-caliber bore. Most of the warnings concerning the use of the Swift on deer came from shooters who never used the cartridge on deer. I cannot recommend the Swift for deer hunting, since I have no experience with it on game larger than rockchucks. The simplest tack is to explain that the bullet is too small for reliable work on big game. That's the easy way out of the dilemma. But it is not an entirely honorable response, in spite of the fact that most detractors of the Swift on deer have taken precisely as many bucks with the cartridge as I have—zero. There are three reasons for not using the Swift for big game: it is against the law in many areas, the bullet is too light, and most gunwriters say not to. More on the Swift as a deer cartridge in the big-game chapter.

Convoluted cartridge history is commonplace. The Swift's siring is no exception. A plausible story gives initial credit for a Swift cartridge to Captain Grosvenor L. Wotkyns, the man associated with 22 Hornet development. Wotkyns necked the 250 Savage to 22 caliber. It seemed a prudent move at the time, and would seem so again to many wildcatters, until that combination would finally find its way to the Remington factory. Wotkyns, it is noted, called his invention the 220 Swift. He brought it to the attention of Winchester engineers. Winchester liked the round, but in initial testing found accuracy

good, velocity indeed in the 4,000-fps realm, but pressures with test powders a trifle high in meeting Winchester's safety criterion; the test rifle had to withstand severe overloads with the test cartridge without evidence of damage or incipient problems. The idea of the necked-down 250 Savage Wotkyns, known as the 220 Swift, was tabled for the moment. The 30-06 case was brought out next, necked to 22

Deer are fair game for the Swift, as long as varmint bullets, which are designed to disrupt on impact, are left out of the picture. One shot in the rib cage of this buck with a Swift will do the job when the right bullet is used.

caliber and tested. Winchester engineers were not too happy with the results. Next in line for testing was a 7 × 57 Mauser case. A new 48-grain soft-point bullet for good ballistic form was used in working up loads for these would-be 220 Swifts. IMR-3031 powder was the most prevalent fuel. But 100-percent loading density, or anything close to it, was not possible with 3031 in light of excessive pressures with case-filling powder charges.

A switch to IMR-4064 powder improved the loading density problem significantly. There was still hope of a 220 Swift, perhaps on the 250 Savage case. But at the time, the 30-06 and 7 × 57 were not yet ruled out either. However, trouble visited the test lab once again—4064 was allowing a good velocity/pressure relationship in the necked-down test cases, but the engineers were unhappy with the erratic ballistics of that powder in each of the three test cases: 250 Savage, '06, and 7 × 57. Unsatisfactory burning qualities were experienced in those big cases necked to shoot little bullets. The original goal, about 4000 fps with a 46-grain Hornet bullet, was achieved, but not with ballistic uniformity and safe pressures. The semi-rimmed 6mm Lee Navy cartridge case was given next consideration. Using the 6mm Lee case necked to 22 caliber and loaded with 3031 proved a workable combination. But the development contained another very

The 220 Swift cartridge compared with the 30-06 (center). Head sizes are identical, but the 1935 Swift has a semi-rimmed case. The Swift gains its impetus from the obviously large case as compared with its small caliber.

important change—the Lee case was vastly improved before it was manufactured as a 220 Swift case. A very strong case emerged, with thick web, deeper under-rim cannelure, and improved shape of the head bunter. The case proved so strong that Dr. Palmisano, the PPC man, has used it considerably in wildcatting. The undeveloped Wotkyns 220 Swift based on the 250 Savage case became known as the WOS, for Wotkyns Original Swift.

The "real" 220 Swift was introduced to the public in 1935. It is interesting that the 220, now more than half a century old, has no factory 22 centerfire boss loaded in the U.S. It whips 'em all, even the 22-250 by a little bit. The 5.6 × 57mm RWS is a shade stronger, but this is a German round (see Chapter 28). Winchester played the role of wildcatter in building the Swift when it used an improved 6mm Lee Navy cartridge case. The final product had less body taper than the parent round and a sharper shoulder. Case length was 2.205 inches, as compared with 2.494 inches for the 30-06. However, the semi-rimmed Swift had a .473-inch head diameter, exactly the same as the '06 case. Factory loads claimed 4140 fps muzzle velocity with a 46-grain hollow-point bullet, and the same for a 48-grain soft-point projectile. The new 220 Swift rifle was the very good Model 54 Winchester, the forerunner of the famous Model 70. Winchester announced a "NEW RIFLE. . . WINCHESTER Super Speed .220 Swift. . . 4140 Feet per Second! Rate of 47 Miles a Minute. . . Over 50% Faster than the 180-grain .30 Govt. '06 Bullet." Choice of sporter or target rifle was offered. However, the Swift was ahead of its time in more than ballistics. It was also ahead of its time in barrel steels.

Ken Waters's study revealed many soft 220 Swift rifle barrels of the era, which certainly were not conducive to good barrel life when 40 grains (or so) of fuel had to be burned through a 22-caliber hole. Waters also discovered undersized flash holes, which may have abetted early pressure problems in some instances. Evidence of 1:16 rate of twist was uncovered, too, rather than the correct 1:14 twist established for the Swift. And there were some Swift rifles with bore diameters of .217/.222 instead of the proper .219/.224. The Model 54 was quite correct in most respects, but it, too, had a distance to go before it could be called a true Swift rifle. When the Model 70 superseded the 54, it was offered with a stainless-steel barrel in 220 Swift. Twist was, of course, 1:14. Therefore, some of the early

Although the Swift has set no bench records, as the 22 PPC USA has, the large-cased 22 has proved itself in the varmint field and even on big game when proper bullets have been used.

complaints against the 220 Swift, which survived beyond their veracity, were quite explainable. But that did not alter the fact that Winchester continued to receive customer complaints about the cartridge. The Swift was phased out of the lineup in 1963-64, with no rifle chambered for it by Winchester after that date.

CONTROVERSIAL CHARACTERISTICS

Barrel Wear. Without a doubt, the 220 Swift was and still is hard on barrels. The relatively large powder charge burning through the small volume of the 22-caliber bore promotes throat demise. On the other hand, modern steel barrels hold up better than barrels of a half-century ago. The 220 Swift is not gentle on bores, but accuracy is not going to deteriorate in 1,000 rounds either, which was the

number associated with early Swifts. Top-notch accuracy can also be maintained by cutting back on the powder charge. This does not mean reducing Swift velocity to 222 stature. Dropping off 100 to 200 fps can lessen bore wear. The bothersome thing about dropping back in velocity to save the Swift barrel is performance; the reason for owning a Swift is bullet speed, with attending benefits. A compromise is in order—for target work and most varminting, a muzzle velocity in the area of 3700 to 3800 fps is sufficient. Push the Swift full-throttle for serious long-range work only.

Cartridge Case Life. Due to the same factors, copious hot gases cutting through a bore of small volume, cartridge cases also take a beating. Brass tends to flow. The biggest problem with brass flow in a cartridge case is neck lengthening. The lengthened neck can cause big problems, with erratic pressure and reduced accuracy. Pressures can reach the problem state, where primers are blown. The answer to improved case life is trimming. Swift brass, as noted above, is very strong. It is in fact quite long-lasting. But it must be trimmed. Outside (or inside) neck-turning is highly recommended for the Swift. By trimming the Swift case neck back and by turning the neck, length and brass thickness remain within safe limits. The bullet is not pinched in the leade. Constant neck friction is maintained.

Serious Swift shooters should buy a supply of cartridge cases, rather than a box here and a box there. Before loading the virgin brass for the first time, chamfer the neck both inside and outside. For professional level case uniformity, outside neck-turn the *new* brass. This maneuver helps bring the cases into uniform specifications. Keep a careful rec-

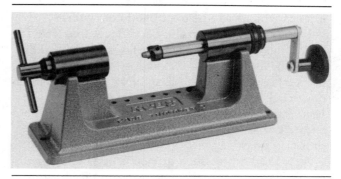

Because case stretch is prominent in "hot" cartridges, this case trimmer becomes an important tool for tailoring any centerfire cartridge, including the Swift, with maximum loads.

ord of case use, marking down how many times each case is reloaded, and the exact components of the reload. It's not a bad idea to trim the Swift case after first reloading. It hurts nothing to cut back to a case length of 2.195 inches. The slightly shorter neck will not impair the load. Shorter necks tend to reduce chamber pressure, in fact. Clean the primer pocket before reloading the case. And watch for signs of case fatigue, especially primers that seat with very little effort, indicating minimum friction. When a primer seats in the pocket so easily it can hardly be felt going in, that indicates a degree of head expansion, and a case that is probably used up.

Swift Accuracy. While the barbs launched against the Swift's bore and case life are somewhat well-earned by the cartridge, denegration concerning accuracy is not legitimately leveled. Dean Zollinger, the custom gunmaker, built a nice 220 Swift that I had access to for two years' worth of shooting. In short order, it was easy to see that Zollinger's custom Swift was accurate. Groups of .70 inch were common. Groups ranging in the half-inch realm were possible at 100 yards. A factory Model 70 Winchester provided groups of about .75 to 1.00 inch at 100 yards from the bench with factory loads. Norma 220 Swift ammo was used. The Swift cartridge is accurate. There are, however, at least three points to consider in regard to maintaining and improving that accuracy.

The first is barrel and barrel bedding. The Swift cartridge can generate a good deal of heat in its operation. After all, any cartridge is a sort of heat engine. Lightweight barrels are not going to dissipate this heat as well as heavier barrels. Furthermore, when a bullet flies downbore at more than 4000 fps, that in itself causes a specific set of harmonics which may be controlled best with a heavier barrel and careful bedding. A free-floated barrel may work best on one rifle, especially if the action is tightly bedded. However, the pressure-point system of bedding may have to be tried in order to achieve best accuracy from other Swift barrels. The accurate Zollinger rifle wore a fairly heavy barrel, and it was closely bedded with a pressure point.

Avoid rapid fire. Such advice is easy to live with on the range, more difficult to observe in the varmint field, especially on prairie dogs where many shots may be fired in a short time from one location. However, heating the steel rapidly and keep-

Factory ammo is available for the Swift, although the cartridge did fall into a period of poor notice for a time. Norma 220 Swift ammo is now offered through Federal Cartridge Company.

ing it hot may cause undue throat wear. The eroded throat will then lead to loss of accuracy. It's that simple.

Something else happens when a bullet screams down the bore at high velocity—it deposits part of itself on the rifling in the form of metal fouling. An "inaccurate" Swift was brought to my attention. It was incapable of producing a two-inch, 100-yard, five-shot group off the bench, with any load. Methods for detecting metal fouling, and removing the copper wash from the lands of the rifling (detailed in Chapter 29) restored that Swift's accuracy.

The 220 Swift is accurate, but it is a highly specialized machine and it requires initially correct construction, good barrels that are well-bedded, and a bit of preventive maintenance to preserve accuracy.

Another means of improving accuracy in the Swift is the reduced load. This is in effect admitting that the Swift does not always operate best at its intended level of performance; however, in all tests (with three Swift rifles) cutting the powder charge back, and thereby reducing the muzzle velocity of the bullet, accuracy was improved. In a sense, this is a negative statement concerning Swift accuracy, for the cartridge does not seem to perform at peak accuracy when loaded "up to snuff." There are some loading problems with the Swift, then, but not all of them are related to the Swift alone. Some of these factors attend all high-velocity cartridges. The high-performance round requires careful management.

Loading Problems. When it comes to reloading, the Swift can be particularly cantankerous. One alleged fault about the cartridge is a supposed propensity for pressure excursions. Adding more powder or a heavier bullet to a load, or even changing from primer A to primer B, may increase chamber pressure. But we expect such changes. The pressure excursion, on the other hand, is a rise that's unexpected. It is difficult to determine its cause. The use of reduced charges of slow-burning powders in large-capacity cases has caused trouble—the Speer bullet company documented incidences of reduced-charge "detonations." The Swift is supposed to be prone to such excursions. None was found in these tests, however. In Speer's remote-control testing of reduced powder charges, including IMR-4350, no pressure problems were experienced. However, this is not offered as proof of anything, but rather as a comment pertaining to test facts. It is difficult to duplicate barrel failure in a short-started muzzleloader, for example, but many researchers are convinced of the danger of such short-started loads in spite of a lack of scientific proof.

The Swift should be loaded "by the book." What's new? That recommendation pertains to all cartridges. For example, the Swift was supposed to act up with reduced loads. But in building reduced test loads for this work, I followed Lyman data and experienced no problems. The Swift has been handed a false negative on this one. Nor did I have any trouble in working up safe maximum loads for this book. The problems that did pop up were the same ones experienced in the loading of all "hot" cartridges. The Swift does digest some powders a little better than others. In our testing, W-760 performed well, for example. But to label the Swift "hard to load for" because it does not work well with all powders is unfair. Case quality must be maintained, as suggested above. So long as cases are kept at proper overall length without thick necks, the rest of the Swift loading game is played with the same reloading rule book that applies to all of the 22 centerfires.

Swift Bullets. All high-velocity cartridges make almost unrealistic demands upon bullets, but high-speed varmint rounds are in a way the worst. The bullet from a hot 22 centerfire must first withstand its flight through the bore without stripping its jacket. The Swift bullet, rushing downbore at more than 4000 fps, for example, must hang together during the trip. Then it exits the muzzle and smacks

The two projectiles on the left are 50-grain varmint bullets, not appropriate in the Swift for big game, but the heavier bullets to the right are big-game strong—of Barnes, RWS, and Allred manufacture.

that invisible wall known as the atmosphere. Many shooters declared that some of the bullets they tried in their Swifts never reached the target. They simply blew up in the air. So make the bullet harder, tougher. That will solve the problem. OK, but then the bullet will not serve properly in the varmint field on two counts. First, it will not maintain proper frangibility on smallish and thin-skinned varmints. The goal of the varmint bullet is to render a spectacular harvest, even at long range. Heavy jackets are out. Second, the harder bullet may ricochet. A major tenet regarding varmint cartridges is bullet disintegration on ground impact. So the Swift bullet must withstand bore speeds exceeding 4000 fps, but it must not be so strongly constructed that it passes through the varmint without imparting its energy, or glances from the earth instead of self-destructing on contact. That's a lot to ask, all right, of a flying, jacketed lead core.

The modern bullet manufacturer has come through, in the main, with such a projectile. There is, however, no short-cut in finding the best Swift bullet for the individual rifle. The Swift fan should make up his mind right now to buy his cartridge cases in a good-sized lot, 60 to 100 rounds, prepare them as suggested above, and then gather samples of various appropriate 22-caliber jacketed bullets in order to run tests of projectile performance. Once the shooter finds that happy combination of powder, primer, and bullet, he simply sticks with it. Don't forget the custom bullet. Many custom bullet-makers are producing specialty projectiles that work admirably in the Swift. Dedicated varminters have also joined the ranks of bullet-makers. Dave Corbin's bullet-making machinery is now offered at reasonable cost, for example, to anyone who wants to handcraft his own missiles. Bullet failure is not Swift failure. Match the correct bullet to the Swift before expecting proper performance. I suggest that most failures in the deer field come when the Swift is loaded with the wrong projectile.

TRAJECTORY AND SIGHT-IN

With a 50-grain bullet starting at 3900 fps, the Swift can be sighted two inches high at 100 yards. The center of the pattern will strike only three inches high at 200 yards with this sight-in. At 300 yards from the muzzle, the bullet lands about 3/4 inch low, and all the way out to 400 yards, it drops about nine inches. This means that even in prairie-dog hunting, shots to 350 yards require that the

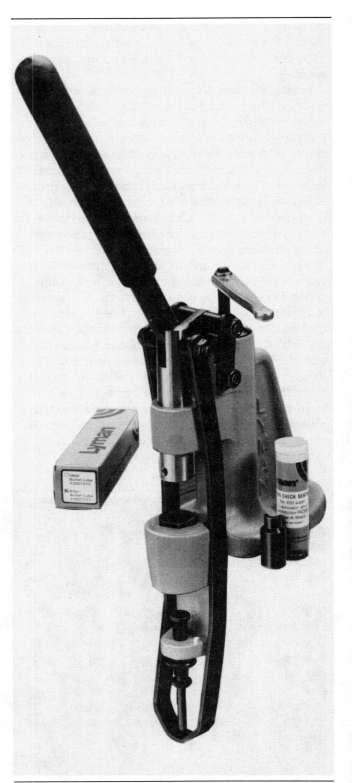

The Swift can be successfully loaded with cast projectiles. This bullet sizer with lubricator is used to ensure proper dimension of the projectile.

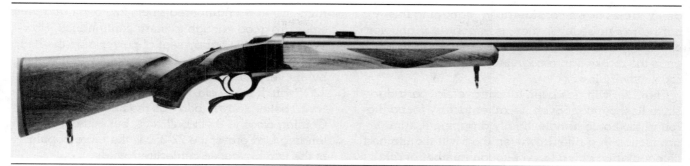

Many different rifle styles have been chambered for the Swift, including the single-shot Ruger No. 1 Special Varmint with 26-inch barrel.

shooter do no more than hold at the top of the target. At 400 yards, the crosswire of the scope can be held under the chin of a standing woodchuck and the bullet will drop into the target. That's flat-shooting. With the 60-grain bullet beginning its journey at 3700 fps, a sight-in 2.5 inches high at 100 yards gives the bullet a strike-high of only 3.5 inches at 200 yards with a zero of 300 and a drop-low at 400 yards of only nine inches. The 60-grain bullet's superior ballistic profile grants it a trajectory very much like the 50-grain bullet, even though the latter starts 200 fps faster.

LOADS FOR THE SWIFT

Factory loads fairly well live up to their paper promises. Winchester's 48-grain bullet slips the muzzle at about 3969 fps (my chronograph and a 26-inch barrel). Norma's 50-grain pill gets away at about 4012 fps in the same barrel. Because of these excellent factory ballistics, gaining a great deal more velocity from handloading is not possible. However, the 220 Swift is widely handloaded for obvious reasons of versatility and economy, not to mention the tailoring of loads to a given rifle's idiosyncrasies.

As noted, several powders work well in the Swift. W-760 is one of them. Forty grains of W-760 pushed a 60-grain bullet at 3556 fps from the 26-inch barrel, with very good accuracy. The 55-grain bullet was chronographed at close to 3800 fps muzzle velocity with 41.5 grains of IMR-4350; however, this load was not as accurate in the test rifle as some others. Most shooting was with 50-grain bullets. A 50-grain spitzer jetted out at 4055 fps with 38.0 grains of IMR-3031. A 50-grain bullet and 44.0 grains of N-204 powder produced an accurate load with a muzzle velocity just over 3900 fps.

A 50-grain bullet cracked a shade over 4000 fps muzzle velocity with 40.0 grains of IMR-4320 powder in one test rifle, but in that particular firearm accuracy was bettered by dropping this charge one grain. Another good load was 39.0 grains of IMR-4064 with the 50-grain bullet. Muzzle velocity was over 3900 fps and accuracy was good.

Two heavier bullets were chronographed and checked for accuracy. The 60-grain Hornady projectile did nicely with 40.5 grains of IMR-4350 powder. Muzzle velocity was just shy of 3700 fps in the test rifle and accuracy was better than an inch center to center at 100 yards. The 70-grain Speer achieved 3412 fps muzzle velocity using 39.0 grains of IMR-4350 powder. The 220 Swift rifles used in testing included a Ruger Model 77 Varmint, which was quite accurate and pleasant to shoot, as well as a Savage single-shot bolt-action varmint rifle, which was also very good. A custom heavy-barrel Swift with a 26-inch barrel was used for all chronographing. Only one reduced load was tried, but it was sufficiently accurate for squirrel and rabbit hunting. The only cast bullet readily available was Lyman's 54-grain No. 225462. The load was seven grains of SR-7625, which chronographed at 1666 fps muzzle velocity. Hornady's 55-grain full-metal-jacket bullet achieved 2425 fps with 16.0 grains of IMR-4227 powder.

BLAST AND RECOIL

The 220 Swift can convince shooters that they are being bucked about. But they are not. Blast is the culprit, not foot-pounds of free recoil. Naturally, a shooter should wear the same hearing protection with the Swift as with all other rifles, but when he combines a solid soft ear plug with muffs to reduce the incoming sound waves to the ear, the Swift suddenly tames down considerably. Managing this cartridge's noise level, then, is important in shooter control. The Swift is actually a pleasure to shoot once the marksman recognizes the fact that actual recoil is very low.

The 220 Swift has been a controversial cartridge since its inception. Even its father factory found the round too hot to handle, finally dropping it from production in a rifle. However, the Swift maintained its popularity with a large enough number of rifle-men to command its return in factory rifles. Several rifles are now chambered in the 220 Swift and their sales are good enough to merit continuance. However, the Swift's happy seat of power atop the heap of hot 22 centerfires has been seriously threatened by the very cartridge that first bore its name—the 220 Swift. It is the old WOS, Wotkyns Original Swift, better known today as the 22-250 Remington. Coming close to Swift ballistics, but without the attending bad press, the 22-250 is the more popular of the two big-cased centerfire rounds.

26 THE 22-250 REMINGTON

The 22-250 has a typically cockeyed evolution, with no clearer birthdate or parentage than other wildcat cartridges of its era. A bevy of inventors laid claim to the round. It is rivaled only by the 25-06 in number of brass-benders associated with its development. It is difficult to find all of its predecessors, which, no matter how remotely, influenced final 22-250 manufacture. Charles Newton was experimenting with a hot 22 centerfire in the very early 1900s, which precipitated further work of its kind. Of course, Harwood's "Hornet .22-20-55" on the 22 Single Shot solid-head case (probably the Maynard design), named by editor A.C. Gould of *Shooting and Fishing* magazine, can't entirely be left out of any 22 centerfire story. All manner of experiments were going on with all manner of cartridges. W.V. Lowe's Hornet with a 1:12 rate of twist, firing 75-grain bullets backed by 20 grains of black powder, gives a hint concerning attitudes. Shooters, wildcatters especially, were looking for something far more exciting than small bullets at modest velocity. The WOS is without a doubt a major 22-250 design of early days. Recall that this is the Wotkyns Original Swift, which was a 250-3000 Savage cartridge necked to hold 22 caliber bullets—no shoulder angle change noted. Remember, too, that Winchester decided to build the Swift on another case, and not from 250 Savage brass.

By 1937, the 22-250 wildcat was more than a little popular among shooters who did not mind the fact that they could not buy factory ammo for the cartridge. J. Gebby and J. Bushnell Smith are credited with producing a particular version of the 22-250 wildcat at this time, although exact individual contributions are not clear. Gebby, according to Ackley and others, copyrighted the name "Varminter," but he probably registered it as a trademark. Many of us growing up in the 1950s, and looking for a hot 22-caliber varmint rifle, highly ad-

mired the Gebby Varminter. The name "Varminter" was attached to the 22-250 design even after Remington introduced its factory version.

Speculation is interesting. Had the Wotkyns Swift become Winchester's Swift, the history of the 22-250 would certainly have been different. Rather than

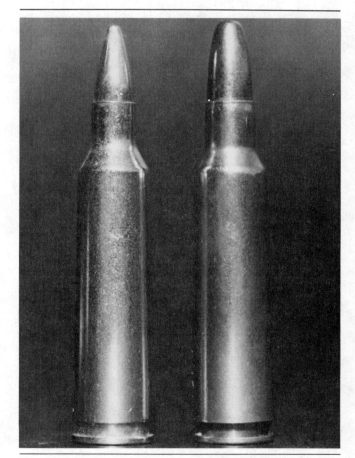

The 22-250 (left) was born of the 250-3000 Savage cartridge (right). It is essentially a necked-down 250 Savage, although the shoulder angle is sharper on the 22-250.

living its early life as a wildcat, the 22-250 would have been a factory cartridge more than 50 years ago. On the other hand, one must wonder what would have become of the 22-250 had it fallen prey to the outlandish praise (much of it deserved) heaped upon the 220 Swift. Many shooters of the time did not know what to make of the Swift. Was it a deer cartridge? One well-known marksman of the day praised it as the *best* round for deer. Did it wear bores out in a heartbeat? Many felt it did. Most of all, the Swift's timing was ill-fated, because the best barrel steels for the cartridge were still a short distance down the pike. All of these faults may have been handed to the 22-250 had it been

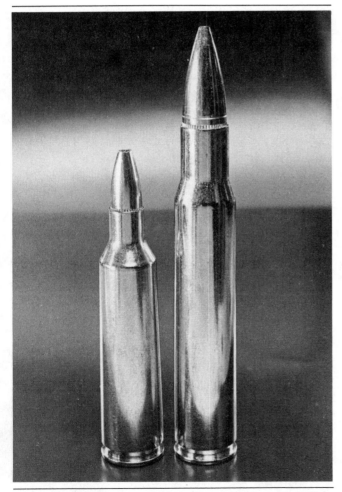

The 22-250 (left) began as a wildcat based on the 250 Savage round, which was a shortened and necked-down 30-06 cartridge. Therefore, ancestry of the 22-250 goes back to the 30-06 (right). Note that the head sizes are the same.

Winchester's Swift.

But the 22-250 would evade such criticism. The marksmen who gravitated to the 22-250 were wildcatters and lovers of handloads. They not only knew quite a bit about shooting, but they also knew what to expect from hot loads. If early 22-250 barrels burned out, there was no Winchester company to complain to. If cases did not last as long as expected, there was no factory ammo to blame. If the 22-250's bullets were less than satisfactory on varmints, or even deer, the fault was often associated with the individual's handload more than the bullet-making company's product. Thus, the 22-250 avoided the criticism attracted by the Swift.

Besides, it was a better balanced cartridge. In reality the 22-250 did not suffer quite the woes of the Swift. Why the beloved little necked-down 250 Savage remained a wildcat for so many years is a wonder. Browning did offer a 22-250 rifle in 1963, before factory ammo was available. Then in 1965, Remington's Model 700 rifle became available in the *Remington* 22-250 caliber. In spite of the name change, the 1970 Speer reloading manual still labeled the cartridge a ''.22-250 or 'Varminter.''' But Remington factory ammo was available in 1965. Remington had tamed this wildcat, and it would become known henceforth as the 22-250 Remington, finalized as a 250 Savage cartridge necked to 22 caliber, but with a slightly sharper 28-degree shoulder.

The factory cartridge gained a great following. Given the same barrel length, the 22-250 was not too far behind the 220 Swift in muzzle velocity. The smaller 22-250 had most of the Swift's velocity without quite the fuss associated with the 220, shooters said. There was to be a takeover. The Swift plummeted from grace, while the 22-250 ascended on angel's wings. The 22-250 was versatile. It handled bullets from as light as 40 grains to as heavy as 70 grains. Reloading was no problem with the 22-250. Case life wasn't bad. Barrels seemed to last fairly long. Few individuals stopped to consider that the Swift did all of these things, too, with modern barrels, and when loaded to duplicate the 22-250's ballistics. The 22-250 was proclaimed the long-range varminter's delight, good to 400 yards if a shooter knew how to hold. Factory rifles were readily available, not only in varminters with heavy barrels, but in all actions and styles.

One rifle tested for this book was an Ultra Light 22-250. Although it weighed under six pounds with

Factory ammo for the 22-250 abounds. Federal Cartridge Company offers 22-250 ammo from Norma.

Remington. Rifle selection is huge. There are several heavy-barrel varmint models made to order for long-range work where repeated fire is the rule, and a host of sporters in 22-250 Remington caliber as well.

ACHIEVING TOP ACCURACY

The 22-250 is so often applauded for its accuracy that this factor was the first to be tested. In one sense, the testing was "loaded" in favor of the cartridge because the rifle selected for accuracy work was a custom heavy-barrel model with floated barrel and very carefully bedded action. All tenets of manufacture were aimed specifically to gain the best bullet groupings possible. The first ammo to be run through the rifle was factory fodder, Winchester's Supreme brand, a product designed for superior bullet-grouping. Both rifle and ammo came through. Groups of 1/2 inch at 100 yards from the bench were commonplace. Groups of 3/8 inch were attained several times. These good groups sizes continued with handloads. One disappointment— full-throttle loads did not produce best accuracy. The notion that cartridges must be mildly loaded in order to attain their best level of accuracy is widely accepted. It is not necessarily true, however, but it seemed to be so with the 22-250 cartridge in several test rifles.

Those who believe that only light loads create good accuracy should check the benchresters at their game. In one shoot, cartridges loaded right up to the safe maximum level earned top places. In testing the 22 PPC for this book, full-throttle fodder proved as accurate as lighter recipes. Making a blanket statement of "fact" about a cartridge based on a few test rifles is hazardous. By the same token, one must present the findings, no matter how risky.

scope, it proved very accurate with its 22-inch barrel. Another 22-250 rifle that made it into the test field often was a Ruger Model 77 International with full-length stock and 18.5-inch barrel, which we used mostly on jackrabbits. Of the three test rifles used for chronographing and benchrest shooting for accuracy, the chief was a custom job built by Dale Storey. This was the "shootingest" 22-250 of the bunch, and was used for accuracy work, although velocity readings were taken from another rifle with a 26-inch barrel. Over the years, many 22-250s have crossed my transom, and I have liked them all. The bottom line is this:
anyone who desires a 22-centerfire rifle for long-range varmint hunting on anything from prairie dogs to coyotes can't go wrong with a 22-250

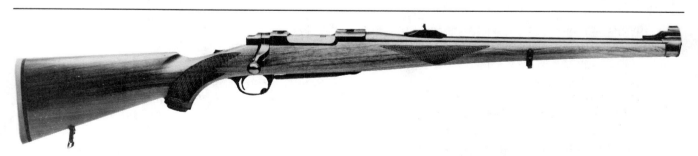

The 22-250 is chambered in many different rifles, including the Ruger M-77 International with 18.5-inch barrel. The author used an International rifle in 22-250 on a successful Montana white-tailed deer hunt.

Dale Storey's custom 22-250 proved very accurate. Dale used a 22-250 long before the round "went factory."

So my recommendation is to load the 22-250 down a peg for best accuracy.

Lack of finest accuracy with highest velocity was disturbing. The original goal in testing the 22-250 began to grow foggy in perspective. The whole idea was to gain stupendous long-range ballistic performance coupled with peak accuracy. But in the test rifles, the most accurate groups were with 52- to 53-grain match bullets at about 3600 to 3700 fps muzzle velocity. Nothing in the 3900-fps range was as accurate in the test rifles. It seemed that velocities over 3700 fps defeated accuracy. I had to conclude my testing before solving the problem. However, many of us believe that there is a solution: the correct combination of rifling twist, bullet construction and design, primer type, and powder type and charge that will deliver optimum accuracy potential and ballistic performance. In the varmint-hunting field, the 22-250s were put up against a very accurate 22 PPC USA rifle. The latter boasted the best shot-for-shot ratio of hits of any rifle/cartridge combination during the duration of field work. Accuracy was the reason. However, top accuracy with the 22 PPC was achieved at maximum performance, with the little scooter pushing 52- to 53-grain missiles at very close to 3600 fps muzzle velocity, quite close to the 22-250 when the latter was loaded for best accuracy.

Forthcoming tests will include a variety of bullets. The reason for continued testing is the high level of accuracy with the 22-250 at high, but not top-end muzzle velocity. If the 22-250 can produce those results at 3600 to 3700 fps, it can produce them at 3900+ with the correct combination of components in the right barrel. At least that is the precept.

Lest anyone think that accuracy deterioration at ultimate velocity meant fist-sized groups at 100 or even 200 yards, let me clear the air. The worst groups provided by the Storey 22-250 rifle were .80 inch for five shots, and these with 50-grain bullets leaving the muzzle at a chronographed velocity of 3964 fps. Furthermore, accuracy held up at long range. Groups at 200 yards settled into about 1.50 inches, for example. However, tests at 300 yards were thwarted by atmospheric conditions and were never satisfactory. Wind prevented good grouping on three occasions, and testing time ran out.

The 22-250 Remington is a very accurate cartridge, capable of producing splendid results in target-shooting as well as in the varmint field. If your 22-250 is not accurate, check the condition of the firearm and your ammunition. If handloads are suspect, give Winchester's Supreme ammo a try.

BALLISTICS

It is interesting to compare the 22-250 with the 220 Swift, because the comparison is a natural. After all, the Swift was kicked off the throne by the 22-250, at least as far as current popularity is concerned. Is one really that much ahead of the other in how fast the bullets fly? Factory ammo provided velocities in the 3700-fps domain for the 22-250. Bullets of about the same weight were driven in the high 3900s and even at a shade over 4000 fps in the factory Swift. If the shooter were looking for the ultimate in velocity from a factory-loaded 22 centerfire, he would have to pick the Swift. But both Swift

Winchester Supreme factory ammo in 22-250 Remington proved very accurate in a Dale Storey custom rifle. Part of the reason for such accuracy is the bullet—a 52-grain match hollow-point.

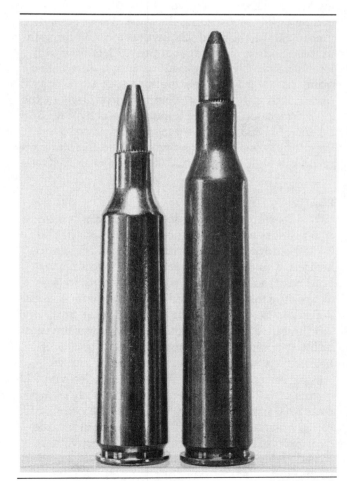

The biggest rival of the 22-250 has been the 220 Swift (right). However, in terms of popularity, today's clear winner is the 22-250.

and 22-250 fans are handloaders. And there the ballistic balance between the two cartridges evens considerably. Remember that velocity variation of 100 fps between any two test rifles is not uncommon. Therefore, view the following as presented and intended—as a general statement only, not an iron-clad guarantee.

Of course, only those loads that achieved allowable pressure levels were compared. It would be easy to stack the deck in favor of one cartridge or the other by simply pushing one at higher pressure level. Both test rifles had 26-inch barrels and bolt actions. The highest velocity reached with the 22-250 and a 50-grain bullet was 3919 fps using 36.5 grains of H-4895 powder. As in all tests, elevation at the site was 6,000 feet above sea level. Temperature was 87 degrees F. Moments later, the 220 Swift sang its song, with the same brand of 50-grain bullet. Top muzzle velocity was 4078 fps with 40.0 grains of IMR-4064 doing the work. What does it mean? Simply, the old 220 Swift remained top gun in this one test. What does it prove? Not an awful lot. However, it bears repeating that ballistics is a game of feet and inches, feet-per-second velocity and inches of trajectory. Using 60-grain bullets, the 22-250 registered 3571 fps muzzle velocity with 37.0 grains of H-380, which seemed to be close to the limit for the test rifle. The Swift shoved the same 60-grain pill at 3644 fps with 37.5 grains of IMR-4064.

LOADS

Winchester brass and Remington standard large-rifle primers were used in every load tested. The 22-250 enjoyed success with a great many combinations. The old broken record plays again—test your personal rifle using various prescriptions okayed by the loading manuals. One of those loads will serve best in your own 22-250 rifle. A gratifying load in one of the test rifles, for both accuracy and ballistic potency, was a charge of 36.0 grains of IMR-4064 with a 52-grain match bullet. Muzzle velocity averaged 3788 fps. A 50-grain bullet with 37.5 grains of H-335 achieved a muzzle velocity of just over 3900 fps. A fairly hot load was 39.5 grains of H-380 powder driving a 50-grain bullet at a trace over 3900 fps. A very accurate and effective load was developed with Hercules Reloader 15 powder. In one test rifle, this powder provided the best accuracy achieved during testing, with a 52-grain match bullet driven at 3666 fps with 35.0 grains of fuel. Although the velocity of the 52-grain bullet

with this load was not equal to others, the combination was very effective in the varmint field for long-range shooting due to excellent accuracy.

Since the 220 Swift had been treated to two reduced loads, one with a lead cast bullet and the other a full-metal-jacket projectile, the 22-250 was given the same opportunity. It proved more accurate with these loads in the particular test rifle than the Swift had been in its. The cast-lead projectile, Lyman's No. 225462, weighing 54 grains, was propelled by 16.0 grains of IMR-4227 powder. Muzzle velocity was 2176 fps. Squirrel or rabbit hunting with a 22-250 and this load would be quite possible (although this shooter still prefers the 22 Long Rifle rimfire for the job). The 55-grain Hornady full-metal-jacket 22-caliber bullet attained a flat 2500 fps muzzle velocity also with IMR-4227 powder, 17.5 grains. The good shot willing to wait for correct bullet placement is going to bag his wild turkey with this load, despite the 22-250's lack of popularity for such work.

Toting Fadala handloads, John Roussalis carried his 22-250 into the field. With the 55-grain soft-point bullet backed by 17.0 grains of IMR-4227 powder, John bagged a fantastic gobbler in the Black Hills of Wyoming with one shot, meat spoilage minimal.

BLAST AND RECOIL

The 22-250 is credited with noticeably reduced recoil and blast as compared with the somewhat larger-cased 220 Swift. In identical barrel lengths, such differences were not discernible. The 22-250 is no 222 in recoil. Nor is it a 30-06. Measurable recoil is very low. Noise is not. The same points made concerning the 220 Swift apply to the 22-250. Foot-pounds of recoil is a hard figure. The amount of powder burned has a good deal to do with the resulting "thrust back" of the firearm. There are many other factors to consider as well. But the 22-250 and 220 Swift are simply too close in components to call one very different from the other in muzzle blast or recoil. Neither "kicks" much. Both are fairly noisy.

THE 22-250 HANDGUN

The 22-250 Remington is chambered in the Ultra Light Model 20 Reb Hunter's pistol. The Ultra Light pistol wears a 14-inch Douglas barrel. It is a bolt-action model, left-hand bolt so that the shooter need not remove his right hand from the grip to work the bolt. While no sights are provided, this pistol comes with a scope mount. It's a handgun

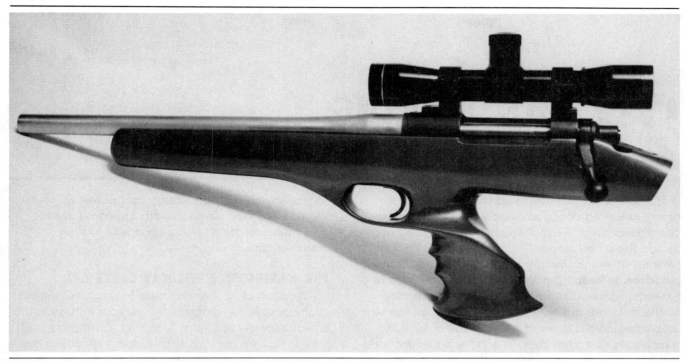

The Ultra-Light pistol is available in 22-250 caliber. This bolt-action model with scope sight proved very accurate in benchtesting.

meant for precision shooting. And it should wear a scope. The four-pound Ultra Light pistol with Timney trigger is a repeater, by the way, with a five-shot magazine. The stock is composed of a graphite-reinforced Kevlar, available in green, brown, black, or camouflage. An interesting pistol for the most popular hot 22 centerfire of the hour, the Ultra Light 20 with scope is capable of varminting when placed in the hands of a good pistoleer. Loads were not worked up for the 22-250 pistol. Powders found ideal in the longer barrel may not prove so in a 14-inch tube, however. Loading data for the 22-250 in the pistol will be seen in forthcoming manuals.

THE WILDCAT TAMED

Of all the hot 22-centerfire wildcats, none has made quite the impact of the 22-250 Remington. It has replaced, for all practical purposes, the wizard of whiz, the big 220 Swift. Swift enthusiasts say there is nothing to recommend the 22-250 over their favorite, not in ballistics, not even in the accuracy department. But the proof of this pudding is in the selling. There are only a handful of modern rifles currently chambered for the Swift, but the 22-250 is chambered in everything from pistols to full-blown varmint rifles with heavy barrels and big scopes. You can argue that the 22-250 has nothing on the Swift. But you can't argue with its success.

27 THE MAKING OF 22 WILDCATS

The alteration of existing cartridge cases into newly designed configurations is wildcatting. The basic question is: Why didn't the factory engineers design the case "correctly" to begin with? The answer is—they did. But they designed it for specific purposes, in keeping with the accepted patterns of the time. Some cartridge shapes were predicated on theories that did not necessarily hold up. For example, we note a tapered body on the old 30-30 Winchester cartridge case. The taper was supposed to aid (some experts say) the withdrawal of the fired case from the chamber, especially if the chamber has become dirty or fouled. However, having owned and fired the straight-wall 30-30 Improved for years, I know that the taper is unnecessary. Besides, there were numerous blackpowder cartridges with straight walls. The 45-70 Springfield was one. It worked fine in its original single-shot rifle, and just as well in the lever-action models later chambered for it.

Hindsight offers 20/20 vision to the near-sighted. Looking back, it is easy to see that many of the factory cartridge designs were unimaginative. The 22 Hornet, for example, was a nifty round. It served its purpose well. The little gem gave good ballistics for medium-range varminting and turned out to be a turkey hunter's delight to boot. However, the wildcat 22 K-Hornet could still be loaded to duplicate original 22 Hornet ballistics, while offering much better ballistic potential for the handloader who sought higher velocity and flatter trajectory from the altered 22 Hornet case. Wildcatters are to shooting what race-car engineers and mechanics are to their sport. The wildcatter fearlessly forges ahead with designs from clever to silly, wild to mundane, useful to useless. Perhaps the greatest recognition that the wildcat cartridge can achieve is factory acceptance. And many of them have. However, wildcatters have also made a direct impact upon the engineers who design factory cartridges. Slope-shouldered, taper-walled cartridge cases are seldom found on the drawing boards of today's ammo-company engineers.

THE MAKING OF A WILDCAT CARTRIDGE

Alteration of an existing case to improve powder capacity and the shape of the powder charge is the basic rationale behind wildcatting. A tapered-wall case is "blown out" straight. Sloping shoulders are sharpened. These changes facilitate greater powder capacity, but they also cause the powder charge to take on a different shape within the case. Accuracy devotees insist that the short, fat, straight-walled case with about a 30-degree shoulder works best for delivering ballistic uniformity. Take a look at what is currently the world's most accurate cartridge, the 6 PPC USA, and you will see that this benchrest winner has the squat shape, as does its 22 PPC USA counterpart. A reamer, which incorporates the straighter wall and sharper shoulder, is introduced to the existing barrel or a new barrel and the resulting chamber matches the specifications of that reamer. Thus, an old chamber is altered to accept (and actually build) the new wildcat, or a new barrel is chambered afresh with the wildcat design.

Fireforming, or the Improved Case. Suppose you have a 22 Hornet rifle. You want to turn it into a 22 K-Hornet. A gunsmith runs the K-Hornet reamer into the chamber, which removes metal and creates the new cartridge shape. When you fire the standard 22 Hornet in the new chamber, the brass case "balloons" out to fill the larger void. The Hornet case is now fireformed to 22 K-Hornet dimensions. Fireforming with factory ammo is perfectly acceptable. Or, you can handload cases for fireforming, using a load fairly close to full throttle (reduced loads used for fireforming sometimes fail to expand the case

Wildcatting brought about the "improved" cartridge. Notice the center cartridge here, a 218 Mashburn Bee wildcat. It was made by fireforming standard 218 Bee rounds (shown on both sides of the Mashburn) in an improved chamber. The resulting neck is much shorter, giving the round greater capacity. Shoulder angle of the wildcat is also steeper.

Cartridge Efficiency. There has always been controversy concerning the efficient cartridge. It is soundly argued that many 22-wildcat rounds are not very efficient. Efficiency entails the best use of the powder charge. It may be looked at as velocity per grain weight of powder. The 222 Remington is more efficient than the 220 Swift, for example. Twenty-seven grains of powder in the 222 Remington can push a 50-grain bullet at 3300 fps muzzle velocity. It takes, with one powder at least, 44 grains to give the 220 Swift's 50-grain bullet 600 fps additional velocity. That is a 15-percent velocity increase for about 40 percent additional fuel—not very efficient, you say, and you are right. However, the family sedan may get 30 miles per gallon of

fully in the new chamber). The fireformed cases are then ready for handloading with the wildcat recipe. Fireforming has brought about an "improved case."

Fireforming can also thrust the latter portion of the neck forward so that it actually becomes a part of the cartridge body, leaving a shorter neck on the round, but increased powder capacity. Necks may also be trimmed to shorten them.

Necking Down. In building 22 wildcats, the major alteration of existing brass comes in necking down the cartridge. The 22-250 Remington is a perfect example. It began life as a 250-3000 Savage cartridge. The major alteration in changing the 250 Savage into the 22-250 was necking the cartridge down from 25 caliber to 22 caliber. The obvious result is the combination of a lighter bullet with the relatively large case capacity of the original cartridge. If the walls of the case are blown out, then the capacity is further improved. And if the slope of the shoulder is sharpened as well, the shape of the powder charge, as it resides in the case, is changed. The original 22-250 round was created by necking down 250 Savage brass to 22 caliber, seating a 22-caliber bullet behind the appropriate powder charge, and firing the cartridge in the 22-250 rifle chamber.

Perhaps the greatest form of recognition for a wildcat is factory manufacture. It took the 22-250 (left) many decades to earn that distinction. The little wildcat, shown here with the 30-06, remained a do-it-yourself round until fairly recent times.

fuel, while the Formula One race car is doing well to get three. But don't enter your family car in the Indy 500. You're going to lose. Select a cartridge, wildcat or factory, based on application, not cartridge efficiency. Some wildcats are very efficient. Others are not. But many that are not efficient do a tremendous ballistic job.

Overbore Capacity. This factor is related to cartridge efficiency. It suggests a balance between the weight of the powder charge and the bore volume of the firearm. Oftentimes, 22 wildcats don't fare well in terms of overbore-capacity relationships. A point of diminishing returns is reached in which the addition of more fuel yields minimal improvement. But once again, as long as the cartridge remains perfectly safe in pressures, the shooter should not concern himself with overbore capacity or the effect of diminishing returns. It is true that certain plateaus are reached. The 22-06, for example, does burn up a lot of extra powder for a minimal return on the investment. Until different powders come along, the 22-06 is not the best choice. One wildcatter, in an effort to show how ridiculous overbore capacity can become, made up a dummy novelty cartridge toy by reducing a 50-caliber machine-gun cartridge necked to hold a phonograph needle. The ridiculous looking (non-shooting, of course) cartridge was a model for the concept of true overbore capacity.

Furthermore, certain overbore-capacity wildcats have been altered by shortening the original cartridge case. The end result was an improved or blown-out case, necked down to 22 caliber, but one not so long as the parent cartridge. For example, the 22 K-Hornet Junior was a short version of the Hornet, but due to sharp shoulder and straight-wall capacity, developed about 2000 fps muzzle velocity. Later, we would see a 228 Ackley Magnum Rimmed, which was the 30-40 Krag cartridge case-necked down and blown out, but also cut off for a shorter overall length. We shall see below that wildcatters have also worked with the interesting 25 Remington case and often shortened it to provide a better relationship of powder to bore size.

IMPORTANT 22 WILDCATS

Many innovative shooters of our recent past were responsible for the great 22 centerfires we enjoy today. Niedner, Donaldson, Mann, Pope, Newton, Ackley, Lovell, Kilbourn, Lindahl, Gebby—these are but a few people we can thank for making the

most interesting branch of cartridges known today, the hot 22s (and their super-accurate 6mm brothers). Harvey Donaldson may have had a 22 wildcat at the turn of the century. History is not entirely clear on the matter. He was supposed to have built a case on his own design, firing a 22-caliber bullet. Some say Savage was offered the design, but went with the 22 Savage Hi-Power instead. The early wildcatters often used expended 22 Short cartridge cases as jackets for their bullets. The goal was clear from the beginning: to make a flat-shooting cartridge for varminting, and even deer hunting, of caliber 22 dimension.

The great Charles Newton, lawyer and cartridge designer, built an interesting wildcat based on the 30-40 Krag cartridge case, which he necked to 22 caliber. It fired a 70-grain bullet at a reported 3276-fps muzzle velocity with 32.0 grains of Lightning No. 1 powder. This was very much like the Savage Hi-Power in ballistic punch. Hervey (not Harvey) Lovell had a 22-32-40 wildcat very early in the 22-centerfire cartridge game as well. This was, as the name implies, a 22 based on the 32-40 Winchester case. We know that as early as 1890, Reuben "Iron Ramrod" Harwood was working on a 22 Hornet design. When the 25-20 Winchester was necked down to 22 caliber by Lovell, he called one version the No. 2 Lovell R-2, the "R" for M.S. Risley, the gunsmith who built the second reamer for the 22-3000 Lovell (improved). The "No. 2" represented the second adaptation of the cartridge. Essentially, here was the old Harwood Hornet blown out to have a nearly straight wall and a 30-degree shoulder. Lovell developed other wildcats: a No. 7, which was an improved Zipper; a No. 9, which was a 25-35 Winchester case necked to 22 caliber and improved; and the Lovell 22-250, the 250-3000 Savage necked to 22 caliber and given a 28-degree shoulder.

Never be surprised when you read various versions of who invented what in the world of wildcatting. Some inventions were quite probably simultaneous, or nearly so, as with Nobel prized awarded to two scientists for the same discovery, though neither scholar knew the work of the other. This is why firearms scholars may claim various inventors for the 22-250 cartridge. There were many other 22 wildcats that shared inventors. Sometimes only the names of the cartridges were different. Sometimes there were only minute differences in the specifications of two very similar cartridges. The "22 Stan-

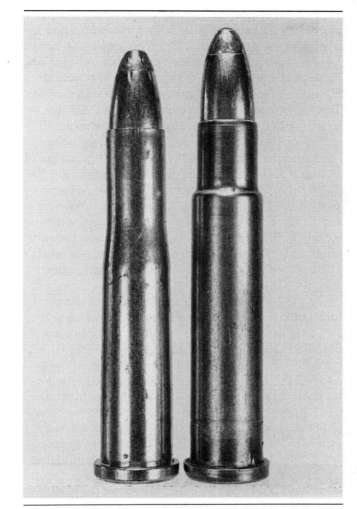

A greatly improved cartridge is the 22 K-Hornet (right) built by "blowing out" the regular 22 Hornet cartridge.

dard Varminter," for example, was built by necking a 250-3000 Savage down to 22 caliber. Sound familiar? Furthermore, not to throw ice water on anyone's flaming idea, but my pickle puss chronograph has not always registered quite the ray-gun velocities claimed by some of the fathers of wildcat cartridges. In fact, velocities at times were not even close to original claims. There may be two good reasons. First, some of the early wildcats were not really chronographed; velocities were computed by bullet drop. Second, pressures developed by some wildcats were no doubt very high. Claimed velocities were true, in such instances, but only at the expense of overly high pressure and short case life.

The data below are for historic purposes only.

Never use any of them in modern loading. The source of the load is given in each instance.

The 22 Hornet. Lysle Kilbourn's blown-out Hornet is indeed a much improved round in performance—an excellent round, provided that additional velocity is needed for the specific shooting task. Kilbourn was a gunsmith and a wildcat chamber specialist. He joined Lyman in the 1950s, but once worked for Remington, beginning for that company at the start of WWI. He also worked for Savage Arms. Savage aided Kilbourn in testing his K-Hornet, in fact. Obviously, the "K" in all of these wildcat cartridges stands for Kilbourn. The fireformed 22 K-Hornet, according to the 1953 publication, *Lyman Ideal Handbook No. 39*, drove a 45-grain bullet at 3000 fps using 11.5 grains of No. 2400 powder, while the standard 22 Hornet pushed the same 45-grain bullet at 2600 fps muzzle velocity with 9.7 grains of No. 2400. The 22 K-Hornet's shoulder angle was 35 degrees. Fireforming left the K-Hornet with a shortened neck (pushed forward), which further increased the powder capacity of the cartridge.

The 218 Mashburn Bee. A.E. Mashburn revised the 218 Bee case through fireforming, resulting in a

The so-called "Hornet problem"—case-head separation—is shown here in a wildcat K-Hornet. This fault occurs in both Hornet and K-Hornet if the case is not sized to headspace on the shoulder, and the firearm has too much headspace for the rim of the round.

case said to propel a 50-grain bullet at about 3300 fps. Such returns from a small case were alluring to anyone who wanted a flat-shooting cartridge in a tiny package. The 218 Mashburn Bee gains considerable added powder space by fireforming the neck out into the upper body portion of the case, leaving a shorter neck with sharper shoulder. Recent chronographings with a short 18.5-inch barrel gave the Mashburn Bee a muzzle velocity of 2972 fps with the 45-grain Hornady bullet backed by 15.0 grains of IMR-4227 powder.

The R-2 Lovell. Also called the 22-3000 Lovell, this is the 25-20 Winchester Single Shot (or Stevens Single Shot) case necked to 22 caliber. One version retained the original long neck and unaltered shoulder angle. But the R-2's neck was shortened, giving more case capacity and a sharper shoulder. The 50-grain bullet was pushed at about 3000 to 3100 fps muzzle velocity with the R-2. Today, this wildcat has few followers. But it was well-received when announced in a May 1934 issue of *The American Rifleman* magazine. Essentially Harwood's Hornet with a shorter neck, the round was picked up by riflemakers Griffin & Howe. Case headstampings read, "G&H 22-3000."

The 218 Bee case (right) is shown in sectioned form. Next to the Bee is a sectioned case formed from the original. On the left is a loaded wildcat round based on 218 Bee brass. Wildcatters have necked down, necked up and blown out just about every case design.

The K-222 Remington. In spite of the nice case design of the 222 Remington, it was indeed treated to a wildcat version in the K-222. The blown-out case design gave a muzzle velocity of about 3450 fps according to the Ideal No. 39 handbook, this with a 50-grain bullet and 22.5 grains of IMR-4198 powder. The same manual credited the standard 222 Remington with a muzzle velocity of 2990 fps using 20.0 grains of the same powder. With W-748 powder, the standard 222 Remington drove a 50-grain bullet at about 3300 fps in a recent test. Therefore, the K-222 data of 1953 seem accurate enough. Ackley improved the 222 Remington Magnum case, increasing powder capacity and sharpening the shoulder. Ackley's 222 Remington Magnum Improved is very much like the K-222, simply blown out to provide a larger powder package, without increasing cartridge neck length.

The 219 Donaldson Wasp. This epochal wildcat captured many a benchrest prize at one time. Now it has been replaced, for all practical purposes, by the 22 PPC and especially by the 6mm PPC, which currently dominate in accuracy circles, as evidenced by the number of shooters who use the latter cartridge in competition. The Wasp begins as a 219 Zipper, a slope-shouldered, taper-bodied case. Quite simply, it is blown out to give minimal body taper and a sharper shoulder. The neck is trimmed back after fireforming, because the long remaining neck is not valuable for any reason. The end result is a clean package that has proved not only accurate, but also very useful in the varmint field, with a 50-grain bullet leaving the muzzle at 3500 fps to almost 3700 fps, according to the load data.

The 219 Wasp was being worked on in 1945. There was speculation of a factory cartridge in this caliber. But there was also speculation of a 22-250 becoming a factory round at this time. As shown in the 22-250 chapter, it would be many years before that round would "go factory."

The original Wasp was built on the 25 Remington case, with a 30-degree shoulder and a final case length of 1.65 inches. It was immediately noted as an accurate cartridge.

A decade earlier, Harvey A. Donaldson—the Fultonville, N.Y., experimenter—was looking for an ideal 22-centerfire cartridge. His goal included a small cartridge case, high-intensity loading (good working pressures), superior accuracy, loading economy, and a very flat trajectory. Donaldson did not wish to use a long case. He tried the 25 Rem-

Dale Storey and his custom 218 Mashburn Bee. Dale used the Thompson/Center action as the heart of this creation. Wildcat rounds often find themselves chambered in interesting firearms.

ington case, but was not happy with it. Pressures seemed too high for the results obtained. He blamed poor case design.

Donaldson decided that a shorter, larger-bodied case would be better suited to his needs, reasoning that it would promote accuracy. So he went back to the 25 Remington case and shortened it to 1⅝ (1.635) inches. Now the case was short, with a "fat" body of little taper. Super accuracy resulted. Witnessed 10-shot groups within a one-inch circle at 100 yards were commonplace. However, Donald-

son decided to wildcat the 219 Zipper. He used the full-length Zipper case, but it was satisfactory in neither muzzle velocity nor accuracy. Through further effort, Donaldson altered the 219 Zipper to produce his famous wildcat, the 219 Donaldson Wasp, with its 1.75-inch trimmed case, a benchrest prize-winner and varmint cartridge deluxe.

The 219 Improved Zipper. While the 219 Donaldson Wasp ends up with a case length of 1.75 inches (the original 219 Zipper has a case length of 1.938 inches, to give an idea of how much neck is cut off in the final operation), the 219 Improved Zipper's cartridge case length is exactly the same as the original's. The 219 K-Zipper is another version of the wildcat. Even though these wildcats prove interesting to study, they offer nothing that cannot be gained with modern standard cartridges, although claims of very high velocities attend them. Most experimenters agreed that ballistics of the improved Zippers fall into the 22-250 domain. One load lists a muzzle velocity of 4080 fps with the K-Zipper. This load, from the *Ideal No. 39* handbook, called for 33.0 grains of IMR-3031 powder. A modern load in the 22-250 with a 50-grain bullet and IMR-3031 powder consists of about 35 grains, but muzzle velocity is listed at 3800 fps, not 4000.

The 22-30-30 Ackley. Of course, the 30-30 Winchester had to serve as a wildcat body for the 22-caliber bullet. Ackley's version offers a blown-out case with sharp shoulder and muzzle velocities in the 4000-fps range with a 50-grain bullet. A 22 Niedner Magnum was built from a 25-35 Winchester case. It was said to drive a 63-grain bullet at about 3250 fps, using 28.0 grains of No. 17½ powder.

The 22 Varmint-R. This cartridge made sense in Canada, where the well-known gunsmith G.B. Crandall developed it. British 303 brass was plentiful in the area. Necked down to 22 caliber, with less body taper and a sharp 29-degree shoulder, the 303 case was shortened to an overall length of 2.31 inches. A 50-grain bullet was reported to achieve over 3700 fps muzzle velocity.

The 22 Marciante Blue Streak. Al Marciante of Trenton, N.J., developed this hot little 22-centerfire wildcat by using the 22 Savage Hi-Power case with a 25-degree shoulder. The Blue Streak was credited with a muzzle velocity of 4000 fps firing the 50-grain bullet.

The 22-250 Varminter. J.B. "Gerry" Gebby legally protected the name 22-250 "Varminter" as a trademark. Early claims showed a 50-grain bullet at close to 4200 fps muzzle velocity in the 22-250. Since the 22-250 has its own short chapter, no fur-

ther details on the cartridge are presented here.

The 22 Hi-Power Improved. This wildcat is the Savage 22 Hi-Power cartridge in a blown-out version. Bullets of .227 to .228 inch are propelled in the 3400-fps realm, quite good for a 70-grain projectile of 22-caliber dimension.

The 220 Swift Improved. This Ackley wildcat offers little advantage over the original. It has a shorter case, but with racier lines. It does develop 220 Swift ballistics from its wildcatted shorter case, however. The 220 Wilsen Arrow is another wildcat Swift. Hosea Sarber, the well-known Alaska Game Commission "Wild Life Agent," said his version of the 220 Arrow was a 220 Swift with sharper shoulder, but the same case length. Other data show the Arrow as a target round with a shorter case length. In 1945, Roy Weatherby offered custom sporter rifles chambered for the 220 Rocket. The 220 Swift had great impact, and it enjoys its own short chapter.

Other 22 Wildcats. The following cartridges, not covered here, will be included in the next chapter on 22-centerfire big-game cartridges: 22 Super Varminter, 22 Newton, 228 Ackley Krag, 228 Ackley Magnum, and 226 Barnes QT.

THE WILDCATTERS' LEGACY

Wildcatters have been responsible for the development of many of our finest cartridges. However, this applause resounds too faintly in their hall of fame, for they've done much more than give us specific high-intensity cartridges to fill gaps in the list of factory rounds. Their efforts have changed the thinking of the shooting world, especially that of designers of factory cartridges. Modern cartridge developments, not only in the arena of 22-centerfire rounds, but in all calibers, can often be traced back to the work of these experimenters. Those of us who enjoy the state of the art in 22-centerfire shooting, as well as in the big-bore field, owe a great deal to the men who altered cartridge cases to suit their own sense of good design and their desire for increased ballistic performance and accuracy.

28 BIG GAME AND THE 22 CENTERFIRE RIFLE

This shooter is not privileged to hunt big game in his home state with a 22-caliber rifle, although it is perfectly legal to use a less powerful, less accurate large-bore sidearm. Therefore, tested information on the use of the 22 centerfire for deer and larger fauna were gathered in two ways: unimpeachable sources and three out-of-state hunts in areas that allow the 22 centerfire for big-game hunting. Argument has arisen from Day One concerning the lethality of the 22 on targets larger than varmints. Those in favor seized upon the little 22 rimfire to back their claims that good marksmen could take venison home with the pipsqueak 22 Long Rifle round, not to mention the hot 22-centerfire number. That argument may have hurt more than helped the 22 centerfire's cause. However, a couple decades past I used to hunt a Mexican ranch frequently. I kept track of the ranch foreman's record of deer harvests with his Stevens 22 rimfire rifle. In the scope of my knowledge, 11 deer were dropped with Don Gustavo's 22 Stevens rifle, all at ranges of 20 to 30 yards. One was a heart shot. Seven were neck-struck. Three fell to head shots. Although I oppose the use of the 22 rimfire for deer, I offer the above facts solely to create a platform for discussion.

Although most hunters agree that the 22 rimfire is wrong for larger animals, the record of 22-rimfire harvests looms large. When game departments outlawed the 220 Swift and other hot 22s for big game, a number of shooters reminded the world about many harvests with the much smaller 22 rimfire-cartridge. Jonas Ahguk, the Eskimo who killed a grizzly with his Woodsman 22-rimfire handgun was remembered. Somebody else recalled the circus elephant that was dispatched with a 22-rimfire cartridge following an accident (that one sounds fictional, but a police report cites it). Dr. H.V. Stent said, "I know personally of several head-shot moose dropped by a single .22 long rifle bullet" (*The American Rifleman*, March 1944, p. 12). Dr. Stent told of two other moose, lung-shot, that went no more than 100 yards after meeting up with a 22-rimfire bullet. I remembered a springbok, duiker, and impala dropped by the little 22 rimfire in Zimbabwe. Paul Bowman, British Columbia guide, used a 22 WMR on wolves, wolverine, and beavers. He dropped a black bear with two shots (75 yards) and killed a grizzly with the same 22 Magnum at 40 paces.

In light of so many harvests with the puny 22 rimfire, when game departments began to outlaw the hot 22 centerfire, some hunters saw red. P.O. Ackley, in the 1962 edition of his *Handbook For Shooters and Reloaders, Volume I,* wrote: "The author has made the statement from time to time that the .220 Swift is the greatest one-shot killer on deer and similar game ever produced." Ackley's temperature was up several degrees. He further commented in the same text: "It is the author's studied opinion that anyone who states the .220 Swift is not a great one-shot killer, is in effect saying he never fired a .220 Swift." One hunter claimed 49 deer for 49 shots with the .220 Swift. Lester Womack, then ranger in Grand Canyon National Park, Arizona, used the 220 Swift for years. He recommended it highly. W.D.M. Bell, the famous ivory hunter, used the Swift on stags in Scotland. An official charged with dispatching deer and other animals struck by vehicles on the highways, but not killed, used the Swift with amazingly uniform results. The Innuit used the 22 Hornet, 222, and 22-250 extensively on large game (but some have since gone to the big 300 Weatherby Magnum, it must be added).

Deer hunters were not alone in using 22-caliber centerfire rifles. Roy Chapman Andrews, the famous naturalist, reported the use of a 22-caliber rifle on tigers in China. Although I have never seen

Don Gustavo, the Mexican rancher/hunter who bags his bucks with a 22-rimfire rifle.

a tiger in the wild, I have seen a lion. I would use nothing so small on such a beast. However, in hunting for "The Great Invisible," a man-eating tiger, Andrews learned that his associate Caldwell had used, and found sufficient, a 22 Savage on a big tiger. Andrews pointed to the lack of good sense in this action, but Caldwell explained, "I killed eight or ten tigers with the .303 [Savage], and thought it was grand, but the Savage Company sent me out this rifle [a 22 Savage] and the first time I ever fired it was at a tiger. You ought to have seen what that tiny bullet did to him. He was a big tiger, too—man-eater that had killed several people in this very village" (from *Heart of Asia*, p. 35). Andrews warned Caldwell to get rid of the 22 Savage for tigers, but the hunter paid no attention. An-

drews learned later that Caldwell gave up on the 303 Savage and stayed with the 22 Hi-Power, killing several tigers with the little peashooter.

CONFIDENCE PLAYS A ROLE

The hunter capable of using a small-caliber firearm, because he is an expert woodsman and a good game shot, gains great confidence in his rifle. Confidence is a strange thing, as the following example shows. I was at the gun range sighting a rifle. During a lull in the shooting, the fellow from the next bench looked over. "Is that a Model 94 Winchester?" he asked. "The action looks like it, but the rest doesn't." I explained that the rifle was a custom Model 94 Storey Conversion, and that it was chambered for the 30-30 Improved, but my handloads

The *average* white-tailed deer is not a large animal. Correct bullet placement, with a proper bullet of big-game construction fired from a 220 Swift or similar cartridge, will drop a deer like this.

were not that far ahead of regular 30-30 ballistics. He smiled. "Used to have a 30-30, but I got rid of it for this." He lifted a pretty little short-barreled rifle from the bench. It turned out to be a 308 Winchester, firing the fellow's handloads with 150-grain bullets. "Never would trust a 30-30 for hunting around here," he assured me. Before the end of the shooting session, my chronograph was set up. And before the instrument was put away, my little 30-30 Improved with the 24-inch barrel using my handloads was compared with my benchmate's 308 Winchester outfit and his handloads. The 308 won, by the width of gnat's antenna. My 30-30 Improved launched a 150-grain bullet, a spitzer single-loaded as the first shot out of the bore, at just short of 2600 fps. The fellow's 308 fired a 150-grain bullet at a

few fps past 2700. He had confidence in his 308. I had confidence in my 30-30 Improved. We would each do well on game with our respective rifles.

That's what has happened with a great many fans of the 22 centerfire on big game. C.P. Wood is one of those fans. His 22-250 has barked many times in the pursuit of deer. When the rifle goes off, get the skillet hot; venison is headed for the table. Woody has a great deal of hunting experience all over the USA, including Alaska. He's a seasoned rifleman. A 22-250 in his hand is a deer rifle. There is no arguing the point. How can you argue with a long string of one-shot kills, never a wounded animal, and no trailing jobs? You can't. Nor can you argue too much with the results taken on a game department damage-control run, in which deer

The 22 Savage Hi-Power cartridge (left and right) has been used even on tigers (not recommended). However, as compared with the 220 Swift (center), the Savage round is much smaller.

were dispatched for management purposes. Several 22-centerfire rifles were put into use. The best of those tested were the 22-250, 220 Swift, and 22 Savage Hi-Power. Of the three, the latter was most effective; however, this was due to its 70-grain bullet of comparatively strong construction. Although the damage-control group did not consider the 222 Remington adequate, in later shooting a 222 with 1: 9 twist barrel was loaded with a 70-grain Speer bullet and the cartridge's effectiveness was vastly improved. Of the bullets tested, the 70-grain Speer semi-pointed projectile was deemed most proficient on deer in the 22-centerfire cartridge by these wardens.

THE AUTHOR GIVES IT A TRY

On one hunt, I dropped two mule deer with the 222 Remington. Neither buck was far. Neither animal was very large. And neither was an impressive

harvest. The deer did not go far, but only because of multiple shots delivered to the rib cage. I was not impressed, at the moment, with the 222 as a deer cartridge. On another out-of-state trip, I harvested a third buck with a 22 centerfire, this one a 22-250 firing a 70-grain Speer bullet. The deer, out about 150 yards, dropped instantly. It never moved. Here was an entirely adequate harvest with a 22 centerfire. I began to sense that the 222's problems lay not so much in the cartridge as with the bullet. My research and field work continued. "I made several pretty sloppy shots. . . It never failed to make me a one-shot kill," said A. Lee Robertson, then of the Information and Education Division of the Arizona Game & Fish Department. He was talking about the 22-250 on deer.

The hot 22 centerfire had to be on par with a rifle we had been using on deer and antelope for years. Fifteen years of bagging deer and antelope with a 6mm-222 (firing an 80-grain bullet at 2900 fps muzzle velocity) proved that the energy levels created with that round were entirely adequate for these animals out to 200 yards. If the 6mm-222 could do it, the 220 Swift could too. That was the next line of logic applied to the question of 22 centerfires on deer and other game. However, there was no arguing with the fact that game departments were not in the process of changing the anti-22-centerfire law. (Arizona did, however.)

A MATTER OF BULLETS

There were problems with the 22 centerfire in the big-game field, all right. And there should have been. Consider a snappy fall day in the Rocky Mountains. The hunter slowly works his way along a high-mountain ridge, glassing the other side of the canyon for mule deer. He spies one. It's a nice buck. Steadying his 300 Magnum, our man takes aim. The big 300 booms. The buck is struck with the surefire behind-the-shoulder shot. But it promptly runs off. Runs off? An unlikely scenario, you say—and you're right. But let's suppose, for the sake of this argument, that the hunter's 300 Magnum happened to be loaded with a 110-grain thin-jacketed varmint bullet. Then the scene is not so fictional after all. It is entirely possible that struck with a varmint bullet, even from a 300 Magnum, a big mountain buck could make a getaway. Few seasoned hunters will deny the validity of that statement. Then why are we surprised when a 22-centerfire rifle, firing a bullet made to blow up on the terrain or,

The hunter who stalks his quarry for a clear shot, and who places the bullet where it belongs, has no problem harvesting big game with the larger 22-centerfire cartridges loaded with bullets of proper jacket thickness. These pronghorn antelope were stalked to within 50 yards for this photo.

for that matter, on a gopher, fails to penetrate properly on big game?

Hunt deer or other big game with bullets designed to explode on contact and you are courting failure, no matter what cartridge you use, including a 300 Magnum.

One more deer became part of research for this work—a buck dropped by a friend using a 220 Swift. The bullet weighed only 55 grains, but it was a "handrolled" missile with core bonded to jacket. The deer fell to one shot. The bullet smacked a limestone ridge behind the animal. The largest single problem with the hot 22s on deer and other game is the bullet. If the hunter is going to employ a 22 varmint rifle for deer, he must take the varminting aspect out of the rifle by using big-game bullets in place of fragile missiles. Many such bullets are available. Winchester is in the process of building a big-game bullet to be factory-loaded in

223 Remington ammunition. The 70-grain Speer is noted as a very good 22-caliber bullet for targets larger than varmints. The 68-grain Hornady and 69-grain Sierra bullets offer 22-caliber projectiles that are heavier than normal.

For tough-jacketed 22 bullets, look to the custom bullet-makers. *The World Directory of Custom Bullet Makers*, by David R. Corbin of Corbin Manufacturing, gives names, addresses and bullet types offered by the makers of handrolled missiles. Also, Frank Washam of Acme Custom Bullets, San Antonio, Tex., makes some tough-jacketed .228-inch bullets in 60-, 70-, and 80-grain weights. Terry Allred makes strong-jacketed 22-caliber bullets in his shop in Logan, Utah. George Hoffman, who runs Custom Bullets by Hoffman out of Seaford, N.Y., makes .224-inch bonded bullets. Merle Kleen, Kleen-Strike Bullets of Sundance, Wyo., also offers bonded .224-inch jacketed bullets. And Harvey Riedel of Wyoming Custom Bullets (Cody) is another bonded-bullet craftsman. These bullets are made to do just the opposite of the varmint bullet. Rather than a quick blow-up, the projectile is engineered to hang together for penetration. It is, after all, the shape of the shock wave attending the bullet that does much of the work in a dispatch. We realize that the exit hole in many instances was caused by the shock wave and not the bullet. An exit hole of two-inch, even three-inch diameter is common with a 30-06, for example, but we know that the 30-06 bullet did not flatten out to a two-inch or three-inch diameter. The exploding varmint bullet imparts tremendous energy upon striking, great for varmints, but not great for larger animals where penetration is vital to harvesting success.

THE BOTTOM LINE

The bottom line in big-game harvesting is power and its transferal to tissue. A bullet may carry a half-ton of remaining energy at 100 yards. If that energy is used up on the surface of the target, that's OK if the target is a prairie dog or a woodchuck. But when the animal is a deer, it's not OK. The energy must reach the vitals of the big-game animal. Game departments have wrestled with the problem of minimum cartridge power for years. No one has found a solution satisfactory to all. A couple of states have no minimum caliber restriction. These states trust that the hunter will not sabotage his own efforts by using a firearm unworthy of the game. If a person has no faith in a 220 Swift for deer, certainly he will not employ that cartridge on deer. Conversely, if the hunter does have faith in the Swift on deer, chances are he has a proper bullet and load for the Swift, and he's a careful hunter who stalks for a good shot and places his bullet properly. But most states don't buy this approach. What they end up with is a can of wriggly worms. For example, consider a handgun firing a 210-grain bullet at 1400 fps muzzle velocity. The muzzle energy of that combination is 914 foot-pounds. At 100 yards, the remaining energy for this bullet is roughly 650 foot-pounds. Now take a look at a 22-250 rifle firing a 55-grain bonded bullet at 3800 fps. The muzzle energy here is 1764 foot-pounds. At 100 yards, remaining energy for the 22-250 bullet is over 1350 foot-pounds, considerably more than the handgun projectile. However, where I hunt the handgun round is legal; the 22-250 is not.

But energy alone does not spell cartridge effectiveness on big game. The 210-grain handgun bullet, some say, will open a greater wound channel than the 55-grain 22-caliber bullet. On the other hand, ballisticians agree that, imperfect as it is, the Newtonian concept of bullet energy is as good a barometer of "killing power" as we presently have to offer. It's a can of worms, all right. The bottom line in harvest effectiveness is a combination of bullet energy *with proper bullet construction*. One without the other is like a canoe without a paddle or a paddle without a canoe. You can deliver a mighty blow to the surface and deal out no more than a nasty "flesh wound." Or you can render a lesser blow to the vitals with a resulting clean harvest. The best combination is both—a powerful blow that reaches the vitals. A proper 22-caliber jacket bullet can deliver that blow to deer-sized game. The true expert woodsman, hunter, or marksman can drop even larger game with strongly made 22-caliber bullets when those bullets are well-placed.

The 222 Clan. When I think of hunting deer or antelope with any 22-caliber rifle, the 222 trio never enters my mind. But the little triple twos enter the minds of many others. The well-known outdoor writer, Bert Popowski, wrote in *American Rifleman* magazine, "A lady neighbor I trained with a .222 Sako was such an apt pupil that she took a total of 12 antelope and deer, all bucks, with just 12 shots. Her shots ranged from 75 to 150 yards, but were so cooly delivered that every animal was fatally hit." A 70-grain Speer achieved nearly 3000 fps in a 222 Remington using H-414 powder, 24-inch barrel. The 222 Remington firing bonded bullets would have to be considered lethal in the hands of hunters willing to stalk and capable of placing their bullets with precision. Mr. Popowski's pupil proves the point. Yet, the 222 should be considered a minimum for deer and antelope where allowed at all. A 223 Remington fired the Sierra 63-grain semi-pointed bullet at more than 3100 fps. The 222 Remington Magnum can do likewise. The 22 Hornet and like cartridges are not mentioned in this chapter, because they are not among the truly hot 22 centerfires. Even with strongly constructed bullets, the Hornet class does not offer the delivery of energy associated with the bigger-cased 22-centerfire numbers.

The 22 PPC. The 22 PPC can blast a well-constructed 55-grain missile away from the muzzle at

The 225 Winchester cartridge never gained great popularity; however, with the right bullet, it has enough ballistic force for deer. The 225 is shown here with a 30-06 round for comparison.

3500 fps. If the 222 can do the trick for Mr. Popowski's neighbor, the 22 PPC can do it with flare.

The 5.6 × 50mm Magnum. This cartridge is essentially a rimmed version of the 222 Remington Magnum. DWM of Germany launched it in 1968. It will propel a 60-grain bullet at 3300 fps muzzle velocity.

The 219 Clan. Letting the first termite through the crack in the wall led to the destruction of the building. The 219 Zipper shoots a 60-grain bullet at 3300, too, just like the 5.6 × 50. Its wildcat cousin, the 219 Wasp, also insists on inclusion.

The 225 Winchester. Here we have a 60-grain missile at 3500 fps muzzle velocity, a better ballistic package than the aforementioned rounds. It must be allowed to enter the domain of deer rifle cartridges.

The 224 Weatherby Magnum. This efficient little hotshot came off the drawing board in 1963, designed to scoot a 50-grain bullet away at 3750 fps, and a 55-grain bullet 100 fps slower. Chambered in the Weatherby Mark V with a 7.5-inch-long action, 54-degree bolt lift, six locking lugs, the 224 was

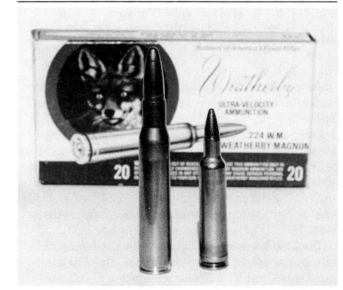

The 224 Weatherby Magnum cartridge, compared here with a 30-06, has the ballistic impetus for deer-sized game when it is loaded with a bullet of correct construction.

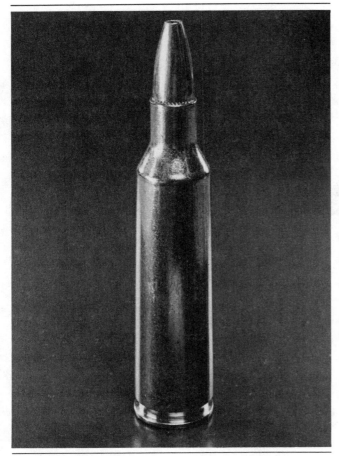

The 22-250 has been used in the big-game field for decades. But its success depends upon two things: proper big-game bullet construction, rather than the use of a varmint projectile, and bullet placement.

unique—Weatherby all the way, including a belted case, the only 22-centerfire factory cartridge (that I know of) with a belt. The belt's use is for precise headspacing. It has no effect on additional case strength. The day the 224 went to the range, a Mark V in 257 Weatherby Magnum was also tested. The latter won the accuracy bout with superlative 1/2-inch 100-yard groups, but the little 224 was just a skip behind with groups of about .65 inch average size.

The 22-250 Remington. Enough has been said of this fellow, except for a brief comment—the 220 Swift has been used by conservation officers, hunters, and explorers on big game for many years. The 22-250 is only a shade behind in muzzle velocity, and it can, of course, shoot the same bullets. Nothing more need be added. Testimonials from deer hunt-

ers who have succeeded with the 22-250 would require a book.

The 220 Swift. The big Swift prepared with properly constructed bullets has dropped enough big game to lift the original cloud of doubt that surrounded the cartridge when hunters went forth with 48-grain varmint bullets against deer and larger fauna. The 220 Swift can propel its 55-grain bullet at 3800 fps for a muzzle energy exceeding 1750 foot-pounds. At 200 yards, the Swift bullet still has a half-ton of remaining energy. But you need a strongly constructed bullet in the Swift for the job of deer hunting, as you do with any other 22-centerfire cartridge, no matter what the energy figures are.

The 5.6 × 57mm RWS. This cartridge outswifts the Swift. It can drive a 60-grain bullet as fast as the Swift can propel a 55-grain pill. Not popular here, this German cartridge was designed for small deer and chamois hunting. The 5.6 × 57 rifle wears a 1:10 rate of twist. In factory form, the cartridge is offered with a 74-grain cone-point bullet by RWS, makers of extremely good ammunition (can be purchased from Old Western Scrounger Co., 12924 Hwy. A-12, Montague, CA 96064). Considering its ballistics and its 74-grain jacketed bullet, the 5.6 × 57 must be considered one of the better 22 centerfires for larger-than-varmint game.

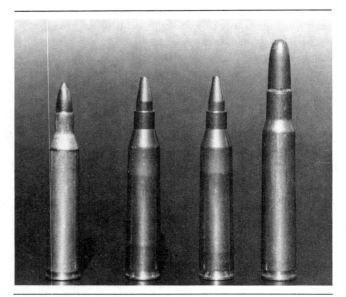

The powerful 5.6 × 57mm RWS cartridge (two center rounds) was designed for hunting deer-sized game. This 22 centerfire is a bit larger than the 220 Swift (left). A 30-06 (right) is included for comparison.

Norma, through the Federal Cartridge Company, offers 22 Savage Hi-Power ammunition with its European title—5.6 × 52 R (the "R" is for "rimmed"). Two 22 Savage rounds (right) compared with a 220 Swift and 30-06.

The 22 Savage Hi-Power (or High-Power). Earlier in this chapter, I mentioned that a tiger hunter used this little fellow on man-eaters. Although no such recommendation flows from these pages, the 22 Savage does drive a 70-grain .227-inch bullet at 3200 fps muzzle velocity. It has more energy than most of the handguns allowed by the game departments that disallow its use. The 22 Savage Hi-Power falls into the same realm as the other 22-centerfire big-game rounds, however—it's for the expert, but it has done the job for decades and still can.

A Few 22 Centerfire Big Game Wildcats. Dozens of wildcats produce Swift or Swift-plus ballistics. The 220 Improved is one. Famed Alaskan hunter Hosea Sarber used a 220 Arrow for big game. The 22 Hi-Power Improved is a blown-out version of that round. It drives the 70-grain bullet a bit faster than its factory brother. The 228 Ackley has been credited with a 70-grain bullet at about 3600 fps. The Ashurst 22-06 pushes a 55-grain bullet at 4000 fps. There is a 22-06 CCC (Controlled Combustion Chamber) that also drives a 22-caliber bullet at Superman speeds. The 22 Newton was based on the 7 × 57 case (just like the 5.6 × 57 RWS above). It was credited with a 90-grain .228-inch bullet at

Savage's Model 99 was chambered for the 22 Savage Hi-Power cartridge. The rifle found its way into the hunting fields of many countries. A bullet weight of 70 grains helped greatly in producing 22 Savage ballistics for deer-sized game.

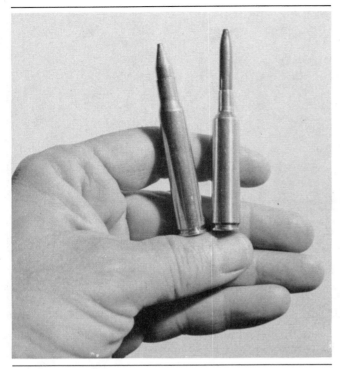

The great 226 Barnes is a true 22-caliber big-game cartridge (right). The long bullet makes this round efficient, not only in maintaining its original velocity, but also in penetration. The most-used bullet in the 226 is a 125-grain *bonded* projectile that retains jacket and core as a unit.

3100 fps muzzle velocity (with a retained velocity of 2891 fps at 100 yards). The rifle bore carries a 1:8 twist to stabilize the long bullet. The muzzle energy of the cartridge with the 90-grain bullet almost cracks the ton mark. The 220 Krag Lightning and 22 Elliot (on the 303 British case) are super 22 centerfires. Ralph Waldo Miller's 22 magnums were based on various cases. There was a 22 formed on the 275 H&H Magnum (free-bored to reduce pressures). There is also the 22-243 Ackley and 22-243 Durham to consider among the wildcats.

The 226 Barnes QT. No 22 centerfire to date equals the 226 Barnes in the 22-centerfire big-game arena. Fred Barnes cooked up his 226 by necking down the 257 Improved cartridge. The 226 is a necked-down, blown-out 7mm Mauser case with a 40-degree shoulder. But there is much more to this cartridge than its being a 22 on a 7 × 57 case. *The bullet weighs 125 grains.* Barnes made a special bonded projectile of that weight in .226 (not .228) caliber. A 125-grain 22-caliber bullet is *long.* The

fantastic sectional density of this bullet required a very fast rate of twist in order to stabilize it—one turn in 5¼ inches. That is why Barnes named his round the QT, for "quick twist." The bullet is very close to 1½ inches long (1.420 inches, I believe). High velocity is out of the question with so much bearing surface and consequent bore drag. The 125-grain .226-inch bullet escapes the muzzle at about 2700 fps using slow-burning powder—not fast, but very effective because of the bullet's profile.

Reports from several reliable sources indicate the same story over and over again concerning the 226 Barnes QT—extremely efficient on big game. Grizzly, elk, moose, and other large animals have been dropped with the 226. One hunter reported five elk and seven mule deer with 12 shots. Every 226 Barnes rifleman further states that bullet recovery is unlikely. The long projectile retains its initial velocity very well, and due to its length, plus attending energy, it penetrates deeply. In a cow elk that was hit in the shoulder with the 226 Barnes bullet, the projectile passed all the way through the animal and exited at the hip. Yet with all of this performance, the 226 Barnes is comparatively mild and easy to shoot.

THE AUTHOR'S OPINION

If you have courage enough to write a book, then you must have sufficient courage to render opinions on controversial subjects within that book. Limited personal experience with 22 centerfires on big game (a few deer, four or five javelina, and an antelope) forces one to rely on the experiences of unimpeachable resources. There are many hunters, world over, who have testified to the worth of the 22 centerfire on deer-sized and bigger game. To say that the 22 centerfire is no good for such game would be tantamount to saying a bumblebee cannot fly, for it should not be able to. Scientific formula says so—too much body, not enough wing. But the bumblebee does fly and the 22 centerfire does dispatch big game.

One question, however, must be broached—why bother? With so many fine hunting cartridges offered, why bother using a 22 centerfire for big-game hunting? Lack of recoil, ease of bullet placement, and excellent results when the right bullet is used form a reply to the question. I shall not leave my favorite 7mm Magnum home this elk season in favor of any 22-caliber centerfire hotshot. I will not be hunting the big mountain deer of Montana with a 22, either. However, there are plans for a 226 Barnes rifle in the works. Its long bullet, which will be properly constructed with a bonded core (home-rolled in a Corbin press), with excellent retained velocity and energy, will be pressed into service in the big-game field without hesitation. I have not used the 226 on big game. But its ballistics and his-tory speak loudly. You don't have to stick your finger in the campfire to know it's hot. Good shooters, using hot 22s loaded with proper bullets, have taken big game for decades. They continue. These hunters like the high accuracy and low recoil of the hot 22. They also savor the lightning-like harvest when the 22 centerfire high-speed bullet is properly placed.

29 MAINTAINING YOUR 22 FIREARMS

Twenty-two maintenance is different from big-bore rifle or handgun cleaning. On the one hand, the 22-rimfire rifle or handgun allows literally hundreds of consecutive shots before cleaning is imperative (although such multiple shooting without cleaning is not recommended). At the same time, improper cleaning methods have been blamed for the early demise of many 22-rimfire guns. The 22 centerfire demands considerable bore attention after a comparatively few shots, however, because the jacketed projectile travels through the bore at very high velocity. Deposits of copper on the rifling (copper wash) are common. Furthermore, even the smaller cased 22 centerfires shove a lot of burning powder (hot gas) through the bore, a bore of limited volume. And it is common to shoot a 22 centerfire numerous times in the varmint field or on the target range without benefit of cool-off periods. These factors promote barrel wear. Therefore, proper maintenance is necessary to thwart early demise of the 22-centerfire bore.

EXTENDING BORE LIFE

The centerfire 22-rifle bore may last 5,000 to 40,000 rounds before accuracy falls below the level of acceptability. Of course, the bore may be ruined after a few hundred shots too. It is impossible to place an exact figure on this because of the multitude of variables. The 22-rimfire bore should last 100,000 rounds. Maybe more. Maybe a lot more. Nobody has derived an exact figure. Erosion of barrel steel depends highly on humidity. In a test conducted in my area, with its very low humidity, a blackpowder firearm underwent long periods of grueling mistreatment and neglect, and yet its bore did not rust. Broadly speaking, a relative humidity of about 50 percent and up causes trouble, while humidity below that level does not wreak nearly the havoc on steel. Metal deterioration comes from chemical attack, but also from electrochemical reaction, the latter abetted by humidity levels in the 50 percent and higher domain.

Humidity is dependent not only on the atmosphere, however, but also the microenvironment. For example, a shooter was surprised to find rust on his rifle following a night in a tent. Food had been cooked within the tent. Water had been boiled. The rifle showed rust in fewer than 12 hours. A storage area may have high humidity. Furthermore, atmospheric purity has much to do with metal corrosion. Even under low humidity conditions, if the air contains chlorates, nitric oxide, sulfur dioxide, and other chemicals, rust is promoted. These chemicals further iron-oxide reaction.

Store In A Safe, Dry Place. The gun safe is as much a safety device as it is a theft-prevention storage chamber for firearms. It keeps children from getting their hands on guns. It also prevents invasion of moisture, to a degree. In short, the gun safe is a dry place to store firearms. Wherever guns are stored, however, there is a short-range consideration and a long-range consideration. The simple wipe-down with a silicone-treated cloth will suffice for short-term storage. The use of a grease or metal preservative will ensure longer protection. For storing of greater duration, the bore can be treated to a heavier coating of grease or metal protecting agent. However, put a sign on the firearm, attached with a rubber band, that reads "Clean Before Shooting" to remind yourself to free the bore of all grease before firing the gun.

Use Clean Ammo. The 22-rimfire bullet is relatively soft and can readily pick up grit. Grit does no favor to a bore. Even the copper-plated 22-rimfire bullet is prone to embedded dirt particles. A sectioned 22-rimfire barrel exhibited the scars of solid particle contaminants. Stuffed in a shirt pocket, your ammo is susceptible to dust. For a handy ammo-carrier, look into a small pouch, such as of-fered by Michaels of Oregon Company. These handy pouches generally attach to your belt. They keep your ammo clean, while allowing easy access to the supply. Plastic ammo containers, as well as other packaging devices, also keep 22-rimfire ammo clean. Of course, 22-centerfire ammo should also be kept grit-free, but it's less of a problem because of the jacketed bullet.

Don't Use Shorts In Long Rifle Chambers. They can do

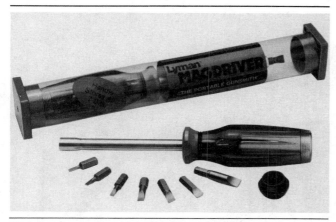

Maintenance requires tools. The correct tools save screw and bolt heads because they fit right. Lyman's Magdriver screwdriver comes with various bits designed to fit different screw and bolt slots.

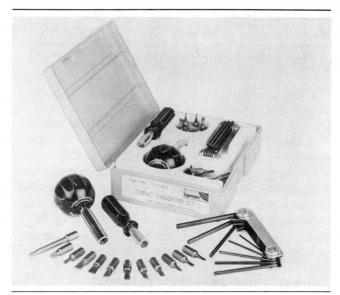

Lyman's Compact Screwdriver Kit fits neatly into any shooting box or bag. A kit like this is as useful on the shooting range as it is in the hunting camp.

damage. In the early days, corrosive priming was used containing potassium nitrate, which left salt residues behind. These salts could etch metal. Old-time ammo also used black powder, which is hygroscopic, meaning its fouling will attract moisture, with consequent ferric oxide (rust) a probable result. When the corrosive Short was fired in the longer chamber, it eroded that portion of the chamber later occupied by the Long Rifle cartridge case. When that happened, the 22 Long Rifle case often stuck in the chamber, because the case walls actually swelled out into the tiny pits in the chamber caused by the corrosive 22 Short ammo.

The advent of non-corrosive 22-rimfire ammo and smokeless powder mitigated problems associated with the use of 22 Shorts in the Long Rifle chamber. To alleviate any possible trouble, avoid using Shorts in Long Rifle chambers. If you do use them—as I do in rifles chambered for Short, Long, and Long Rifle ammo—clean the bore soon afterwards with a bristle brush and the proper solvent. Or, avoid the problem by shooting the Long when you want Short ballistics, since the Long has the same case length as the 22 Long Rifle, but uses the same 29-grain bullet as the Short, at very close to the same muzzle velocity.

How Often To Clean? Although it has been proved that a 22-rimfire firearm may shoot many hundreds, even thousands, of shots before damage is done to the bore, don't try it. Powder residue can cake up in the action, causing malfunctions. And even though the lubricated 22-rimfire bullet coupled with non-corrosive priming mixture is easy on the bore, continued shooting without cleaning does cause a buildup of powder residue in the rifling, just as in the action of the firearm. The only thing worse than abject neglect of the 22-rimfire bore is improper cleaning. Better not to clean at all than to clean improperly.

There is no set number of rounds that can be fired in the 22-centerfire rifle or handgun before cleaning is required, because numerous factors influence it, including the type of powder used (some powders leave more deposit in the bore than others), the weight of the powder charge, the hardness of the bullet jacket, the speed at which the projectile is driven, even the number of lands and grooves and rate of twist of the rifling. However, wise is he who cleans his 22-centerfire rifle or handgun after each long shooting session. The job

One rule of thumb to prevent damage from improper cleaning is to clean the firearm from the breech, not the muzzle, if at all possible.

is quick and easy, and well worth the little trouble it takes.

FIREARM DISASSEMBLY

Disassembling the rifle or sidearm for cleaning requires knowledge of its working parts. If in doubt as to the fine points of field-stripping your firearm, seek the paid advice of a professional gunsmith and learn the procedure correctly. Consult the firearm manual that came with your gun. Or look into one of the texts on the subject. The NRA has several textbooks on field-stripping many different models. These are entitled *Firearms Assembly*, and they are offered in several editions. In order to clean the action (ejector, extractor, working parts),

you must know how to remove bolts and in general gain access to the working parts. Keep the magazine clean too. That goes for clips as well. A wipe-down with a metal preservative is generally enough, but you can also blow dust from the workings of the clip with an air hose. Keep the cylinder chambers of the revolver clean. Learn to take down the 22 semi-auto pistol for complete cleaning. In short, see to it that all working parts receive attention.

DAMAGE FROM IMPROPER CLEANING

Ruining a firearm in the name of maintenance is pointless and unnecessary. First, use only those chemicals prescribed for cleaning, and follow the manufacturer's directions. A shooting friend depended on a name-brand sewing machine oil for every aspect of gun cleaning, which included swabbing the bore and sprucing up the stock of the rifle. Sewing machine oil is a good lubricant, but it is neither a bore solvent nor a protector of wood. Use the appropriate chemicals formulated for firearm maintenance. Second, clean from the breech whenever possible. There is a good reason for this. The crown of the muzzle is a sensitive area of the bore. As the crown goes, so goes the bullet. The last touch to the bore that the projectile experiences is at the crown.

Damage to the crown can send a missile off course. Cleaning a bore from the muzzle end may lap (polish) the rifling at that position, rounding the lands, and even causing them to lose symmetry (one land may be rounded more than another, or even chipped). Pistols, some lever-actions and single-shots, as well as a few others, must be cleaned from the muzzle. Use a muzzle protector. Or employ a nylon-coated rod (more on coated rods below). Or use an undersized rod, being careful to keep it centered in the bore, rather than allowing it to scrape against the crown at the muzzle. Third, for premier care, employ a bore guide in the 22 centerfire. More on this soon, too. Fourth, clean the rimfire, but don't overdo it. My best-loved rimfire rifles get a wipe-down following even a short range session, but they do not receive a full-blown bore scrubbing after every 50-pack of ammo. Running a rod up and down the bore needlessly is—needless. Fifth, do not over-lubricate. Excess oil can be damaging. It may cause hydraulic problems in the bore or action. Leave only a trace of oil in the action, and even less in the bore. Remember that machine oil can soften wood. Furthermore, excess oil in a bore may cause bullets to go astray. Sixth, remove fingerprints from metal parts of the firearm. Fingerprints may be acidic, causing etching of metal. A wipe-down with a silicone-impregnated cloth will remove fingerprints.

PROPER MAINTENANCE TOOLS

The Cleaning Kit. There are numerous excellent cleaning kits on the market that are fairly complete and compact. Hoppe's Deluxe Wooden Presentation Kit was used in testing a cleaning kit for this work. The wooden box proved sturdy, with a proper latch. The well-made, brass break-down rod of small diameter worked well for 22s. Lubricating oil,

Hoppe's No. 9 solvent (good for removing powder residue), appropriate jags and brushes, plus cleaning-patch cloth rounded out the kit's contents. Added to the kit was Flitz (its use explained later under "metal fouling cleanup") and a small tube of Gunslick grease.

The Cleaning Rod. Takedown or one-piece rod? The takedown rod is handiest in the field, and was used for all field-cleaning. But the one-piece rod is best for cleaning at home. The break-down rod can't be as strong as the one-piece model. The one-piece rod used in testing cleaning methods for this book was the J. Dewey model (from the J. Dewey Mfg. Co. of Southbury, Conn.). The nylon-coated Dewey rod does not pick up abrasives, nor does the coating peel off. It is a one-piece spring-steel unit with ball bearing handle that swivels as the rod progresses downbore and is turned by the rifling twist. Dewey also has a stainless steel cleaning rod with a built-in bore protector. The bore protector is a cone-shaped device that centers on the rod. The point of the metal cone is introduced to the muzzle of the firearm when cleaning from the muzzle is required. The shaft of the rod is thereby centered in the bore. It cannot scrape along the sides of the bore, or against the crown of the muzzle. A pull-through cleaning cord can also be used in the field,

A good gun cleaning kit, such as this Hoppe's Wooden Presentation model, will give the 22 fan the majority of cleaning tools and chemicals necessary for good maintenance.

The use of a bore guide ensures that the cleaning rod will not lap the chamber area. Shown is a special bore guide designed for the 22-rimfire rifle.

or at home for pistols, semi-auto rifles and others usually cleaned from the muzzle. This is a plastic-coated wire fitted with a tip that will accept cleaning jags or brushes. The wire is snaked through the bore from the muzzle; the cleaning patch is attached to the slotted jag, or a brush is installed; then patch or brush is pulled back through the bore and out of the muzzle. This device is compact, and as stated, will not cause crown damage. It is not, however, as handy to use as a standard rod.

Jags. Many shooters prefer the standard jag, which is a metal unit with a sharp tip and (often) knurled rings. This jag guides the patch through the bore, but drops the patch when the rod is pulled back toward the breech of the firearm. The dirty patch does not travel back through the bore. The slotted jag, on the other hand, is popular because it hangs onto the patch and the patch can be passed through the bore several times. In the main, the nylon slotted jag (also called a slotted cleaning tip) was used for this work. It is easy on the bore, and the patch cannot get caught in the breech or chamber area as it is guided upbore. Most precision shooters, however, prefer the standard jag.

Bore Guides. A bore guide keeps the cleaning rod centered at the breech of the firearm. The one used for this work was an M&M model, called an ''in-line bore guide.'' If a shooter lifts up on the cleaning rod as he drives it through the bore, he can seriously damage the chamber and throat area of his firearm, and may actually wear a groove into the chamber or leade of the rifle.

Many shooters feel that the hard rod is safer than a soft one because soft rods tend to pick up grit. The bore guide allows the use of a very hard rod,

because the rod does not scrape against the chamber area of the 22-centerfire firearm. Even with the coated rod, a bore guide was used in cleaning the varmint rifles field-tested for this book. Precision shooters believe that a bore guide is essential for accuracy preservation.

The Bore Brush. Shooters use nylon or metal-bristle brushes mainly to reach fouling trapped in the grooves of the rifling, but the brush also serves to clean the tops and sides of the lands as well. Even a tight-fitting patch may not always reach deeply into the groove of the rifling. The 22 rimfire's major problem is powder residue, since there is no jacket metal to foul the bore. Also, comparatively low velocity and proper bullet lubrication prevent major leading problems with the 22 rimfire. A nylon bristly brush coupled with solvent is sufficient medicine to attack most 22-rimfire cleaning problems. The 22-centerfire bullet, on the other hand, will eventually leave metal wash behind, especially on the lands of the rifling. The nylon bristle brush won't always remove this metal coating. In a moment, more on the detection and removal of metal fouling.

Patch Material. Soft clean cloth is used for cleaning patches. Cut size and patch thickness are important. Patches that are too thin or too small in diameter do not offer sufficient friction in the bore to pick up fouling. But those that are too thick or too large are even worse—they require so much effort to drive them through the bore that cleaning rods may

The bolt of the rifle is wiped down with solvent, then lightly oiled for preservation and prevention of friction. A film of oil or grease allows the bolt to work more freely.

At the close of a cleaning session, the entire firearm is wiped down with a soft cloth. In this case, the cloth has been pre-treated chemically with a rust inhibitor.

bend or break in the process. Furthermore, when a patch requires too much effort to drive it downbore, the rod may bend in the process, which can cause it to make contact with the chamber of the firearm, or the rifling. If you cut your own patches, carefully determine by trial and error the best size for each firearm. Keep the patches properly sorted out. When it comes time to cut more patches, use the correctly sized examples as patterns. Factory-cut patches are even handier.

Brushes. A toothbrush is excellent for reaching into the action for removal of fouling. Coupled with solvent, the toothbrush will remove even stubborn residue. Dewey and Outers offer special cleaning brushes. Three Outers brushes tested for this work were: nylon bristle, stainless-steel bristle, and bronze bristle. The metal-bristled brushes are for heavy-duty fouling. A soft mop (as sold in music shops for the cleaning of wind instruments) swabs loose powder residue from the chamber of the 22-centerfire rifle or pistol.

The Gun Cloth. A gun cloth may be any clean, soft rag used to wipe away fingerprints and other contaminants, mainly from metal parts, but also from stocks. The cloth may be impregnated with a silicone spray. The easy way to come up with a good cloth is to buy one ready-to-go, such as the Outers Silicone Gun & Reel cloth, which is a soft, large cloth impregnated with proper chemicals for gun maintenance. It is advertised as good for cleaning, polishing, and protection. It comes in a zip-closure plastic container and may be carried in a vehicle or taken to the gun range. Keep the cloth encased. It must not pick up abrasive grit from the atmosphere.

Chemicals. Hundreds of chemicals have been used for firearms cleaning over the years. Modern chemicals, however, are the best. There are specially formulated solvents that break down powder residue, and many metal-saving oils and greases as

Product	Lubricant	Rust Protection	Cleaning Powder Fouling	Cleaning Grease & Crud	Water Displacement
Tri-Lube	Superior	Excellent	Excellent	Excellent	Excellent
Metal Seal	Excellent	Superior	Good	Good	Superior
Crud Cutter	N/A	N/A	Not Recommended	Superior	N/A
Nitro Solvent	Not Recommended	Not Recommended	Superior	Good	Not Recommended
Gun Oil	Excellent	Good	Not Recommended	Not Recommended	Excellent
Gunslick	Superior	Good	N/A	N/A	Good
Gun Grease	Excellent	Superior	N/A	N/A	Good

well. So many special chemicals have been introduced for gun care that Outers was obliged to print a chart (see above) pertaining to the uses of that company's chemical products. The two-major duties of firearms chemicals are to attack fouling for breakdown and removal, and to preserve metal and wood gun parts.

Solvent. These days, there are several solvents that truly attack powder fouling. For this book, Shooter's Choice MC#7 was used at great length and found to be excellent for cleaning bores of both 22-rimfire and centerfire guns. It not only reduced powder residue for easy pick-up on the cleaning patch, but also attacked metal fouling.

Grease. Grease thwarts moisture, especially condensation, which is a natural phenomenon in just about any setting, including the gun range, hunting camp, and the shooter's home. Grease is a good lubricant and is highly useful for long-term arms storage. We used many excellent greases in our tests, including Gunslick, Shooter's Choice, and Outers Gun Grease.

Metal Protectors. Today, there are many sophisticated chemicals used in the preservation of metals. Accragard, from Jonad Corporation, was the product tested for this work and one we have used for more than a decade. While proof of metal longevity is a difficult commodity, the high-tech Accragard preservative seems to have done its job very well, especially on test metals, which were treated with various agents, and then allowed to stand in a small room for several days with a humidifier going. The metal test strips treated with Accragard were last to show signs of rust.

Lubrication. Several oils were used to lubricate the moving parts of actions. All seemed to work perfectly, including Hoppe's, Jonad's Accralube Precision Lubricating Oil, and Tri-Lube, a spray-on chemical from Outers.

Gunstock Chemicals. Many agents can help preserve the gunstock. One used with satisfaction was Birchwood Casey Gun Stock Wax. Furniture polishes were found to remove dirt adequately, but were wiped down and not allowed to remain on the

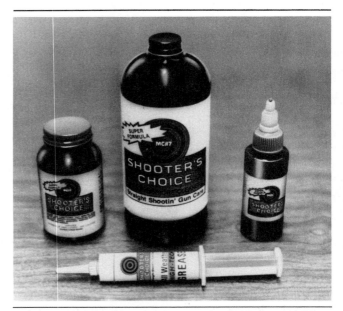

Shooter's Choice is a modern chemical solvent used in removing powder and metal fouling from the bore. It comes in various packagings. The company also offers gun grease in a plunger-tube.

wood after cleaning. If left on the wood as a coating, the agents seemed to hold dust particles.

Touch Blue. For minor touchup work of blued metal surfaces, Birchwood Casey Super Blue proved very satisfactory. Directions, especially pertaining to pre-application of the blue, were followed to the letter.

Copper Fouling Agents. For heavy metal fouling, JB Compound and Flitz were used in the bore. These chemicals reduced stubborn copper wash for removal from the rifling.

22-RIMFIRE CLEANING PROCEDURE

The following is but one suggested procedure. Many different methods work equally well. This particular sequence happens to be the one chosen for this work's testing. It has the advantage of being simple, fast, and effective.

1. Make certain that the firearm is unloaded.

2. Run a solvent-soaked patch through the bore.

3. Allow the solvent to work for 15 minutes.

4. Pass the bristle brush through the bore several times.

5. Use dry patches to remove fouling.

6. Run a solvent patch through the bore several passes.

7. Follow with dry patches.

8. If the last patch emerges clean, apply a trace of preserving oil to a fresh patch and run that through the bore two or three passes.

9. Be certain to wipe the bore with a dry patch before shooting the firearm. Oily bores are not recommended.

22-CENTERFIRE CLEANING PROCEDURE

The same treatment as described above will take care of the 22 centerfire if the rifle or pistol has not seen heavy action on the range or in the varmint field. Shooter's Choice MC#7 worked well for both rimfire and centerfire guns in breaking down powder fouling, and in removing traces of metal fouling and leading. For 22-centerfires that have been fired numerous times, try the following procedure.

1. Make certain that the firearm is unloaded.

2. Run a solvent-soaked patch through the bore.

3. Allow the solvent to work for 15 minutes.

4. Pass a dry patch through the bore to remove fouling.

5. Wet a bristle brush with solvent and pass through bore about a dozen times.

6. Remove fouling with dry patches. If the last dry patch emerges fairly clean, the bore may be treated to a trace of preserving oil.

7. Run a dry patch through the bore before firing the gun.

METAL FOULING

Generally speaking, there are two kinds of fouling—powder and metal. Metal fouling includes tiny fragments of metal deposited upon the rifling, mainly the lands, as the high-speed jacketed bullet passes through the bore of the 22-centerfire rifle or handgun. Metal fouling can leave a rough spot in the bore and can also ruin accuracy. A fellow who had a custom rifle built for him at first praised its accuracy. After a few months, however, he was saying that the rifle's fine accuracy had deteriorated. He blamed the rifle maker for it. The unhappy customer returned to the custom shop, demanding satisfaction. The gunmaker placed the rifle's forend in the padded jaws of his bench vice for a thorough bore cleaning. The customer returned later. "Sorry. I guess I hadn't gotten the bore clean after all," he admitted. Accuracy was restored once metal fouling was removed.

How To Check For Copper Wash. Insert a bit of cotton or clean white cloth into the muzzle. A piece of cotton swab is satisfactory. Use a kitchen match to

Detect metal fouling by inserting clean white cotton into the muzzle, then shining light against the walls of the bore. Metal fouling will usually show up as a golden layer on the lands.

push the white material down into the muzzle about ⅛ inch. With a bore light, direct a beam into the muzzle of the firearm, against the interior walls of the bore. The white cotton or cloth will reflect this beam of light in such a manner that copper fouling will readily show up. It will appear on the land as a gold plating.

Removing Copper Wash. Follow all of the procedures above, especially using the bristle brush soaked with Shooter's Choice MC#7 solvent. Allow the solvent extra time to do its work. Then dry the bore completely with several patches. Now apply either JB Compound or Flitz to a clean patch and work this patch through the bore several times. Flitz is described as a non-abrasive metal polishing agent. After applying JB Compound or Flitz to the bore, clean the residue away with solvent, followed by dry patches. Now run the white cotton test again. If traces of gold appear, use JB's or Flitz again, this time applied to a phosphorus-bristle brush. Follow with dry patches. And then be certain to remove all traces of JB's or Flitz with solvent. *None must remain in the bore.* This procedure will remove even fairly severe metal fouling. If it does not, see your gunsmith.

MAINTAINING THE WOOD

Wood can be spruced up with "scratch remover" from time to time, or treated to a light coating of gun wax. Minor defects in blued surfaces can be touched up with cold blue. There are several stock finishing kits on the market that contain all of the basic necessities to bring a stock back into form. Follow directions carefully, and your gunstock will look, if not new, at least much better than it did. Of course, when a complete, first-class refinishing job is desired, check into the talents of your local custom gunmaker. He will lift (steam) dents from the stock and apply a professional finish to the wood.

CLEANING THE SCOPE SIGHT

The "wipe her down with your shirttail" trick will eventually destroy the very thin, and very important, coating on the lenses of the scope sight. The scope can be cleaned by first aiming a jet of air

"Canned air" is useful in blowing away minor dust that may cling to the glass surface of the scope sight. It is also useful in blowing dust out of the action of the firearm.

against the lens to blow away clinging dust as gently as possible. Canned air (as sold by Outers) works well here. A camel-hair brush can be used to flick away more stubborn adherents. When the grit is gone, use a soft clean cloth, one intended for lens cleaning (see your camera shop) to polish the lens surfaces. Do not press hard. Breathe on the lens to deposit moisture and work the cloth gently in circles from the outside of the lens inward.

Accuracy deterioration is a very sad fact of shooting. The shooter can do nothing to prevent the direct wear of bullets flying through bores, but he can do a great deal to prolong the life of the bore. The 22-rimfire firearm should actually last several lifetimes with the original barrel intact. The 22-centerfire barrel cannot be expected to fare as well, but once its barrel is used up, it can be replaced with a new barrel, giving the rifle a brand new life. Proper maintenance promotes longevity, however, and even though the 22 centerfire sees much more action than the average big-bore firearm, it does not mean that its life need be short.

30 SAFE SHOOTING

Never gloss over safety information. The only worthwhile shooting is safe shooting. The entire gamut of this subject is too sweeping for our scope. A compendium of safety rules would weigh enough to knock out a gorilla. This is no such compendium. The information offered below may serve to prevent a mishap. The only way to truly enjoy the fascinating world of 22-rimfire and centerfire shooting is the safe way. The following rules are a representation only, but a very important representation. Be safe. Teach your young shooters to be safe too.

HOW FAR WILL THEY SHOOT?

The 22 Long Rifle rimfire cartridge will fire well over a mile when the angle of the bore is directed at 45 degrees. It is difficult to give an exact figure because there are many variables to consider. The extreme-range warning on a 1950 box of Winchester Super-X 22 Long Rifle high-velocity ammunition read "Range 1 Mile Be Careful." A box of Peters 22 Long Rifle high-velocity ammo from the same time frame read, "Range-One Mile *Be Careful!*." Remington Hi-Speed 22 Long Rifle ammo from a little later date gave the same warning. So did Federal's Power-Flite 22 Long Rifle high-velocity ammo. But at a somewhat later date, Western's Super-Match Mark IV 22 Long Rifle ammo read, "Caution: Dangerous within 1½ Miles." New Winchester T22 Target ammo carries the same caution. Imported Sovereign (Mexico) 22 Long Rifle high-velocity ammo carries a two-mile warning. The extreme-range 22-rimfire warning is prudent.

As for 22-centerfire ammunition, an extreme range of three miles is certainly no exaggeration. The upshot of the whole extreme-range concept is to consider where the projectile will end up when a rifle or handgun is fired. There are generally adequate backstops in field shooting, such as small-game hunting. When there is not, don't shoot.

Squirrels are usually perched on tree limbs with literally hundreds of woody backstops to capture the fired bullet. Cottontail rabbits and snowshoe hares usually live in a maze of backstops. In target shooting and plinking, the shooter posts his targets in front of butts that will hold any bullet. So be mindful of extreme range, and also of the glancing bullet, or ricochet.

The Ricochet. Winchester ballisticians tested the remaining velocity of a 22 Long Rifle bullet (Super-X high-velocity ammunition) fired at an angle into a body of water. The bullet left the muzzle at 1240 fps. After the bullet glanced off of the water, its remaining velocity was 1195 fps. Only 43 fps were lost from the striking of the bullet against the water, indicating that contact with such a surface does not absorb so much of the bullet's impetus as might be expected. The missile remains lethal *after* a ricochet. Never shoot a bullet into a body of water, with the exception of frog hunting where the projectile is aimed straight downward and there is a backstop

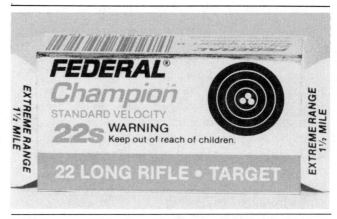

The extreme range warning on these 22 Long Rifle cartridges states that the bullet will fly as far as 1½ miles. Take these warnings seriously.

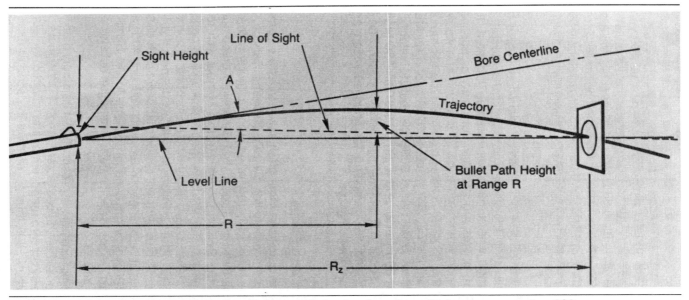

Trajectory is the path taken by the bullet. If the muzzle is aimed at about 45 degrees upward, a 220 Swift may launch its missile well over two, even three, miles depending upon the bullet and the load. Know the extreme range of your cartridge. Use a backstop to capture the fired bullet.

to catch the bullet. The 22-rimfire cartridge also has a tendency to glance off of hard objects, such as the ground. It is more susceptible to ricochet from these surfaces than is the 22-centerfire cartridge, which tends to self-destruct upon contact with hard surfaces.

When the 22-centerfire cartridge began to gain popularity with shooters all over the country, it was soon found that its bullet reduced ricochet to a minimum. These jacketed bullets designed for varminting were thin-skinned. They were frangible, made to come apart. Combining high velocity and a thin-jacketed bullet made an ideal self-destructing missile for farm country. In a recent demonstration conducted for this chapter, several rifles were fired against "hard pan," earth that had been rained on, turned to mud, and then literally baked hard by the sun afterwards. The beauty of the test sight was a solid dirt cliff behind the hard pan. Bullets fired at an angle downward into the compacted earth could be seen knocking dirt out of the background wall. Various distances between the bullet strike zone and the wall were observed. Bullets were fired into the hard pan from distances of 100, 50, and 25 yards from the wall, using varied, but non-specific angles of the rifles' muzzles.

As expected, the 22 Long Rifle glanced from the hard pan and into the dirt wall with the greatest

frequency. More accurately, it should be stated that the bullet from the 22 Long Rifle was the only one to make it to the wall intact. As part of the little study, a 17 Remington was included, firing hand-loads with the Remington 25-grain bullet (purchased as a reloading commodity from Midway Arms Company) at a chronographed muzzle velocity of 4075 fps. There was never any sign of so much as a bullet fragment reaching the wall from

Use a backstop. An earthen hill should have a sufficiently steep angle to catch the projectile. Watch for rocks. Check the area behind your target to ensure that it will stop a bullet.

The 22-centerfire varmint bullet flies at such high speed and is so lightly constructed that it generally explodes upon contact with the ground, as shown here. The bullet missed the prairie dog, but it did not ricochet from the hard ground—it fragmented.

any firing distance, 100 down to 25 yards, with the fast little 17 Remington. The 22 Hornet did not reach the wall either. The only 22-caliber centerfire bullet to fly from strike zone to wall was the full-metal-jacketed projectile loaded into military 223 ammo. Full-metal-jacket Hornady bullets fired from a 22-250 Remington rifle did not reach the wall. Be cognizant of bullet ricochet. Be especially watchful of the 22 rimfire and any extra hard bullets, or full-metal-jacket military ammo.

TAMPERING WITH AMMUNITION

It was noted that shooters at a silhouette range were altering 22 WMR ammo by exchanging the factory bullet with another harder projectile. This practice was immediately put to an end because of the extreme danger it represented. Ammunition is made to very rigid specifications, with absolute attention paid to *combinations* of correct case, powder, bullet, and priming mixture or primers. Tampering with any one of these components can bring

Enjoy the benefits of a proper gun range. This range is set up for silhouette shooting. In addition to the correct rails for the targets, it also has efficient backstops behind every target.

disaster. Replacing softer-jacketed bullets with harder-jacketed bullets can be very dangerous because it takes more energy to drive harder bullets through the bore, and therefore, may raise pressures significantly. This situation presented itself at the range recently when a very hard military projectile was used in a hot load for a 22-250. Although no damage was done, the warnings were clear—case extraction became difficult with the hard-bullet handload, and finally a primer was pierced. So even though the weight and diameter of two bullets may be identical, this does not mean that a hard-jacketed missile can be installed in place of a softer-jacketed one. As for the rimfire cartridge, never tamper with it at all. It was put together very specifically. As one NRA staff member said recently, "Doing something because 'no one's been hurt yet' is extremely foolish—the first one hurt could be you." (*The American Rifleman*, April 1988, p. 67.)

MATCH AMMO TO FIREARM

It was proved that the 22 Long Rifle cartridge could "go off" in the chamber of a 22 WMR rifle. The case split badly. Fragments of brass could have been expelled from the rifle. Shoot only that ammo designed for the firearm and no other.

OLD AMMUNITION

Usually old ammunition fails through misfiring. It simply does not "go off." However, it is not inconceivable that very old ammo may be damaged through powder alteration. Excessive heat may have changed the detonation quality of the propellant. In one test of outdated ammunition, another problem arose. The powder charge was rendered less powerful. Instead of the bullet exiting the muzzle, it lodged in the bore and had to be driven out. If a person were firing several rounds in succession, and such an event occurred, the lodged bullet would have become a bore obstruction. Damage to the firearm could have resulted, and perhaps to the shooter as well. In one report, a bullet was lodged in the bore. The result of firing the next round was a "ring" in the bore of the rifle, according to the examining gunsmith. Old ammunition is best retained in an appropriate collection or safely destroyed, rather than fired. Remember that some ammunition made in the past used a very hot priming mixture. This priming mixture sometimes caused the head of the 22 rimfire cartridge to burst.

Getting Rid Of Old Ammunition. Never toss unwanted ammunition away where anyone, especially a curious young person, can find and tamper with it. In most cases, it is best to take unwanted ammo to the local shooting club for disposal. Centerfire ammunition may be dismantled safely with a commercial bullet-puller (such as the RCBS kinetic model). A hundred old centerfire cartridges were broken down with bullet puller as described above. The bullets were retained, but the old brass and the powder were turned over to a range officer, who deposited these in a small private pond where the water would destroy the primers and the powder. The pond, devoid of fish or other life, was a good repository for the ammo components. Do not dismantle rimfire ammo. Take it to your range officer or other authority in the area for proper disposal.

SAFE AMMUNITION STORAGE

Ammunition is far safer to store than many solvents, and immeasurably safer than gasoline. All the same, ammo of any type should be stored where it is not exposed to a water heater or any other source of ignition. Being extra safe is smart. At the same time, the dedicated shooter should know about unconfined cartridge detonation. Here are the results of an NRA test as conducted by Major Julian S. Hatcher:

Studies showed that cartridges that go off in a fire generally propel pieces of the case, not the bullet. The bullet has more mass than the bits of brass which result when the powder charge detonates. Therefore, the bullet remains close to its original location, while bits of brass cartridge case fly away. The velocity of a bullet departing from an unconfined detonation is quite low. In one instance, two unsupervised boys located a 22-rimfire cartridge and decided to apply a match flame to it. When the cartridge exploded, small pieces of brass, one about 1/8-inch long, another about 1/16-inch long were embedded in one lad's neck and later re-

moved. The bullet was not propelled by the explosion. It was suggested that reports from a person declaring he was shot by a bullet from an exploding unconfined cartridge be investigated through studying the bullet for rifling marks. If the projectile has rifling marks, then it was obviously fired from the bore of a firearm. Even if fired from a smoothbore, such as a rifle designed for the use of 22 Long Rifle bird shot, the bullet will bear marks from the bore.

In a test, 22 Long rifle cartridges were fired unconfined by placing them in a pot designed for melting lead. The cartridge was placed on its head in the bottom of the pot, bullet pointed upward. On top of the pot, a single layer of corrugated cardboard was located. The bullet did strike the cardboard, but not forcefully enough to penetrate it. There was only a shallow dent in the cardboard to indicate where the bullet had struck. A 22 Remington Rocket Short was used in this experiment, because these cartridges, which were manufactured in the 1950s, used a very light bullet at about 1600 fps muzzle velocity. It was thought that this light bullet, having such small mass, might be propelled by the detonated cartridge with sufficient force to penetrate the cardboard lid on the melting pot, but it, too, made a shallow dent only. The upshot of the discussion is this: never store ammo near a source of detonation. On the other hand, suspect stories concerning 22 bullets flying all over the place when the cartridges were detonated outside of a firearm chamber and without benefit of a bore.

Safe Ammo Storage Practices

1. Store ammo in a clean area free of flammables.

2. Be certain that the ammunition is stored in a secured area where children are unlikely to reach it, and where it cannot be stolen.

3. Maintain temperature in the storage area. Temperature extremes can damage ammunition. In one test of centerfire ammo, 50 cartridges were handloaded. Twenty-five of them were subjected to a temperature of 120 degrees F. (via a small closed area with a heat source and a thermometer) for 10 days. The accuracy of that ammo fell off sharply from the norm. The heated ammunition was compared with the control ammo. While the control ammunition maintained a standard deviation averaging only 14 fps, the heated ammo registered a standard deviation of 148 fps.

4. Store ammunition in a dry area. Moist basements are not ideal storage areas. If there is no storage location other than a damp environment, place ammo in a sealed container. The Army Surplus store usually sells metal containers, originally designed for ammunition, which have rubber liners used to prevent moisture invasion. These GI containers come in various sizes.

5. Store ammo out of direct sunlight.

6. Store ammo in a no-smoking area. Although it has been shown that ammunition detonated outside of a chamber does not send singing bullets all over the place, as in the B western movie, nonetheless, fire and ammo should be kept apart from each other.

7. Be certain that the labels on all of your ammunition and powder cans are correct. Never trust to memory. For example, even if you have only one handload for your 22-250 varmint rifle, mark all boxes with that load anyway, using a data sticker relating powder type and charge weight, primer, brand of cartridge case, specific bullet, seating depth, muzzle velocity if you know it, and any idiosyncrasies of the load. Include the date that the ammo was handloaded and the number of times the cases have been reloaded.

SAFE RELOADING

The Reloading Bench And Area. Keep all of your components stored as safely as your loaded ammunition. Ensure that your reloading bench is clean.

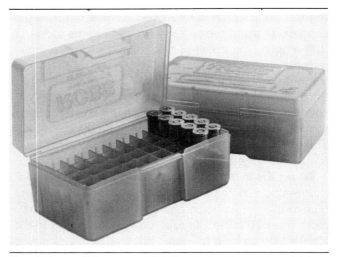

Store ammunition properly. Do not leave ammo within reach of children. Storage boxes like these keep ammunition clean and prevent contamination from outside sources.

Do not allow any spillage of powder or a dropped primer to remain. Clean the powder up. Find the primer. Maintain your reloading area in an organized and neat fashion.

Use Exact Loading Data. A shooter reported that his 220 Swift was unsafe with a particular load he discovered in a reloading manual. However, when questioned, he admitted that he did not use the same brand case as mentioned in the original

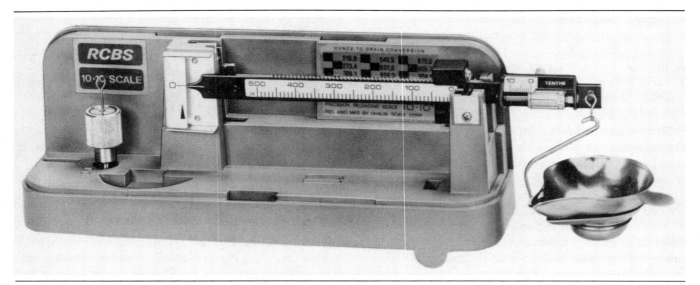

Always use a powder scale to weigh your charges, or to set your powder measure for dumping charges. Check often to ensure that the powder charge your 22 centerfire is getting is the correct one.

loading data, and the powder was not of the same exact brand. Adding to the problem, his bullet was not the one suggested by the manual either, nor was his primer. And yet he insisted that his load was taken from the manual because he used the powder number stated in the book and a bullet of the same weight. Be exact. Do not alter loading data at will. Watch out for reduced loads. Detonation or pressure excursions have been known to occur when very small charges of slow-burning powder have been used in specific cases. Be especially watchful of this in the large-capacity 22-centerfire cartridge, such as the 220 Swift, 5.6 × 57mm RWS, and 226 Barnes. If you wish to use a reduced load, follow the data for reduced loads as given in a manual on the subject.

Case Length. Trim your brass. Be sure that your cartridge case has not lengthened out unduly from firing. If it has, use either the rotary trimmer or trim die to return the cartridge to normal length. An overly long neck can pinch the bullet in the throat of the rifle, raising pressures significantly. Furthermore, be careful about neck thickness. As the brass flows from continued firing, the neck area may grow thicker. This may cause an increase in neck friction, which will raise pressures because the bullet can no longer escape up the bore with the same ease it once did. There are tools designed for neck reaming (inside and outside) which will insure that thick necks are returned to proper specs.

Cast Bullets. An oversized cast bullet may cause the same pinched-projectile condition described above. The bullet cannot normally move upbore when the initial thrust of powder gasses strike it and pressures may rise due to increased friction. Cast bullets are usually larger than the bore to insure accuracy. Therefore, it is imperative that the shooter watch out for thick necks on his cartridge cases. Necks may have to be turned to reduce thickness. Outside neck turning is quite common in the game of benchrest shooting and tools are available for the job.

SAFETY WITH THE FIREARM

The Tubular Magazine. The tubular magazine of the 22-rimfire rifle must be operated specifically. A shooter pulled the follower tube from his 22-rimfire rifle, poured the contents of the magazine into the palm of his hand, replaced the rod, rotated it in place and put the rifle away. Later, the rifle was being shown to a friend. Before handing it over, the

owner of the rifle pulled the bolt back a couple of times as a safety gesture. A live round plopped onto the floor. Simply pulling the tube out of these rifles and emptying the contents of the magazine does not make for a safe condition. A round may still be in the carrier. In removing ammo from a 22-rimfire rifle with a tubular magazine, empty the rounds, but after replacing the follower tube, work the action several times to insure that no cartridge remains in the rifle. Visually inspect the chamber area to see that no cartridge is lodged there that the extractor failed to pull away.

Be Sure The Action Is Closed. It is possible with some rifles to explode the cartridge without the action of the rifle being fully closed. An older lever-action 22-rimfire rifle was fired in this manner. The cartridge case erupted, sending tiny fragments of brass back toward the shooter. Some of these fragments lodged in the shooter's right eye, which, fortunately, was not permanently damaged. Make certain that the action of the rifle is fully closed before shooting.

Old Firearms. Guns are so long-lasting that we have many examples of very old 22 rifles and handguns remaining in shooting condition. However, just because these guns fire does not mean that they are safe to shoot. Have a gunsmith inspect any old gun before using it. Some old-time 22s were designed for the original 22 rimfire black-powder cartridge. These guns may not be safe with modern ammunition. Also, there could be internal damage that's difficult to detect without stripping

Trim your cases. A trimmer, such as this Lyman model, is easy to use and will prevent a rise in breech pressure caused by a long neck invading the rifling portion of the firearm's throat.

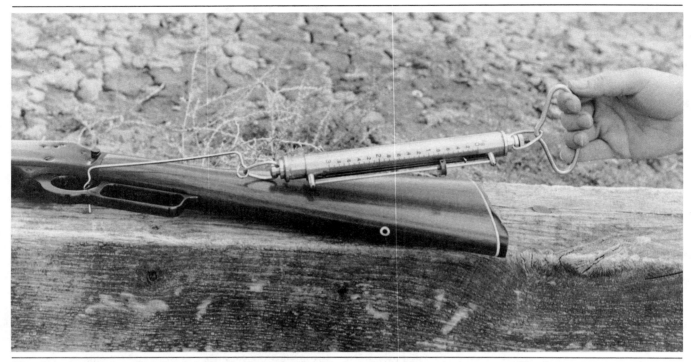

Check your trigger pull or have it checked by a gunsmith, but do not alter triggers yourself unless you are duly qualified. The job of altering trigger pull is best left to an expert.

Have that old firearm inspected by a gunsmith if you have any doubt about its condition. Guns may last a long time; but damage can occur through abuse, neglect, and even normal wear.

the rifle down for a thorough examination. If in doubt, have the old gun fired first by remote control. Many venerable 22s deserve retirement. They should be enjoyed as collector's items, not shooting instruments. Be certain that an old rifle is safe before firing it.

EYE AND EAR PROTECTION

Shooting glasses will prevent eye injury should gasses or particles of brass fly back toward the face of the marksman. Ear plugs—simple synthetic devices made to fill the canal completely—work very well. Some sort of plug or muff is necessary to prevent hearing loss. Ear plugs coupled with ear muffs (headset type) offer excellent protection. There are various types of muffs, including models with liquid-filled ear cushions that seal nicely to block out sound.

Being safe is being smart. Make shooting safety a habit. Don't tolerate unsafe shooting practices at the range or in the field. The shooting sports have an enviable record of safety. Shooting accidents are far fewer than mishaps that occur in many other areas of either work or recreation. Let's do our best to keep it that way. Better yet, let's try to improve the record.

31 FASCINATING FACTS FOR THE 22 FAN

This brief catalogue of interesting and useful 22 facts is offered to the reader as a self-help guide—a body of data he can apply to improve his shooting. But the chapter is also designed to promote the *enjoyment* of 22 marksmanship. Useful facts constitute the framework of shooting. But interesting, if not necessarily applicable data, give the sport form and often promote understanding. Synthesized here are a number of 22 shooting facts, some of them touched on elsewhere, but encapsulated again for quick and easy reader reference.

THE CARTRIDGE THAT WORKS IN SPITE OF ITSELF

The 22-rimfire bullet has the same diameter as the case. For example, a micrometer showed a currently manufactured 22 Long Rifle bullet as having a diameter of .2235 inch. The case diameter of the very same cartridge was also .2235 inch. What other cartridge fires a bullet the same diameter as its case? Because of this fact, 22-rimfire ammo is more difficult to manufacture. The bullet must be rebated in order to fit within the case. Therefore, the projectile is reduced in diameter toward the base so that it will slip into the case neck. If the 22 Long Rifle were being designed today, it would be more like the 22 WRF or 22 WMR cartridge. The bullet diameter would be *smaller* than the case diameter. But designers of the late 1800s apparently did not see things that way. The 22-rimfire case is also very weak and very light. Today's engineers would have it otherwise, if only for enhancement of manufacture.

22-RIMFIRE HOLLOW-POINT ACCURACY

In testing for this book, many 22 Long Rifle hollow-points were matched against their solid-nose counterparts, same brand in each instance. Generally, the hollow-point is supposed to be less accurate than its solid-nose brother. However, such was not generally the case in these tests, and often, the reverse was true. Once again, it pays to test ammunition in a particular rifle to see which fodder works best. Hollow-points were more accurate in 60 percent of the above tests, as compared with high-velocity solids, but of course they were no match for target ammunition. A possible reason for hollow-point accuracy is the change in weight distribution toward the base of the bullet.

22-RIMFIRE VERSATILITY

The importance of correlating a given brand of ammunition to a specific rifle or handgun has been hammered home. At the same time, this must not imply that a 22-rimfire firearm will shoot only one

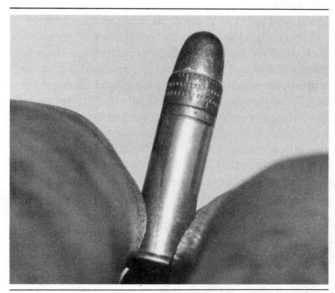

The bullet of the 22 Short, Long, or Long Rifle rimfire cartridge is the same diameter as the body of the case. Therefore, the base of the projectile must be reduced in size in order to fit into the mouth of the cartridge.

brand of ammunition with accuracy. In testing, a Kimber 22 rifle proved accurate with no fewer than 12 loads. Top accuracy happened to be with RWS R-50 ammo in this rifle, followed by Eley Tenex. However, the rifle also achieved splendid accuracy with several other brands, including Winchester Silhouette ammo, Winchester's T22s, and Federal's Champions. Match the ammo to the firearm, but do not lose sight of the fact that the 22-rimfire rifle or handgun will usually group with several loads, even though it prefers one or two for its closest clusters. Versatility of the 22-rimfire is greatly enhanced by matching several different loads to a given rifle or sidearm, from low velocity, quiet, close-range plinker or cottontail rounds to hyper-velocity varmint loads.

22-RIMFIRE BULLET SHAPE

Testing with numerous bullet shapes revealed that the present form is the best to date in terms of accuracy. Bullets of spire point and spitzer configuration gave no better accuracy than the round-nose projectile that has been loaded for so long in our 22-rimfire ammunition. The round-nose form offers a high-density pack, the most mass per shape of the bullet styles tested in the 22-rimfire cartridge. The round-nosed bullet was also the most accurate tested in the 22 Long Rifle.

PRIMING

Methods of priming vary among manufacturers. Fiocchi of Italy is now using a "squashed primer" method. Fiocchi draws the brass cartridge case first, *without a rim*. Wet priming mixture is installed within this metal closed-end tube, and then the rim is formed through a hydraulic effort. The wet priming mixture supplies the fluid for the hydraulic forming of the rim. Priming mixture now ends up along the inside edge of the rim only. In this manner, there is no additional pyrotechnic influence from additional priming mixture left on interior case walls.

THE COPPER-COATED 22-RIMFIRE BULLET

Many gun writers, including the great Townsend Whelen, were not quite on the mark when they lauded the copper-coated 22-rimfire bullet in terms of improved performance (*See also* Chapter 9). A copper-plated bullet without lube will rapidly foul the bore. Therefore, copper plating does not act as a lubricant. These bullets are lubed, often with

There have been so many designs built to chamber the 22-rimfire cartridge that a large book would be needed to list them all. This "different" model was a four-barrel top-break handgun chambered for 22 Long Rifle or 22 magnum. It is double-action (fires each time the trigger is pulled) and it carries a rotating firing pin.

some form of wax. While copper plating may aid somewhat in keeping a bullet surface cleaner, it can reduce accuracy because the extra step in plating the bullet requires rotation in a basket. The bullet may become slightly dented during this process. Copper-plated bullets are not used in match-grade 22-rimfire ammo. The plating, according to one source, is only .0003-inch to .0005-inch thick. Other sources suggest different thicknesses; however, all experts agreed that the plating is very thin. Copper plating does serve two functions, though. It helps identify a specific ammunition (many high-velocity loads are copper-plated), and it beautifies the product. None of this is meant to suggest that copper-plated 22 bullets are of poor quality. They are not, but neither are they superior to lead projectiles.

22-RIMFIRE BULLET LUBES

Many synthetic bullet lubes have been tried, but none has worked any better than the waxes and lubes in present use. The 22-rimfire bullet is difficult to lube in the first place. Synthetic lubes that worked well on the 38 Special at velocities in the 900-fps range failed on 22 Long Rifle bullets at 1250 fps. Currently, the long-used lubes and lubrication methods stand as best.

AUTOMATION AND 22-RIMFIRE MANUFACTURE

Automation has become so refined in the manufacture of 22-rimfire ammo that machines are taking over in quality control. Where people used to inspect loaded 22 ammo to ensure quality, machines can now detect certain problems. And the sophistication of these machines is growing in sensitivity. The human technician is still the prime mover in 22-rimfire manufacture, but man's metal and electrical slaves are taking over some very sophisticated operations.

22-RIMFIRE MARKETING

The 22 rimfire is no longer a cartridge for only hunting, or competitive target shooting, or even Sunday plinking. It has become a high-use commodity worldwide. Packaging changes reflect this new stature. A great deal of ammo is sold by the "brick" of 500 rounds now. Waxed cartons containing 250 shots are being tried. Plastic belt-containers of 275 rounds are also successful. Considering inflation, the cost of 22-rimfire ammunition is very low. If the entire population of America shot 22 rimfires, each man, woman, and child would have to shoot about 16 rounds per year to equal the current use of 22-rimfire ammo. World consumption is expected to soon reach six billion rounds annually.

SWITCHING AMMUNITION

The company Kimber of Oregon was test-firing as many as 40,000 rounds of 22-rimfire ammo monthly in a research program. Kimber ballisticians found a lack in accuracy when switching from one brand of ammunition to another. The Kimber report precipitated an interesting side test during ammunition accuracy testing for this book. Ammunition known for its accuracy was not living up to its sterling reputation. This situation occurred only after long runs of testing, following brand switching, which was the case with Kimber. For example, 100 rounds of RWS Silhouette ammunition was tested in a very accurate rifle. Following this test, Eley Tenex was fired in the same rifle. Accuracy was not up to par with the Tenex ammo. A retest was conducted. This time, the bore of the test rifle was thoroughly cleaned after shooting R-50. When Tenex was fired in the test rifle again, excellent accuracy resulted. Lubrication variation could be the cause of the problem. The bore becomes conditioned to a given type of lubrication, or combination of lube, powder type, and charge. Switching

Ever-changing, the 22 Long Rifle has been offered in literally hundreds of different loads. Here is Federal's Spitfire, for example, a hyper-velocity 22 Long Rifle cartridge. Note the packaging.

Packaging of 22 ammo continues to change. The plastic tray of 100 rounds is comparatively new. Cardboard boxes of 50 rounds prevailed for decades. Now, 22 ammo is packed into plastic belt containers, wax-coated cartons, and in many other packages as well.

to the next batch of ammo reduces accuracy until the bore is conditioned to *that* lube, powder type, and charge. For the testing in this book, bores were cleaned in between *all* ammo tests.

DRESSING THE BORE

In conjunction with switching brands of test ammunition, it was discovered that accuracy from a "squeaky-clean" bore was not always best. In many instances, accuracy improved after a given number of shots were fired. The exact number was never isolated. However, in dressing the bore, the firing of five shots through a clean barrel is suggested before expecting a long string of good groups.

THE WAXED HOLLOW-POINT

Tampering with loaded ammunition is taboo. However, the cleaning and reshaping of the 22 Long Rifle hollow-point cavity does not require tampering in any form. A tiny drill bit is *inserted by hand* into the cavity and slowly twisted a couple of times to remove the lubrication normally captured there. Then warm paraffin is pressed into the hollow-point cavity by hand. The wax is warm, but never hot. On test media, especially clay blocks, the filled cavity gave more uniform expansion. In the field, it was sometimes difficult to discern the value of the waxed hollow-point bullet, but of 10 shooters who used the ammo on jackrabbits and prairie dogs, nine felt that expansion was more reliable, with improved uniformity of results. Exit holes were large and the apparent effect upon the varmint improved. Some shooters reported greater accuracy with the waxed hollow point (four testers), while others felt there was neither gain nor loss of accuracy with the wax-filled cavity. The idea is to clean and shape the hollow-point cavity, *not drill it out*. The drill bit is turned slowly by hand only.

22 LONG RIFLE MATCH AMMO VELOCITY

Everyone knows that the 22 Long Rifle standard-velocity cartridge experiences less wind drift for its bullet than does the 22 Long Rifle high-velocity projectile. However, tests have revealed that the discrepancy between the two can be very significant, with the high-velocity bullet drifting a full 50 percent more than the standard-velocity missile. Target shooters in the 1930s expected an improvement in wind drift when the new high-velocity 22 Long Rifle round was announced. But these shooters were greeted instead with greater wind drift. The region-of-disturbance theory explaining this factor (discussed previously) is accompanied by another suggestion—wind drift being governed not by time of flight alone, but also by relative loss of speed. The high-velocity 22 Long Rifle bullet loses more of its initial velocity, proportionally, over 100 yards than the standard-velocity projectile. Of course, its bullet still arrives at 100 yards going faster than the standard-velocity missile, but not by much. One series of chronographings revealed a velocity loss from muzzle to 100 yards of 14 percent for standard-velocity 22 Long Rifle ammunition, a velocity loss of 20 percent for 22 Long Rifle high-velocity ammo, and a loss of 30 percent for hyper-velocity Long Rifle. Regardless of the hypotheses, the tested fact remains that 22 Long Rifle high-velocity ammo drifts more in the wind than standard-velocity 22 Long Rifle ammunition.

MATCH AMMUNITION AND SMALL-GAME HUNTING

In spite of complaints to the contrary, a well-placed 22 Long Rifle bullet on squirrels or rabbits will cleanly drop that game with one shot. Those who find otherwise are not making head shots. Therefore, bullet placement becomes paramount to clean small-game harvesting. For one entire season, we hunted cottontails and tree squirrels with CCI and RWS match-grade ammunition. The results were gratifying. Head shots from the accurate test rifle, the author's faithful Kimber, were no big trick. While impact was not as pronounced as delivered by high-velocity ammo, the final reward was meat on the table. This is not an endorsement for match ammo in all small-game hunting, and it is especially no suggestion for 22 rimfire varminting. In most small-game arenas, the high-velocity solid-nose round, or high-velocity hollow-point, is still king, more powerful, and flatter-shooting than target fodder. But consider target ammunition when bullet placement is more important than bullet impact. Wind drift is less with this standard-velocity ammunition, and bullet penetration is excellent, partly because of the three-percent antimony alloy used in match ammo, making a relatively hard projectile.

T-42 AMMO

As an oddity only, remember the full-metal-jacket 22 Long Rifle round loaded by Remington. It was

The 22-rimfire round is so versatile that it functions in numerous firearm styles, including the semi-auto design exhibited by this Weatherby Mark II.

noted as "Cartridge, Ball, Caliber .22, Long Rifle, M24" in one of its designations and used in the Army Air Force E12 or E14 "Jungle Kit." The full-metal-jacket bullet, .008-inch-thick jacket, had a lead-antimony alloy core.

WINGO AMMUNITION

If you locate a rimfire shot cartridge with a large "W" headstamp, you may have a Wingo round for your collection. It is not 22 caliber, however. Rather, it is 20 caliber and was used in a special Winchester single-shot, lever-action shotgun for a skeet-like indoor shooting game called "Wingo." Introduced in 1970 by Winchester-Western, the odd little shot-gun and its 20-caliber ammo did not remain long in the marketplace.

THE "A&W" SHORT

A 22 Short cartridge with the headstamp "A&W" is a rare cartridge produced by the Allen & Wheel-ock Company of Worcester, Mass., from 1856 to 1866. This company was reorganized into the better known Ethan Allen & Company in 1866.

THE REMINGTON DOT HEADSTAMP

These cartridges carry the normal "U" head-stamp; however, there is also a small dot, some-times beneath the U. The dot's significance is loca-tion of manufacturer, which is Cartuchos Deporti-vos De Mexico, S.A., Cuernavaca, Morelos, Mexico—CDM for short. The dot is the only mark denoting a difference between this Mexican-manu-factured ammo and American-made Remington 22-

rimfire rounds. If the dot is located below the U, it denotes Mexican manufacture as stated above. However, if the dot appears in the center of the U, it means something else entirely. The inside dot signifies that the cartridge case is slightly longer than ordinary. These cartridge cases are used for stunner guns in humane dispatch of livestock, 22 Long Rifle shot cartridges, and power tools that are operational through a powder charge.

LESMOK POWDER

Du Pont Lesmok was a semi-smokeless powder used in very accurate match ammunition from the 1920s into the 1930s. As with black powder, Lesmok was easy to ignite. Oddly, Lesmok was in the long run less ruinous to barrels than early smokeless powder, because smokeless powder, coupled with corrosive priming mixtures, was very hard on steel. Meanwhile, Lesmok's blackpowder content left a heavy residue in the bore that joined with the leftover chemicals of the corrosive priming mixture. When the bore was cleaned, the corrosive chemicals from the priming mixture tended to be lifted away with the blackpowder residue. Lesmok also

The world of the 22 includes the world of the 30 caliber. The Accelerator cartridge from Remington gives the shooter a high-velocity 22-caliber bullet encapsuled in a sabot. This is the 30-30 Accelerator firing a 55-grain 22-caliber soft-point bullet. Note the 30-caliber plastic sabot holding the smaller bullet.

offered better loading density with the Long Rifle cartridge, and being somewhat less efficient than smokeless powder, it actually offered excellent shot-for-shot consistency, whereas a highly efficient fuel would fail to give consistency if not loaded in exacting amounts in every case. Finally, practical smokeless powder and non-corrosive priming brought an end to Lesmok manufacture in the 1930s.

DAISY'S CASELESS 22

The Daisy Company, maker of famous air rifles, developed a caseless 22 that really can't be called a cartridge. It's simply caseless ammunition. The propellant was devised by Jules Langehoven, a Belgian chemical engineer. The solid-propellant cylinder was attached to the base of a lead, 29-grain, 22-caliber bullet. Ignition was caused by a jet of hot air supplied by a spring-piston air-rifle mechanism (see *The Rifleman's Bible* by Sam Fadala for details of this air gun type). A spring-piston air rifle compresses air in a cylinder, expelling the air at great speed. The hot air was used to ignite the solid propellant attached to the Daisy caseless bullet.

Several firearms were designed, including a lever-action repeater, for the caseless ammo. Finally, a rifle did emerge, but it was not a repeater. It was the Daisy V/L single-shot rifle, the only rifle to date using commercially loaded caseless ammo. Today, both rifle and ammunition are collector's items. The single-shot rifle was an under-lever air gun in a sense, because cocking it compressed the air, which would serve as a hot jet to ignite the propellant. The 29-grain lead projectile left the muzzle at about 1150 fps (22 Short ballistics). Daisy offered the 4.75-pound rifle in 1968, but discontinued it in 1969. The Daisy V/L was the only commercial 22-caliber caseless-ammo rifle; however, considerable research went into other caseless-ammunition gun designs, none of which became a standard over-the-counter arm.

THE 22 WCF SHOT CARTRIDGE

Another oddity of the 22 world was the 22 WCF (Winchester Center Fire) shot cartridge, which used a wood-encased shot charge, or wooden bullet with shot in it, if you prefer. The thin wooden shell was bullet-shaped and filled with fine shot. The round was manufactured by the Union Metallic Cartridge Company and is headstamped U.M.C., followed by

The 30-30 Accelerator worked quite well in the field, with its 55-grain 22-caliber projectile.

S.H. .22 C.F. The S.H. stands for solid head, meaning that the head of the case (the part that held the primer) was not a folded type, but rather the rim was a solid part of the brass case. This made for a stronger cartridge case. Of course, the .22 C.F. meant 22 caliber, centerfire. The "wooden bullet" is flat-nosed.

THE 5.6MM VELO DOG

Since this little round played a minor role in the development of the 22 Hornet (bullets were withdrawn from 5.6mm Velo Dog rounds to be used in experimental Hornet ammo), it is mentioned here. Developed in 1894 by Galand of Paris, this small revolver cartridge was devised to aid the cycler who was chased by vicious dogs, a use that would certainly be frowned upon today. The term "velo" was a slang expression for bicycler. When coupled with the English word "dog," you had "gun for bicycler to use against attacking dogs." Hundreds of Velo Dog revolvers were manufactured. A metal-cased 45-grain bullet was propelled at about 660 fps velocity at 15 feet, fired from a two-inch barrel. The 5.6mm Velo Dog was manufactured into 1940. Blanks and shot-cartridge loads were also available for the 5.65mm Velo Dog, which, by the way, was also known as the 5.5mm, 5.75mm, 6mm, and 6.5mm. The bullet diameter was actually .224 inch (5.68mm), so the Velo Dog was indeed a 22-caliber cartridge of varied history.

THE ACCELERATOR

Three Accelerator cartridges were tested for the book: the 30-30 Winchester, 308 Winchester, and 30-06 Springfield. Each becomes a 22-caliber in Remington's Accelerator form in which a 22-caliber 55-grain bullet is encased in a plastic 30-caliber sabot, or form. The sabot guides the 22-caliber bullet to the muzzle, and then soon falls away as the bullet speeds toward the target. In chronographed tests, advertised velocities proved quite realistic. The 30-30 fired its 55-grain bullet at about 3400 fps. The 308 pushed its 22-caliber pill out of the muzzle at more than 3700 fps, and the 30-06 drove its projectile beyond 4000 fps. Accuracy in all three rifles was respectable. The 30-30 was used on a jackrabbit hunt with considerable success.

The fascinating world of the 22 carries with it a myriad of interesting facts. The 22 rimfires were of so numerous design and manufacture that books have been written specifically on the subject of their designs and peculiarities. The centerfires have also occupied a large space in shooting literature. As described in Chapter 27 on wildcats, a great deal of experimentation has taken place in the development of high-velocity, flat-shooting, 22-caliber centerfire cartridges. All 22s are fascinating, some more than others, but each 22-caliber development, whether the short-lived Daisy caseless 22 or the perpetual 22 Long Rifle, has enriched the world of shooting.

DIRECTORY OF 22 ARMS AND AMMO MANUFACTURERS

This directory is concerned with 22-caliber guns and 22-caliber ammunition only. Addresses are provided for those who wish to write for catalogs or further information.

22 FIREARMS

AMT
536 N. Vincent Avenue
Covina, CA 91722
The AMT Automag II is a 10-shot semi-automatic pistol offered in 22 WMR caliber. The AMT Lightning semi-auto pistol comes in 22 Long Rifle only.

ANSCHUTZ
Precision Sales International
PO Box 1776
Westfield, MA 01086
The Anschutz Model 54 Sporter series includes the Bavarian, Custom, and Classic, calibers 22 Long Rifle, 22 WMR, 22 Hornet, and 222 Remington. Also a similar Match 64 series, and a Mark V Sporter semi-auto in 22 Long Rifle. The Achiever is a junior-sized 22-rimfire rifle that "grows" with its user with buttstock extensions. Match-grade target rifles, intermediate to competition-grade levels, including silhouette and biathlon models. The Exemplar pistol in 22 Long Rifle and 22 Hornet.

Beeman Precision Arms, Inc.
3440-SBL Airway Drive
Santa Rosa, CA 95403
There is the Model 69 Target pistol—22 Long Rifle and the Match 2000-U in 22 Short by Beeman, as well as the Beeman/Krico Model 700 L in 222, 223, and 22-250 calibers. Also a Model 640 Varmint rifle in 222 and a 60J BA in 222. The Beeman/Krico M400 bolt-action rifle is a five-shot 22 Hornet made in West Germany.

Beretta Corporation
17601 Indian Head Highway
Accokeek, MD 20607
The Beretta 500 Series bolt-action rifle is available in 222 Remington. Also Beretta's Model 950 semi-automatic in 22 Short only and a Model 21 in 22 Long Rifle.

Browning Arms
Route One
Morgan, UT 84050
There is a Browning A-Bolt rifle in 22-250 Remington caliber, a lever-action Model '81 in 222, 223, and 22-250. The Model 1885 Single-Shot in 22-250. The A-Bolt 22 rimfire repeater. The Browning Semi-Auto 22-rimfire rifle. And the Buck Mark 22-rimfire semi-auto pistols in various styles.

Charter Arms
430 Sniffens Lane
Stratford, CT 06497
The 22-rimfire AR-7 Explorer survival rifle—also the Pathfinder revolver in 22 Long Rifle and 22 WMR calibers. The Pathfinder is the same as the Charter Undercover model, except for calibers.

Chipmunk Manufacturing
114 East Jackson
Medford, OR 97501
The Chipmunk Single Shot is a scaled-down bolt-action rifle with 16⅛-inch barrel chambered for 22 Short, Long, and Long Rifle cartridges. Also a Deluxe version of the Single Shot and a Silhouette pistol in 22 Long Rifle.

Colt Firearms
150 Huyshope Avenue
PO Box 1868
Hartford, CT 06102
The Colt AR-15A2 H-Bar is a heavy-barrel, semi-auto, military-type rifle in caliber 223 Remington. There is also

Colt Firearms (cont.)

a standard model as well as the AR-15A2 Carbine with 16-inch barrel weighing under six pounds and wearing a telescoping aluminun stock.

Freedom Arms Company
PO Box 1776
Freedom, WY 83120

A Mini-Revolver in 22 Short, Long, and Long Rifle calibers, five-shot, along with a four-shot Boot Gun revolver in 22 WMR—stainless steel—barrels of one to three inches in length.

Heckler & Koch
14601 Lee Road
Chantilly, VA 22021

Heckler & Koch's Model 300 Auto Rifle is a semi-automatic chambered for the 22 WMR cartridge.

Interarms Ltd.
10 Prince Street
Alexandria, VA 22313

The Mark X bolt-action rifle in 22-250 caliber, made in Yugoslavia, as well as the Mini- Mark X built on a miniature Mauser 98 action, 20-inch barrel, under 6.5 pounds, 223 Remington caliber.

Ithaca Gun Company
123 Lake Street
Ithaca, NY 14850

The X-Caliber single-shot pistol in calibers 22 Long Rifle and 223 Remington.

Iver Johnson
2202 Redmond Road
Jacksonville, AR 72076

The Iver Johnson Model 3112 is a 15-shot M1 Carbine-like rifle in 22 Long Rifle caliber. Also the Wagonmaster, Targetmaster, and the Li'l Champ 22 single-shot bolt-action rifle in 22 Short, Long, and Long rifle (16 1/4-inch barrel) and a TP22 Auto Pistol, semi-automatic, 22 Long Rifle.

Kimber of Oregon
9039 S.E. Jannsen Road
Clackamas, OR 97015

The Kimber Model 82 Government Match Rifle is a target model capable of sub 1/3-inch groups at 50 yards with selected match ammo. Kimber's 82 or 84 Super America is a super-grade rifle in 22 Long Rifle caliber, 22 Hornet, or 223 Remington. The 84 Sporter is available in 221 Fireball, 222, or 223 Remington. The Ultra Varminter with mini-Mauser action is offered with laminated stock, heavy stainless-steel barrel, 223 Remington. A Model 84B Custom Classic is available in 221 Remington, 222, or 223 Remington calibers. There is also the Kimber Predator, a single-shot bolt-action pistol in 221 Fireball and 223 Remington.

Llama Firearms
55 Ruta Court
South Hackensack, NJ 07606

The Llama Small Frame Auto is a semi-automatic pistol in 22 Long Rifle caliber only.

Marlin Firearms Company
100 Kenna Drive
New Haven, CT 06473

Marlin's famous Model 39 lever-action is offered in takedown version, as well as the 39AS Golden Mountie with 24-inch barrel, 22 Short, Long, and Long Rifle, tubular magazine. The Model 60 is a tubular magazine semi-auto, the 70HC a 25-shot semi-auto, the Papoose (70P) a takedown, 25-shot semi-auto; many bolt-action 22s, including a Midget Magnum in 22 WMR. The Marlin 1894M is a lever-action 22 magnum rifle.

Pachmayr Ltd.
1875 South Mountain Ave.
Monrovia, CA 91016

Pachmayr's Dominator pistol is available in calibers 22 Hornet and 223 Remington.

Remington Arms Company
1007 Market Street
Wilmington, DE 19898

Remington's Model 552 BDL is a tube-fed semi-auto firing 22 Short, Long, and Long Rifle ammo. The 572 is a pump-action rifle that handles the same ammo, tube magazine. Remington's 40XR Custom bolt-action wears a 24-inch barrel, 22 Long Rifle, grades I through IV. The bolt-action 541-T replaces the S model, with 24-inch barrel. The 40XR is a target rifle with heavy 24-inch barrel, 22 Long Rifle. The 40XC is a 20-inch barreled benchrest rifle in calibers 22 BR Remington centerfire, 222 and 223 Remington. The XP-100 Varmint Special Pistol comes in 223 Remington caliber. The 700 ADL bolt-action rifle chambers the 22-250, while the Sportsman 78 and Model Seven come in 223 caliber.

Ruger
Sturm, Ruger & Company
Lacey Place
Southport, CT 06490

Ruger's 10/22 carries a 10-shot rotary clip, semi-auto. A similar clip feeds the bolt-action Model 77/22. The Ruger No. 1 is offered in 22-250 and 220 Swift, as is the No. 1V, Special Varminter rifle. Ruger's bolt-action Model 77R and International are offered in calibers 22-250. The 77 Varmint model comes in 22-250 or 220 Swift. The semi-auto Mini-14 is built in many different styles, in 223 caliber. The Mark II semi-auto pistol, 22 Long Rifle, is also offered in various styles, including a Target and Government Target model. Ruger's New Model Super-Six Convertible revolver shoots 22 Short, Long, and Long Rifle, as well as 22 magnum shells with its additional cylinder.

Sako Arms
55 Ruta Court
South Hackensack, NJ 07606
The Sako heavy-barrel bolt-action single-shot varmint rifle in caliber 22 PPC USA is acclaimed, along with its bigger brother in caliber 6 PPC USA, as the most accurate factory rifle in the world. Sako has a long line of bolt-action sporter and heavy barrel rifles, such as the Hunter in calibers 222 and 223 with a short action, and 22-250 with medium-length action (left-hand action available). The Carbine with 18½-inch barrel comes in 22-250. There is a Mannlicher carbine in 222 Remington. Sako's Trace Match Pistol is a six-shot semi-auto handgun offered in two models, 22 Short or 22 Long Rifle.

Savage Arms
Springdale Road
Westfield, MA 01085
The Savage over/under rifle/shotgun Model 389 comes in 222 Remington and 20 gauge, while the 24V is offered in 222 or 223 over a 20-gauge barrel. The 24 and 24C combine a 22 Long Rifle barrel with a 20-gauge tube. The 24 is also available with a 22 magnum top barrel.

Smith & Wesson
2100 Roosevelt Avenue
Springfield, MA 01101
The Model 17 K-22 six-shot revolver in 22 Long Rifle is offered along with a Model 22/32 Kit Gun, also a six-shot revolver, in 22 Long Rifle. The S&W Match H.B. M-41 is a 22 Long Rifle semi-auto with heavy barrel; the M-41 is the same with a standard barrel. There is also an M 422 semi-auto S&W in 22 Long Rifle.

Dan Wesson Arms
293 Main Street
Monson, MA 01057
The Dan Wesson Model 22 six-shot Revolver is offered in 22 Long Rifle and 22 WMR calibers.

Thompson/Center Arms
Farmington Road, PO Box 2426
Rochester, NH 03867
The TCR Hunter single-shot break-open rifle is offered in 22 Hornet, 222 and 223 Remington, and in 22-250 calibers. The break-open T/C Contender pistol comes in 22 Long Rifle, 22 WMR, 22 Hornet, and 223 calibers.

Ultra Light Arms Company
PO Box 1270
Granville, WV 26534
Ultra Light offers a wide range of calibers, including custom chambering. The UL rifle is a super lightweight model with special miniaturized action and composite stock. Accuracy without weight is the company's thrust. The UL Model 20 Reb Hunter's Pistol is a bolt-action model in 22-250 caliber.

Valmet Sporting Arms Div.
55 Ruta Court
South Hackensack, NJ 07606
Valmet has a Hunter Auto Rifle with 15- and 30-shot magazines and 20.5-inch barrel. This Finnish-made semi-auto rifle comes in caliber 223 Remington. Valmet also has an over/under combination rifle, 222 Remington on top of a 12-gauge shotgun barrel.

Winchester
U.S. Repeating Arms Company
275 Winchester Avenue
New Haven, CT 06504
Winchester's Model 9422 is a trim version of the famous Model 94 lever-action deer rifle. It is chambered for 22 Short, Long, and Long Rifle, with tubular magazine, straight grip. The 9422 XTR Pistol Grip wears a longer barrel, along with its pistol grip stock. Winchester's Model 70 Lightweight, Sporter, and Featherweight are all offered in calibers 223 and 22-250 Remington.

Weatherby's
2781 East Firestone Blvd.
South Gate, CA 90280
The Weatherby Mark II semi-automatic rifle is available in 22 Long Rifle in a tube-fed or clip-fed version. Weatherby's bolt-action rifles include calibers 223 Remington and 22-250, as well as the Mark V in Weatherby's 224 Magnum, the only belted 22 centerfire available.

Wichita Arms
444 Ellis
Wichita, KS 67211
The Wichita Classic bolt-action rifle is offered in all 22-centerfire chamberings upon customer request. There is also a Varmint model, again available in all 22-centerfire calibers. The Wichita Silhouette Pistol is chambered in 22-250 Remington caliber—various models. The Wichita Hunter International Pistol is offered in 22 Long Rifle and 22 magnum, single-shot.

TWENTY-TWO AMMUNITION

Dynamit Nobel—RWS
105 Stonehurst Court
Northvale, NJ 07647

RWS rimfire ammunition is available in many different styles, from 22 BB and CB Caps through 22 WMR. Biathlon, silhouette, hunting ammo, and numerous target grades are available. RWS also offers various 22-centerfire loadings, including the 5.6 × 50 Magnum, 5.6 × 57 and the 22 Savage (5.6 × 52R).

Eley-Kynoch
ICI - America
Wilmington, DE 19897

Eley 22-rimfire target ammunition has long been used worldwide in countless matches. This ammo comes in various grades for different shooting purposes.

Federal Cartridge Company
900 Ehlen Drive
Anoka, MN 55303

Federal Cartridge Company has a complete line of 22-rimfire ammunition, with the exception of a match grade. The company offers a 50-grain bullet for the 22 WMR, and it also has a long list of 22-centerfire cartridges, including the Premium line 22-250. Federal imports Norma ammunition, including Norma's 220 Swift and 22 Savage H.P. loads.

Fiocchi of America
Route 2, Box 90-8
Ozark, MO 65721

Sub-sonic, standard-velocity, hyper-velocity (WASP), Free Pistol, several match loads, and more fill the 22-rimfire lineup for Fiocchi. Solid or hollow-point, lead or copper-plated.

Hansen Cartridge Company
244 Old Post Road
Southport, CT 06490

Hansen's rimfire line includes a 22 Long Rifle standard-velocity cartridge, a 22 Long Rifle high-velocity hollow-point load, and a 22 Short standard-velocity target-grade load. Each load is available in a 5000-round package. The 223 Remington is also offered with a 55-grain full-metal-jacket bullet in 1000-round quantities.

Hornady Mfg. Company
PO Box 1848
Grand Island, NE 68802-1848

The company offers a 222 Remington with 50-grain SX Hornady bullet, 52-grain boattail hollow-point, 55-grain SX; 223 Remington loaded with a 55-grain full-metal-jacket projectile, or a 60-grain bullet; several 22-250 loads and two 220 Swift loads.

Kendall International Arms
418 Fithian Avenue
Paris, KY 40361

Lapua ammunition is imported from Finland through Kendall. Lapua has been known for a very long time as high-quality match 22-rimfire ammo. A 22 Long Rifle hollow-point match load serves for target shooting, but also works well on the tree-squirrel hunt.

Omark Industries
PO Box 856
Lewiston, ID 83501

CCI rimfire ammunition, including a highly regarded Pistol Match load, is offered in an extremely wide variety, from Mini CB Cap and CB Long with less than 800 fps muzzle velocity, through Stingers with about twice that speed. There is a Belt Pak plastic container of 275 Long Rifle cartridges, Long Rifle shot, 22 WMR shot, 22 Short hollow-point, WMR with 40-grain full-metal-jacket or hollow-point bullet, and the Green Tag Competition Long Rifle for match shooting.

PPC Corporation
625 East 24th Street
Paterson, NJ 07514

This company deals in 22 PPC ammunition as well as researching the area of benchrest competition accuracy loads.

Remington Arms Co.
1007 Market Street
Wilmington, DE 19898

From 22 Short hollow-point to 22 Long Rifle hollow-point, in both target and high-velocity configurations, the Remington ammunition line is long and highly praised. Remington also offers a great number of 22-centerfire loads with various bullet types. The 222 Remington Magnum is still available as a factory load through Remington.

Weatherby's
2781 East Firestone Blvd.
South Gate, CA 90280

Source of ammunition for the 224 Weatherby Magnum cartridge.

Winchester (Olin/Winchester)
427 N. Shamrock Street
East Alton, IL 62024

Numerous 22-rimfire cartridges complete the Winchester line, including a 22 Short hollow-point and 22 WMR ammo with 40-grain full-metal-jacket or hollow-point bullet. Twenty-two centerfire ammunition runs from 22 Hornet through 220 Swift. Winchester's Supreme line includes a 22-250 load that gave match-winning accuracy in tests.

INDEX